STUDIES IN CONTEMPORARY JEWRY

The publication of
Studies in Contemporary Jewry
has been made possible through the generous assistance
of the Samuel and Althea Stroum Philanthropic Fund
Seattle, Washington
and of the
Ben-Eli Honig Family Foundation

THE AVRAHAM HARMAN RESEARCH
INSTITUTE OF CONTEMPORARY JEWRY
THE HEBREW UNIVERSITY OF JERUSALEM

BECOMING POST-COMMUNIST: JEWS AND THE NEW POLITICAL CULTURES OF RUSSIA AND EASTERN EUROPE

STUDIES IN CONTEMPORARY JEWRY AN ANNUAL XXXIII

2022

Editor: Eli Lederhendler

OXFORD
UNIVERSITY PRESS

OXFORD
UNIVERSITY PRESS

Oxford University Press is a department of the University of Oxford. It furthers
the University's objective of excellence in research, scholarship, and education
by publishing worldwide. Oxford is a registered trade mark of Oxford University
Press in the UK and certain other countries.

Published in the United States of America by Oxford University Press
198 Madison Avenue, New York, NY 10016, United States of America.

Library of Congress Cataloging-in-Publication Data
Names: Lederhendler, Eli, editor.
Title: Becoming post-Communist : Jews and the new political cultures of russia
and eastern europe / edited by Eli Lederhendler.
Description: New York, NY : Oxford University Press, [2023] |
Series: Studies in contemporary Jewry | Includes bibliographical references.
Identifiers: LCCN 2022053504 (print) | LCCN 2022053505 (ebook) |
ISBN 9780197687215 (hardback) | ISBN 9780197687239 |
ISBN 9780197687222 (epub) | ISBN 9780197687246
Subjects: LCSH: Antisemitism—Europe, Central—History—21st century. |
Antisemitism—Europe, Eastern—History—21st century. |
Europe, Central—Politics and government—21st century. |
Europe, Eastern—Politics and government—21st century. |
Post-communism—Europe, Central—21st century. |
Post-communism—Europe, Eastern—21st century. |
Jews—Migrations—History—21st century.
Classification: LCC DS146.E8515 B43 2023 (print) | LCC DS146.E8515 (ebook) |
DDC 305.892/4043—dc23/eng/20221108
LC record available at https://lccn.loc.gov/2022053504
LC ebook record available at https://lccn.loc.gov/2022053505

ISBN 978-0-19-768721-5

DOI: 10.1093/oso/9780197687215.001.0001

Printed by Integrated Books International, United States of America

STUDIES IN CONTEMPORARY JEWRY

Preface

Across the landscape that until 1939 housed most of the world's Jewish population, the closing decade of the 20th century witnessed dramatic upheavals: the overturning of the East European Communist governments and the fall of the USSR, accompanied by a major Jewish emigration movement. The legacy of the Jewish presence in those countries, and the ways in which it became enmeshed in the quest by people of the region—Jews and non-Jews alike—to secure their future, highlights fundamental issues about the politics of memory, national identity, and the relative stability of regimes in the region.

If those questions were important even before the Russian invasion of Ukraine in 2022, understanding their implications now seems even more crucial. In a field fraught with conflicting narratives, the challenges of social and political reconstruction are primary concerns for peoples and governments. The experts contributing to this volume apply interdisciplinary approaches to analyze and interpret a multiplicity of post-communist social realities and aid our understanding of recent events.

On a personal level, I wish to reflect on the process that led me to imagine and create this volume. My travels and attendance at academic events over the years in countries that were once "behind the Iron Curtain" have stimulated my re-engagement with the East European realm. Those sojourns were always facilitated and enhanced by individuals and institutions too numerous to list and to thank here, although I would like to make special mention of the Nevzlin Research Center for Russian and East European Jewry, which is deeply immersed in academic work related to Jewish life under (and after) communism.

Each new volume of *Studies in Contemporary Jewry* is the result of much preparation and teamwork. I wish to express my hearty thanks to the authors of all these essays—those that feature in our symposium as well as the separate essay in this volume by Janiv Stamberger that deals with the Jewish communities of Antwerp and Brussels in the interwar period—all of whom have, collectively and individually, given our volume its character and high academic quality. In the same vein, I extend my thanks to all the reviewers of current scholarly literature whose critiques of new and recent works comprise a large and standard section of *Studies*, enabling the annual to function as a "town commons" for academic discourse in our field.

Publication of these volumes has been materially supported by the Ben Eli–Honig Family Foundation and by a Jacob and Hilda Blaustein Foundation endowment at the Hebrew University. We in the editorial office and at the Avraham Harman

Research Institute of Contemporary Jewry are indebted to them and grateful for their contributions.

I am forever conscious of the legacy of our founding editors, the late Jonathan Frankel and Ezra Mendelsohn, who, together with Peter Medding (long life and good health to him!), placed this publication on its firm footing and created a standard to which I try to aspire. My gratitude goes to my co-editors, Richard I. Cohen, Anat Helman, and Uzi Rebhun, whose initiative, advice, team spirit, and assistance in reviewing submitted manuscripts allows this journal to carry on smoothly from year to year. Each and every volume is meticulously edited by Laurie Fialkoff, ably seconded by the efforts of our managing editor, Robin Zalben, so as to shepherd each new volume through the publication process. They are what I might call the "hard core" of a demanding operation, to which they bring ever-renewed dedication, and I am grateful to them for all that they do.

E.L.

Contents

Symposium

Becoming Post-Communist:
Jews and the New Political Cultures of Russia and Eastern Europe

Essay

Review Essay

Book Reviews (arranged by subject)
Antisemitism, Holocaust, and Genocide

Cultural Studies, Literature, and Religion

History, Biography, Social and Gender Studies

Zionism, Israel, and the Middle East

Symposium

No Small Matter: Features of Jewish Childhood

Introduction: Jews, Communism, and Post-Communism: Short- and Long-term Aftereffects

Eli Lederhendler

(THE HEBREW UNIVERSITY)

The essays in this volume limn the aftermath of the Jewish encounter with communism, viewed in retrospective through the prism of the fall of state socialism in Russia and Eastern Europe just over three decades ago. The history of Jews and communism—and of Jews *under* communism—is a well-established field of inquiry, but relatively less has been written about post-communist life and its ramifications for Jewish history. Since the 1990s, the beginnings of a historical evaluation has emerged, but thus far the bulk of new scholarship derives mainly from an ever-growing body of political and sociological studies with a contemporary focus.[1]

One salient subject under study is the crucial matter of large-scale Jewish emigration from the former Soviet Union (FSU) and other former Eastern-bloc countries, along with studies of the new diaspora of those émigré communities. Because these subjects have drawn relatively wide attention, we decided not to focus on them in this volume, although the post-emigration and "post-Jewish" aspects of life in the region inevitably color the character of life there for both Jews and non-Jews alike. This fact—the emigration as well as the reality left in its wake—lies in the background of several of the inquiries presented here: for example, those by Mark Tolts, Marcin Wodziński, and Vladimir Levin, which explore the cultural and demographic imprint of the Jews in the social and material landscape of the region.

Apart from treating the post-communist realm as a habitat for Jews and a space in which Jewish heritage can be explored, we also highlight in this volume the ubiquitous attention that is paid to the image and figure of "the Jew(s)," as this is manifested in popular and political discourse, particularly within the larger sphere of the politics of memory. The implications of this for the emergent post-communist polities are crucially important, insofar as the politics of memory are mainly about establishing (or

Eli Lederhendler, *Introduction: Jews, Communism, and Post-Communism: Short- and Long-term Aftereffects* In: *Becoming Post-Communist.* Edited by: Eli Lederhendler, Oxford University Press. © Oxford University Press 2023. DOI: 10.1093/oso/9780197687215.003.0001 denying) identity and legitimacy. As Michael Bernhard and Jan Kubik, two scholars engaged in defining the stakes in this field, have pointed out:

> A radical regime change, such as that experienced in Eastern Europe . . ., is not only about the reconfiguration of economic interests, redistribution of political power, and reordering of social relations. It is also about the reformulation of collective identities and the intro-duction or reinvigoration of the principles of legitimizing power. These two tasks cannot be realized without a re-examination of the group's past—their historical memory.[2]

Jews and their relation to communism in the past, as well as Jewish victimhood during the Holocaust, have become staple items in this process of reconstruction and realignment of new national civic ideologies, summoned to redefine and defend the restored boundaries of collective identity. That is so, because a great deal of this process entails arraigning both of the 20th century's totalitarian systems—National Socialism and Soviet Communism—for crimes that seem to warrant comparable types of political recognition.[3] Yet setting these histories in tandem with each other arouses ambiguities, competing memories, and the continued purveying of stereo-typed images. At times, actors in East Central and East European public sphere deflect the debate over these issues onto the "Jew" in the picture. This has occurred despite the very small numbers of Jews currently living in the region, whether measured in absolute or in relative figures.

The blatant asymmetry between the actual Jewish presence and the high pro-file of "Jewish" issues—that is, public issues in which "Jews" feature as narrative elements—is, in itself, less of a conundrum than one might think. The sparse Jewish presence does nothing, apparently, to mitigate the super-sensitivity of public debate surrounding "the Jews," as it seems there is much in the Jewish case that prompts the memory of the 20th century's wars, revolutions, occupations, dictatorships, and depredations.[4] These issues and their salience in both Polish and Hungarian politics are discussed in the essays by Jelena Subotic and Jonathan Zisook. They also figure importantly in the essay by Marcin Wodziński, who considers the dynamics of Jewish studies in post-Communist Poland's academic scene.

Insofar as Jews continue to reside across the region, they, as much as their neigh-bors, are stakeholders in the redress of historical grievances and the pursuit of new self-understandings. Some of their responses to the fraught discourse of identity and memory are explored in an essay contributed by András Kovács, who discusses changes over time and across generations since the collapse of state socialism in Hungary. Moving from East Central Europe to the FSU, Mark Tolts sheds light on the social and demographic data in post-Communist Russia, where some new features and modes of life emerged among the Jews in recent years. We are struck by such phe-nomena as the new role played by Hebrew as an ethnic Jewish language (but also as a language mastered by those whose ethnic classification is Russian); by the apparent sex-ratio imbalance between Jewish men and women; and by the slippage in higher educational attainments (especially among Jewish males), as well as the decreasing number of Jewish residents of Moscow who are employed in medicine, technology, and science, as opposed to their rather strong base in businesses, including hi-tech as well as more traditional business ventures.

The watershed events of 1989–1991, though of paramount significance, do not entirely account for the ways in which issues connected to Jews and Jewish life have taken shape. One might, in fact, point to unanticipated continuities that are only now beginning to be perceived, in social and cultural experiences that straddle the purported gap dividing the era of Communist rule from the post-Communist era. Vladimir Levin presents a nuanced argument here, demonstrating that several countries in the region have maintained core elements of Soviet-era policies toward sites of Jewish culture and Jewish memory, with but slight modification, while in other instances, the politics of change have had a more profound impact. Semion Goldin, for his part, documents a case in point that similarly bridges both sides of the seismic crisis surrounding the fall of Soviet rule: the story of the erstwhile Jewish University in Leningrad (now St. Petersburg), whose career began as part of a renaissance of legal Jewish cultural activity in the 1980s, in the context of Mikhail Gorbachev's *perestroika*.

This matter of continuities that span the historical divide represented by the events of 1991, which is considered by several of our authors, has gained even greater significance and applicability due to recent events in Russia and Ukraine. The essays in this volume were written during the second half of 2021, but prior to their publication, just as the manuscript was being prepared for the book production stage, Russia invaded Ukraine on February 24, 2022. Events on the ground being subject to constant change, I will not venture to comment on the eventual outcomes either over the short or the long term. However, in the context of a volume dealing with the transition to post-communism and its consequences, we would be remiss if we did not pause to observe that Vladimir Putin's assertion of Russia's putative "right" to displace borders and send its troops across sovereign nation's frontiers—despite the time that has elapsed since the fall of the USSR—was uncannily reminiscent of Soviet actions ever since 1939 (Poland), 1940 (the Baltic states), 1956 (Hungary), and 1968 (Czechoslovakia). Indeed, Putin publicly reminded the world that the contours of Ukrainian territory had been (re)configured a century ago by none other than Lenin and Stalin during the establishment of the USSR. Moreover, as the Russian invasion played out, the so-called "de-nazification" pretext (repeated in print by Moscow spokesperson Timofey Sergeytsev in the authoritative RIA Novosti early in April 2022) speciously and ironically reconnects the historical loop between the memory-culture surrounding World War II and subsequent events.[5]

It is, therefore, hard to avoid the close parallels between Putin's actions and Soviet-era practices and, in that sense at least, it seems reasonable to conclude that some long-term phenomena or processes did not so much cease or disappear at one stroke, as much as evolve along a continuum of sorts. That proposition, which appears to have been reinforced by the events of February 2022, clearly has a bearing on the Jewish issues that we raise in our discussion.

**

As editor, I have had the advantage of previewing these fascinating discussions and considering how they dovetail and engage with one another in overlapping explorations. From that vantage point, I highly recommend that readers take a similarly broad view of this entire forum of essays. The quest for renewed Jewish academic studies in Russia and in Poland—two instances that differ individually in form and import yet also share some common relation to "Jewishness" as a form of oppositional culture—also shares something crucial with the exploration of material and visual Jewish culture in the region. Indeed, to take that overlap to a specific and personal level, we might note that Vladimir Levin, whose study of public policy toward the preservation of Jewish heritage sites and objects we are publishing here, is both a former active participant in, and retrospective informant on, the career of the Jewish University and its ethnographic field expeditions, as described in the article by Semion Goldin.

In analogous ways, a number of continuities and comparisons may be made among the three essays about East Central Europe (chiefly, Poland and Hungary), written by Kovács, Subotic, and Zisook. Reading them in tandem gives us a detailed and rounded picture not only of the Jewish dimension of the post-communist experience but also of the region's ongoing political and social reconstruction as a whole.

Notes

1. A selection would include: Michael Burawoy and Katherine Verdery (eds.), *Uncertain Transition: Ethnographies of Change in the Postsocialist World* (Lanham: 1999); Ruth Ellen Gruber, *Virtually Jewish: Reinventing Jewish Culture in Europe* (Berkeley: 2002); Padriac Kenney, *A Carnival of Revolution: Central Europe, 1989* (Princeton: 2002); Geneviève Zubrzycki, *The Crosses of Auschwitz: Nationalism and Religion in Post-Communist Poland* (Chicago: 2006); Zvi Y. Gitelman, Musya Glants, and Marshall I. Goldman (eds.), *Jewish Life after the USSR* (Bloomington: 2003); Zvi Y. Gitelman, *Jewish Identities in Post-communist Russia and Ukraine: An Uncertain Ethnicity* (New York: 2012); Mark Kramer, "The Demise of the Soviet Bloc," *Journal of Modern History* 83, no. 4 (2011), 788–854; Piotr Forecki, *Reconstructing Memory: The Holocaust in Polish Public Debates* (Frankfurt: 2013); Katka Reszke, *Return of the Jew: Memory Narratives of the Third Post-Holocaust Generation of Jews in Poland* (Brighton, Mass: 2013); Serhii Plokhy, *The Last Empire: The Final Days of the Soviet Union* (New York: 2014); Jelena Subotic, *Yellow Star, Red Star: Holocaust Remembrance after Communism* (Ithaca: 2019).

2. Michael Bernhard and Jan Kubik (eds.), *Twenty Years after Communism: The Politics of Memory and Commemoration* (New York: 2014), 8; cf. Anna Manchin, "Jews in Museums: Narratives of Nation and 'Jewishness' in Post-Communist Hungarian and Polish Public Memory," *Polin* 31: *Poland and Hungary Jewish Realities Compared*, ed. François Guesnet, Howard Lupovitch, and Antony Polonsky (New York: 2019), 481–501; Georges Mink and Laure Neumayer (eds.), *History, Memory, and Politics in Central and Eastern Europe: Memory Games* (New York: 2013); Muriel Blaive, Christian Gerbel, and Thomas Lindenberger (eds.), *Clashes in European Memory: The Case of Communist Repression and the Holocaust* (Innsbruck: 2013); Małgorzata Pakier and Bo Strath (eds.), *A European Memory? Contested Histories and Politics of Remembrance* (New York: 2010); John-Paul Himka and Joanna Michlic (eds.), *Bringing the Dark Past to Light: The Reception of the Holocaust in Postcommunist Europe* (Lincoln: 2013); Michael Steinlauf, *Bondage to the Dead: Poland and the Memory of the Holocaust* (Syracuse: 1997). On the pre-1989 background, see Tony Judt, "The Past Is Another Country: Myth and Memory in Postwar Europe," *Theoria: A Journal of Social and Political Theory* 87 (June 1996), 36–69; Jan T. Gross, "A Tangled Web: Confronting Stereotypes Concerning Relations between Poles, Germans, Jews, and Communists," in *The Politics of Retribution in Europe: World War II and its Aftermath*, ed. István Deák, Jan T. Gross, and Tony Judt (Princeton: 2000).

3. Tzvetan Todorov, *Hope and Memory: Lessons from the Twentieth Century* (Princeton: 2003), originally published as *Mémoire du mal. Tentation du bien. Enquête sur le siècle* (Paris: 2000), esp. ch. 2; cf. Małgorzata Pakier and Joanna Wawrzyniak, "Introduction: Memory

and Change in Eastern Europe: How Special?," in *Memory and Change in Europe: Eastern Perspectives*, ed. Małgorzata Pakier and Joanna Wawrzyniak (New York: 2018), 1–19, and two of the articles in that volume: Piotr Tadeusz Kwiatkowski, "The Second World War in the Memory of Contemporary Polish Society" (231–245) and Jackek Chrobaczyński and Piotr Trojański, "Auschwitz and Katyn in Political Bondage" (246–263).

4. Apart from the essays in this volume, see Anna Seleny, "Revolutionary Road: 1956 and the Fracturing of Hungarian Historical Memory," in Bernhard and Kubik (eds.), *Twenty Years after Communism*, 48–49; Emmanuel Droit, "Le Goulag contre la Shoah: Mémoires officielles et cultures mémorielles dans l'Europe élargie," *Vingtième Siècle. Revue d'histoire*, 94, no. 2 (2007), 101–120.

5. Timofey Sergeytsev, "Chto rossiia dolzhna sdelat' s Ukrainoi" [What Should Russia do with Ukraine?], https://ria.ru/20220403/ukraina-1781469605.html; for English translation, see: https://medium.com/@kravchenko_mm/what-should-russia-do-with-ukraine-translation-of-a-propaganda-article-by-a-russian-journalist-a3e92e3cb64.

Historical Memory and Antisemitism in Post-Communist East Central Europe

Jelena Subotic

(GEORGIA STATE UNIVERSITY)

During the 2020 presidential election in Poland, the state television and leading politicians from the ruling Peace and Justice (PiS) party accused the main opposition candidate Rafał Trzaskowski, then mayor of Warsaw, of being an "agent of a powerful foreign lobby" trying to "satisfy Jewish claims" by means of his support for the restitution of property stolen from Polish Jews murdered in the Holocaust.[1] In Lithuania, a local politician claimed on Holocaust Remembrance Day that "Jews shared the blame for the Holocaust."[2] In Hungary, an article (later retracted) by the national commissioner of culture offered a lament that Poland and Hungary today were Europe's "new Jews," while characterizing Jewish financier and philanthropist George Soros as "a liberal Führer" responsible for the "poisonous gas" of "multiculturalism and open society, which is deadly to the European way of life."[3]

While there was a moment in the scholarship of contemporary Europe that considered antisemitism to be largely removed from the political discourse, even referring to it as a "dead prejudice" mostly replaced by Islamophobia and anti-Romism,[4] this is clearly no longer the case. Antisemitism is alive and well, even thriving, although it manifests itself in new mutations that reflect contemporary political realignments, strategies, and historical legacies.

This essay surveys the current manifestations of antisemitism in post-Communist East Central Europe by linking antisemitism to historical memory, especially the still contested memory of the Holocaust. Antisemitism, obviously, is not new and has provided a foundation to many nationalist and exclusionary movements throughout history. The objective here is not to reiterate that obvious point. Instead, it is to analyze the changing forms of antisemitism in East Central Europe since the collapse of Communism and to explain its relationship to unresolved questions of historical memory, especially the memory of what was once a vibrant Jewish presence and is now an overwhelming Jewish absence.

The essay proceeds as follows. First, I provide a framework for understanding the political context of contemporary antisemitism. Next, I link the problem of antisemitism to the contested issues of historical memory in East Central Europe. I then

Jelena Subotic, *Historical Memory and Antisemitism in Post-Communist East Central Europe* In: *Becoming Post-Communist*. Edited by: Eli Lederhendler, Oxford University Press. © Oxford University Press 2023.
DOI: 10.1093/oso/9780197687215.003.0002

offer a few brief snapshots of contemporary historical revisionism regarding the Holocaust and the place of the Jews in the region, as well as examples of contemporary antisemitism.

Changing Manifestations of Antisemitism

There is much evidence that antisemitism is on the rise around the world. Survey after survey shows that there is an increase in expressions of antisemitism, especially on social media.[5] This rise has coincided with the emergence and strengthening of populist movements—those that separate social groups into "the people" vs. "the elite"—which have deployed elements of the transnational antisemitic repertoire, most often the idea of Jewish control of capital, Jewish globalism and cosmopolitanism and, increasingly, the threat of Jewish-financed and facilitated international migration flows.

As its own system of meaning, as an epistemic code, antisemitism provides an immediately useful ideological framework for nationalist populist agendas. It easily separates "the pure people" (the national ethnic majority) from a "corrupt elite" (Jews, with their outsized power, and also their allies and co-conspirators), and it defines who belongs, who is alien, who is morally righteous, and who is corrupt. Antisemitism is useful for populist nationalist state-building because it is plastic and adaptable, but also because it is inherently contradictory and can thus be utilized in seemingly any context, in pursuit of any argument. There are no wrong answers: Jews are weak and pathetic but they are also super-powerful; they are inferior, but they also control the world. It means everything and nothing; it is about constructing the perfect enemy, the perfect elite, and the perfect counterfoil to the people (the *volk*). Contemporary antisemitism, then, often has very little to do with the actual Jews *as Jews*, and more to do with the contemporary construction of what "the Jews" represent in the current international order. In the context of post-Communist East Central Europe, antisemitism's enduring power lies in its ability to construct "the Jews" to represent whatever it is that current majorities reject—whether "Communism," "capitalism," "neoliberalism," "multiculturalism," "pluralism," "feminism," or "cosmopolitanism."

Contemporary antisemitism is often implicit. It manifests itself in a coded or latent form that often does not mention Jews directly, but rather engages in dissemination of easily recognizable antisemitic tropes, sometimes referred to as "antisemitism without Jews and without anti-Semites."[6] Often these tropes involve global market financiers or "greedy speculators conspiring against nations" without explicit mention of Jews (so that a charge of antisemitism can be easily refuted). In addition, antisemitism in contemporary East Central Europe is often directly related to a sense of cultural identity and identity politics; it has become a marker of political identity, a shorthand for a particular set of political views that transcend attitudes toward the Jews. This issue also relates to the domestic struggle over whether or to what extent post-Communist societies should liberalize after the end of Communism. Many studies have noted the significant decline in the perceived legitimacy of liberalism as a form of social order in post-Communist East Central Europe.[7] Manifestations of this illiberal turn are the shrinking public space for dissent; increasing control over media, academic and cultural institutions and civil society; opposition to the expansion of rights for women and sexual minorities; state capture of courts; and one-party domination with largely non-competitive elections. Among the factors accounting for this turn to illiberalism are the general dissatisfaction with the consequences of economic reforms of the 1990s and the more recent Great Recession of 2007–2009, and the sense of threat posed by the refugee crisis of 2015. Illiberalism as a form of social order has taken root in many post-Communist societies and has become a dominant social and political force that has produced further nationalist and conservative politics across the region, perhaps most visibly in Poland and Hungary.[8]

Such developments relate to antisemitism in that the main adversary of illiberal movements is the project of liberal democracy in its cosmopolitan, international, and multicultural form—and Jews have often been perceived as embodiments of liberal democratic values and as beneficiaries of liberal policies. Thus, as post-Communist societies turned to illiberalism, this had consequences for the perception and status of Jews in these countries. For example, as a number of studies of Hungary have shown, antisemitism is a form of cultural code, a communicative function through which not merely (or even not primarily) the Jews, but also a range of issues that the Jews have come to represent, are rejected.[9] This context includes economic and cultural liberalization and globalization, specifically the "conflict between cosmopolitan and national interests, the consequences of joining the process of international integration as the loss of national sovereignty, and the social consequences of the economic and political transition as the result of being at the mercy of colonial masters."[10] The Jews, then, come to be represented as symbols of this national destruction and as a demarcation of what is "anti-national" as opposed to "national."[11]

It follows that antisemitism in contemporary East Central Europe is best understood as a frame through which nationalist movements in the aftermath of Communism imagine a new and desirable post-Communist cultural and social order. This involves recasting the political stakes into a conflict over radically different visions of the role of the nation-state, sovereignty, and pluralism after Communism. The antisemitic framework with its ready-made concepts of incompatibility, hostility, and threats presented by Jews (or their national agents) taps into an existing deep reservoir of local popular antisemitism.[12] It offers a response to the dislocations of economic and cultural globalization in the aftermath of the Communist collapse by presenting these real social problems as a result of a conspiracy between globalist unaccountable elites (often, the Jews) and the immigrants and other cultural minorities they allegedly support, guide, and finance.[13] An additional factor feeding into persisting antisemitism is historical memory—in particular, the highly contested memory of the Holocaust and the role, place, and status of East European Jews in the 20th century. It is to this problem that I turn next.

Historical Memory and the Antisemitic Repertoire in Post-Communist Europe

While there are many social and cultural sources that continue to nourish antisemitism in East Central Europe, contemporary antisemitism in the region cannot be properly understood outside the context of the Holocaust and its contested memory.[14] In the aftermath of the Communist collapse, as East Central European states started to apply for membership in various European bodies, and especially in the European Union, they were expected to adopt the West European narrative of the 20th century. One of the most important elements of this narrative was the Holocaust, perceived as the singular and most consequential event of 20th-century Europe. Its story of genocide and the promise of "never again" became a foundational story of the European Union[15] and a broadly shared and accepted "cosmopolitan memory" that transcended national borders, even those of countries that had little or no direct relationship to the events of the Holocaust.[16] The memory of those events has also become something of a "memory template."[17] Its universal lesson about the disastrous consequences of intolerance, racism, and "othering" of minorities is frequently invoked to warn against contemporary manifestations of bigotry, intolerance, and political violence.

In fact, the EU made membership of East Central European countries conditional on their carrying out a number of domestic reforms, among them, Holocaust education and memorialization.[18] While many governments in East Central European states, anxious not to jeopardize the delicate process of EU accession, accepted this new condition, signing the necessary documents and adopting major parameters of the memory framework, they also rejected much of the established canon of European memory politics.[19] This was especially the case with conservative and populist governments in countries such as Poland, where the initial, more liberal embrace of West European memory practices was quickly marginalized.

The main point of rupture after Communism was the fact that the cosmopolitan memory of the 20th century as developed in the West—with its emphasis on the universal value of memorializing specifically Jewish suffering in the Holocaust, and its embrace (even if only rhetorical) of postwar multiculturalism and ethnic pluralism—did not align with the very different set of memory traditions in post-Communist Europe.[20] This lack of fit was evident in the lack of centrality of the Holocaust as the defining memory of the 20th-century experience across the post-Communist space. As Tony Judt put it, "the really uncomfortable truth about World War II was that what happened to the Jews between 1939 and 1945 was not nearly as important to most of the protagonists as later sensibilities might wish."[21] Instead, East Central European states after Communism constructed their national identities on the memory of Stalinism and Soviet occupation, as well as on the search for continuity with pre-Communist nation states. The problem, after Communism, became one of "multiplicities of memories" that were often at odds with one another.[22]

Emerging post-Communist narratives that focused on ethnic nationalism and rejection of all Communist legacies clashed with the established Western narrative of the Holocaust that began to trickle into the East Central European cultural space in the 1990s. The Western historical narratives, and perhaps none more so than the cosmopolitan narratives of the Holocaust, became threatening and destabilizing to the more conservative post-Communist regimes. Many East Central European governments rejected what they regarded as the dogmatism of Western narratives of minority rights, cultural pluralism, and ethnic co-existence, and they resented the attempt to replace the centrality of anti-Communist and ethnic nationalist frames in their national narratives. An additional source of discontent was the perceived necessity of "performing" cultural pluralism in the form of Holocaust memorialization. Finally, and most consequentially, the Western historical narrative of the 20th century elevated Jewish victimhood above that of regional majority ethnic groups and also brought to the fore two sensitive matters that had long been suppressed, namely, the extensive and deep local complicity in the Holocaust, and the material and political benefits of the nearly complete Jewish absence across Eastern Europe.[23]

Indeed, much of post-Holocaust East Central Europe has been described as a purposeful "site of nonmemory," a "landscape of erasure."[24] Writing about Poland, Ewa Płonowska Ziarek offers an apt description for the entire post-Communist political space characterized by "the erasure of collective and individual memories of Jewish life . . ., the lack of mourning for the Jewish tragedy, and the overwhelming loss of awareness of the absence of Jews and Jewish culture."[25] The fact that post-Second World War Jewish communities in these countries are negligible in numbers and have limited political clout is not incidental to this condition.[26] These once multicultural societies had large Jewish minorities, but today are mostly ethnically homogeneous, making Eastern Europe a site of "dismembered multiethnicity."[27]

East Central Europe is not only the main site of the Holocaust, but also the main witness to, and the main beneficiary of, the Holocaust. The annihilation of European Jewry was carried out not only behind the barbed wire of concentration camps, hidden from plain sight. It also took place in the public view of non-Jewish citizens on the streets, squares, and farms across the region. Non-Jews benefited from this Jewish erasure—often for generations after the Holocaust.[28] Decades of looting followed by Communist seizures resulted in the slow morphing of Jewish businesses, homes, and property into the general economy, with only sporadic attempts at restitution. These, in turn, led to growing resentment and nationalist entrenchment. The Jews of East Central Europe again became inconvenient, their demands for remembrance raining on the parade of post-Communist independence and ruining the moment that was supposed to be triumphant, liberating, and hopeful.

The unresolved and contested memory of the Holocaust in post-Communist Europe intersected with the growing forces of populism. At a time of post-Communist identity crisis, populism sought to reposition national historical narratives in opposition both to those of Communism and to those historically embraced by Western Europe. References to Communist history disappeared, replaced by frequent harkening back to an imaginary pre-Communist national golden age (often imperial or at least monarchic, and often very Christian). The narrative continuity offered by populist movements linked the present-day country to a mythical national past with its central narratives of righteousness, honor, sacrifice, and heroic suffering.[29] This nationalist narrative left very little space for minorities, and almost no space whatsoever for the millions of Jews who were once citizens of these countries.

The discussion of historical memory, especially historical memory of the Holocaust, is relevant for explaining the rise of nationalist populism in the region. It demonstrates that the basis of nation-building after Communism was ethnic and exclusionary. And while this new populist national identity construction may not be about the Jews or about the Holocaust, it unquestionably is related to the exclusion of others—both the nonexistent Jews and those who are the "new others"—refugees, migrants, or other ethnic minorities such as the Roma or Muslims.

The exclusionary concept of the nation in post-Communist East Central Europe came to sharp focus after the 2015 refugee crisis, when politics became intensely ethnic and old antisemitic tropes morphed easily into different forms of prejudices, whether the (already existing) anti-Romism or the newer and increasingly main-streamed Islamophobia. It is within this context of old prejudices now directed against different groups of people that we can understand the attraction of a popu-list far-Right party such as People's Party Our Slovakia, which originally built its support on nostalgia for the Slovak fascist state during the Nazi era, and which dis-played open antisemitism. Once the party won seats in the parliament for the first time in 2016, its rhetoric shifted from antisemitism to attacks against immigrants and the Roma.[30] The targets may have shifted, but the sentiment remains the same. This shape-shifting of ethnic and racial prejudice has caused great anxiety among European Jews since, in the words of a Hungarian Jewish human rights activist: "When a Roma person is targeted, I feel less safe because I know they will come for me next."[31]

In sum, the politics of memory has played a momentous role in the rise of popu-list and far-Right movements in East Central Europe since at least 2010. The sharp tilt to authoritarianism and illiberalism in Hungary and Poland, and also encroach-ing illiberalism in Bulgaria, Serbia, and Croatia, cannot be explained without under-standing the strength of the appeal to a particular type of memory politics. History, quite simply, has become a "handmaiden of populism,"[32] in that the question of who are the "real victims" of history has been central to the populist enterprise, which claims that East European victimization under Communism is neither adequately un-derstood nor appreciated.[33]

In the next section, I illustrate this dynamic with some brief examples of contempo-rary manifestations of antisemitism in East Central Europe.

Antisemitism in Contemporary East Central Europe: Snapshots

The political consequences of politicized historical memory, and especially the reha-bilitation of fascist movements that supported and often directly participated in the Holocaust, have been evident both in the stunning rise of the populist far-Right across post-Communist Europe (which is part of a much broader global far-Right resurgence that has also destabilized politics in the West), and in growing manifestations of anti-semitism. The precise determination of causal factors that link historical memory and the rise in antisemitism is beyond the scope and methodology of this essay.[34] What I want to showcase, however, are some examples of the ways in which histor-ical memory builds on and further entrenches local antisemitism in post-Communist Europe.

In Hungary, the major turn to illiberalism since the rise of the Fidesz Party under Viktor Orbán has been marked by overt and covert expressions of antisemitism. A report published in 2019 by the Organization for Security and Cooperation in Europe (OSCE) noted a significant uptick in antisemitism and antisemitic violence in Hungary,[35] while the European Union survey on antisemitism found that a large majority of Hungary's Jews—up to 77 percent—considered antisemitism to be a major problem in their country.[36] Antisemitism in contemporary Hungary follows closely the populist blueprint presented above. One of the main far-Right populist grievances—the "invasion" of migrants, refugees, and foreigners and their "pollution" of the national body politic—expresses itself in the attitude of about 25 percent of Hungarians who blame the Jews for bringing more migrants to their country.[37]

The claim that Jews are behind Europe's migrant crisis is what animates Orbán's sustained nationwide campaign against Hungarian-born Jewish philanthropist George Soros,[38] under the slogan "Let's not let Soros have the last laugh." Orbán has repeatedly accused Soros of orchestrating the surge of migrants (especially Middle Eastern migrants) into Europe. In addition, Orbán has made the unsubstantiated claim that Soros was somehow involved in the murder of Slovak journalist Ján Kuciak in 2018. "I see George Soros and his organizations' fingerprints on the events in Slovakia," Orbán declared, adding: "I don't doubt it for a minute that this network does everything to overthrow governments opposing migration."[39] The issue of migration, alongside Soros' support of rights of the Roma and other minorities, and his huge investment in the Central European University in Budapest, has been at the heart of Fidesz's attacks on Soros, the foundations he funds, and Hungarian opposition parties that are branded as having been "paid by Soros."[40] One of Fidesz's campaign advertisements warned that, on "the day after the election, the opposition will start to settle migrants in the country," urging voters to stop "Soros' people" from forming the government.[41]

Orbán's anti-Soros campaign can thus be understood as an activation of one of the elements of the antisemitic platform—the accusation that Jews, as enemies of the nation, work to destroy it from within by "diluting" the nation with external, alien elements. Orbán came very close to a direct spelling-out of this accusation in his 2018 tirade directed at Soros: "They are not national, but international; they do not believe in work, but speculate with money; they have no homeland, but feel that the whole world is theirs."[42] While Orbán was careful not to mention "the Jews" (and in fact has also made repeated overtures of friendship toward Israel), this statement encompassed a number of known antisemitic tropes such as financial speculation and globalized, anational control, and it was broadly understood as such by Hungarian Jews as well as by the international public.[43]

Antisemitism most clearly intersects with historical memory in contemporary Hungary in state-sponsored acts of historical revisionism, especially with regard to the Holocaust in Hungary. For example, the Memorial to the Victims of the German Occupation erected in Budapest in 2014 memorializes Hungary (that is, the country) as the main victim of the German occupation by means of a not very subtle depiction of Germany's imperial eagle crushing Hungary, as represented by the Archangel Gabriel.[44] The memorial was unveiled overnight and with no accompanying official opening ceremony, in order to avoid any public debate and expected protests.[45] However, it immediately produced deep domestic contestation. Outside the memorial, Holocaust survivors or their family members have placed hundreds of handwritten notes, pictures, and objects that tell the story of 430,000 Jews who were deported from Hungary, mostly to Auschwitz—the quickest rate of deportation in the history of the Holocaust, taking less than two months, and carried out with the active participation of Hungarian civil servants.

The memorial makes use of architecture as a tool to express myths of nationhood, as part of the populist strategy of visual remembrance that the Fidesz government has been promoting for more than a decade.[46] More specifically, it narratively replaces the memory of the Holocaust, and the catastrophe of Hungarian Jewish annihilation as the central memory of the Second World War in Hungary, with the memory of Hungarian victimhood and innocence. It also purposefully removes responsibility for the murder of Hungarian Jews from Hungary's Axis-allied government, placing the blame firmly on Germany and presenting fascism and its extermination policies as alien, foreign intrusions into the Hungarian body politic.

This intervention is important because it provides the current Hungarian far-Right government with a brick-and-mortar visual device to claim a mythical continuity with the pre-Axis sovereign Hungary and its (illiberal, fascist, and antisemitic) regime.[47] In so doing, it presents the history of the Second World War as being exclusively the history of Hungary's victimization—through the loss of state sovereignty—and not as the history of genocide of Hungarian Jews. Here, the principal victims of the German occupation, Hungarian Jews killed in the Holocaust, are erased to make room for the memory of the Hungarian state, which not only was *not* the main victim of the German occupation, but in fact directly participated in the genocide. The very purpose of this type of historical memory, this "pathological mourning,"[48] was to produce competitive victimization, which itself served as an attack on liberal cosmopolitan politics of remembrance.

Similarly, the House of Terror museum that opened in 2002 in Budapest narrates the story of Hungary's 20th-century experience as a nation-victim of a foreign Communist regime and, and to a much lesser extent, a foreign fascist regime. The museum truncates Hungary's 20th century to 1944–1989, such that the fascist era begins with the German occupation in 1944, rather than 1940, when Hungary joined the Axis alliance. This shift completely removes the history of the Holocaust in Hungary before 1944, despite the fact that some 60,000 Hungarian Jews were killed as early as 1942—not by Germans, but by Hungarian forces under the rule of regent Miklós Horthy.[49] At the same time, rehabilitation of the Horthy era, including its well-documented and deeply entrenched antisemitism, provides post-Communist Hungary with a mythologized connection to its pre-Communist past, conveniently sidestepping the 44 years of Communism and deriving contemporary state legitimacy from national continuity with an earlier, more "authentic" (and therefore more legitimate) Hungary. These kinds of historical erasures do not merely reflect on a country's relationship with its past; they are also manifestations of the country's present: its attitude toward its minorities, cultural inclusion, and diversity.

Croatia is another post-Communist state with a deeply problematic relationship to the memory of the Holocaust on its own territory. A survey conducted by the Anti-Defamation League (ADL) in 2014 indicated that 33 percent of citizens displayed antisemitic attitudes; more recently, in 2019, the Office for Democratic Institutions and Human Rights (ODIHR), a unit of the OSCE, reported an increase in antisemitic crimes in Croatia.[50] In 2017, a group of Croatian war veterans affiliated with the Croatian Defence Forces (HOS)[51] erected a memorial plaque with the unit's call to arms, "Ready for the Homeland!" (*Za dom spremni!*) near the memorial site of the Jasenovac concentration camp.[52] This slogan was identical to that of the Ustasha, Croatia's fascist militia, which had killed more than 80,000 Serbs, Jews, and Roma at the Jasenovac death camp during the Second World War; it was as if a plaque reading *Sieg Heil!* had been placed next to Auschwitz.[53] Although this act led to a public outcry that resulted in the plaque being removed from Jasenovac, it was then mounted a few miles down the road, in the town of Novska.[54]

Ustasha chants and insignia are not banned, and thus they have become ubiquitous in post-Communist Croatia. Marko Perković-Thompson, one of Croatia's most popular rock singers, performs regularly dressed in Ustasha gear, riling his supporters into Ustasha chants. At soccer games—a notorious hotbed of racist invective across Europe—the fans often break into the Ustasha salute "Za dom spremni!" or "Let's go, Ustasha" (this happened, for instance, at a March 2016 match against Israel, with Israel's ambassador to Croatia in attendance).[55] Croatian President Kolinda Grabar Kitarović and Prime Minister Tihomir Orešković explicitly condemned the employment of Ustasha slogans and symbols only in March 2017, following a meeting with Tom Yazdgerdi, the U.S. special envoy on the Holocaust.[56] According to Yazdgerdi, Utasha symbols were "especially offensive to the Holocaust survivors and their family members. ... It is hard, especially for the Holocaust survivors, to watch those symbols."[57]

There are also increasingly loud voices in support of the Ustasha and the Independent State of Croatia (ISC)—as the Second World War fascist puppet state was called—from within the Croatian Catholic Church. In a well-publicized case in 2016, a priest on a popular televised Sunday sermon program spoke with nostalgia about the ISC, asking: "Whom have we really ever killed outside our borders?"—as if to indicate that there was nothing wrong with killing *inside* ISC borders.[58] Such sentiment appears to be widespread within the Church, whose stance has contributed in no small part to the growing acceptance of the Ustasha among the Croatian mainstream; the apparent logic behind the Church's tolerance is that most members of the Ustasha were Catholic as well as anti-Communist.

Croatia's far-Right surge and especially its increasingly problematic official memory of the Second World War have destabilized its relationships with traditional allies and friends. Israel's ambassador to Croatia wrote an open letter of protest against an award-winning Holocaust revisionist film.[59] Since 2016, in response to the surge of neo-fascism in Croatia, Serbian and Jewish communities have boycotted the annual memorial events at the Jasenovac site. Instead, they each have organized their own, separate memorials, whether at Jasenovac or at other sites.[60]

There is increasing general anxiety in the Croatian Jewish community about the rise of antisemitism and the normalization of fascist rhetoric. "When fascist events start happening in a society, this brings about a sense of uneasiness among Jews. But when institutions don't react, this causes fear because you don't know where that really can lead us," noted Sanja Zoričić Tabaković, a representative of the Jewish community in Zagreb.[61] Daniel Ivin, a well-known Croatian Holocaust survivor and activist said: "We know that with the new government we don't have a future, but in recent times, they are starting to take our past."[62]

In other parts of East Central Europe, antisemitism is no longer latent, but has instead become quite overt. In Poland, the most explicit antisemitic groups are the All-Polish Youth and the National-Radical Camp, which together in November 2017 organized a massive rally in Warsaw, a gathering of some 60,000 participants that welcomed neo-Nazis and where participants carried banners that asserted "only white Christians belong in Europe."[63] The Polish government supported the rally, and while condemning the openly racist and antisemitic banners on display, nonetheless called it "a great celebration of Poles" and "a beautiful sight."[64]

Extreme xenophobia is not only of far-Right provenance. The mainstream populist PiS (Law and Justice) party has become radicalized, moving farther to the right, especially since coming to power in 2015. A PiS member of parliament wondered in 2018 why there were "so many Jews among the abortionists, despite the Holocaust."[65] Another PiS political figure shared on his Facebook page a link to a Nazi propaganda film that depicted the Jews as controlling and cruelly abusing those confined in the Warsaw ghetto. This narrative about "Jewish perpetrators" of the Holocaust is prevalent and was repeated in Polish Prime Minister Mateusz Morawiecki's defense of the 2018 Holocaust bill, the now notorious law that penalized (originally criminally, later modified to civil penalties) any insinuation that the "Polish nation" participated in the Holocaust.[66] In a 2015 survey conducted by the Polish state polling agency, the Public Opinion Research Center, only 23 percent of the respondents agreed that the record of Poles' crimes against Jews was "still valid and needed to be disclosed and publicized."[67] A recent social scientific experiment with Polish respondents who were confronted with the evidence of Poles' murder of their Jewish neighbors in Jedwabne indicated that presenting this historical evidence to today's Poles can quickly lead to further cycles of denial, claims of Polish-only victimhood, and even an uptick in antisemitic attitudes, further complicating efforts at historical accountability and reconciliation.[68]

In Ukraine, 46 percent of the respondents in the 2015 survey conducted by the Anti-Defamation League displayed signs of antisemitism.[69] There was a wave of antisemitic and anti-Roma incidents in 2018, including a far-Right politician's call for "cleansing Ukraine of *zhidi*," vandalism of a Holocaust memorial in Ternopil, a neo-Nazi march in honor of an SS unit in Lviv, and an especially violent attack on a Roma encampment in Kyiv—all in the span of a few weeks.[70] Members of the National Squad far-Right militia marched along the streets of Ukrainian cities dressed in black, promising to "establish order in Ukraine" and to fight the "alcoholic genocide of the Ukrainian people." A smoke grenade was thrown at a bookshop in Lviv during a lecture on the Holocaust.[71] These incidents may be isolated and marginalized, but they caused Ukrainian Jews to note a "disturbing correlation between Holocaust revisionism and violence against living Jews."[72] And yet, in 2019, Ukraine elected Volodymyr Zelensky president, the first Jewish Ukrainian ever elected to that post. Even though Zelensky himself hardly ever brought up his Jewish background during the campaign (his unlikely ascent to power had much more to do with his TV popularity than his ethnic background), prior to the Russian invasion of 2022, some Ukrainian Jews have expressed apprehension about his political future and its consequences for Ukrainian Jews.[73] Since the Russian invasion, however, his conduct as the leader has gained him national hero status in Ukraine, and any questions about his Jewishness seem to have dissipated.

In Bulgaria, the most recent Anti-Defamation League survey conducted in 2014 determined that 44 percent of the population displayed negative attitudes vis-à-vis Jews.[74] In the annual hate crime data compiled by the Office for Democratic Institutions and Human Rights of the OSCE, an upsurge in violent antisemitic crimes in Bulgaria was reported for 2019.[75] The capital city, Sofia, is littered with antisemitic graffiti and swastika images (even inside at least one government administration building), with seemingly no effort on behalf of the authorities to clean them up. The leader of the high-profile Bulgarian populist party, Ataka—which, for a while, was part of the coalition government—has referred to the Holocaust as a "plot" and has said that "Western talmudic circles, headed by the Rothschild family," are responsible for a "genocide" against predominantly Orthodox Christian countries such as Bulgaria.[76]

In Romania, a Jewish cemetery was desecrated in the town of Husi in 2019. Romania's capital city of Bucharest ranks third in a global listing of number of antisemitic social media posts, while data from 2015 and 2017 indicated that only 39 percent of Romanians would accept a Jewish person as a family member.[77] The 2015 ADL survey found that 47 percent of Romanians harbored antisemitic sentiments, up from 35 percent in 2014.[78]

In Slovakia, as well, antisemitic incidents are on the rise. Recent research shows that Jews face negative attitudes from a significant percentage of the Slovak population (23 percent did not want a Jewish neighbor), and there has been an uptick in desecration of Jewish graveyards and graffiti scrawled on Jewish landmarks.[79] In 2019, as many as 75 gravestones were toppled in the town of Námestovo, and 20 Jewish graves were desecrated in the town of Rajec. In a village near the capital city, Bratislava, a Jewish graveyard was being used as a playground and site of a local festival.[80]

And on and on. Almost every country in the region has examples of overt antisemitism, physical abuse of Jewish landmarks and sites, and a broad and seemingly intractable discomfort with inclusion of Jews as fully equal members of the national body.

Conclusion

In post-Communist East Central Europe, the deeply contested memory of the Holocaust, coupled with an almost complete absence of sizable Jewish communities, has shaped both the exclusionary nation-building that occurred after the end of Communism and contemporary attitudes about past and present Jews. The history of Jews in East Central Europe, and their annihilation under the German occupation (but also with the help of the local population), casts a long and dark shadow over the region. Attempts to reconcile very different memories of the 20th century, especially the memories of Communist oppression with memories of the Holocaust, have led to deep and sustained resentment and a particular form of backlash in the form of historical revisionism in both historiography and museum and memorial practices.

While historical revisionism is not the same as antisemitism, it effaces and erases the Jewish experience in East Central Europe. In consequence, Jews in the region feel as though they never belonged, nor are they accepted today, as full-fledged members of the nation.

In evaluating the political changes in the aftermath of Communism, it appears that they also brought about a complete rearranging of historical memory, as well as rearrangement of how ethnic minorities are accommodated and managed. In fully rejecting Communism and its legacies, post-Communist governments likewise rejected Communist commitment, however superficial and fleeting, to multiculturalism and pan-nationalism. Post-Communist societies were organized in opposition to this Communist legacy, and thus turned to ethnic majoritarianism and nationalist exclusion. This choice has opened up the political space for the marginalization of Jewish life and an alarming rise in antisemitism. If populism and nationalism were never good news for the Jews, their newly emerging strength in East Central Europe is indeed cause for apprehension.

Notes

I would like to thank Ben Stanley and editors of this volume for very helpful comments and suggestions, as well as Saad Khan for research assistance.

1. Edit Inotai and Claudia Ciobanu, "Antisemitism Creeps Back as Hungary and Poland Fail to Draw Red Lines," *Balkan Insight* (11 September 2020). This is an online publication.

2. Cnaan Liphshiz, "In Holocaust Memorial Day Speech, Lithuanian Lawmaker Says Jews and Communists Share Blame," *Jewish Telegraphic Agency* (27 January 2021).

3. *Radio Free Europe* (29 November 2020), online at: https://www.rferl.org/a/hungary-museum-retracts-article-george-soros-nazi-gas-chambers-holocaust-hitler-orban-eu/30974375.html (accessed 1 August 2021).

4. Ruth Wodak, "The Radical Right and Antisemitism" in *The Oxford Handbook of the Radical Right*, ed. Jens Rydgren (Oxford: 2018), 61–85.

5. Sergio DellaPergola, "Jewish Perceptions of Antisemitism in the European Union, 2018: A New Structural Look," *Analysis of Current Trends in Antisemitism—ACTA* 40, no. 2 (2020).

6. Karin Stögner and Karin Bischof, "International High Finance against the Nation? Antisemitism and Nationalism in Austrian Print Media Debates on the Economic Crisis," *Journal of Language and Politics* 17, no. 3 (2018), 428–446, 430.

7. Don Kalb, "Upscaling Illiberalism: Class, Contradiction, and the Rise of the Populist Right in Post-socialist Central Europe," *Fudan Journal of the Humanities and Social Sciences* 11, no. 3 (2018), 303–321.

8. Lenka Bustikova and Petra Guasti, "The Illiberal Turn or Swerve in Central Europe?," *Politics and Governance* 5, no. 4 (2017), 166–176.

9. András Kovács and Anna Szilágyi, "Variations on a Theme: The Jewish 'Other' in Old and New Antisemitic Media Discourses in Hungary in the 1940s and in 2011," in *Analysing Fascist Discourse: European Fascism in Talk and Text*, ed. John E. Richardson and Ruth Wodak (London: 2013), 203–227; András Kovács, "From Anti-Jewish Prejudice to Political Anti-Semitism? On Dynamics of Anti-Semitism in post-Communist Hungary," in *A Road to Nowhere? Jewish Experiences in Unifying Europe*, ed. Julius H. Schoeps and Olaf Glöckner (Leiden: 2011), 247–267.

10. Kovács, "From Anti-Jewish Prejudice to Political Anti-Semitism?," 258.

11. Ibid., 260.

12. Volha Charnysh, "Historical Legacies of Interethnic Competition: Anti-Semitism and the EU Referendum in Poland," *Comparative Political Studies* 48, no. 13 (2015), 1711–1745.

13. Dani Filc, "European Populism and Minorities," in *The Jewish Contribution to European Integration*, ed. Sharon Pardo and Hila Zahavi (New York: 2020), 47–62, 52; Michal Bilewicz, Mikołai Winiewski, Adrian Wójcik, and Mirosław Kofta, "Harmful Ideas: The Structure and Consequences of Anti-Semitic Beliefs in Poland," *Political Psychology* 34, no. 6 (2013), 821–839.

14. For a full elaboration of this argument, see Jelena Subotić, *Yellow Star, Red Star: Holocaust Remembrance after Communism* (Ithaca: 2019).

15. Aleida Assmann, "Transnational Memories," *European Review* 22, no. 4 (2014), 546–556.

16. Daniel Levy and Natan Sznaider, "Memory Unbound: The Holocaust and the Formation of Cosmopolitan Memory," *European Journal of Social Theory* 5, no. 1 (2002), 87–106.

17. Ljiljana Radonic (ed.), *The Holocaust/Genocide Template in Eastern Europe* (Abingdon: 2020).

18. For example, back in 1995, the European Parliament passed a resolution pertaining to the return of plundered property to Jewish communities, which contained explicit demands for East European states to return property looted in the Holocaust. European Parliament, "Resolution on the Return of Plundered Property to Jewish Communities" (Brussels: 1995).

19. Maria Mälksoo, "The Memory Politics of Becoming European: The East European Subalterns and the Collective Memory of Europe," *European Journal of International Relations* 15, no. 4 (2009), 653–680; Annabelle Littoz-Monnet, "Explaining Policy Conflict across Institutional Venues: European Union-Level Struggles over the Memory of the Holocaust," *JCMS: Journal of Common Market Studies* 51, no. 3 (2013), 489–504.

20. Levy and Sznaider, "Memory Unbound"; Małgorzata Pakier and Joanna Wawrzyniak, "Introduction," in idem (eds.), *Memory and Change in Europe: Eastern Perspectives* (New York: 2015), 1–22.

21. Tony Judt, "From the House of the Dead: On Modern European Memory," *New York Review of Books* (6 October 2005).

22. Pakier and Wawrzyniak, "Introduction," 7.

23. Alejandro Baer and Natan Sznaider, *Memory and Forgetting in the Post-Holocaust Era: The Ethics of Never Again* (Milton Park: 2017); John-Paul Himka, "Obstacles to the Integration of the Holocaust into Post-Communist East European Historical Narratives," *Canadian Slavonic Papers* 50, no. 3–4 (2008), 359–372.

24. Omer Bartov, "Eastern Europe as the Site of Genocide," *The Journal of Modern History* 80, no. 3 (2008), 557–593; Baer and Sznaider, *Memory and Forgetting*, 105.

25. Ewa Płonowska Ziarek, "Melancholic Nationalism and the Pathologies of Commemorating the Holocaust in Poland," in *Imaginary Neighbors: Mediating Polish–Jewish Relations after the Holocaust*, ed. Dorota Glowacka and Joanna Zylinska (Lincoln: 2007), 301–326, 302.

26. Today, Hungary is the only country in the region with a sizable Jewish population (75,000–100,000). Jewish communities in the rest of post-Communist Europe are reduced to miniscule numbers. Michael Shafir, *Between Denial and "Comparative Trivialization": Holocaust Negationism in Post-Communist East Central Europe* (Jerusalem: 2002).

27. Karolina S. Follis, *Building Fortress Europe: The Polish–Ukrainian Frontier* (Philadelphia: 2012).

28. Volha Charnysh and Evgeny Finkel, "The Death Camp Eldorado: Political and Economic Effects of Mass Violence," *American Political Science Review* 111, no. 4 (2017), 801–818.

29. Aleida Assmann, "Europe's Divided Memory," in *Memory and Theory in Eastern Europe*, ed. Uilleam Blacker, Aleksandr Etkind, and Julie Fedor (New York: 2013), 25–41.

30. Rick Lyman, "After Years in the Shadows, Europe's Neo-Fascists Are Stepping Back Out," *New York Times* (20 March 2017).

31. Jewish Telegraphic Agency and Cnaan Liphshiz, "European Jews Watch on in Fear as Italy Targets Roma People," *Haaretz* (24 June 2018).

32. István Rév, "Liberty Square, Budapest: How Hungary Won the Second World War," *Journal of Genocide Research* 20, no. 4 (2018), 607–623, 621.

33. Jelena Subotić, "The Appropriation of Holocaust Memory in Post-Communist Eastern Europe," *Modern Languages Open* 1 (2020), 1–8.

34. For an insightful attempt at teasing out the causal mechanism between Holocaust memory and antisemitism in Greece, see Georgios Antoniou, Elias Dinas, and Spyros Kosmidis, "Collective Victimhood and Social Prejudice: A Post-Holocaust Theory of Anti-Semitism," *Political Psychology* 41, no. 5 (2020), 861–886.

35. Organization for Security and Cooperation in Europe (OSCE), "Hate Crime Reporting: Hungary" (2019), online at: https://hatecrime.osce.org/hungary (accessed 13 July 2021).

36. European Union Agency for Fundamental Rights, "Experiences and Perceptions of Antisemitism: Second Survey on Discrimination and Hate Crime against Jews in the EU" (Luxembourg: 2018).

37. Anti Defamation League global survey (21 November 2019), online at: adl.org/news/ press-releases/adl-global-survey-of-18-countries-finds-hardcore-anti-semitic-attitudes-remain (accessed 13 July 2021).

38. A child Holocaust survivor, Soros acquired considerable wealth in the United States as a hedge fund manager; he has spent the last 40 years investing in liberal and progressive causes around the world. Inspired primarily by Karl Popper's vision of an "open society," Soros was especially attracted to the idea of multiculturalism, free press, and human rights, and it is on this basis that his network of Open Society foundations was established across East and Central Europe after the fall of Communism. See Kenneth P. Vogel, Scott Shane, and Patrick Kingsley, "How Vilification of George Soros Moved From the Fringes to the Mainstream," *New York Times* (31 October 2018).

39. "Hungary's Orban Says George Soros Behind Mysterious Death of Slovak Journalist," *Haaretz* (11 March 2018).

40. Fidesz is not even the party furthest to the right in Hungary. On that extreme is Jobbik, whose representative in the Hungarian parliament suggested in 2012 that Hungary should create lists of Jews to be registered as threats to national security. See Marton Dunai, "Outrage at 'Jewish List' Call in Hungary Parliament," *Reuters* (27 November 2012). Increasingly, however, Jobbik's extremism has been mainstreamed by Fidesz. See Cathrine Thorleifsson, "Disposable Strangers: Far-right Securitisation of Forced Migration in Hungary," *Social Anthropology* 25, no. 3 (2017), 318–334.

41. Michael Colborne, "Orbán Blamed All of Hungary's Problems on a Jew—and Won, Big Time," *Haaretz* (9 April 2018).

42. Ibid.

43. Shaun Walker, "Hungarian Leader Says Europe is Now 'Under Invasion' by Migrants," *Guardian* (15 March 2018).

44. This issue is discussed as well in Jonathan Zisook's essay in this volume (pp. 33–34).

45. Andrea Pető, "'Non-Remembering' the Holocaust in Hungary and Poland," *Polin: Studies in Polish Jewry* 31 (2019), 471–480.

46. Emilia Palonen, "Millennial Politics of Architecture: Myths and Nationhood in Budapest," *Nationalities Papers* 41, no. 4 (2013), 536–551.

47. Rév, "Liberty Square, Budapest," 610.

48. Jeffrey Stevenson Murer, "Four Monuments and a Funeral: Pathological Mourning and Collective Memory in Contemporary Hungary," in *Fomenting Political Violence: Fantasy, Language, Media, Action*, ed. Krüger Steffen, Karl Figlio, and Barry Richards (Cham: 2018), 189–218.

49. Randolph L. Braham, "Hungary: The Assault on the Historical Memory of the Holocaust," in *The Holocaust in Hungary: Seventy Years Later*, ed. Randolph L. Braham and András Kovács (Budapest: 2016), 261–309.

50. Croatia, in Anti Defamation League, "ADL Global 100 Survey: An Index of Anti-Semitism 2014," online at: global100.adl.org/country/croatia/2014 (accessed 12 July 2021);

Organization for Security and Cooperation in Europe (OSCE), "Hate Crime Reporting: Croatia" (2019), https://hatecrime.osce.org/croatia (accessed 13 July 2021).

51. HOS (Hrvatske obrambene snage), a paramilitary unit active during the Croatian war of independence (1991–1995), was affiliated with the far-Right Croatian Party of Rights. It also shares the acronym HOS with the Second World War-era Croatian Armed Forces (Hrvatske oružane snage)—the armed forces of the Ustasha, the fascist movement of the Independent State of Croatia.

52. Sven Milekic, "Croatia Removes Fascist Slogan Plaque from Jasenovac," *Balkan Insight* (7 September 2017).

53. Jelena Subotic, "Political Memory, Ontological Security, and Holocaust Remembrance in Post-Communist Europe," *European Security* 27, no. 3 (2018), 296–313.

54. Milekic, "Croatia Removes Fascist Slogan Plaque."

55. Goran Penić, "S osječkih tribina se orilo 'Za Dom Spremni' i 'Ajmo, Ustaše,'" *Jutarnji list* (24 March 2016). The same thing happened at a Croatia–Israel soccer match in 2012. See Dario Brentin, "Ready for the Homeland? Ritual, Remembrance, and Political Extremism in Croatian Football," *Nationalities Papers* 44, no. 6 (2016), 860–876.

56. Lajla Veselica, "Croatia's Jews Fear Growing Intolerance under Conservatives," *Times of Israel* (29 April 2016).

57. "US Holocaust Envoy Warns Croatia About Fascist Symbols," *Balkan Insight* (24 March 2017). An especially ironic event took place at a rally in February 2017 in Croatia's capital, Zagreb, when the Croatian far-Right party A-HSP marched in a rally with the American flag, apparently identifying President Donald Trump as a possible ideological ally. See "US Embassy Condemns Far-right March With US Flag in Croatia," *Voice of America* (27 February 2017), online at: voanews.com/usa/us-embassy-condemns-far-right-march-us-flag-croatia (accessed 8 August 2021).

58. Quoted in Nebojša Blanuša, "Trauma and Taboo: Forbidden Political Questions in Croatia," *Politička misao* 54 (2017), 170–196, 180.

59. Sven Milekic, "Croatian Director Reported for Jasenovac Camp Film," *Balkan Insight* (15 July 2016).

60. Sven Milekic, "Boycott Overshadows Croatian Concentration Camp Memorial," *Balkan Insight* (22 April 2016).

61. Quoted in Tamara Opacic, "Selective Amnesia: Croatia's Holocaust Deniers," *Balkan Insight* (24 November 2017).

62. Quoted in Sven Milekic, "Croatia Govt Criticised at WWII Death Camp Commemoration," *Balkan Insight* (23 April 2016).

63. Volha Charnysh, "The Rise of Poland's Far Right: How Extremism Is Going Mainstream," *Foreign Affairs* (18 December 2017).

64. Rick Noack, "How Poland Became a Breeding Ground for Europe's Far Right," *Washington Post* (14 November 2017).

65. Charnysh, "Rise of Poland's Far Right."

66. Leonid Bershidsky, "Why Polish Jews Are Growing Uneasy," *Bloomberg News* (27 February 2018).

67. Volha Charnysh and Evgeny Finkel, "Rewriting History in Eastern Europe: Poland's New Holocaust Law and the Politics of the Past," *Foreign Affairs* (14 February 2018).

68. Volha Charnysh, "Remembering Past Atrocities—Good or Bad for Attitudes toward Minorities?" in *Politics, Violence, Memory: The New Social Science of the Holocaust*, ed. Jeffrey S. Kopstein, Jelena Subotić, and Susan Welch (Ithaca: 2022).

69. Ukraine, in Anti Defamation League, "ADL Global 100 Survey," online at: global100. adl.org/country/ukraine/2015 (accessed 13 July 2021).

70. Lev Golinkin, "Violent Anti-Semitism Is Gripping Ukraine—And The Government Is Standing Idly By," *Forward* (20 May 2018).

71. Anna Nemtsova, "The Frightening Far-Right Militia That's Marching in Ukraine's Streets, Promising to Bring 'Order,'" *Daily Beast* (5 February 2018).

72. Lev Golinkin, "How the Holocaust Haunts Eastern Europe," *New York Times* (26 January 2018).

73. Andrew Higgins, "Ukraine's Newly Elected President Is Jewish. So Is Its Prime Minister. Not All Jews There Are Pleased," *New York Times* (24 April 2019); Cnaan Liphshiz, "For Ukrainian Jews, Having a Jewish President is a Source of Pride—and Fear," *Times of Israel* (12 November 2019).

74. Bulgaria, in Anti Defamation League, "ADL Global 100 Survey," online at: https://global100.adl.org/country/bulgaria/2014 (accessed 13 July 2021).

75. Organization for Security and Cooperation in Europe (OSCE), "Hate Crime Reporting: Bulgaria" (2019), online at: hatecrime.osce.org/bulgaria (accessed 13 July 2021).

76. Michael Colborne, "The European Capital With a Swastika Epidemic," *Haaretz* (1 November 2018).

77. Stephen McGrath, "Anti-Semitism Threatens Romania's Fragile Jewish Community," *BBC News* (15 April 2019), online at: bbc.com/news/world-europe-47865369 (accessed 13 July 2021).

78. Romania, in Anti Defamation League, "ADL Global 100 Survey," online at: https://global100.adl.org/country/romania/2014 (accessed 13 July 2021).

79. Peter Salner, "Anti-Semitism in Slovakia after the Velvet Revolution of 1989," *Occasional Papers on Religion in Eastern Europe* 40 (2020), 32–43.

80. Ibid.

The Politics of Holocaust Memory in Central and Eastern Europe: Contemporary Poland as a Comparative Case Study

Jonathan Zisook

(UNIVERSITY OF PITTSBURGH)

Following the collapse of Communism in 1989, a preoccupation with history and national memory developed in Central and Eastern Europe as a means of strengthening political support for post-Communist governments. In a new political environment in which the "former mechanisms of legitimacy" were socially and politically undermined and where major economic transformations resulted in mass unemployment in the immediate post-Communist years, a return to history helped strengthen democratic national movements.[1] Post-Communist governments were tasked with instituting some sort of transitional justice whereby perpetrators of previous regimes were held accountable and, in some cases, reparations were offered to victims.[2] Part of this process also included the adoption of a pan-European or transnational Holocaust memory, which served as a starting point for the institutionalization of a system of universal human rights across postwar Europe. Throughout the transitional 1990s and early 2000s, the Holocaust thus emerged as a European "negative founding myth"—encompassing not only Western Europe but also members of the former Eastern bloc.[3] Consequently, the "Europeanization" of the Holocaust, especially in the aftermath of European Union (EU) enlargement in 2004, has forced numerous countries to confront their silenced pasts of dispossession, complicity, and active participation in genocide.[4]

Despite many transnational Holocaust memory initiatives, the attitudes of post-Communist countries are often tactical and do not necessarily entail a genuine commitment to addressing the difficult pages of the region's past. Instead, post-Communist societies have often internalized the not entirely unfounded notion that their own suffering during the Second World War and under Communist regimes has been overlooked by Western Europe. This has resulted in a battlefield of memory in which competing narratives of the past are constitutive features of the region's contemporary political consciousness. It is within this context that discussions of the Holocaust in Central and Eastern Europe are taking place.[5]

Jonathan Zisook, *The Politics of Holocaust Memory in Central and Eastern Europe: Contemporary Poland as a Comparative Case Study* In: *Becoming Post-Communist.* Edited by: Eli Lederhendler, Oxford University Press. © Oxford University Press 2023. DOI: 10.1093/oso/9780197687215.003.0003

In this essay, I address contemporary Poland and its "contentious politics" of Holocaust memory as a comparative case study. By contentious politics, I refer to what historical sociologists term "episodic, public, collective interaction among makers of claims and their objects when (a) at least one government is a claimant, an object of claims, or a party to the claims and (b) the claims would, if realized, affect the interests of at least one of the claimants."[6] While broadly conceived, my focus on public episodes of contentious politics serves as a narrowing principle, which thereby excludes from my investigation "regularly scheduled events such as . . . parliamentary elections."[7] To be sure, the outcomes of elections often produce contentious politics, which then fall into the purview of my analysis. Consequently, I begin by sketching three recent controversies and their dynamics of public contention, followed by an analysis of the Jedwabne debate of the early 2000s, which continues to shape present-day political discourse in Poland. I then address the comparative politics of Holocaust memory in Hungary as a means of elucidating and broadening the Polish case. Finally, I conclude with a short discussion of the ascendance of the Law and Justice Party (Prawo i Sprawiedliwość [PiS]) in 2005–2007 and from 2015 to the present, and its concomitant implications for the role of Holocaust memory in shaping the political future of Poland in particular and the region in general.

Recent Episodes of Contention

As elsewhere in Central and Eastern Europe, Holocaust memory in Poland is subject to distortion and political instrumentalization. In the wake of PiS's second electoral victory in October 2015, a flurry of highly contentious new controversies emerged. Here, I discuss three recent episodes in the spheres of education, culture, and law.

On July 13, 2016, TVN24 (arguably the most influential private television company in Poland) featured an interview conducted by prominent TV broadcaster Monika Olejnik with Anna Zalewska, the minister of national education. The subject of the interview was the PiS government's proposed education reform (later approved by the Sejm, Poland's lower house of parliament, and signed into law), which sought to dissolve middle schools, extend primary school education, and modify school curricula.[8] Several days before, there had been commemorations of both the Jedwabne and Kielce pogroms. Olejnik asked Zalewska whether the history of anti-Jewish violence should be taught in the Polish school system, and she pressed the minister to acknowledge that Polish Catholic citizens had murdered their Jewish neighbors in both pogroms. Zalewska, however, refused to incriminate non-Jewish Poles. Concerning Kielce, Zalewska declared that the event should be left "to historians to sort out" and that "Poles have differing opinions on the matter." Olejnik's follow-up question was who, specifically, committed the crime, to which Zalewska retorted: "The antisemites committed the crime." Olejnik asked if those antisemites were also Poles. Zalewska evaded a direct answer, replying that "you cannot compare antisemites to Poles" because "there was a different political and historical background then. . . . I am trying to demonstrate the respect I have for different opinions."[9] In reality, however, the historical events are not in dispute: in the aftermath of the Second World War, a pogrom was unleashed in the city of Kielce in July 1946, during which at least 42 Jews—mostly destitute Holocaust survivors—were murdered by their fellow Polish citizens in response to a ritual murder accusation.[10]

Olejnik also asked Zalewska about the Jedwabne pogrom, which had taken place during the war, in July 1941. Not surprisingly, Zalewska once again refused to acknowledge who committed the crime, stating that "Jedwabne is a historical fact that has led to many misunderstandings and very biased opinions." Olejnik's blunt retort: "Poles burned Jews in a barn." Zalewska countered: "That is your opinion, repeated after Mr. Gross," whose book, she said, was "full of lies."[11] Here Zalewska was referring to Jan Tomasz Gross, a Polish-born emeritus professor of history at Princeton University, whose book *Sąsiedzi* (Neighbors) triggered a fierce public debate on the history of Polish–Jewish relations in the early 2000s.[12] Despite the well-documented historical record, Zalewska, who at the time was overseeing one of the most significant education reforms in Poland since the fall of Communism, repeatedly refused to acknowledge that individual Polish Catholic citizens were responsible for murdering fellow Jewish citizens during and in the aftermath of the Second World War. In the face of fierce challenges on the part of the interviewer, Zalewska would not budge from her version of the past. Immediately following the broadcast, Poland's chief rabbi, Michael Schudrich, along with representatives of other Jewish institutions in Poland, invited the minister to the POLIN Museum of the History of Polish Jews in Warsaw to learn about the events under question. Zalewska, however, never responded to the invitation.[13]

The Zalewska–Olejnik interview revealed a certain political form of Holocaust negationism that serves to undermine previous, gradual processes of coming to terms with the past in the context of Poland's educational system.[14] Such negationist approaches have had consequences for cultural institutions as well. In April 2017, shortly after the grand opening of the Museum of the Second World War (Muzeum II Wojny Światowej) in Gdańsk, the museum's director, Paweł Machcewicz, was dismissed from his position by the minister of culture, Piotr Glinski, for not expressing a "Polish point of view." Following a protracted legal battle, the Museum of the Second World War was merged by the government with the Museum of Westerplatte and the War of 1939 (Muzeum Westerplatte i Wojny 1939), an institution existing in name and on paper only at the time.[15] According to Machcewicz, the Museum of the Second World War was "formally liquidated" and immediately "re-founded under the same name . . . [as] a legal trick to discontinue my contract."[16] The museum was then reopened with a new, PiS-appointed director, Karol Nawrocki, a historian specializing in the Solidarity movement. The government's claim was that the museum in its original format had failed to satisfactorily present the bravery of Polish fighters and their suffering at the hands of German and Soviet occupiers—a position that was in fact expressed throughout the core exhibition, though not in an exclusive manner. In contradistinction to other Second World War museums in Europe, the museum in Gdańsk was founded to present a global perspective of the war, with an emphasis on the suffering of civilian populations. Within this larger framework, the museum, in its original form, situated the tragic and heroic Polish story of the Second World War within a global context while also openly addressing difficult topics such as the pogrom at Jedwabne and the blackmailing of Jews by Poles who threatened to expose them to the authorities (*szmalcownicy*).[17]

Notwithstanding the museum's seemingly evenhanded approach to the Second World War, it was lambasted by Jarosław Kaczyński, the co-founder and undisputed leader of PiS, for being insufficiently patriotic and thus contributing to the "disintegration of the Polish nation."[18] According to Kaczyński, as explained by Machcewicz, in presenting the "wartime experiences of other nations alongside the Polish experience," the museum "jeopardize[d] the exceptional status of the Polish nation."[19] Accordingly, the new PiS-appointed director and curatorial team quickly set out to redesign the core exhibition. While the original exhibition remains largely intact— a pragmatic reality, given the enormous financial costs of creating an entirely new exhibition—more than 20 significant and symbolic changes were introduced between October 2017 and March 2018. Some of these changes are not merely cosmetic but both subtly and deliberately distort the history of the Holocaust and politicize the history of Poles who rescued Jews during the war. Here, one representative example will suffice.

In the newly modified museum exhibition, visitors are informed that Poles saved "several dozen thousand to more than one hundred thousand Jews."[20] To be sure, righteous Poles did save thousands of Jews and assisted many more who ultimately perished; these Poles should rightly be recognized for their heroism. However, the historically accepted estimates of the number of Jews saved by Poles are nowhere near 100,000. Israel Gutman, for instance, determined that between 30,000–35,000 Jews were saved by Poles, accounting for approximately 10 percent of the surviving Jewish population (some 70 percent of the survivors had found refuge in the Soviet Union), whereas Teresa Prekerowa's calculation is that between 30,000 and 60,000 Jews survived the war among the Polish population.[21] Barbara Engelking and Jacek Leociak have a similar estimate of between 40,000 and 60,000.[22] Jan Grabowski writes that "the number of survivors [due to Poles' assistance]" is "no more than 50,000 people"; Saul Friedländer, agreeing with the calculation of Antony Polonsky, maintains that "40,000 at most survived in hiding on Polish territory."[23] Paweł Machcewicz further concurs with Friedländer and Polonsky and places the upper estimate at 40,000, stating that "historians know that not more than 40,000 Jews survived the war in Occupied Poland" hiding among non-Jewish Poles.[24] Consequently, even if we accept the high-end estimate of 60,000 people, it remains far below the higher number cited in the emended core exhibition of the Museum of the Second World War.[25]

While subtle, the museum's inflation of the number of Jews saved by Poles is not only a historical manipulation. It also appears to be constitutive of a politics of Holocaust memory, in which the Polish government seeks to present an exclusively sympathetic, self-celebratory, and sanitized narrative of Polish–Jewish relations during the Second World War, whereby Poles universally sacrificed to help Jews and therefore cannot be implicated in crimes against them during the Holocaust. This uncritical narrative, also expressed by Minister Zalewska, is, however, increasingly complicated by historians of the Holocaust. In fact, according to a recent path-breaking, two-volume collection of studies edited by Barbara Engelking and Jan Grabowski on "the fate of Jews" in nine counties in German-occupied Poland, "the Polish population directly or indirectly contributed to the deaths of thousands of Jews who were seeking rescue on the 'Aryan' side," after escaping deportation to concentration camps and death camps between 1942–1945. In the counties analyzed, two out of every three

Jews seeking shelter among the Polish population wound up perishing, "most often with the involvement of their [Polish] Christian neighbors."[26] The exact number of Jews who were murdered or betrayed by Poles assisting the Germans remains unknown. However, according to historian Jan Grabowski's work on the *Judenjagd*— Jew hunts—the number "could reach," and might even exceed 200,000.[27] This fact, however, is at odds with the new curation of the museum, which seemingly attempts to negate critical approaches to the Polish past while overemphasizing a narrative of Polish heroism, suffering, and innocence, what sociologist Geneviève Zubrzycki has called Poland's "martyrological paradigm."[28]

Coming on the heels of the government takeover of the Museum of the Second World War in 2017, the most audacious manifestation of Poland's contentious politics of Holocaust memory was the 2018 "Holocaust law." Seeking to "defend the good name of the Polish nation," Minister of Justice Zbigniew Ziobro first introduced the amendment to the "Act on the Institute of National Remembrance–Commission for the Prosecution of Crimes against the Polish Nation"—referred to internationally as the "Holocaust law" or the "memory law"—in September 2016. Eventually signed into law in 2018, article 55.a.1. of the amendment states:

> Whoever publicly and against the facts ascribes to the Polish Nation, or to the Polish State, the responsibility or complicity for Nazi crimes committed by the III German Reich . . . or other crimes that constitute crimes against peace, humanity, or war crimes, or [whoever] otherwise greatly diminishes the responsibility of the real perpetrators of these crimes, shall be subject to fine or three years of imprisonment. The sentence shall be made public. It will be, of course, the police and the prosecutors who will, henceforth, establish the facts and what can be said and written.[29]

Government representatives have claimed that the amendment is a necessary deterrent for those who inaccurately refer to Nazi concentration camps and death camps as "Polish concentration camps" and "Polish death camps." On the surface, this is not unreasonable. After all, it was Germany that implemented the plan to systematically annihilate Polish Jews (Operation Reinhard) in the so-called Generalgouvernement in occupied Poland. Poles, of course, had nothing to do with the creation of concentration camps and were themselves persecuted alongside Jews. The problem, however, is that the legislation indicates nothing about concentration camps specifically and is in fact far broader. It outlaws discussions of Poles' complicity with the Nazi regime during the Holocaust and applies the law even to those who might unintentionally break it, as well as to foreigners whether in Poland or abroad. This fact, according to one political commentator, makes the law explicitly illiberal because it is "designed to punish people who make historical mistakes," as determined by the government, even if the government is unlikely to prosecute foreigners.[30] Further, as Jan Grabowski astutely notes, perhaps even more problematic than criminalizing ignorance is that the Holocaust law poses "a threat to the freedom of public and scholarly discussion."[31]

In reaction to the Holocaust law, an explosion of criticism was leveled at the PiS government by scholars and politicians in Poland and abroad. In Israel, Prime Minister Benjamin Netanyahu claimed at the time that it was tantamount to Holocaust denial.[32] The U.S. State Department urged the Polish government to consider the legislation's possible "repercussions ... on Poland's strategic interests and relationships—including with the United States and Israel" and "to reevaluate the legislation in light of its potential impact on the principle of free speech."[33] In Poland, dozens of prominent professors, politicians, and religious leaders, including former president Aleksander Kwaśniewski, criticized the law in an open letter, asking: "Why should the victims and witnesses of the Holocaust have to watch what they say for fear of being arrested, and will the testimony of a Jewish survivor who 'feared Poles' be a punishable offence? Why must this be argued based on paragraphs from the criminal code and not through the merits of debate?"[34] Finally, Holocaust museums and academic centers across the globe, including the Center for Holocaust Research of the Polish Academy of Sciences (Centrum Badań nad Zagładą Żydów), Yad Vashem, and the United States Holocaust Memorial Museum, denounced the legislation.

Despite the international and domestic condemnation of the legislation, the law was passed in the Sejm, on January 26, 2018—on the eve of International Holocaust Remembrance Day!—in the Senate on February 1, and signed into law five days later. Prior to signing the legislation into law, President Andrzej Duda defended it, stating that "we, as a state, as a nation, have a right to defend ourselves from an evident slander, an evident falsification of historical truth."[35] At the same time, noting that "it is extremely important to be sensitive to opposition voices and those who fear that it will not be possible to proclaim the truth, that it will muzzle the mouth of survivors," Duda announced that he had referred the law to the Constitutional Tribunal.[36] The Constitutional Tribunal, however, never ruled on the constitutionality of the law.[37]

Shortly after the passage of the law, Prime Minister Mateusz Morawiecki, through the Chancellery of the Prime Minister of Poland, initiated a social media campaign in support of the legislation with the hashtags "#GermanDeathCamps" and "#PolishRighteousness."[38] He further inflamed the discussion in response to a question by Israeli journalist Ronen Bergman at the Munich Security Conference on February 17, 2018, by equating Polish perpetrators with "Jewish perpetrators." Bergman asked: "Both my parents were born in Poland. My late mother and my father. . . . Then the war started, and they lost much of the[ir] families because their neighbors, their Polish neighbors, snitched to the Gestapo. . . . If I understand correctly, after this law is legislated, I will be considered criminal in your country for saying this. What is the purpose? What is the message that you are trying to convey to the world? You are creating the opposite reaction and just attracting more attention to these atrocities."[39] Assuring Bergman that he would not be subject to the law when telling his parents' survival stories, Morawiecki stated: "It's not going to be seen as criminal to say that there were Polish perpetrators, as there were Jewish perpetrators, as there were Ukrainian; not only German perpetrators."[40]

Since then, the topic has consistently featured in public and political discussions throughout Poland and abroad. In late June 2018, in what many have deemed a surprising decision, some five months after the law was initially passed by the Sejm, Morawiecki proposed amending the memory law by forgoing its criminal provisions. While upholding the government's rhetoric, stating that "those who say that Poland may be responsible for the crimes of World War II deserve jail terms," Morawiecki nevertheless recognized the necessity of walking back the legislation's most controversial component because "we operate in an international context, and we take that into account."[41] The amendments were quickly passed in both houses of parliament and President Duda signed them into law shortly thereafter, on June 27, 2018. On the same day, a "Joint Declaration of Prime Ministers of the State of Israel and the Republic of Poland" was signed by both Morawiecki and Netanyahu to put an end to the diplomatic dispute between the two countries that the legislation had created. Among other things, the declaration condemns "every single case of cruelty against Jews perpetrated by Poles during World War II," while emphasizing that the "Polish underground" and the "Polish Government-in-Exile created a mechanism of systematic help and support to Jewish people."[42] The declaration concludes with a statement ostensibly equating antisemitism with "anti-Polonism" and calling upon both the Israeli and Polish governments to "return to civil and respectful dialogue in the public discourse."[43]

Although the declaration has been criticized by historians in Israel, Poland, and the United States, the chief historian at Yad Vashem, Dina Porat, conceded that while she did not agree with the entire declaration, "we can live with [it]."[44] As a political compromise, therefore, the joint declaration appears to be a positive outcome of Polish–Israeli diplomatic discussions, even though Israel largely acquiesced to the Polish narrative against the recommendation of several senior scholars at Yad Vashem who disagreed vehemently with Porat. As to the status of the amended law, it remains unclear how it will be implemented, and it continues to be a source of consternation among many. While the criminal provisions have been removed, violators of the memory law are still subject to heavy fines under civil proceedings.

The above controversies illustrate how the memory of the Holocaust and the Second World War in Poland are instrumentalized for political purposes—seemingly to promote a singularly positive image of Poland, where Poles are considered the consummate victims and heroes of the war. The ruling party appears to be rewriting history, creating its own state-sponsored national memory while rejecting previous approaches to coming to terms with the past that had emerged with the fall of Communism and Poland's accession into the EU. In this regard, the most significant national debate dealing with the memory of the Holocaust in Poland was conducted in the early 2000s following the aforementioned publication of Jan Tomasz Gross' *Neighbors*, a shocking historical telling of the murder and plunder of the Jews of Jedwabne. The current politics of Holocaust memory in Poland are, to a large degree, an extension of this earlier debate and a reaction to the progressive stocktaking among Poland's intellectual and political elite.

The Jedwabne Debate

On July 10, 1941, in the little town of Jedwabne in the Łomża region of today's northeastern Poland, the majority of the town's Jews were rounded up and burned alive in a barn by their Polish Catholic neighbors. While largely an open secret in Jedwabne, until recently this atrocity was forgotten; the Communist-era monument commemorating the event placed the blame on the Nazi regime and thus had it subsumed under the umbrella of German crimes. The discovery that the Jews of Jedwabne were massacred by Poles and not principally by Germans came as a shock to Polish society. Gross' exhaustively researched and gruesome account, based upon trial records, archival documents, and Jewish and Polish testimonies, sparked a vigorous national debate concerning Polish complicity and culpability for crimes committed against Jews during the Second World War. Antony Polonsky, a veteran historian of Polish Jewry, went as far as to state that "the debate on Jedwabne has been the most serious, protracted, and profound on the issue of Polish–Jewish relations since the end of the war."[45]

The debate over Gross' *Neighbors* played out in multiple media and with many different actors, including politicians, clergy, historians, and journalists. The crux of the debate rested on whether Polish society was ready to come to terms with its own difficult past. By publishing *Neighbors*, Gross challenged the uncritical narrative of Polish victimhood and heroism during the Second World War, demonstrating that victims could also perpetrate horrific crimes. In addition, Gross disputed the antisemitic canard of "Judeo-Communism" (*Żydokomuna*), according to which Jews were both pro-Communist and anti-Polish.[46] According to Gross, "like several other nations, in order to reclaim its own past, Poland will have to tell its past to itself anew. . . . We have reached a threshold at which the new generation, raised in Poland with freedom of speech and political liberties, is ready to confront the unvarnished history of Polish–Jewish relations during the war."[47] Gross is thus representative of a self-critical approach to the Polish past, albeit not the first, nor the only one.

In the immediate postwar years, self-critical Polish intellectuals reflected upon the murder of Jews on Polish soil, but by 1948–1949 they were largely silenced by the Communist state.[48] Not until the waning years of Communism in the 1980s was there any significant public discussion of Polish–Jewish relations. Of considerable importance was Jan Błoński's essay, "The Poor Poles Look at the Ghetto," which was published in the January 1987 issue of *Tygodnik Powszechny*.[49] Błoński's essay challenged the Polish self-image of heroic sacrifice and solidarity in suffering with their Jewish compatriots by highlighting the widespread indifference among Poles to the plight of Polish Jewry. According to Błoński, Poles always saw themselves as the ultimate victims of the German occupation and were therefore incapable of critically examining their own moral neglect of the Jewish population during the Holocaust. As significant as this critique was, Błoński could not fathom a scenario in which Poles were responsible for mass murder. Morally, in Błoński's judgment, Poles "share the responsibility for the crime without taking part in it."[50]

Błoński had a major impact on a small group of intellectuals, including Gross, but his introspective analysis of Polish indifference was summarily rejected by most opinion makers. By contrast, the debate initiated by Gross was both more intense and more influential in shaping public and intellectual discourse. Gross' conclusions were also far more radical than those of Błoński. In demonstrating that Poles actively and voluntarily murdered the Jewish population of Jedwabne, Gross overturned the historiography of the Holocaust and Polish–Jewish relations in Poland. In so doing, he engendered support from large segments of the intellectual, cultural, and political elite, but also stimulated fierce apologetic and ethnonationalist opposition.

The scholarly responses that shaped the public discourse surrounding Gross' publication, and the literature produced in its aftermath, can be classified under two

ideal-typical camps: the *self-critical camp* and the *apologetic camp*.[51] Historian
Joanna Michlic emphasizes the historiographical studies of Andrzej Żbikowski and
Dariusz Libionka, as well as others who were associated with the Institute of National
Remembrance (Instytut Pamięci Narodowej [IPN]) under the leadership of Leon
Kieres (2000–2005), as representative examples of the self-critical scholarship that
emerged in the years following the publication of *Neighbors*.[52] One might also point
to more immediate self-critical responders such as anthropologist Joanna Tokarska-
Bakir, journalists Anna Bikont and Konstanty Gebert, and sociologist Hanna Świda-
Ziemba, among many others, whose pieces were prominently featured in the Polish
press.[53] Finally, the establishment of the Center for Holocaust Research of the Polish
Academy of Sciences in Warsaw in 2003, as well as the publication of the center's
scholarly yearbook, *Zagłada Żydów: Studia i Materiały* (Holocaust Studies and
Materials), contributed to the development and institutionalization of self-critical his-
torical writing in Poland. In particular, the writings of Barbara Engelking and Jan
Grabowski of the Center have been extremely important to this endeavor.[54]

   The self-critical camp recognizes that Polish history includes both positive and
negative periods of ethnic and religious interaction, and that Jedwabne represents
the worst of Polish–Jewish relations. In fact, scholars would later determine, the
Jedwabne massacre was not an isolated occurrence. Similar pogroms, some insti-
gated by Germans and some with only marginal German participation (or none at all),
occurred in at least two dozen towns and villages in the Łomża and Białystok regions,
including Goniàdz, Grajewo, Kolno, Radziłów, Szczuczyn, and Wąsosz.[55] According
to the self-critical camp, regardless of the number of Jews murdered in Jedwabne[56]
or any other site of atrocity, the realization that Polish Jews were murdered and dis-
possessed by their neighbors should compel Poles to reflect sincerely upon the past
in order to create a more tolerant and democratic present. In short, as the sociologist
Sergiusz Kowalski astutely notes: "The point is not to humiliate the Poles, to suddenly
transform them from victims and heroes into a nation of blackmailers and torturers.
. . . The point is . . . to recognize . . . a more ordinary society—sometimes heroic,
sometimes ignoble—like every other sensible nation."[57] The self-critical camp thus
exposed Polish society to an unvarnished picture of its past, not altogether different
("sometimes heroic, sometimes ignoble") from other German-occupied countries
during the Second World War.

   In contrast to the self-critical camp, an apologetic, defensive, and sometimes radically ethnonationalist group of scholars emerged in response to Gross' uncovering
of the Jedwabne massacre. The apologetic camp either refuses to accept that Poles
were actively involved in the murder of Jedwabne's Jews, preferring to reassert the
Communist-era position that the Germans bear sole responsibility for the crime, or
else they directly invoke *Żydokomuna* as an apologetic defense of Polish violence
against Jews. Poles of the Łomża region, according to these perspectives, were universally heroic in their dual stance against the Soviets and the Germans, as well as in
their relationship with Jews prior to and during the Second World War. And if indeed
there were any crimes committed by Polish Catholics against Polish Jews during this
period, this was regrettable but understandable, given that Jews had "supported" the
Soviet occupation of eastern Poland, thereby betraying the Polish nation. In defending "the good name of Poland" against the self-critical camp, the apologetic camp

couches a classic antisemitic canard in an academic veneer, downplaying Polish anti-semitism in favor of guilt-free and triumphant historical narratives. Chief among the apologetic camp are historians Marek Jan Chodakiewicz, Tomasz Strzembosz, and Bogdan Musiał.

Chodakiewicz presents a reinterpretation of the Jedwabne massacre, whereby Germans alone orchestrated and carried out the massacre. Aside from a few petty criminals and *Volksdeutsche* Polish collaborators, Poles did not participate in the murderous events, in Chodakiewicz's rendering.[58] Similarly apologetic in its conclusions is the late Tomasz Strzembosz's study of an anti-Soviet Polish underground unit in the Biebrza river region.[59] Strzembosz neglects to examine how Jews were massacred in the surrounding Łomża villages in 1941, including Jedwabne, and he paints the local Jewish population as Communist supporters and betrayers of Poland. Despite this supposed Jewish betrayal, Polish anti-Communist partisans heroically protected and saved Judeo-Communist Jews, according to Strzembosz. Finally, in Bogdan Musiał's examination of the German invasion of Soviet-occupied Poland in the summer of 1941 and of the accompanying anti-Jewish pogroms that occurred in cities and villages in Eastern Galicia, he too employs the stereotype of Judeo-Communism as a key element to understanding anti-Jewish violence.[60] Consistent with their positions, both Strzembosz and Musiał directly invoke *Żydokomuna* as an apologetic defense of Polish violence committed against Jews in Jedwabne.[61]

It seems evident that these apologetic views continue to shape the contentious contemporary discussions of the Holocaust in Poland. During the height of the Jedwabne debate, however, the position emanating from the highest officials of the Polish government sided chiefly with the self-critical camp. The prime minister of Poland at the time, Jerzy Buzek (1997–2001), declared that "the slaughter . . . in Jedwabne of Polish Jews, our fellow citizens, is terrifying in its savagery. Our duty is to honor the victims in a dignified way and to establish the truth. . . . The participation of Poles in the crime in Jedwabne is indisputable; it isn't questioned by any respectable historian."[62] Furthermore, in a speech in Jedwabne commemorating the 60th anniversary of the Jedwabne massacre delivered on July 10, 2001, President Aleksander Kwaśniewski (1995–2005) asked for forgiveness:

> Because of this crime, we must beg the shadows of the dead and their families for forgiveness. This is why today, as a citizen and as the President of the Republic of Poland, I apologize. I apologize in the name of those Poles whose conscience is moved by that crime. In the name of those who believe that we cannot be proud of the glory of Polish history without feeling, at the same time, pain and shame for the wrongs done by Poles to others.[63]

Although these anguished responses by the president and prime minister of Poland were not universally accepted by the Polish public, they substantiated the need for Polish society to confront the more problematic aspects of its past. Knowledge regarding the Jedwabne pogrom was by then widespread among the general population—as of April 2001, fully 83 percent of the population had become aware of this historical event.[64] The president and prime minister sensitively addressed a painful episode in Polish–Jewish relations without asserting collective blame on all

Poles for the crime of Jedwabne. They additionally broadcast to international observers that Poland had matured from its days as a Communist tyranny into a democratic state capable of openly debating difficult topics and achieving a level of self-examination rarely present in the region of Central and Eastern Europe.

Despite mainstream academic consensus and previous apologies from leading politicians, the Polish *Historikerstreit*, or "historian's controversy,"[65] over Jedwabne in the early 2000s has continued to shape public discourse and remains a highly fraught political topic up to the present day. Further, the contentious politics of Holocaust memory in Poland are not completely isolated from contemporaneous developments in the region. The apologetic camp in Poland is emboldened by a regional turn to "illiberal" democracy in Central and Eastern Europe, especially in Hungary.

Orbán's Hungary

The prominent Hungarian-born historian István Deák recently noted that "the conservative right-wing interpretation of history is a significant force today in both Hungary and Poland." This, Deák maintained, is "because the right-wing governments champion an official ideology that claims that their nation was not guilty of any war crimes."[66] Under the stewardship of Prime Minister Viktor Orbán, Holocaust memory in contemporary Hungary has been distorted and instrumentalized in pursuit of a narrative of innocence, in which the Hungarians are transformed exclusively into victims of German oppression. Similarly, under the leadership of Jarosław Kaczyński, Poland has perpetuated its own myth of innocence. A fundamental difference between the Polish and Hungarian cases concerns their historical positions vis-à-vis Germany during the Second World War. Whereas Hungary was allied with the Germans until March 1944, Poland was occupied by the Germans for the entirety of the war. Hungary instituted a collaborationist government; Poland's government was forced into exile. To be sure, local Polish collaboration was far greater than previously understood, as Jan Gross, Jan Grabowski, Barbara Engelking, and others have demonstrated, but the Polish state cannot be implicated directly in genocide. Instruments of the Hungarian state, by contrast, played an active role in the liquidation of provincial Jewish communities. These historical differences notwithstanding, the issue of Hungarian participation in the Holocaust has animated post-Communist discussions of Hungarian–Jewish relations, as is the case with similar debates in Poland. The scale of complicity differs, but the contemporary political mechanisms of obfuscation of guilt mirror each other. For this reason, it is useful to consider the politics of Holocaust memory in Hungary, paying close attention to the instrumental strategies of Holocaust distortion, in order to elucidate the Polish case.

On July 26, 2014, Prime Minister Viktor Orbán delivered a now famous speech detailing his outlook on the future of Hungary as an "illiberal" state. Orbán declared that Hungary was abandoning the liberal principles of Europe, instead adopting the approach of what he termed "the stars" of the international community—Singapore, China, India, Russia, and Turkey.[67] Only an "illiberal" democracy, according to Orbán, could be properly patriotic and serve the interests of the entire nation. Accordingly,

Orbán's Fidesz Party, building upon previous governmental attempts, has overseen an effort to rehabilitate the Second World War-era regime of Admiral Miklós Horthy by squashing criticism pertaining to Hungary's behavior during the Holocaust. Instead of assuming responsibility for the collaborationist government and the mass deportations of Jews to Auschwitz–Birkenau in 1944 under the authority of Horthy, Fidesz has used legal means to blur this history. The "legal façade," according to the late historian and political scientist Randolph L. Braham, was initiated by the Fundamental Law of Hungary, a new Hungarian constitution adopted on April 25, 2011.[68] Its preamble states: "We date the restoration of our country's self-determination, *lost on the nineteenth day of March 1944*, from the second day of May 1990, when the first freely elected organ of popular representation formed. We shall consider this date to be the beginning of our country's new democracy and constitutional order."[69]

Braham astutely observed that one of the main objectives of this constitutional provision was to "convince the world that Hungary lost its sovereignty in the wake of the beginning of the German occupation" in 1944.[70] According to this negationist line of thinking, Hungary—as a victim of occupation that did not regain full sovereignty until the fall of Communism—could not be held co-responsible for the genocide of its Jewish population. Rather, Germany was solely responsible. This interpretation, of course, is contrary to historical reality, as many Hungarian and international scholars have pointed out. Hungary instituted anti-Jewish legislation akin to Germany's Nuremburg Laws in 1938; it deported 18,000 to 20,000 thousand "alien" Jews to German-occupied Eastern Galicia in 1941, where they were murdered by the Einsatzgruppen with the assistance of local Ukrainians and auxiliary units near Kamianets-Podilskyi; and by 1942, it had forced some 100,000 men, mostly Jewish, into the Hungarian labor service; by the time of the German occupation, more than 40,000 of them had already died in Ukraine.[71]

In March 1944, as part of the Horthy–Hitler pact signed at Schloss Klessheim, the Hungarian leader agreed to deliver hundreds of thousands of Jews to the Germans. In the wake of the pact, Hungary was occupied by the Germans. The occupation, Braham notes, "took place without any resistance . . . and the Hungarian army and the law-enforcement agencies continued to serve the Axis war effort."[72] Further, "the Horthy-appointed government placed the instruments of state power—the gendarmerie, police, and civil service—at the disposal of those in charge of the Final Solution," while Horthy "continued to represent the sovereignty of the nation as head of state."[73] Although Horthy halted the deportations in July 1944, thereby largely saving the Jews of Budapest from annihilation, he was directly implicated in the liquidation of the provincial Jewish communities of Hungary, most of whose members were gassed upon arrival at Birkenau prior to the far-Right Arrow Cross Party's brutal seizure of power in October 1944.[74] By war's end, approximately 75 percent of Hungarian Jewry had been murdered—close to 600,000 out of 800,000 people.

In July 2014, in another attempt to transfer exclusive responsibility for the Holocaust to the Germans, Orbán erected the controversial Monument to the Victims of German Occupation (the German Occupation Monument) in Budapest's Liberty Square. The monument features a statue of the Archangel Gabriel, whose wings are frayed and broken, being crushed by the imperial eagle of Germany. The symbolism is both clear and politically instrumental—Hungary as a helpless and innocent victim of Germany—belying the historical fact that Hungary was a member of the Axis alliance for most of the Second World War. From the moment the government announced its intention to erect the monument in January 2014, it came under attack by activists, scholars, and opposition politicians. Although it was intended to be unveiled as part of an extensive series of events in commemoration of the 70th anniversary of the Holocaust in Hungary, no such ceremonial unveiling occurred. Instead, the monument was erected, without prior notice, in the dead of night.

Shortly thereafter, a makeshift counter-monument—the Living Memorial—was erected directly in front of the German Occupation Monument. The Living Memorial is a dynamic challenge by ordinary citizens to the narrative created by Fidesz. It consists of family photographs, flowers, rocks, votive candles, chairs, book excerpts, and personal mementos. It is a continuously evolving and ephemeral memorial, to which anyone can add objects. The Living Memorial is accompanied by a Facebook group that allows members to share stories and organize public protests, readings, performances, and symposia in the memorial's vicinity in Liberty Square. During the height of activity between 2014 and 2016, these memorial initiatives were well attended by university faculty and students throughout Budapest, but it was not, and is not, exclusively the endeavor of critical academics. According to memorial activists, apart from mostly minor incidents of vandalism, "respect towards the victims of the Holocaust [has] always protected the memorial from the worst attacks."[75] The Living Memorial has remained virtually untouched by the Hungarian authorities, and events continue to be organized there periodically.[76]

The similarities between the political rhetoric and instrumental strategies deployed in Hungary and Poland concerning the history of the Holocaust are striking. Both countries have promoted negationist conceptions of the Holocaust and contend that this is necessary in order to enhance patriotism and national solidarity in the face of Western provocations. Additionally, both utilize their legal systems to determine an official version of events at odds with the prevailing academic consensus, and both advance cultural initiatives in support of these distortions. In so doing, the Polish and Hungarian governments effectively exculpate their citizens for crimes committed against Jews during the Second World War. Although Hungary's attempt to rewrite its wartime history may be more brazen than Poland's perpetuation of its singular victimhood in the face of contradictory evidence, the governments of both countries appear to have adopted "illiberal" policies in support of mythical national pasts; while differing in its degree of negationist revisionism, the Hungarian example emboldens Poland to continue promulgating its own "assault on the historical memory of the Holocaust."[77] At the same time, self-critical opposition movements exist in both countries, offering a challenge to the regimes' current politics of Holocaust memory.

Conclusion

In the early years of the 21st century, Poland reckoned with its past in a manner unlike any other nation in Central or Eastern Europe. Today, however, rather than being resolved, the battle over Poland's historical memory rages on. The apologetic camp gained official legitimation with the ascent to power, in October 2005, of the Kaczyński brothers and their political party, PiS. During the first PiS-led coalition government (2005–2007), a "policy on history" (*polityka historyczna*) was implemented to reassert a positive image of the Polish past, the claim being that, in a period of rapid political and economic transformation following the collapse of Communism in 1989 and enlargement of the European Union in 2004, a shift in historical thinking was imperative in order to further social solidarity. Accordingly, the Institute of National Remembrance was restructured by PiS. The previous government led by the Democratic Left Alliance Party (Sojusz Lewicy Demokratycznej) had tasked the IPN with investigating the Jedwabne crimes; in 2002, the Institute had published two volumes of in-depth studies and documents, titled *Wokół Jedwabnego*, which, with some minor differences, had confirmed and expanded upon Jan Gross' general conclusions. These findings were fiercely challenged by some PiS representatives. As of late 2020, the newly restructured IPN was promoting an apologetic line by historians who reaffirmed the pre-Gross Polish historiography. According to the IPN's director, Jarosław Szarek, Poles were not responsible for the Jedwabne massacre; he blamed the Germans exclusively for the crime, despite ample evidence to the contrary.[78]

Although PiS suffered defeat in 2007, its "policy on history" persisted as a competing narrative of national identity, helping the party regain power in 2015. The polarization of views regarding Jedwabne and subsequent debates over Jan Gross' later publications, as well as those of other critical scholars at the Polish Center for Holocaust Research,[79] mobilized an apologetic backlash. As was the case during its first government, PiS has placed Holocaust negationism front and center in its post-2015 political agenda. The reality of Polish suffering under German occupation is instrumentalized to seemingly obfuscate culpability for crimes committed against Jews by Poles. Thus, as previously indicated, some PiS officials continue to deny Polish involvement in the murder of Jews during the Second World War and have enacted legislation to this effect, threatening academic and journalistic freedom. Critical approaches and opposition voices, however, have not disappeared with the political ascendance of PiS. Critical perspectives are, in fact, as present as they have ever been. At the same time, Polish society now appears to be more divided. At stake is the collective memory of Poland.

Back in the 1920s, the sociologist and father of memory studies, Maurice Halbwachs, famously argued that collective memory is a constitutive feature of social solidarity.[80] It is shaped through the creation of collective myths reinforced by commemorative rituals—what Émile Durkheim referred to as "collective representations."[81] Collective memory thus requires group membership, be it religious, ethnic, or national. In Poland, collective memory is a feature of all three, as it was constructed along ethnoreligious (Catholic) and national lines (Polish) under years of foreign rule during the partition periods, the Second World War, and Communism. The Jedwabne debate shattered the *Polak-Katolik* (Polish-Catholic) collective memory and exacerbated growing divides over national identity already visible during previous politically contentious controversies in the late 1980s and 1990s.[82] No longer can Polish society conceive of its collective self as the endlessly suffering *Polska Chrystusem narodów*—Poland, the Christ of nations—so poetically articulated by Adam Mickiewicz in the 19th century. After the Jedwabne revelations, Polish society began to come to terms with its past. Some have faced this history directly, while others twist the past in the service of the political present.

As the last survivors and witnesses of the Holocaust die and as the Holocaust grows ever more distant in time, battlefields of Holocaust memory continue to intensify in Central and Eastern Europe. The politicization of the Holocaust in Poland has its own domestic specificity, but it also has clear regional parallels to Hungary, where negationist and rehabilitory movements predominate in defense of unvarnished mythical pasts, as indicated by the changes to the Hungarian constitution and the construction of the German Occupation Monument.

The Polish attempt at rewriting history is, in fact, even more convoluted and far-reaching than the Hungarian case because it cannot be reduced to the question of complicity of state organs during the Second World War. Hungarian collaboration with the Nazi regime occurred primarily at the state level and with direct participation of the Hungarian authorities.[83] Viktor Orbán therefore boldly "resolves" this issue precisely by rehabilitating the Horthy era and by fallaciously claiming that Hungary lost its independence in 1944 with German occupation. In Poland, collaboration occurred in defiance of the government-in-exile. Poles' wartime crimes against Jews were decentralized, episodic, and were often manifested in intimate spaces by "ordinary people," including firefighters, night watchmen, police officers, and town officials. These perpetrators represented a broad interface of close relations among neighbors, friends, and families, and their crimes cannot be easily offloaded onto dispassionate state actors who then receive clemency through distortionist contemporary political policies, as Orbán is doing in Hungary.

Moreover, the history of anti-Jewish animus in Poland further predates the Second World War and extends throughout the postwar period, as evidenced most prominently in the Kielce pogrom of 1946 and the "anti-Zionist" political campaign of 1968, when some 15,000 of the remaining 30,000 Jews were expelled from the country.[84] This reality presents an enormous challenge to Polish collective memory, which the present government in power seeks to reinforce politically by instrumentalizing a highly distorted and contentious version of the past.

The line between history and politics continues to be blurred in Central and Eastern Europe as the optimism of the 1990s and early 2000s dissipates. The instrumentalization of the Holocaust both in Poland and elsewhere has been politically productive for nationalist and populist parties, such as PiS in Poland and Fidesz in Hungary. Scholars must interrogate this as a sociological phenomenon at the heart of national and transnational politics in post-Communist Europe.

Notes

I am grateful to those who offered advice, encouragement, or comments on this essay, including John Torpey, Shelley Salamensky, Debórah Dwork, Rebecca Pollack, Maciek Zabierowski, Eli Lederhendler, and Laurie Fialkoff. I presented this research at the 22nd Workshop on the History and Memory of National Socialist Camps and Extermination Sites in Budapest (2017) and the Future of Holocaust Research conference at the CUNY Graduate Center (2018). I thank the panelists and participants at these conferences for their questions and feedback. I especially want to acknowledge the late Randolph L. Braham, the preeminent scholar of the Holocaust in Hungary, who at 95 years old carefully read an earlier version of this article. With generosity and kindness, Professor Braham, himself a Holocaust survivor, encouraged me to think comparatively and to pursue doctoral research on the politics of Holocaust memory. This essay is dedicated to his memory.

1. See, for instance, Gábor Gyáni, "Political Uses of Tradition in Postcommunist East and Central Europe," *Social Research* 60, no. 4 (1993), 893–914; idem, "The Memory of Trianon as a Political Instrument in Hungary Today," in *The Convolutions of Historical Politics*, ed. Alexei Miller and Maria Lipman (Budapest: 2012), 91–115; Robert Traba, *The Past in the Present: The Construction of Polish History*, trans. Alex Shannon (Frankfurt: 2015).

2. See extensive analysis of the topic in Tina Rosenberg, *The Haunted Land: Facing Europe's Ghosts after Communism* (New York: 1995); Elazar Barkan, *The Guilt of Nations: Restitution and Negotiating Historical Injustices* (Baltimore: 2000), 112–156; Constantin Goschler, *Schuld und Schulden. Die Politik der Wiedergutmachung für NS-Verfolgte seit 1945* (Göttingen: 2005), esp. 361–475; John Torpey, *Making Whole What Has Been Smashed: On Reparations Politics* (Cambridge, Mass.: 2006).

3. See, for example, Daniel Levy and Natan Sznaider, "Memory Unbound: The Holocaust and the Formation of Cosmopolitan Memory," *European Journal of Social Theory* 5, no. 1 (2002), 87–106; idem, *The Holocaust and Memory in the Global Age* (Philadelphia: 2005); Tony Judt, *Postwar: A History of Europe since 1945* (New York: 2005), 803–831; Jan Eckel and Claudia Moisel (eds.), *Universalisierung des Holocaust? Erinnerungskultur und Geschichtspolitik in internationaler Perspektive* (Göttingen: 2008); Claus Leggewie, *Der Kampf um die europäische Erinnerung. Ein Schlachtfeld wird besichtigt* (Munich: 2011); Aleida Assmann, "Transnational Memories," *European Review* 22, no. 4 (2014), 546–556.

4. Among many excellent treatments of this topic, see especially Dan Stone, "The 'Final Solution': A German or European Project?" in *Histories of the Holocaust*, ed. Dan Stone (Oxford: 2010), 13–63; Constantin Goschler, "The Dispossession of the Jews and the Europeanization of the Holocaust," in *Business in the Age of Extremes: Essays in Modern German and Austrian Economic History*, ed. Hartmut Berghoff (New York: 2013), 189–203. See also the extremely methodical and voluminous material on anti-Jewish violence perpetrated by local Ukrainian pogromists and nationalist militias in Eastern Galicia in 1941, especially the Lwów pogrom, in Kai Struve, *Deutsche Herrschaft, ukrainischer Nationalismus, antijüdische Gewalt. Der Sommer 1941 in der Westukraine* (Berlin: 2015).

5. Most recently, see Jelena Subotić, *Yellow Star, Red Star: Holocaust Remembrance after Communism* (Ithaca: 2019), which analyzes this topic in Serbia, Croatia, and Lithuania. I thank Eli Lederhendler for bringing this new work to my attention.

6. Doug McAdam, Sidney Tarrow, and Charles Tilly, *Dynamics of Contention* (New York: 2004), 5.

7. Ibid.

8. During the 2015 campaign season, one of PiS's political promises was to reform the education system. This was deemed necessary in order to promote education "strongly rooted in our tradition" and to facilitate greater equality in education outcomes among students. The reform, adopted by the Sejm in December 2016 and signed into law by the president in early January 2017, was (and is still) highly controversial, not least because of changes made in the history curriculum that have direct implications for the study of the Holocaust and the Polish Jewish past. For more information, see Ministerstwo Edukacji Narodowej [Ministry of National Education], "Reforma edukacji," online at: https://www.gov.pl/web/edukacja/refo rma-edukacji (accessed 30 December 2020); interview (by Michał Gostkiewicz) with Anna Dzierzgowska, "Czego dzieci nauczą się na historii? Nauczycielka nie ma złudzeń: 'Od mamuta do Bieruta,'" *Gazeta Weekend* (1 September 2017); Justyna Wojniak and Marta Majorek,

"Polish Education System under 2017 Reform: Assumptions, Aims and Controversies," *ERPA International Congresses on Education* 48 (2018), 1–12, online at: shs-conferences.org/articles/shsconf/abs/2018/09/shsconf_erpa2018_01043/shsconf_erpa2018_01043.html (accessed 28 October 2020).

9. "Kto odpowiada za pogrom kielecki? 'Różne były zawiłości historyczne,'" *TVN24* (13 July 2016), online at: tvn24.pl/wiadomosci-z-kraju,3/anna-zalewska-w-kropce-nad-i-o-jedwabnem-i-pogromie-kieleckim,660799.html (accessed 28 October 2020); Ofer Aderet, "Two Senior Polish Ministers Deny Poles' Involvement in Massacres of Jews," *Haaretz* (English ed.) (17 July 2016).

10. On the Kielce pogrom, as well as other instances of violence against Polish Jews in the postwar period, see, for example, Yisrael Gutman, *Hayehudim bepolin aharei milhemet ha'olam hasheniyah* (Jerusalem: 1985), 27–41; Bożena Szaynok, *Pogrom Żydów w Kielcach 4 lipca, 1946* (Warsaw: 1992); David Engel, "Patterns of Anti-Jewish Violence in Poland, 1944–1946," *Yad Vashem Studies* 26 (1998), 43–85; Natalia Aleksiun, "Jewish Responses to Antisemitism in Poland, 1944–1947," in *Contested Memories: Poles and Jews during the Holocaust and Its Aftermath*, ed. Joshua D. Zimmerman (New Brunswick: 2003), 247–262; Jan T. Gross, *Fear: Anti-Semitism in Poland after Auschwitz—An Essay in Historical Interpretation* (New York: 2007); Joanna Tokarska-Bakir, *Pod klątwą: Społeczny portret pogromu kieleckiego* (Warsaw: 2018).

11. "Kto odpowiada za pogrom kielecki?"; Aderet, "Two Senior Polish Ministers Deny Poles' Involvement in Massacres of Jews."

12. Jan Tomasz Gross, *Sąsiedzi: Historia zagłady żydowskiego miasteczka* (Sejny: 2000); idem, *Neighbors: The Destruction of the Jewish Community in Jedwabne* (Princeton: 2001).

13. Interview with Rabbi Michael Schudrich (16 August 2016).

14. For an extensive treatment of the emergence of Holocaust negationism in post-Communist Central and Eastern Europe, see the many works of historian and political scientist Michael Shafir, including, for example, *Between Denial and "Comparative Trivialization": Holocaust Negationism in Post-Communist East Central Europe* (Jerusalem: 2002); "Denying the Shoah in Post-Communist Eastern Europe," in *Holocaust Denial: The Politics of Perfidy*, ed. Robert S. Wistrich (Berlin and Jerusalem: 2012), 27–65; "The Nature of Postcommunist Antisemitism in East Central Europe: Ideology's Backdoor Return," *Journal of Contemporary Antisemitism* 1, no. 2 (2018), 33–61. Most recently, see also Yehuda Bauer, "Creating a 'Usable' Past: On Holocaust Denial and Distortion," *Israel Journal of Foreign Affairs* 14, no. 2 (2020), 209–227.

15. The merger bill was initially signed by the minister of culture and national heritage in April 2016, but the Provincial Administrative Court in Warsaw rejected the merger of the two museums, preventing, for a time, the seizure of the Museum of the Second World War by the government. In April 2017, however, the Supreme Court ruled "that the legal controversy was beyond the jurisdiction of the administrative courts," which allowed PiS to officially merge the museums. Interview (by Monika Heinemann) with Paweł Machcewicz, "Politics of History – Politicians against Historians," *Verband der Historiker und Historikerinnen Deutschlands* (10 July 2018), online at: blog.historikerverband.de/2018/07/10/739 (accessed 1 November 2020); Ministerstwo Kultury i Dziedzictwa Narodowego, "O zamiarze i przyczynach połączenia państwowych instytucji kultury Muzeum II Wojny Światowej w Gdańsku oraz Muzeum Westerplatte i Wojny 1939," *Dziennik Urzędowy Ministra Kultury i Dziedzictwa Narodowego*, item 18 (2016), online at: http://bip.mkidn.gov.pl/media/dziennik_urzedowy/p_18_2016.pdf (accessed 28 December 2020).

16. Personal correspondence with Paweł Machcewicz (7 May 2020).

17. Paweł Machcewicz, the former director of the Museum of the Second World War, describes the origins of the museum, its history, and the political battle over its opening in his monograph, *Muzeum* (Kraków: 2017).

18. Wiesław Władyka, "Gorące muzeum," *Polityka* (5 December 2017).

19. Interview (by Monika Heinemann) with Paweł Machcewicz, "Politics of History – Politicians against Historians."

20. Text of the multimedia display, "Poles Saving Jews," installed between October 2017 and March 2018 in the redesigned core exhibition of the Museum of the Second World War.

21. Israel Gutman, "Historical Introduction," in *The Encyclopedia of the Righteous among the Nations: Rescuers of Jews During the Holocaust: Poland*, 2 vols., ed. Sara Bender and Shmuel Krakowski (Jerusalem: 2004), xx; Gutman, *Hayehudim bepolin*, 12; Teresa Prekerowa, "Wojna i okupacja," in *Najnowsze dzieje Żydów w Polsce w zarysie (do 1950)*, ed. Jerzy Tomaszewski (Warsaw: 1993), 384.

22. Interview (by Aleksandra Pawlicka) with Barbara Engelking-Boni, "Spójrzmy prawdzie w oczy," *Wprost* (2 January 2011), online at: wprost.pl/tygodnik/224996/Spojrzmy-prawdzie-w-oczy.html; interview (by Michał Okoński) with Jacek Leociak and Dariusz Libionka, "Sny o Bezgrzesznej," *Tygodnik Powszechny* 3 [3210] (2011), online at: tygodnikpowszechny.pl/sny-o-bezgrzesznej-140526 (both sources accessed 18 January 2021).

23. Antony Polonsky, "Beyond Condemnation, Apologetics and Apologies: On the Complexity of Polish Behavior toward the Jews during the Second World War," in *Studies in Contemporary Jewry*, vol. 13, *The Fate of the European Jews, 1939–1945: Continuity or Contingency?* ed. Jonathan Frankel (New York: 1997), 192; Saul Friedländer, *The Years of Extermination: Nazi Germany and the Jews, 1939–1945* (New York: 2007), 632; Jan Grabowski, *Hunt for the Jews: Betrayal and Murder in German-Occupied Poland* (Bloomington: 2013), 2.

24. Paweł Machcewicz, "Museum of the Second World War in Gdansk: Crossroads of History, Memory and Politics," Lecture delivered at the Munich Documentation Centre for the History of National Socialism (9 July 2019), online at: youtube.com/watch?v = IS177vsRbT4 (accessed 18 January 2021).

25. It is not clear how the museum derived the upper estimate of "more than one hundred thousand Jews." Perhaps the new curators relied upon the scholarship of Polish Jewish historian Szymon Datner. Writing during the politically fraught and antisemitic period of the late 1960s and early 1970s, Datner maintained that approximately 100,000 Jews survived the war in Poland with the help of local Poles. See Szymon Datner, *Las Sprawiedliwych: Karta z dziejów ratownictwa Żydów w okupowanej Polsce* (Warsaw: 1968), 86; idem, "Zbrodnie hitlerowskie na Żydach zbiegłych z gett," *Biuletyn Żydowskiego Instytutu Historycznego* 75 (1970), 29.

26. Barbara Engelking and Jan Grabowski, "Wstęp," in *Dalej jest noc: Losy Żydów w wybranych powiatach okupowanej Polski*, 2 vols., ed. Engelking and Grabowski (Warsaw: 2018), 41–42. Engelking and Grabowski have increasingly come under attack in Poland for openly discussing the history of Poles' participation in crimes against Jews during the Second World War. In 2019, along with Jan Gross and Jacek Leociak, PiS-controlled state television TVP 1 publicly labeled the scholars "anti-Polish." Engelking and Grabowski were also sued by Filomena Leszczyńska at the behest of "Maciej Świrski, the Chairman of the Supervisory Board of the Polish Press Agency, the head and founder of the Polish Anti-Defamation League, and former deputy head of the Polish National Foundation." Engelking and Grabowski were accused of "slandering the memory" of Edward Malinowski, Leszczyńska's uncle, by citing allegations made against him by a Holocaust survivor when they published their work *Dalej jest noc*. See Wojciech Czuchnowski, "The Plan to Destroy Holocaust Scholars: Polish Anti-Defamation League Goes after the Authors of the Book 'Night Without End,'" *Gazeta Wyborcza* (English ed.) (23 January 2021).

27. Grabowski, *Hunt for the Jews*, 3, 172. This figure is in fact a conservative estimate because it does not consider the number of Jews murdered or captured by the collaborationist Polish Blue Police. According to Emanuel Ringelblum (writing in 1943–1944), this group was responsible or co-responsible for the murder of "hundreds of thousands of Polish Jews." See Joseph Kermish and Shmuel Krakowski (eds.), *Polish–Jewish Relations during the Second World War*, trans. Dafna Allon, Danuta Dabrowska, and Dana Keren (Evanston: 1992), 135. See also the more recent works by Jan Grabowski: *Hunt for the Jews*, 101–120; "Powiat Węgrówski," in Engelking and Grabowski (eds.), *Dalej jest noc*, 416–457, 500–517; "Rural Society and the Jews in Hiding: Elders, Night Watches, Firefighters, Hostages and Manhunts," *Yad Vashem Studies* 40, no. 1 (2012), 49–74; *Na posterunku: Udział polskiej policji granatowej i kryminalnej w zagładzie Żydów* (Wołowiec: 2020).

28. Geneviève Zubrzycki, "The Politics of Jewish Absence in Contemporary Poland," *Journal of Contemporary History* 52, no. 2 (2017), 256. In an effort to reverse the changes to the permanent exhibition, Machcewicz and three other founding historians filed a lawsuit against the new Museum of the Second World War for copyright infringement. The Gdańsk district court ruled largely in favor of Machcewicz and his co-claimants on October 15, 2020 and ordered the new director of the museum to remove an apologetic and historically misleading film that was added to the concluding gallery of the exhibition, though it did not mandate the removal of other contested additions. See Estera Flieger, "PILNE! Film IPN musi zostać usunięty. Jest wyrok w procesie o wystawę w Muzeum II Wojny Światowej," *OKO.press* (15 October 2020), online at: https://oko.press/pilne-film-ipn-musi-zostac-usuniety-jest-wyrok-w-proce sie-o-wystawe-w-muzeum-ii-wojny-swiatowej/ (accessed 24 January 2021). It should also be noted that the Museum of the Second World War is not the only cultural institution to be heavily scrutinized by the Polish government. Almost every museum in Poland that deals with the Holocaust and the Polish Jewish past has been subject to intense political interference by PiS since 2015, including most recently the POLIN Museum of the History of Polish Jews, whose director, Dariusz Stola, was forced out of his position by the minister of culture in February 2020, following a year-long dispute. See interview (by Michał Okonski) with Dariusz Stola, "Powód za pięć milionów," *Tygodnik Powszechny* (24 February 2020); Emilie van Outeren, "Is the Polish Government Holding a Jewish Museum Hostage for Being 'Disobedient'?" *Haaretz* (3 October 2019) (Eng. ed.). See also Jan Grabowski and Dariusz Libionka, "Distorting and Rewriting the History of the Holocaust in Poland: The Case of the Ulma Family Museum of Poles Saving Jews during World War II in Markowa," *Yad Vashem Studies* 45, no. 1 (2017), 29–60, which offers an in-depth review and critical analysis of Holocaust negationism in that particular museum (which opened in 2016 in the Subcarpathian village of Markowa).

29. Cited in Jan Grabowski, "The Holocaust and Poland's 'History Policy,'" *Israel Journal of Foreign Affairs* 10, no. 3 (2016), 483. For the full text of the bill, see Kancelaria Sejmu, "USTAWA z dnia 26 stycznia 2018 r. o zmianie ustawy o Instytucie Pamięci Narodowej—Komisji Ścigania Zbrodni przeciwko Narodowi Polskiemu," *Dziennik Ustaw*, item 369 (2018), online at: isap.sejm.gov.pl/isap.nsf/download.xsp/WDU20180000369/T/D20180369L.pdf (accessed 1 November 2020).

30. Interview with a prominent political commentator in Poland who wishes to remain anonymous (5 May 2019).

31. Grabowski, "The Holocaust and Poland's 'History Policy,' " 483.

32. Prime Minister Netanyahu's full statement reads as follows: "The law is baseless; I strongly oppose it. One cannot change history and the Holocaust cannot be denied. I have instructed the Israeli Ambassador to Poland to meet with the Polish Prime Minister this evening and express to him my strong position against the law." Israel Ministry of Foreign Affairs, "PM Netanyahu's Statement on Draft Polish Law" (27 January 2018), online at: mfa.gov.il/MFA/PressRoom/2018/Pages/PM-Netanyahu's-statement-on-draft-Polish-Law-27-January-2018.aspx (accessed 1 November 2020).

33. U.S. Department of State, "Legislation in Poland Regarding Crimes Committed during the Holocaust" (31 January 2018), online at: state.gov/legislation-in-poland-regarding-crimes-committed-during-the-holocaust (accessed 1 November 2020).

34. "Polish Law Denies Reality of Holocaust," *The Guardian* (5 February 2018).

35. As quoted in Marc Santora and Joanna Berendt, "Poland Tries to Curb Holocaust Speech, and Israel Puts Up a Fight," *New York Times* (1 February 2018).

36. As quoted in Maciej Orłowski, "Andrzej Duda: Podpiszę ustawę o IPN. Ale skieruję ją też do Trybunału Konstytucyjnego," *Gazeta Wyborcza* (6 February 2018). The Constitutional Tribunal (Trybunał Konstytucyjny) is the judicial body that determines whether a given piece of legislation adheres to the Polish constitution. This should not be confused with the Supreme Court (Sąd Najwyższy), which exercises judicial review of lower courts and generally hears cassation appeals in civil and criminal cases.

37. Because the Holocaust law was later amended to remove the threat of prison terms, the Constitutional Tribunal discontinued its evaluation of the constitutionality of the legislation.

See Constitutional Tribunal of the Republic of Poland, "Wyrok z dnia 17 stycznia 2019 r. o Nowelizacja ustawy o Instytucie Pamięci Narodowej," *Wyroki* Ref. Act K 1/18 (2019), online at: https://trybunal.gov.pl/postepowanie-i-orzeczenia/komunikaty-prasowe/komunikaty-po/art/10463-nowelizacja-ustawy-o-instytucie-pamieci-narodowej (accessed 22 January 2022).

38. See, for example, the viral YouTube video of February 2018 titled "Today, We Are Still on the Side of Truth," whose concluding frame reads: "#GERMANDEATHCAMPS"; online at: youtube.com/watch?v = NrkQ20SjHoU (accessed 1 November 2020).

39. Munich Security Conference, "Statements by Mateusz Morawiecki and Sebastian Kurz" (17 February 2018), online at: youtube.com/watch?v = bk9k5KyZmT0 (accessed 1 November 2020).

40. Ibid.

41. As quoted in Rick Novak, "Poland's Controversial 'Holocaust Law' Set to be Reversed after Global Outcry," *Washington Post* (27 June 2018).

42. Chancellery of the Prime Minister of Poland, "Joint Declaration of Prime Ministers of the State of Israel and the Republic of Poland" (27 June 2018), online at: https://www.gov.pl/web/premier/joint-declaration-of-prime-ministers-of-the-state-of-israel-and-the-republic-of-poland.

43. Ibid.

44. "Yad Vashem's Top Historian Says 'We Can Live with' Joint Israel–Poland Holocaust Declaration," *Jewish Telegraph Agency* (10 July 2018).

45. Antony Polonsky, *Polish–Jewish Relations since 1984: Reflections of a Participant/ Stosunki polsko-żydowskie od 1984 roku: refleksje uczestnika* (Kraków: 2009), 45 (English section).

46. The myth of Judeo-Communism—the conspiracy theory that asserts a uniquely Jewish–Communist plot against the nations of Europe—emerged during the Russian Revolution and has since spread across the continent despite being routinely debunked. The Polish variety has its own idiosyncrasies and historical origins, but it is not exceptional. For an analysis of the history of this myth, see Paul A. Hanebrink, *A Specter Haunting Europe: The Myth of Judeo-Bolshevism* (Cambridge, Mass.: 2018).

47. Gross, *Neighbors*, 169, 173.

48. See Hanna Świda-Ziemba, *Urwany lot: Pokolenie inteligenckiej młodzieży powojennej w świetle listów i pamiętników z lat 1945–1948* (Kraków: 2003); Natalia Aleksiun, "Polish Historiography of the Holocaust—Between Silence and Public Debate," *German History* 22, no. 3 (2004), 406–432; Joanna Michlic, "The Holocaust and Its Aftermath as Perceived in Poland: Voices of Polish Intellectuals, 1945–1947," in *The Jews Are Coming Back: The Return of the Jews to Their Countries of Origin after WWII*, ed. David Bankier (Jerusalem: 2005), 206–230.

49. A translated version appears in *My Brother's Keeper: Recent Polish Debates on the Holocaust*, ed. Antony Polonsky (London: 1990), 34–48.

50. Ibid., 46.

51. Both the self-critical and apologetic camps can be further subdivided in many ways; these are typological approximations of the many multifaceted responses to Gross' publication. I opt to simplify the categories into two competing camps, allowing for clear historical-sociological comparisons as per the Weberian methodology of "ideal types." For slightly different delineations of categories, see Andrzej Paczkowski, "Debata wokół 'Sąsiadów': Próba wstępnej typologii," *Rzeczpospolita* (24 March 2001), A6; and Antony Polonsky and Joanna B. Michlic, "Introduction," in *The Neighbors Respond: The Controversy over the Jedwabne Massacre in Poland*, ed. Polonsky and Michlic (Princeton: 2004), 33.

52. Joanna B. Michlic, "Anti-Polish and Pro-Soviet? 1939–1941 and the Stereotyping of the Jew in Polish Historiography," in *Shared History—Divided Memory: Jews and Others in Soviet-occupied Poland, 1939–1941*, ed. Elazar Barkan, Elizabeth A. Cole, and Kai Struve (Leipzig: 2007), 81–84.

53. A selection of key responses are republished in English in Polonsky and Michlic (eds.), *The Neighbors Respond*.

54. See, most recently, Barbara Engelking, *Such a Beautiful Sunny Day . . . : Jews Seeking Refuge in the Polish Countryside, 1942–1945* (Jerusalem: 2016); idem and Grabowski (eds.), *Dalej jest noc;* Grabowski, *Na posterunku.*

55. Gross, *Neighbors,* 54–71; Paweł Machcewicz, "Wokół Jedwabnego," in *Wokół Jedwabnego,* vol. 1, ed. Paweł Machcewicz and Krzysztof Persak (Warsaw: 2002), 31–35; Andrzej Żbikowski, "Pogromy i mordy ludności żydowskiej w Łomżynskiem i na Białostocczyźnie latem 1941 roku w świetle relacji ocalałych Żydów i dokumentów sądowych," in ibid., vol. 1, 159–272; Anna Bikont, *My z Jedwabnego* (Warsaw: 2004), 345–352; Timothy Snyder, *Bloodlands: Europe between Hitler and Stalin* (New York: 2010), 195. See also the documents preserved in the Archive of New Records (Archiwum Akt Nowych) in Warsaw, which have been reproduced, selected, and introduced by Waldemar Grabowski in the third section of *Wokół Jedwabnego,* vol. 2, 123–154. See especially the reproduced documents on pp. 130 and 132, which indicate that the Home Army and the Polish government-in-exile had real-time knowledge of massacres of Jews in the Podlasie region by non-Jewish Poles during the second half of 1941. Gross emphasizes this point in his 2013 Copernicus Lecture delivered at the University of Michigan, later published in Jan Tomasz Gross, *Collected Essays on War, Holocaust and the Crisis of Communism* (Frankfurt: 2014), 22.

56. Gross provides 1,600 as the number of Jews murdered in Jedwabne by their Polish neighbors. He relies upon the 1945 testimony of Szmul Wasersztajn, a survivor of the pogrom, as well as the number included on the original monument to the massacre. There are also variant numbers recorded in other historical sources, such as 1,200, 1,460, 1,500, and 1,640. The Institute of National Remembrance (IPN) conducted what the Chief Rabbi of Poland Michael Schudrich called a "partial exhumation" that "uncover[ed] the grave" to document the crime forensically. In deference to Rabbi Schudrich's halakhic recommendations, the IPN agreed not to exhume the bones because Jewish law generally prohibits the removal of human remains from their place of burial. As a consequence, the IPN could not ascertain precisely the number of victims of the Jedwabne massacre; however, according to Dariusz Stola, "reasonable estimates range from five hundred to fifteen hundred." See Michael Schudrich, "Jewish Law and Exhumation," in *Killing Sites: Research and Remembrance,* ed. Thomas Lutz, David Silberklang, Piotr Trojański, Juliane Wetzel, and Miriam Bistrović (Berlin: 2015), 79–84, esp. 82–83; Dariusz Stola, "Jedwabne: How Was It Possible?" in Polonsky and Michlic (eds.), *The Neighbors Respond,* 387.

57. Sergiusz Kowalski, "It's Obvious," in *Why Should We Teach about the Holocaust?* ed. Jolanta Ambrosewicz-Jacobs and Leszek Hońdo (Kraków: 2005), 64. I thank Tomasz Kuncewicz for pointing me to this work.

58. Marek Jan Chodakiewicz, *The Massacre in Jedwabne, July 10, 1941: Before, During, After* (New York: 2005).

59. Tomasz Strzembosz, *Antysowiecka partyzantka i konspiracja nad Biebrzą: X 1939–VI 1941* (Warsaw: 2004).

60. Bogdan Musiał, *"Konterrevolutionäre Elemente sind zu erschiessen." Die Brutalisierung des deutsch-sowjetischen Krieges im Sommer 1941* (Berlin: 2000).

61. Tomasz Strzembosz, "Collaboration Passed Over in Silence," in Polonsky and Michlic (eds.), *The Neighbors Respond,* 220–236; Bogdan Musiał, "The Pogrom in Jedwabne: Critical Remarks about Jan T. Gross's *Neighbors,*" in ibid., 304–343. For an extensive analysis of Strzembosz, Musiał, Chodakiewicz, and other historians of the apologetic camp, see Michlic, "Anti-Polish and Pro-Soviet?" 85–100.

62. Jerzy Buzek, "Living in Truth," in Polonsky and Michlic (eds.), *The Neighbors Respond,* 125.

63. Aleksander Kwaśniewski, "Sąsiedzi sąsiadom zgotowali ten los," *Gazeta Wyborcza* (11 July 2001), 4.

64. For a summary of various opinion polls taken during and after the Jedwabne debate, see Polonsky and Michlic, "Introduction," in Polonsky and Michlic (eds.), *The Neighbors Respond,* 38–40.

65. Here I am alluding to the West German *Historikerstreit* of the middle and late 1980s. For a discussion, see John Torpey, "Habermas and the Historians (Introduction to Special Issue on the *Historikerstreit*)," *New German Critique* 44 (1988), 5–24; as well as the classic work, Charles S. Maier's *The Unmasterable Past: History, Holocaust and German National Identity*

(Cambridge, Mass.: 1997). The national fault lines that surfaced during the Jedwabne debate in Poland have striking parallels to this earlier intellectual–political debate revolving around the history of the Holocaust and German national identity. However, a thorough comparison is beyond the parameters of this essay.

66. Interview (by Howard Lupovitch) with István Deák, "Polish and Hungarian Jews: So Different, Yet So Interconnected," *Polin: Studies in Polish Jewry* 31 (2019), 511.

67. Office of the Prime Minister of Hungary, "Prime Minister Viktor Orbán's Speech at the 25th Bálványos Summer Free University and Student Camp," (26 July 2014), online at: http://2010-2015.miniszterelnok.hu/in_english_article/_prime_minister_viktor_orban_s_speech_at_the_25th_balvanyos_summer_free_university_and_student_camp (accessed 30 December 2020).

68. Randolph L. Braham, "Hungary: The Assault on the Historical Memory of the Holocaust," in *The Holocaust in Hungary: Seventy Years*, ed. Randolph L. Braham and András Kovács (Budapest: 2016), 286.

69. Ibid., my emphasis.

70. Ibid., 286–287.

71. According to Braham, "of the approximately 50,000" Jews forced to work in military detachments deployed in Ukraine, "only 6–7,000 returned to Hungary." Consequently, "the losses of Jewish labor servicemen [in Ukraine] were staggering"—this, in addition to the execution of 18,000 to 20,000 "alien" Hungarian Jews. Scholars of the Holocaust in Hungary estimate that a total of 50,000 to 60,000 Jewish forced laborers across the various labor service companies were killed during the Second World War. See Randolph L. Braham, "The Hungarian Labor Service System (1939–1945): An Overview," in *Forced and Slave Labor in Nazi-Dominated Europe* (Washington, DC: 2004), 55, 60. See also the many other works of Randolph L. Braham that address this subject: "The Kamenets–Podolsk and Delvidek Massacres: Prelude to the Holocaust in Hungary," *Yad Vashem Studies* 9 (1973), 133–156; *The Politics of Genocide: The Holocaust in Hungary* (New York: 1994), 205–218; "Hungary," 264. See also Zoltán Vági, László Csősz, and Gábor Kádár, *The Holocaust in Hungary: Evolution of a Genocide* (Lanham: 2013), 7–10, 50–53; Robert Rozett, *Conscripted Slaves: Hungarian Jewish Forced Laborers on the Eastern Front during the Second World War* (Jerusalem: 2013); Tamás Csapody, "Bor Forced Labor Service as Reflected in Diaries," *Hungarian Historical Review* 9, no. 3 (2020), 391–407.

72. Braham, "Hungary," 287.

73. Ibid.

74. In the war's final months, Horthy unsuccessfully attempted to break his alliance with Nazi Germany. This led to a German-orchestrated coup, the removal of Horthy from office, and the installment of Ferenc Szálasi, the founder and leader of the far-Right fascist Arrow Cross Party, on October 15, 1944. During its short period of rule, the Arrow Cross terrorized Budapest, ghettoizing the city's Jewish population, shooting as many as 20,000 Jews along the banks of the Danube river, and deporting more than 70,000 Hungarian Jews on death marches to concentration camps in Austria and Germany, especially Mauthausen and Dachau. The collaboration of the Arrow Cross has been extensively documented. See, for example, the discussion in Braham, *The Politics of Genocide*; Vági, Csősz, and Kádár, *The Holocaust in Hungary*, 147–176; Krisztián Ungváry, *The Battle for Budapest: One Hundred Days in World War II*, trans. Ladislaus Löb (London: 2010), 236–251; Andrea Pető, *The Women of the Arrow Cross Party: Invisible Hungarian Perpetrators in the Second World War* (Cham: 2020).

75. As quoted in Christopher Adam, "Antisemitic Attack in Hungary—Holocaust Memorial Vandalised," *Hungarian Free Press* (11 September 2016).

76. On the significance of the German Occupation Monument and the Living Memorial, as well as other political touchstones in Hungary's battles over Holocaust memory, see Éva Kovács, "The Hungarian Holocaust Memorial Year 2014: Some Remarks," *S:I.M.O.N.–Shoah: Intervention. Methods. Documentation* 4, no. 1 (2017), 109–121, esp. 116–118; Andrea Pető, "'Hungary 70': Non-remembering the Holocaust in Hungary," *Culture & History Digital Journal* 3, no. 2 (2014), 1–8; idem, "'Non-Remembering' the Holocaust in Hungary and Poland," *Polin: Studies in Polish Jewry* 31 (2019), 471–480; Braham, "Hungary," 261–309, esp. 297.

77. Braham, "Hungary," 261.

78. See "Przyszły szef IPN o mordzie w Jedwabnem: Wykonawcą tej zbrodni byli Niemcy," *Wprost* (20 July 2016).

79. See, for example, Engelking, *Such a Beautiful Sunny Day*; Grabowski, *Hunt for the Jews*; Grabowski, *Na posterunku*; Gross, *Fear*; Engelking and Grabowski (eds.), *Dalej jest noc*; Barbara Engelking, Jacek Leociak, and Dariusz Libionka (eds.), *Prowincja noc: Życie i zagłada Żydów w Dystrykcie warszawskim* (Warsaw: 2007); Barbara Engelking and Dariusz Libionka, *Żydzi w powstańczej Warszawie* (Warsaw: 2009); Jan Tomasz Gross and Irena Grudzinska-Gross, *Golden Harvest: Events at the Periphery of the Holocaust* (New York: 2012).

80. See Maurice Halbwachs, *On Collective Memory*, ed. and trans. Lewis Coser (Chicago: 1992); idem, *The Collective Memory*, trans. Francis J. Ditter, Jr. and Vida Yazdi Ditter (New York: 1980).

81. Émile Durkheim, *The Elementary Forms of Religious Life* (New York: 1995).

82. Perhaps the most contentious disputes in the period prior to Jan Gross' publishing of *Neighbors* concerned the Auschwitz convent, the papal cross, and the "war of the crosses." In 1984, Carmelite nuns established a convent in a building on the periphery of the former Auschwitz concentration camp. In 1988, the "papal cross"—part of an altar used by John Paul II when he celebrated mass at Birkenau in 1979 during his first papal visit to Poland—was taken out of storage and re-erected in the vicinity of the convent. The establishment of the convent and the erection of the papal cross at Auschwitz triggered fierce protests from Jewish leaders, most prominently Rabbi Avi Weiss of New York City, and spurred internal Polish discord. With the pope's intervention, the nuns eventually relocated to a new building outside of the camp in 1993, while the papal cross remained. Five years later, with talk of the Polish government removing the papal cross, Polish nationalists planted more than 300 hundred crosses around the papal cross, which sparked another related controversy that became known as the "war of the crosses." By the year 2000, the vigilante crosses had been removed, but the papal cross has remained on the grounds of Auschwitz. For extensive analyses of these controversies, see Władysław T. Bartoszewski, *The Convent at Auschwitz* (London: 1990); Debórah Dwork and Robert Jan van Pelt, *Auschwitz: 1270 to the Present* (New Haven: 1996), 354–378; Avi Weiss, "Raising a Voice of Moral Conscience against the Christianization of Auschwitz–Birkenau," *Cardozo Law Review* 20, no. 2 (1998), 671–676; Janine P. Holc, "Memory Contested: Jewish and Catholic Views of Auschwitz in Present-Day Poland," in *Antisemitism and Its Opponents in Modern Poland*, ed. Robert Blobaum (Ithaca: 2005), 301–325; Geneviève Zubrzycki, "'Poles-Catholics' and 'Symbolic Jews': Jewishness as Social Closure in Poland," in *Studies in Contemporary Jewry*, vol. 21, *Jews, Catholics, and the Burden of History*, ed. Eli Lederhendler (New York: 2005), 65–87; idem, *The Crosses of Auschwitz: Nationalism and Religion in Post-Communist Poland* (Chicago: 2006).

83. Hungarian collaboration with the Nazi regime also occurred in local contexts beyond the jurisdiction of state and political authorities. "Ordinary" Hungarians, to borrow Christopher Browning's well-known terminology, perpetrated crimes against Jews during the Second World War; among them were female members of the Arrow Cross Party, who until recently were largely "invisible." See Pető, *The Women of the Arrow Cross Party*, esp. 19–78.

84. See, especially, literature on Roman Dmowski's antisemitic nationalism during the early 20th century, including, for example, Israel Oppenheim, "The Radicalization of the Endecja Anti-Jewish Line during and after the 1905 Revolution," *Shvut* 9 (2000), 32–66; Grzegorz Krzywiec, "Eliminationist Anti-Semitism at Home and Abroad: Polish Nationalism, the Jewish Question and Eastern European Right-Wing Mass Politics," in *The New Nationalism and the First World War*, ed. Lawrence Rosenthal and Vesna Rodić (London: 2015), 65–91. On the interwar period, see the classic works: Raphael Mahler, *Yehudei polin bein sheteh milḥamot 'olam: hisṭoryah kalkalit-sotsyalit leor hasṭaṭisṭikah* (Tel Aviv: 1968); Ezra Mendelsohn, *The Jews of East Central Europe: Between the World Wars* (Bloomington: 1987), 11–84; Emanuel Melzer, *No Way Out: The Politics of Polish Jewry, 1935-1939* (Cincinnati: 1997). On postwar pogroms, see the literature cited in n. 10. On the anti-Zionist and antisemitic campaign of 1968, see the many writings of Dariusz Stola, including *Kampania antysyjonistyczna w Polsce 1967-1968* (Warsaw: 2000); "Anti-Zionism as a Multipurpose Policy Instrument: The Anti-Zionist Campaign in Poland, 1967-1968," *The Journal of Israeli History* 25, no. 1 (2006), 175–201; "The Hate Campaign of March 1968: How Did It Become Anti-Jewish?" *Polin: Studies in Polish Jewry* 21 (2009), 16–36.

Jewish Revival in Post-Communist Hungary: Expectations and Reality

András Kovács

(CENTRAL EUROPEAN UNIVERSITY)

After the fall of Communism, a general expectation prevailed that in the wake of the advent of Western-style pluralist democracy, a Jewish revival was imminent in Hungary. The fact that political obstacles hindering the manifestation of particular personal identities had disappeared together with the monolithic Communist party-state played an obvious part in this anticipation. The early 1990s saw a resurgence of ethnic and religious identities, movements, and organizations throughout the former Eastern bloc. However, forecasts based on extrapolations from the demographic trends of the period following the Shoah were pessimistic about the chances that this revival would manifest in the Jewish societies of the region.[1] The exception was Hungary, the only country where the size of the Jewish population was large enough to reach the level of critical mass required (aside from other factors) for such changes. Numerical estimates tended toward 100,000 people with Jewish parentage, and ranging upwards of 150,000 for those of partial Jewish descent.[2]

During the 1990s, the "Jewish revival" indeed seemed to pick up rapidly in Hungary.[3] Numerous religious, cultural, and Zionist organizations were set up or relaunched, and local Jewish communities were reestablished in several provincial towns. In 1991, Mazsihisz (Federation of Hungarian Jewish Communities), an umbrella organization of the dominant Neolog branch of the Hungarian Jewry (a moderate Reform branch of Judaism, roughly equivalent to the American Conservative movement) was established, with the aim of representing the interests of religious Jews in their contacts with the Hungarian state, society, and churches, as well as with foreign governments and actors. In the early 1990s, the Chabad–Lubavitch movement also established a presence in Hungary; subsequently, the first Reform congregations, among them Szim Salom and Bet Orim, were established. In the next decade, a wide array of religious, educational, cultural, and social institutions were founded under the auspices of, and funded by, various religious branches. Additionally, around 1990, several foreign—mainly Israeli and American—Jewish organizations (among them, the Ronald S. Lauder Foundation and various Zionist groups) launched their activities in Hungary. Although the rapid and impressive development of this Jewish

András Kovács, *Jewish Revival in Post-Communist Hungary: Expectations and Reality* In: *Becoming Post-Communist*. Edited by: Eli Lederhendler, Oxford University Press. © Oxford University Press 2023. DOI: 10.1093/oso/9780197687215.003.0004 institutional framework seemed a clear indication of a Jewish revival, statistical data have shown that this institutional framework has turned out to be somewhat hollow and underused.[4]

Information gathered in the general population censuses of 2001 and 2011 corroborate this observation. The census surveys contained questions on the religious and ethnic affiliation of the respondents. Religious affiliation and national–ethnic self-identification were classified on both occasions as sensitive personal data or special category data and thus the response to such questions was made voluntary. The 2001 census reported a total of 12,871 people and the 2011 census a total of 10,965 people—that is, about 10 percent of the Jewish population in the country—who self-identified as "Israelite" (i.e., Jewish) on the question regarding religious affiliation.

Similar data can be found in the Hungarian tax administration's statistical database. Hungarian tax regulations allow taxpayers to designate 1 percent of their personal income taxes to any of the religious denominations recognized by the state. The list of officially registered churches contained five Jewish denominations until 2011; since then, the list has contained three (and, after 2020, four).[5] Between 2010 and 2020, the highest number of all taxpayers who designated such a donation in a given year to any of the Jewish denominations was 11,000, which basically equals the number of self-declared individuals of Jewish religion in the censuses.

As part of a research project conducted between 2016 and 2017,[6] we set out to collect data on synagogue attendance both in Budapest and in several other towns.[7] According to our hypothesis, the number of attendees in synagogues during the major Jewish holidays can serve as an indicator of how many people feel the need to express their attachment to the religious and cultural community at least through some symbolic act. Similarly, the number of attendees at a random Friday evening service can inform us about the approximate number of people with a stronger religious commitment who attend religious services relatively frequently. According to the results of our survey, the total sum of attendees in all synagogues in the country on major Jewish holidays was about 4,000, and the total number of attendees at weekly Shabbat services was 1,000, about 4 percent and 1 percent of the estimated total Jewish population, respectively.

Comparing the estimated size of the Jewish population in Hungary (73,000–138,000) both with the number of Jews officially defining themselves in the census as Jewish in a religious and/or an ethnic sense (around 11,000 and 13,000) and with the number of people participating in religious life regularly (1,000) or symbolically (4,000), there is obviously a major difference in the figures. Even if we consider statistical uncertainty, it is fair to state that, at most, 10 percent of the total Jewish population in Hungary express Jewish self-identification on an institutional level, as in the case of the census; only about 4 percent express belonging to the Jewish religious-cultural community through symbolic attendance at religious services on major holidays; and only about 1 percent of the total Jewish population attend religious services regularly. Thus, it seems legitimate to ask whether the expectations of communal renewal following the fall of Communism were illusory, whether the rapid and diverse institutional development created false impressions, and whether it is possible that below the surface there were no developments underway that could be really regarded as a Jewish revival.

Jewish revival as a concept encompasses a wide array of processes and modes of behavior: an interest in and return to religious traditions, a heightened national (ethnic) consciousness, and the deliberate fostering of Jewish culture as broadly conceived through the cultivation of Judaism's intellectual legacy and material cultural heritage. The most commonly defined aim embedded in the idea of such a revival was to bring Judaism back into the life of Jews brought up in secular families during the Communist era. As one of the many Jewish revival projects declared, the purpose was to allow students to "explore their Judaism in meaningful and relevant ways, to foster their Jewish identity development, to deepen their Jewish knowledge and understanding, and to motivate them to live passionate Jewish lives."[8]

During the final decades of the 20th century, a significant number of young American and Israeli Jews raised in non-religious families became practicing Orthodox Jews. This phenomenon seemed to encourage similar expectations among East Central European proponents of a movement for Jewish revival. However, as early as the beginning of the 1990s, many researchers in the field of Hungarian Jewish studies, including myself,[9] expressed concern regarding the (over)optimism of activists working toward the renewal of Jewish religious and national identity.

As a result of a long process of secularization and assimilation (dating back, in the long-term sense, to the 1867 law of emancipation of Jews in Hungary), the main body of Hungarian Jewry was characterized even before the Holocaust by the prevalence of the Neolog communities over those that were hasidic or Orthodox. This socio-demographic profile was greatly amplified by the selective impact of the Holocaust and the subsequent postwar emigration. During the Holocaust, all the Jews in rural parts of the country—most of whom were traditional and observant—were deported, and only a few returned. These transports, however, were halted before the systematic deportation of the more assimilated and secularized Jewry of the capital city could be started. As a result, the postwar Jewish population of Hungary (around 200,000 individuals) was composed almost entirely of urban residents, and the proportion of strictly observant religious groups sharply declined. By the early 1960s, the majority of strictly observant Jews who remained left the country, the last large-scale wave of emigration taking place in the aftermath of the 1956 Hungarian revolution. Another group, comprising active participants in the postwar Zionist movements and parties that were subject to political persecution after the Communist takeover, also left the country by the end of the 1950s. The anticlerical politics of the Communist regime and the compelled collaboration of the only officially recognized Jewish religious congregation with the regime increased people's alienation from Jewish traditions and religious institutions.[10] This was particularly characteristic of the new generation born after the Holocaust, whose members might have been the target population for a Jewish revival.

As far back as a study we carried out in the mid-1980s,[11] there were already indications that the chances of a religious and/or national Jewish revival were very limited. According to the interviews, among the members of the second generation, only 7 out of the total 117 respondents observed Jewish traditions, with an additional 22 people "looking for their roots" who had begun to engage with Jewish history, culture, and religious heritage in one way or another. About two-thirds of the respondents said that their family followed a conscious strategy to get rid of the perceived stigma of Jewishness. "Stigma management," as I termed it in a previous study, following Erving Goffman's term[12] consisted essentially of a set of behaviors developed and passed down in a family in order to conceal or keep Jewish ancestry secret. Of the interviewees, 31 either found out about their Jewishness from strangers rather than from family members, or they inferred the fact from certain clues. In the parents' generation, 66 families tried to conceal their Jewishness as much as possible, and they also tried to pass on their example to their children. Among these families, 20 attempted a strategy of "total passing," while 46 carefully evaluated the situation first before deciding whether they would reveal the secret of the family's Jewish background. Systematic and consequent stigma management puts a heavy burden on the individual and, additionally, does not offer a real escape from a stigmatized identity. Indeed, during interactions with others, this very behavior may become the means of external and internal identification among members of the group. A striking example of how systematic stigma management triggers a feeling of "groupness" was the account of many of our interviewees about the formation of their circle of friends in high school. In many cases, they learned years afterward that their friendship circles turned out to be exclusively Jewish, even though they never spoke about their Jewish backgrounds and many of them were even unaware of it at the time. However, in certain crucial situations, they could identify striking similarities in their friends' reactions and behavior.

After the collapse of the Communist regime, many of the members of the second generation, and especially their children, the representatives of a "third generation," seemed about to break free from the burden of an identity created or conditioned by stigma. One reason for this was the aforementioned general trend of ethnic revival. Another important factor, somewhat paradoxically, was the resurgence of antisemitism in the Hungarian political and cultural discourse—a consequence of which was that people who conceived their Jewish identity only through the challenges of personal interactions with the outside, non-Jewish world were more frequently "obliged" to feel Jewish. As a result, stigma management and information control required much more effort and constituted a heavier burden than before. Considering all these changes, in 1990, while remaining skeptical about religious or national revival, I made a cautious forecast about the possible emergence of ethnic consciousness among Jews in Hungary, and as a consequence, a strengthening of Jewish group cohesiveness that could eventually counterbalance the predicted trends toward full assimilation.[13] Now, two decades later, we must ask again: What do the results of the latest studies, such as the large-scale population surveys conducted in 1999 and 2016–2017, indicate about the expectations formulated around the fall of Communism? Were these fulfilled, or was the prospective advent of a Jewish revival yet another illusion of that period that never came to fruition? Based on a comparison of data collected during the 1999 and 2016–2017 Jewish population surveys in Hungary, I aim to reconsider whether Jewish group identification increased in the decades after the fall of Communism, and how developments in this respect may be related to the functioning of the Jewish institutions in Hungary.[14]

1. Identity Theories

The role of identities in the formation of social groups and of group consciousness has been widely discussed. Though they differ in many aspects, constructivist theories dominating the field ever since the publication of Fredrik Barth's seminal study[15] agree that the primary factor that needs to be addressed is not the supposedly "inherent" group traits or cultural contents, but how these contents are used for setting boundaries between one group and others. Boundaries are usually constructed on the basis of a set of perceived differences between interacting groups; in this way, the groups also define the *content* of their collective identity. However, there may not actually be a consensus among group members regarding the content of their identity; this, consequently, affects the interpretation and perception of group boundaries. Therefore, debates over the criteria for belonging to the group play an important role in its collective self-perception and in the self-awareness of its members. These debates may also define the issues and topics that seem most relevant in the eyes of those who perceive the group externally. The commonality of these relevant issues is an important factor of group belonging.[16]

In the perception of cohesive or bounded groupness, two factors play a key role. The first is perceived sameness, which is often a function of the frequency with which situations occur in which the markers of internal and external group identification become salient and group belonging is strongly felt. The second is the density of the network among group members. Rogers Brubaker and Frederick Cooper—based on Charles Tilly's argument—suggest that instead of the overly pluri-semantic concept of identity, we apply the concepts of commonality and connectedness when examining the emergence of groupness.[17] According to Tilly, whose main interest was how collective action comes into being, groupness is a joint product of what he refers to as "catness" and "netness"—that is, categorical commonality and relational connectedness. As Brubaker and Cooper summarize it:

" 'Commonality' denotes the sharing of some common attribute, while 'connectedness' denotes the relational ties that link people. Neither commonality nor connectedness alone engenders 'groupness'—the sense of belonging to a distinctive, bounded, solidary group. But commonality and connectedness together may indeed do so."[18] At the same time,

> categorical commonality and relational connectedness need to be supplemented by a third element, what Max Weber called a *Zusammengehörigkeitsgefühl*, a feeling of belonging together. Such a feeling may indeed depend in part on the degrees and forms of commonality and connectedness, but it will also depend on other factors such as particular events, their encoding in compelling public narratives, prevailing discursive frames, and so on.[19]

In what follows, I apply these concepts elaborated for the analysis of group constitution to analyze the changes in both self-identification with the group and feelings of groupness among Hungarian Jews. I will compare the results of the 1999 and 2016–2017 surveys in order to determine whether the salience of commonality, connectedness, and perceived groupness has increased during the post-Communist period, and whether the changes should be interpreted as indicators of Jewish revival.

I will begin with a brief overview of the elements that serve as tools for setting boundaries between Jews and their surroundings, which in turn create commonality. Among these, the initial ones to mention are religion and religious-cultural tradition. Additionally, I consider group-specific historical memory and the idea of an "imaginary homeland"—Israel and the attitude toward it—as tools of boundary creation, as well as typical group norms and group choices that are not directly related to Jewishness but, by ruling out certain options as inappropriate for one's identity, may influence choices.[20]

Following this I will outline of the development of "netness," that is, whether the weight of the Jewish network has increased in the field of interaction in which the group members are active. Next, I identify and examine situations in which Jewish self-identification become salient, i.e., where the Jews as social actors perceive that they interact with the social environment as group members. If, according to the perception of the potential group members, the frequency of such situations has increased, this points to an increased intensity of group identification. Finally, I examine the intensity of the subjective identification with Jewish collectivity.

2. Commonality: Setting Group Boundaries

2.1 Religion and Religious-cultural Tradition

The presence of religion, fostering of religious tradition, and religious-cultural heritage in family life are undoubtedly important factors in setting the boundaries between "Us" and "Them." Such indicators of identity were examined in detail during both the 1999 survey[21] and that conducted in 2016–2017.[22] In a previous study comparing the results of the two surveys,[23] we examined whether the typical markers of the process called Jewish religious revival could be identified. To this end, we classified yearly participation in Hanukah celebrations and Passover seders as indicators of relatively "thin" identification, whereas Sabbath observance (of unspecified nature), keeping kosher, and circumcision (*brit milah*) were classified as indicators of a relatively "thick" religious identification, as these demand a larger and long-lasting "investment" in Jewish identity.[24] According to the results of the 1999 survey, all these traditions were kept more frequently in the respondents' childhood families than at present. For this study, the cohort older than age 56 (that is, those born before 1943) comprised about one-third of the sample, and this explains the high level of reported experience of tradition in the parental family. "Passing" and stigma management, which would work to reduce levels of childhood experiences of the tradition, were mostly characteristic for the childhood families of the younger members of the sample, who were children under Communism. In the case of circumcision, celebrating bar/bat mitzvot, and Jewish burials, the differences between childhood families and those of the present exceeded 20 percentage points, and there was no single tradition for which the difference was less than 10 percentage points in the whole sample. At the same time, we could identify a relatively large group of mostly young people in the sample who have reverted to some Jewish traditions that were not present in their childhood families. However, a complete revival of religious tradition affecting all aspects of life has only been characteristic for a smaller subgroup. For the majority, the elements of revived tradition belonged to the group of "thin" identity markers, and these seemed destined to serve merely as tokens of group belonging/ group identity.

After the completion of the 2016–2017 survey, we investigated whether the tendencies observed 18 years ago remained consistent over time—that is, do the connections to Jewish religious traditions occur more frequently among members of the younger generation or among the parents' generation? The most frequently kept religious-cultural practices in 2017 were Hanukah celebration (52 percent), Jewish burial (48 percent), and Passover seder (47 percent), while the least frequently kept practices were keeping kosher (12 percent), Sabbath observance (21 percent) and circumcision (21 percent).[25] Twice as many respondents reported celebrating Hanukah or conducting a Passover seder as compared with respondents in the earlier survey, whereas there was only a slight increase in the numbers of those reporting keeping kosher, Sabbath observance, or circumcision. The greatest increase can be seen in the case of the two middle-aged cohorts, those aged 25–44 and 45–64. The latter represents the "revival" generation who were aged 18–37 in 1990, whereas the former (aged 7–26 in 1999) represents mainly the second generation since the "revival." According to our data, members of both generations adhere to these traditions more so now than was true during the childhood of the older cohort (who had been raised under Communism). For the youngest generation, who are today between 18 and 24, the presence of religious-cultural practices remained basically on the same level as compared with their parental families. Thus, data show that the revival tendencies recorded 18 years ago have had an impact on the two younger cohorts; I suggest, however, that those indicators mainly describe "thin" markers of Jewish identity—that is, expressions of a symbolic identity rather than practices that systematically regulate everyday life. Such markers serve as a tool for expressing identification and allow for setting symbolic group boundaries.[26]

2.2 Historical Memory

Group-specific historical memory plays a crucial role in setting boundaries between the in-group and the out-group. It is an especially important factor in the case of the Jewish diaspora, and all the more so in countries where there is a strong historical tradition of antisemitism and where the societies' majority groups bore either major or minor historical responsibility for the devastating effects of the Holocaust. Hungary is one of those countries.

In 2017, the vast majority of the respondents said that their family was affected by the Holocaust: of all respondents, 82 percent said that there were victims of the Holocaust among their close relatives—great-grandparents, grandparents, parents, or siblings. It is no wonder that among Hungarian Jews, the strongest element in Jewish group identity content is a sense of common destiny stemming from historical persecution. When we asked respondents (both in 1999 and in 2017) to define what was the most important element of their identification with Jewishness, the most frequent answer was consciousness of the historical persecution of Jews and memory of the

Holocaust. This was true whether the individual belonged to the group of respondents fostering cultural and/or religious traditions or to the more secular group, and regardless of whether they were younger or older. Practically all respondents to the later survey agreed that memory of the Holocaust had to be preserved. More than four-fifths of the respondents agreed as well with the statement that more should be taught in the schools about persecution of the Jews. Almost two-thirds agreed that Holocaust denial should be legally prosecuted. The strength of the group boundaries is clearly suggested by comparing those figures with responses among non-Jews in a survey conducted in 2014. Only 43 percent of the non-Jewish adult population of Hungary reported being in favor of maintaining the memory of the Holocaust, and only 37 percent agreed that the Holocaust should have a more significant place in school curricula. Moreover, whereas 38 percent of non-Jewish respondents agreed with the statement that, after so many years, the Holocaust should no longer be treated as an important topic, 90 percent of Jewish respondents in 2017 disagreed.[27]

2.3 Diaspora Consciousness

Diaspora consciousness used here in the sense of homeland orientation also functions as constituent of boundary-setting. Group boundaries set on this basis are clearly perceivable in the attitude of Hungarian Jews toward Israel. While in 2017, 89 percent of Jewish respondents agreed with the statement that the existence of Israel gave them a feeling of security, and 75 percent agreed that they were emotionally attached to Israel via a feeling of collective belonging, non-Jewish respondents hardly shared the same feelings, as expected. Although about one-fifth (19 percent) of Jewish respondents were critical about Israeli policy with regard to the Palestinians and agreed with the statement that "the Israeli government's policy toward the Palestinians is morally unacceptable," the rejection of Israel's policy in the non-Jewish population was much stronger. The majority of non-Jews (76 percent) accepted, or at least did not reject the statement that "Israel is doing the same thing to Palestinians as the Nazis did to Jews."

Emotional attachment to Israel, however, does not correlate with a national minority consciousness, as it does in the case of other minorities that—according to their perception—live outside of their homeland. Only a minority of Hungarian Jews (44 percent) think that Israel is the real homeland of Jews and only 13 percent said they would ever consider emigrating to Israel (and excluded emigration to any other country). These proportions and the level of emotional attachment to Israel are only slightly higher than in 1999. Thus, Israel serves as a point of reference and tool for boundary-setting for a much wider Jewish group than for those who actually perceive themselves as members of a diasporic national minority.

2.4 Worldview, Value Choices, Political Preferences

Group members may also perceive the boundaries between in-groups and out-groups in contexts only indirectly related to their identity "content" (the in-group's religious or ethno-cultural traditions and history). If a large enough portion of the group members consistently and repeatedly follow ethical norms and ideological choices that are available for everyone, including the out-group, yet the social environment considers them to be specifically characteristic of the group in question (and especially if members of the group are also inclined to consider them so), then these choices can serve as tools or materials for boundary-setting and boundary perception. The results of the 2017 study indicate that this is true for Hungarian Jewish society today.

In the 2017 survey, we asked the participants to mark their sympathies or antipathies concerning certain attitudes characteristic of conservative, liberal, or leftist worldviews and of certain political camps. In an earlier survey, we put the same questions to members of a non-Jewish national sample group, which enabled us to compare the answers given by Jews with the answers of non-Jewish university graduates, the group closest in socio-demographic status to the Jewish population. According to our results, the overwhelming majority of Jewish respondents reject authoritarianism, political conservatism, law-and-order attitudes, and all expressions of xenophobia. Their values diverged significantly from the values of the highly educated members of Hungarian majority society, who manifest the abovementioned attitudes in significantly higher proportions. While two-thirds of the majority-society respondents holding a graduate degree would tighten immigration provisions, 43 percent regard the death penalty as justified in serious cases, and more than half (52 percent) would imprison drug abusers, only around one-tenth of the Jewish respondents would do the same in all three cases. Similarly, indices of sympathy toward all other ethnic groups that are present in Hungary were much higher among Jews when compared with majority-society respondents with a similar educational status. Jewish respondents view even the least favored ethnicity group, defined in the questionnaire as "Arabs," more favorably than do respondents from the majority population holding a graduate degree. Moreover, the gaps between Jewish and non-Jewish respondents with lower educational levels were even wider.

Concerning political attitudes and opinions, there were significant differences between Jewish and non-Jewish respondents regarding political preferences: Jewish respondents were more pro-EU (in the sense of favoring greater integration of Hungary within the European Union) and regarded support for Hungarian minorities in the neighboring countries as being less important than did non-Jewish respondents. In light of the previous data, it is not surprising that on a left–right bipolar rating scale, the vast majority of Jewish respondents categorize themselves on the left side (7.6 average score on a 10-point scale) and, on the liberal–conservative bipolar rating scale, closer to the liberal pole (8.3 average score on a 10-point scale). Average points so close to the extremes indicate that only 3–4 percent of all respondents marked themselves on the conservative or right side of the scale, and even the neutral midpoint was rarely chosen compared to the left, and especially compared to the liberal extreme.

The political preferences of the Jewish population also reflect these attitudes. In most places in the world, Jews hold more liberal political views than does the average population, and hence they are more likely to vote for liberal or left-wing parties. However, it is uncommon that they do so in such an overwhelming majority as in Hungary: in 2017, only 1 percent of all Hungarian Jewish respondents said that they would vote for the ruling right-wing party, Fidesz (in power since 2010) or for other rightist parties that, when added together, received about three-quarters of the national vote in 2020. In sum, concerning their values and political choices, the Jews appear as a homogenous group in the society, strikingly different from the majority.

All these indicators—the (at least symbolically maintained) religious and cultural tradition, historical memory, diaspora consciousness, and group-specific value choices—clearly demonstrate the presence of content that serve as indicators of group boundaries separating "Us" and "Them" required for group identification.

3. Netness

In addition to the aforementioned mechanisms of internal and external categorization on the basis of perceived commonalities, there is a second basic component and indicator of groupness: the density of the in-group network. In the case of high density, in-group members interact significantly more frequently with other perceived group members than with members of out-groups in those spheres of everyday life in which interaction partners can be relatively freely chosen, such as friendships. Being continuously present and active in in-group networks entails a high level of readiness for self-identification as a group member and for identification of potential partners in interactions as in-group members. Thus, netness is a substantial component of group identity.

An analysis of the survey results from 1999 showed that netness has a strong presence in Hungarian Jewish society.[28] According to the results, the size of the respondents' personal network in the Jewish population was significantly larger than among non-Jews, and also conspicuously homophilic: 60 percent of the network members were Jewish, whereas the proportion in comparable religious minority groups was much lower: 49 percent among Calvinists, and 37 percent among Lutherans.[29] Even in the case of those whose Jewish identity proved to be weak in all other dimensions, the extent of their Jewish network was typically about 40 percent. Another indicator of the correlation between network size and groupness is that the weight of family network in the Jewish case is weaker than in the non-Jewish one, and the weight of "chosen" contacts is stronger than the weight of the "given" contacts. Interestingly, the extension of Jewish network was greatest among the youngest age group (66 percent of those aged 18–25), which could be regarded as a sign of a relatively strong groupness.

The results of the 2017 survey similarly substantiated the importance of netness in Jewish identity. In this survey, too, we sought to estimate how strong the in-group coherence in Hungarian Jewish society is perceived by the respondents and how many Jewish contacts are to be found in their personal network. According to 50 percent of the respondents, Jews form a more cohesive group than other social groups; only 5 percent felt that Jews had weaker cohesion. The 1999 survey's results were similar in proportion, so we can state that the intensity of the perception of network has not decreased since then.

In the 2017 survey, respondents had to address only one question regarding their personal network: how many Jews were to be found in their circle of friends. Of all respondents, 55 percent said that their circle of friends consisted mostly of Jews; 6 percent said their circle of friends was exclusively Jewish. If we compare these results to those of the 1999 survey, we can see that more respondents report having mostly Jewish friends (48 percent in 1999), but fewer said that their circle of friends was exclusively Jewish (the corresponding figure was 10 percent in 1999).[30] A strongly Jewish network was most characteristic of those belonging to families in which Jewish cultural and religious traditions are present (68 percent). At the same time, it is also strong in families in which Jewish traditions are relaxed or abandoned altogether: more than 50 percent of respondents in such families have a majority of Jewish friends in their circle. What is striking is that the Jewish network has the same level of weight among a quarter of those belonging to families in which Jewish traditions were already absent in the lives of the parental generation. The significance of belonging to the network for the contours of self-identification is also indicated by the fact that not only does the great majority (77 percent) of families who observe Jewish traditions regularly visit Jewish websites, but also 30 percent of those who have fully abandoned traditions.

These data indicate that the majority of Jews in Hungary live in a dense Jewish network. Even in the case of those raised in families that had already given up Jewish religious or cultural tradition, there is a strong and conscious sense of belonging to this network, which plays a key role in maintaining Jewish identification.

4. Groupness

4.1 Groupness in Social Interaction

In this section, based on the responses of the participants of the 2017 survey, I examine how frequently respondents engage in interactions with the non-Jewish out-group in which they perceive themselves to be representatives of the (Jewish) in-group, and therefore, a sense of group belonging is salient. Such a situation occurs in two possible contexts. In the first, the actor perceives the out-group as hostile toward the in-group, and this reinforces the sense of group belonging. Put somewhat differently, those who perceive the immediate social environment as strongly antisemitic will encounter more situations in their interactions with their social environment in which they categorize themselves as representatives of the in-group, that is, in which they identify as Jewish. In the second context, the actor does not perceive the out-group as hostile, simply as "other." Notwithstanding, in situations in which "otherness" plays a key role in the interactions, in-group identification is enhanced.

4.1.1 The Perception of Antisemitism

The analysis of the survey results point to a peculiar contradiction. In the 2017 survey, a lower ratio of all respondents stated that they had personally encountered antisemitism (they were asked to specify where such incidents occurred: in the location where they live, at their workplace, in institutions, or among their neighbors) than was the case in the 1999 survey. Whereas only one-fifth (21 percent) of all respondents in the 1999 survey stated that they had *not* encountered such situations in the previous year, the comparable figure was 42 percent in 2017. And yet, in the 2017 survey, more respondents agreed with the assertion that that there was a high—or very high—level of antisemitism in the country. More than half of them (55 percent) felt that antisemitic prejudice was strong, and an additional 10 percent felt that it was very strong. When we asked them to offer an estimate of the proportion of antisemites in Hungary, a quarter of the respondents (23 percent) answered that at least half of the population was antisemitic. In addition, they estimated that about two-thirds (64 percent) of Hungarian Jews would say that antisemitism was strong in the country, and that a quarter (25 percent) would call it very strong; hence, according to their perception, almost *all* Hungarian Jews feel that there is strong antisemitism in their country. What this means is that the respondents of 2017 had a more negative view of the situation than did respondents in 1999, even though they personally encountered fewer incidents of antisemitism in their interactions than did respondents to the earlier survey.

This perception of the surrounding society has an obvious impact on interactions with the out-group. The presence of the feeling of a perceived threat triggers permanent readiness to face it, and, consequently, the salience of group belonging was stronger in 2017 than before.

4.1.2 Interaction with "Others"

As indicated, the perception of a threatening out-group may serve to strengthen the salience of group belonging. In addition, however, the perception of systematic disturbances in interaction and communication with members of the out-group can have the same impact even if the out-group is *not* perceived as hostile. In this case, in-group members attempt to determine whether members of the out-group identify them regularly on the basis of their group belonging; in which sort of situation this identification happens frequently; and what consequences this may have for their interactions. Thus, they enter these interactions as group members. If Jews, for instance, sense that entering interactions with the out-group *as Jews* would in some way disturb the interaction, they are apt to devise strategies such as "passing" or withholding personal details that could identify them as Jews (information control), or they would simply avoid such interactions. The more frequent these disturbances are expected to be, the greater the salience of in-group belonging. In our survey, we tried to determine how strongly this factor contributes to the feeling of Jewish groupness.

In the survey, Jewish respondents were asked to answer questions about whether they experienced disturbances in situations in which they had to be in contact and communicate with non-Jews. The responses indicated that a significant portion of contemporary Hungarian Jewry perceives disturbances in situations of in-group–out-group communication. According to the majority of Jewish respondents (57 percent), there are certain things a non-Jewish person cannot understand; one-third of the respondents (33 percent) found certain topics embarrassing to discuss with non-Jews. The reason for the disturbance, according to the responses to the survey, is to be found partly in the reciprocal attitudes of Jews and non-Jews. Nearly two-thirds of the respondents (61 percent) agreed with the statement that Jewish people are often overly sensitive, and 42 percent agreed that Jewish people take any unfriendly remark as antisemitic—that is, they enter situations that require interaction with the social out-group with group-specific attitudes. A significant portion of the respondents assume the same about out-group members: almost half of the respondents (49 percent) agreed with the statement that non-Jewish people often get embarrassed about the topic of persecution of Jews, because they have not yet personally settled these issues of the past. More than one-third of the Jewish respondents agreed with the statement that many non-Jewish people think that Jews conspire against them. A relatively high proportion of the Jewish respondents (20 percent) found interactions with the out-group difficult in almost all spheres of life, because, according to them, non-Jewish people are often embarrassed when they have to interact with Jews. These results indicate that about one-third to a half of Hungarian Jews interact as representatives of the in-group with the out-group and think that the members of the out-group also consider them as such. This mechanism, when repeatedly reenacted, reconstitutes perceived group boundaries.

4.2 Feeling of Groupness

As Brubaker and Cooper have pointed out, the previously analyzed factors—commonality and netness—significantly contribute to the feeling of groupness.[31] This subjective sense of belonging is a basic indicator of groupness. Our 2016–2017 survey has shown that this feeling was rather strong in the group under examination, and its level was mostly stable compared with the 1999 results. Almost three-quarters (71 percent) of all respondents replied that they had strong (53 percent) or very strong (18 percent) feelings of Jewishness. The significance of subjective identification for in-group identification is also demonstrated by the fact that a strong emotional Jewish identification was declared even by one-third of those respondents whose family had been out of touch with Jewish religious and cultural traditions for two generations. A subjective sense of belonging is the strongest factor in in-group identification even in comparison with other dimensions of identification. The survey contained a question on the subjective importance of ten factors (on a scale of 1–5) in the respondents' self-identification as Jews—that is, in their subjective (Jewish) identity. The respondents found that a subjective sense of belonging to Jewry (4.2 average score) and Jewish historical memory (4.3 average score) were the most important factors. They also found the following factors important: an interest in Jewish culture (4.1 average score) and friendships with other Jews (3.5 average score). In contrast, the two identity elements related to religion—religious practice (2.3 average score) and active participation in Jewish religious community life (2.2 average score)—were relegated last in order of importance.

Overall, the elder generations found all identity elements more important than did the younger ones, with three exceptions: there was no difference in how different generations evaluated the importance of religious practice and the subjective sense of belonging to Jewry, and both younger and elder generations equally regarded friendships with other Jews as important. These three factors in in-group identification were not dependent on age.

5. Jewish Groupness and Jewish Revival

As the findings of the 1999 survey have shown, the fall of the Communist regime and the post-Communist transition period were marked by certain transformations in Hungarian Jewish society that could be regarded as signs of a Jewish revival, even though these did not conform totally to expectations. The return to the religious-cultural tradition did not manifest itself in a substantial growth of the proportion of strictly observant Jews, as in many cases in Western Jewish societies, but rather in the renewal of certain elements of Jewish tradition that could serve as vehicles for the expression of Jewish identification on a symbolic and occasional basis, and thus also as tools of group boundary-setting. This "Judaism à la carte"[32]—a rough equivalent of the phenomenon of symbolic identity in the scholarship on ethnicity—serves as a tool of boundary-setting much more frequently than in the Communist period.

Mechanisms for the creation/formation of secular group identity, such as group-specific historical memory and group-specific value choices, function more widely as boundary-setting tools than do religious-cultural traditions. Through these secular tools, group identity is reinforced by "particular events, their encoding in compelling public narratives, [and] prevailing discursive frames."[33] Examples of this abound in public debates and conflicts over museums, memorials, and commemoration of the Shoah, in particular with regard to the question of Hungary's historical responsibility. All these mechanisms largely contribute to the preservation and reproduction of the ethnic network, and thus—along with it—help maintain the intensity of a subjective sense of group belonging.

Hence, based on our data, we can state that self-categorization rooted in external and internal identification, a developed group network, intergroup interactions, and a strong subjective feeling of group belonging became more salient and visible among Jews in Hungary in the post-Communist period as opposed to the period preceding it. All these factors substantially contributed to the perception of bounded groupness that is characteristic of a much larger group than that of affiliated Jews in Hungary. This is reflected by the opinions about the role of Jewish organizations in politics.

The results of the survey in 2016–2017 indicate that, in the eyes of the majority of respondents, Jews are an ethnic group that should be represented as an interest group in politics. Only a minority thought there was no need for autonomous Jewish representation in politics and that national political parties could provide adequate political representation for Jewish issues in present-day Hungary. The majority (66 percent) considered this to be the task of Jewish organizations. Moreover, the overwhelming majority of religious Jews rejected the statement that Jewish organizations should represent them, religious Jews, alone; in a clear indication of ethnic self-identification, the majority would rather entrust Jewish political representation to organizations independent of religious communal institutions. Furthermore, the majority of Jews expect Jewish organizations to take an active part in shaping public policy in the country. Three-quarters of the sample thought that Jewish leaders should feel free to express their opinions on their own initiative, without waiting to be invited to do so by the authorities, whereas only one in five respondents thought otherwise. Indeed, only a minority (33 percent) of our respondents thought that the Jewish organizations should take stands only on Jewish issues.

It is striking that these opinions contradict the previously observed fact that only a small proportion of Hungarian Jews support the Jewish organizations active in the country and an even smaller proportion are members of these organizations. This is equally true for Jewish congregations and Jewish associations. As noted, only about

10 percent of the Jewish population takes advantage of the option to have 1 percent of their taxes directed toward the support of a Jewish congregation, and in the past 10 years, the annual number of similar tax-support donations earmarked for Jewish civil societies fell to somewhere between 2,000 and 3,000.[34] This indicates that the role of Jewish institutions is not what one might expect among members of a Jewish society with a dominant ethnic identity: the institutionalization of ethnic identification is lagging far behind the development of ethnic group consciousness that has taken place since the 1990s. Analyzing the causes of this lag is beyond the scope of this study. However, I suggest that while the limits of a religious revival are conditioned by the predominantly secular character of the Jewish population, the dynamics of a possible ethnic revival are mainly influenced by the fact that Hungarian Jewish institutions have not sufficiently adapted to the changes in post-Holocaust Hungarian Jewish society in the post-Communist period.

This is the main reason why Jewish institutional leaders have become "powerless shepherds whose flocks are deserting the fold."[35] The respondents from the Jewish sample of the survey expect more of Hungarian Jewish organizations in the field of interest-group representation and beyond. According to our data, the largest discrepancy between the demand and the supply side—the expectations of self-identifying Jews and the activity of the Jewish organizations—appears in the fields of social work, education, and culture. While a number of studies have shown that effective ethnic interest representation and mobilization can significantly increase ethnic identification,[36] it seems highly likely that weak institutionalization and a related lack of ethnic policy is significantly impeding the dynamics of a possible Jewish ethnic revival.

Independent of the future prospects of a Jewish ethnic revival in Hungary, the original question of this study remains: even if important indicators of a Jewish revival can be observed, can these tendencies counteract the demographic decline of the Jewish population? Might the growing number of self-identifying Jews previously belonging to the group of "Jews in hiding," along with an increase in the sense of ethnic groupness, counterbalance the effects of low birth rates, intermarriage, and emigration? On the one hand, several scholars investigating the identity patterns and future perspectives of East and East Central European Jews around the turn of the 21st century responded in the negative. Charles Liebman, for example, regarded the separation of Judaism and Jewishness as a determinative first step toward assimilation.[37] Similarly, Zvi Gitelman, an eminent scholar of contemporary Russian and Ukrainian Jewry, argued that a durable, transgenerational, and, in his words, "thick" Jewish culture as a solid ground for identity in the diaspora could become viable only if it included the religious tradition, which regulates all spheres of everyday life. Accordingly, such Jewish identities as the ones mapped by our surveys in Hungary would typically be classified as culturally "thin," since both Orthodox and Neolog Judaism have lost ground while, at the same time, Zionism or national minority self-consciousness has remained marginal, and the weight of the memory of the Shoah is changing with the disappearance of the survivors' generation.[38] According to Gitelman, a "common and distinct system of understandings and interpretations that constitute normative order and world view and provide strategic and stylistic guide to action" cannot serve as basis of "thick" identities.[39] What remains at the end is a "thin," a-religious Jewish culture, which, for its consumers is akin to opera in the eyes of an opera fan: "[a]

pastime, not a vocation. . . . Occasional rather than constant and all-embracing. . . ."[40] Following that line of reasoning, what we observe in Hungary today (and elsewhere in the post-Communist world) cannot serve as the basis of a thorough or lasting Jewish revival.

However, other sociologists researching diasporic identity find that it is an overly substantialist stance to hold that durable, transgenerational Jewish identity can be built only on religious Orthodoxy and that diasporic Jewish communities are condemned to slow disappearance through assimilation, apart from those small groups adhering to, or returning to, traditionalist Orthodoxy. The results of the Hungarian surveys presented above seem to contradict this forecast. It is true that global aspects of modernity and post-modernity—rationalization, secularization, and individuation—have fundamentally transformed the processes of ethnic group construction, but this has not resulted in the thorough absorption or amalgamation of ethnic groups. Instead, such processes have led to new types of ethnicity, and in certain cases, have even stimulated ethnic group construction.[41] In an overview of such social transformations in the post-Communist Jewish diaspora, Lars Dencik has asked whether there is no way to react to these developments other than by leaving Jewishness behind: might it rather be the case that Jews simply "change their way of being Jewish"?[42]

Analyzing social developments in post-transition Jewish society in Poland, Marius Gudonis revisited Benedict Anderson's concept of imagined community to understand the role that can be played by a "thin" Jewish culture consumed by a widening circle of Jews (and non-Jews) in a process of group reconstruction. Gudonis argues that the "thin" Jewish culture offered by Jewish institutions and by cultural and commercial enterprises can engender identity construction, as it carries a different meaning for Jews and non-Jews, even if they are merely individual consumers of cultural goods. As he sees it, a book by a Jewish author or a play performed by a Jewish theater troupe may attract non-Jewish consumers or meet a general cultural demand, but it might also take on a different connotation for consumers attracted to Jewish culture as a result of their ethnic self-identification. The Jewish character of an institution links together Jewish consumers of diverse backgrounds and thus creates a meaningful community. This community is based on a shared commonality both among them and, symbolically, between them and "those previous generations who were the originators of the culture: [thus] consumption acts as both a spatial and temporal link to other Jews."[43] The cultural content disseminated by these institutions might include elements of Jewish religious and ethno-cultural traditions, a combination of these, or even be newly invented. As Eric Hobsbawm demonstrated, invented traditions were important tools in the construction of modern nations,[44] and as Shulamit Volkov pointed out, they are not unknown in Jewish history, either:

> The invention of tradition was the most comprehensive, perhaps even the most formidable Jewish "project of modernity." Unlike other aspects of modernization, this was not an unintended outcome of individuals' decisions and actions but a conscious collective effort, designed to reshape and modernize that ever-present but often so elusive, even mysterious entity, Judaism. . . . [It] had been undergoing deep transformations since the last decades of the 18th century, these, contrary to established wisdom, were not inevitably leading to its disintegration or decay but included a massive collective effort at a

cultural rejuvenation, resulting in what might readily be subsumed under the title of an "invented tradition."[45]

The invention of tradition is mostly the task of intellectuals and ethnic institutions that serve as the arena for debates over the authenticity of identities offered in the cultural marketplace. These debates represent an important part of identity construction, since even if they are not able to dissolve the contradictions between the different identity options, they can present, in Claire Rosenson's words, "a set of core issues or questions that the members of an ethnic group consider 'their own', . . . questions that are more or less relevant to each member, but more relevant to the members of the group than to outsiders in general." Moreover, if they fulfill this function well enough, "it is precisely the areas of controversy that drive the evolution of ethnicity."[46]

As Stephen Miller, who carried out the most comprehensive empirical study on the relationship of Jewish ethnicity and identity in Great Britain, summarized the results of his investigation: "the mental and affective components of ethnicity can be intense and personal, but virtually irrelevant to practical involvement in Jewish life . . . Behavioral ethnicity [that is, the strength of involvement in social-institutional activity and the performance of light rituals] is the most effective determinant of transgenerational identity behaviors."[47] Thus, if the institutional supply side can adequately answer the needs of the individual demand side, the subjective cognitive and affective components of ethnicity—the individually felt and perceived groupness that we identified in the Hungarian case—can be turned into "behavioral ethnicity" that was present to a much smaller extent among the Jews in Hungary.

A quantitative survey of the Jewish community in postwar Poland[48] found that the strength of in-group ties was the strongest predictor of involvement in the ethnic minority community in both its secular and its religious forms. Thus, the transformation of subjectively felt groupness into engagement in ethnic activities is most likely when strong netness is a substantial component of perceived groupness, as in the Hungarian case. The first step in this direction can be the regular consumption of ethnic cultural offerings perceived by the consumers as systematic participation in Jewish institutional life. According to Miller's observations, this could be an important move towards a more solid transgenerational identity.

In the Hungarian case, the most striking indicator of readiness for such an engagement is the development of Jewish schooling. Currently, there are three Jewish schools in the country, with a total number of about 1,200 students aged 6–19. The largest one—located in Budapest with a student enrollment of 900 students in preschool, elementary, middle, and secondary school—is a private school called Lauder Javne, founded in 1992. It has no formal links to any of the Hungarian Jewish congregations; according to its self-definition, it is an independent, secular institution. Our surveys contained questions directed at respondents whose children were or had been attending a Jewish school, asking about their expectations from the school and the most important aspects they considered when choosing a school. According to the responses, the parents who chose the Lauder Javne School attached much greater importance to aspects unrelated to the school's Jewish character—its liberal atmosphere and the prospects and training for an international career—than to such aspects as having the opportunity to get acquainted with Jewish religion and cultural traditions. Nevertheless, all respondents who themselves attended this school after 1990 had a stronger sense of group belonging, according to all indicators of Jewish identification, than those attending non-Jewish schools. They had a much denser Jewish personal network, and they were significantly more active in Jewish organizations than were students who attended non-Jewish schools. Thus, if Jewish educational institutions can reach their target group through such means as offering high-quality education and proxies for Jewish social traits such as liberal attitudes and an international outlook, they can contribute to the transformation of subjectively felt ethnic belonging into behavioral ethnicity, which is directly linked to the intensification of identification. However, the example of the Lauder Javne schools points to an opportunity more than to a general trend: as with several similar initiatives (for instance, JDC summer camps and the "March of the Living" initiative), the school functions outside the institutional realm of Jewish denominations, and a significant portion of its funding is based on foreign (Jewish) subsidy.

Jews in Hungary are apparently more "Jewish" than they were three decades ago. As this study has demonstrated, instead of passing and hiding, Jews perceive themselves much more frequently as members of a bounded group and are increasingly open to being identified as Jewish in interactions with their environment. Yet these changes are less the consequence of a return to traditional religious observance in the strict sense, and more the products of enhanced ethnic consciousness and identification. They can be considered as features of a Jewish ethnic revival. However, due to a lack of dynamic ethnic institutions, Hungarian Jews have not yet been able to translate their cognitive-emotional ethnicity into behavioral ethnicity so as to appear as an assertive ethnic group in Hungarian public life. Under those conditions, even if ethnic groupness becomes stronger in the future, it may not be able to counterbalance persisting demographic trends: the numerical decline of the group due to low birth rates, emigration, and intermarriage. At the same time, perceived groupness based on ethnic identification among a majority of the remainder may become more strongly articulated and institutionalized. Over the longer run, this might reverse the causal chain: stronger ethnic groupness could have an impact on the religious-cultural renewal by redefining and changing the criteria and symbols of belonging. Whether this will happen is an open question.

Notes

1. Bernard Wasserstein, *Vanishing Diaspora: The Jews in Europe since 1945* (Cambridge, Mass: 1996).

2. According to our calculations, the estimated number of Jews according to matrilineal descent was between 58,000 as a minimum and 111,000 as a maximum, and the number of individuals with at least one Jewish parent was between 73,000 as a minimum and 138,000 as a maximum; according to the broadest definition of Jewishness, out of the total adult population (aged 18 or above) of Hungary, 160,000 people had at least one Jewish grandparent. See András Kovács and Ildikó Barna (eds.), *Zsidók és zsidóság Magyarországon 2017-ben: Egy szociológiai kutatás eredményei* [Jews and Jewry in Hungary in 2017: Results of a sociological survey] (Budapest: 2018), online at: szombat.org/files/2019/05/Zsidok-es-zsidasag-Magyarorszagon-2017-ben.pdf (accessed 20 December 2021). According to calculations based on the concepts

developed by Sergio DellaPergola, the size of the Jewish population in the country with one Jewish grandparent is 130,000; see Sergio DellaPergola and L. Daniel Staetsky, "Jews in Europe at the Turn of the Millennium: Population Trends and Estimates" (London: 2020), online at jpr.org.uk/publication?id = 17623 (accessed 23 August 2021), 31–32.

3. András Kovács and Aletta Forrás-Bíró, *Jewish Life in Hungary: Achievements, Challenges and Priorities since the Collapse of Communism* (London: 2011).

4. Ibid., 47–49.

5. The five were Mazsihisz (Neolog), Maoih (Orthodox), Emih (Chabad), Szim Salom and Bet Orim (Reform). Between 2011 and 2020, the Reform branches were excluded; after 2020, Szim Salom was once again included.

6. Kovács and Barna (eds.), *Zsidók és zsidóság Magyarországon 2017-ben.*

7. Data was collected through participant observation in 2016. The researchers visited the synagogues on three occasions, Rosh Hashanah (New Year), Yom Kippur (Day of Atonement), and on a non-holiday Shabbat (both at *kabalat shabbat* Friday evening service and Shabbat morning service, on 3–4 November 2016). Attendees were counted several times according to a standardized method.

8. Jewish Renaissance Project, online at https://www.jrp.com (accessed 29 August 2021).

9. András Kovács, "Changes in Jewish Identity in Modern Hungary," in *Jewish Identities in the New Europe*, ed. Jonathan Webber (London: 1994), 150–160.

10. András Kovács, "Hungarian Jewish Politics from the End of the Second World War until the Collapse of Communism," in *Studies in Contemporary Jewry*, vol. 19, *Jews and the State: Dangerous Alliances and the Perils of Privilege*, ed. Ezra Mendelsohn (New York: 2004), 124–156.

11. Between 1984 and 1987, we collected 117 family history interviews with members of the "second generation"; the total volume of the interview material exceeded 10,000 typewritten pages. For details regarding survey results, see Ferenc Erős, András Kovács, and Katalin Lévai, "How Did I Find Out that I Was a Jew? Interviews," *Soviet Jewish Affairs* 17, no. 3 (1987), 55–66; Kovács, "Changes in Jewish Identity in Modern Hungary"; idem, "Anti-Semitism and Jewish Identity in Post-Communist Hungary," in *Anti-Semitism and the Treatment of the Holocaust in Postcommunist Eastern Europe*, ed. Randolph L. Braham (New York: 1994), 125–142.

12. Erving Goffmann, *Stigma: Notes on the Management of Spoiled Identity* (London: 1968).

13. Kovács, "Changes in Jewish Identity in Modern Hungary," 159.

14. The data presented and analyzed in this study were recorded as part of two questionnaire-based surveys of the Hungarian Jewish population conducted in 1999 and 2016–2017. During the first survey, 2,015 individuals aged 18 and above were interviewed; during the second survey, 1,879 individuals aged 18 and above were interviewed. These face-to-face interviews lasted, on average, 1.5 hours. Since there is no general database on Jews in Hungary, sampling via random selection was impossible. We thus used the so-called "snowball" sampling technique, for which the sample frame was basically defined according to the "Law of Return" (i.e., the individual has at least one Jewish grandparent), excluding non-Jewish family members and including converts to Judaism. Because of the sampling method used, there are several reasons to believe that the sample consists of people who are more strongly attached to Judaism and who possess a stronger Jewish identity than the overall Hungarian Jewish population. Nevertheless, each characteristic subgroup of the Hungarian Jewish community is represented in our sample, though probably not exactly in the same proportion as would correspond to their numbers in reality. For more details regarding the study, see András Kovács (ed.), *Jews and Jewry in Contemporary Hungary: Results of a Sociological Survey* (London: 2004); Kovács and Barna (eds.), *Zsidók és zsidóság Magyarországon 2017-ben.*

15. Fredrik Barth, *Ethnic Groups and Boundaries: The Social Organization of Culture Difference* (Oslo: 1969).

16. See Rawi Abdelal, Yoshiko M. Herrera, Alastair Iain Johnston, and Rose McDermott, "Identity as a Variable," *Perspectives on Politics* 4, no. 4 (December 2006), 695–711; Claire A. Rosenson, "Polish Jewish Institutions in Transition," in *New Jewish Identities: Contemporary Europe and Beyond*, ed. Zvi Gitelman, Barry Kosmin, and András Kovács (Budapest: 2003).

17. Rogers Brubaker and Frederick Cooper, "Beyond 'Identity,'" *Theory and Society* 29, no. 1 (2000), 1–47.

18. Ibid., 20.

19. Ibid.

20. Abdelal, et al., "Identity as a Variable."

21. András Kovács (ed.), *Jews and Jewry in Contemporary Hungary: Results of a Sociological Survey* (London: 2004).

22. Kovács and Barna, *Zsidók és zsidóság Magyarországon 2017-ben.*

23. Ildikó Barna and András Kovács, "Jewish Religious-Cultural Traditions and Identity Patterns in Post-Communist Hungary," in *Being Jewish in 21st Century Central Europe*, ed. Haim Fireberg, Olaf Glöckner, and Marcela Menachem Zoufalá (Oldenbourg: 2020), 103–114.

24. On the methodology employed, see n. 14.

25. Upon analyzing the data, it must be taken into account that, as noted above with regard to our sample of 1,879 respondents, the proportion of religious and affiliated Jews was in all likelihood higher among the respondents to the survey than among Hungarian Jews as a whole. See Kovács and Barna, *Zsidók és zsidóság Magyarországon 2017-ben.*

26. Herbert Gans, "Symbolic Ethnicity: The Future of Ethnic Groups and Cultures in America," *Ethnic and Racial Studies* 2, no. 1 (January 1979), 1–20.

27. Data for the non-Jewish respondents are taken from a study based on a 2014 survey sample representative for the adult population of Hungary. See Endre Hann and Dániel Róna, "Antiszemita előítéletesség a mai magyar társadalomban (2014)" [Anti-Semitic prejudice in contemporary Hungarian society (2014)], Brüsszel Intézet–Tett és Védelem Alapítvány (TEV), online at: https://tev.hu/wp-content/uploads/2014/04/Median_2015_HU_web.pdf (accessed 29 August 2021).

28. Róbert Angelusz and Róbert Tardos, "Társas kötelékek és kulturális tradíciók a magyar zsidóság különböző nemzedékeiben [Social networks and cultural traditions in different generations of Hungarian Jews], in *Zsidók a mai Magyarországon* [Jews in contemporary Hungary], ed. András Kovács (Budapest: 2002), 41-76.

29. Ibid., 53.

30. In the 1999 survey, we investigated the subject's personal network not only by means of questions about the circle of friends but also through additional questions about family network and more distant personal relationships. Hence, there is a discrepancy in the data for network belonging (60 percent in 1999).

31. Brubaker and Cooper, "Beyond 'Identity.'"

32. András Kovács, Ildikó Barna, Sergio DellaPergola, and Barry Kosmin, "Identity à la Carte: Research on Jewish Identities, Participation and Affiliation in Five Eastern European Countries," JDC International Centre for Community Development (2011), online at: https://archive.jpr.org.uk/object-eur103 (accessed 29 August 2021).

33. Brubaker and Cooper, "Beyond 'Identity,'" 20.

34. Hungarian tax regulations allow citizens subject to personal income tax (PIT) to designate an additional 1 percent of their annual PIT to support officially registered, public benefit civil society organizations. There are more than 50 registered Jewish public benefit organizations in Hungary.

35. Régine Azria, "A Typological Approach to French Jewry," in Gitelman, Kosmin, and Kovács (eds.), *New Jewish Identities*, 66.

36. Peter Vermeersch, "Theories of Ethnic Mobilization: Overview and Recent Trends," CRPD Working Paper No. 3 (September 2011), online at: https://soc.kuleuven.be/crpd/files/working-papers/wp03.pdf (accessed 29 August 2021).

37. Charles S. Liebman, "Jewish Identity in Transition: Transformation or Attenuation?" in Gitelman, Kosmin, and Kovács (eds.), *New Jewish Identities*, 341–350.

38. Zvi Gitelman, "Conclusion: The Nature and Viability of Jewish Religious and Secular Identities," in *Religion or Ethnicity? Jewish Identities in Evolution*, ed. Zvi Gitelman (New Brunswick: 2009), 303–322, here 316.

39. Ibid.

40. Ibid.

41. See Joane Nagel, "Constructing Ethnicity: Creating and Recreating Ethnic Identity and Culture," *Social Problems* 41, no. 1 (February 1994), 152–176; Lars Dencik, "'Jewishness' in

Postmodernity: The Case of Sweden," in Gitelman, Kosmin, and Kovács (eds.), *New Jewish Identities*, 75–104.

42. Dencik, " 'Jewishness' in Postmodernity," 77.

43. Marius Gudonis, "Particularizing the Universal: New Polish Jewish Identities and a New Framework of Analysis," in Gitelman, Kosmin, and Kovács (eds.), *New Jewish Identities*, 258.

44. Eric Hobsbawm and Terence O. Ranger (eds.), *The Invention of Tradition* (Cambridge: 1983).

45. Shulamit Volkov, "Inventing Tradition," in idem, *Germans, Jews, and Antisemites: Trials in Emancipation* (Cambridge: 2006), 278–281.

46. Rosenson, "Polish Jewish Institutions in Transition," 266.

47. Stephen Miller, "Changing Patterns of Identity among British Jews," in Gitelman, Kosmin, and Kovács (eds.), *New Jewish Identities*, 59.

48. Michal Bilewitz and Adrian Wójcik, "Does Identification Predict Community Involvement? Exploring Consequences of Social Identification Among the Jewish Minority in Poland." *Journal of Community & Applied Social Psychology* 20, (2010), 72–79; Published online in Wiley InterScience (www.interscience.wiley.com) DOI: 10.1002/casp.1012

Prospects for Jewish Studies in Poland: An Update for a New Decade

Marcin Wodziński

(UNIVERSITY OF WROCŁAW)

"Small numbers, big presence," a phrase coined by the Polin Museum of the History of Polish Jews in Warsaw, is the key message about Jews in contemporary Poland. This slogan might be applied as well to academic Jewish studies in the country. Around 100 books concerning Jewish subjects appear in Poland every year alongside several hundred articles, many of them written in widely accessible languages. Three universities offer high-quality BA and MA programs in Jewish studies, two others in Hebrew studies.[1] Several dozen doctoral dissertations on Jewish topics are defended each year at Polish universities. More than 200 members of two associations of Jewish studies focus on Jewish history and culture, mostly pertaining to Eastern Europe. There are seven scholarly journals specializing in Judaica that appear on a quarterly, semi-annual, or annual basis. There is also a significant, and growing, presence of Jewish topics in mainstream academic publishing houses and periodicals in various fields, including history, literature, sociology, and anthropology. A tangible expression of the high status of Jewish studies in the Polish academy is the proportion of books on Jewish subjects nominated in the most prestigious academic book contests. Typically, among the finalists of the top academic book contest in Poland, every sixth book deals with Jewish history or culture; in the contests for historical books, the figure is closer to 10 percent.[2] With regard to the two state-run research-granting programs in the humanities and social sciences, the number of grants awarded to projects on Jewish subjects accounts for 3 to 4 percent of the total; in history, it is as high as 5 percent, as will later be illustrated.

This remarkable development of academic Jewish studies in Poland (and in Eastern Europe more generally) has been the subject of a number of scholarly and popular studies over the last two decades.[3] A majority of these have focused on the transition from the ban on studying Jewish history and culture in most of the Soviet bloc countries before 1989 to the institutional maturing of academic centers and teaching programs in the period after the fall of Communism. Attention has also been given to the startling success of old, new, and refurbished Jewish museums and their associated academic activities—in particular, in Warsaw and Moscow, but also in other cities

Marcin Wodziński, *Prospects for Jewish Studies in Poland: An Update for a New Decade* In: *Becoming Post-Communist*. Edited by: Eli Lederhendler, Oxford University Press. © Oxford University Press 2023. DOI: 10.1093/oso/9780197687215.003.0005 and smaller towns of Eastern Europe, from Riga, Chernivtsy, and Kraków to Sighet, Chmielnik, and Dolní Kounice.[4] Specifically for Poland, it seems we have a relatively comprehensive picture of these developments thanks to a series of insightful publications, some of them by leading scholars in the field who have engaged in a kind of "participant observation," if it is appropriate to borrow this phrase from the language of anthropology.[5] My intention in this essay is, therefore, not to reflect on these long-term changes but rather to consider what are the most recent developments and where these are possibly heading.[6]

I shall begin with an analysis of the changing interests and motivations of undergraduate students who have chosen to major in Jewish history and culture over the past ten years. As I hope to demonstrate, their motivations remain strongly correlated with wider public debates and developments among liberal segments in Poland, though at the same time they have become increasingly pragmatic. This section is followed by a short bibliometric analysis of research interests among Polish scholars as reflected in two databases: articles in academic journals of Jewish studies published in Poland; and research grants distributed by the two state-run research-granting programs. Here I trace three main characteristics of the research on Jewish history and culture conducted in Poland: ethnocentrism; a focus on a selected set of topics (mostly connected with Holocaust and antisemitism); and an increasing interest in contemporary issues to the detriment of historical studies. The concluding section will turn to the question of the future and what are the possible research interests of the emerging generation of scholars, as reflected in doctoral dissertations on Jewish topics currently being written in Poland.

Students' Interests

As noted by a number of scholars, the status of Jewish studies in Poland reflects the special attention to Jewish-related matters in Polish society, which in turn is dependent on a variety of historical and contemporary factors. Dozens of permanent museums and temporary exhibitions; nearly forty annual festivals of Jewish culture; films and theatre performances; klezmer and Israeli music concerts; workshops on Jewish cooking, Yiddish singing, or Hebrew calligraphy—such activities aim at filling the void of Jewish life in Poland, informing a powerful "mnemonic awakening" as a response to Jewish absence in contemporary Poland.[7] As Geneviève Zubrzycki has demonstrated, all of this is part of a broader socio-political project aimed at transforming the orientation of Polish national identity into something that is more liberal and progressive, less nationalist and xenophobic. That project involves wide and diverse groups within Polish society with varying objectives and levels of involvement, ranging from occasional visitors to a klezmer concert to life-long activists in organizations dedicated to the preservation of Jewish heritage, as well as converts to Judaism (whose numbers are modest but steadily growing).[8] Enrollment in one of the leading university programs for three to five years, during which time students spend hundreds of hours studying Hebrew and Yiddish (and, at one university, Ladino) in addition to rabbinical literature and Jewish history, is certainly not a conversion, but nonetheless ought to be counted as signifying a high degree of involvement. In that sense, the motivations and interests of those choosing to do a major in Jewish studies are not necessarily characteristic of "average" participants in the "mnemonic awakening." What are they, then? And what do they represent?

For nearly two decades, I have carried out a survey at the beginning of the "Introduction to Jewish Studies" course, on average some thirty students each year, that I teach at the University of Wrocław. The students are asked about their personal interest in the culture and history of the Jews, and the reasons that led them to select our BA program in Jewish studies. Ten years ago, when I first summarized the outcome of the survey, I separated the students into five dominant groups: 1) "children of *Fiddler on the Roof*," who were motivated both by a sense of the exoticism of Jewish culture and by the closeness or even intimacy that it evoked, given the historic proximity of Jews and non-Jews in Poland; 2) "children of the Second Vatican Council" who, motivated by religious convictions, wanted to learn more about Jews as Jesus' fellow believers; 3) "seekers," that is, young Jews in search of their identity, or, more often, individuals who suspected that one of their ancestors might have been "of Jewish origin," as the common Polish phrase has it; 4) students who, while critical of the position of Jews and Jewish society in the contemporary world, were nonetheless open to questioning the stereotypes they held; and 5) young people disenchanted with the official, dominant vision of Poland, Polishness, and Catholic-dominated Polish national culture.[9]

Much of this remains true today, but several significant alterations have appeared in students' responses in recent years. These seem to be indicative of a transformation of the status of Jewish studies in Poland, which in turn may point toward more general changes taking place in Polish society.

Many of the students still declare that they were drawn to Jewish studies by its mixture of exoticism and proximity, seeing it as "a completely separate civilization existing in the midst of everything that is so Polish," or "a melting pot of cultures, so distant and yet so close." Quite a number refer to a personal fascination with klezmer music (or "Jewish" music more generally), and some cite the film/play *Fiddler on the Roof* or the writings of Sholem Aleichem as the source of their fascination. Others mention iconic figures such as Marc Chagall, Simone Weil, Isaac Bashevis Singer, Martin Buber, or else they refer to Jewish mysticism and the Kabbalah (sometimes with reference to very dubious literature that they have encountered).

One might argue that the image of Jewish culture that is reflected in these motivational statements seems to replicate anti-Jewish Orientalist stereotypes, even if prompted by Judeophile fascination.[10] It also might resemble what has been dubbed "virtually Jewish culture," that is, the appropriation of authentic Jewish culture by popularized products manufactured by non-Jews for non-Jews *about* Jews.[11] I will refrain from delving into these speculative and somewhat spurious interpretations. Studying three Jewish languages demands much more of the students than could possibly be provided by a mere touch of naïve exoticism. As noted, pragmatic motivations have been coming to the fore, such that the "impractical" impulse of studying something that is fascinating and exotic is now often paired with the goal of pursuing a professional career. A surprisingly large number of students, several dozen out of approximately 150 who take the survey, use the word "niche"—in unequivocally positive terms—in characterizing the field of Jewish studies. Many indicate that the field offers them a distinct and competitive edge in the job market in such realms as diplomacy, international relations, translating or interpreting, or simply working abroad. Maybe the most picturesque was the case of a student whose stated goal was to engage in arms trading with Israel. More typically, students note that they have checked the number of certified translators of Hebrew in Poland or the number of job offers with Hebrew language skills among the requirements.

The category of "children of the Second Vatican Council" is still a sizable group among our students, but it, too, is evolving in an interesting way. As before, many refer to their desire to read the Hebrew Bible in its original language; some also mention their regular religious studies of the Scripture. They say: "as a Christian I have many warm feelings toward Jews," or "I should learn more about the religion that gave birth to Christianity." Judging by the students of Jewish studies in Poland, one does not discern much evidence of secularization among the young generation. But this group is undergoing a significant transformation. Whereas Protestants make up as little as 0.4 percent of the Polish society today, they are at least seven times more populous among our students in the last ten years.[12] In addition, several students in recent years have identified themselves as Russian-Orthodox, one as a former Jehovah's Witness, and there is at least one member of a new Judaizing religious movement (unfortunately, not specified in the student's answer to our general query). Considering that these are unsolicited statements of religious belief made in response to a question about their motivations in choosing their area of studies (with no specific question about their faith), one might infer that the actual number of students belonging to religious minorities is even higher, and that this contrasts strikingly to averages in the general population. In other words, religious motivation remains an important factor when choosing to do a BA in Jewish studies, but the particular religious background does not necessarily remain the same as it had been in the past.

The next group of students, namely those seeking their Jewish identity, is also prominently visible in the recent class surveys. In recent years, more than 10 percent of our students mentioned being Jewish or, more often, "of Jewish origin," quite frequently offering complex stories of a grandparent's Holocaust survival, mixed marriages, and hidden or lost identities. In a country with fewer than 15,000 Jews, this is a fantastically high percentage, even if not totally surprising. In a personal communication, David Basok, the Israeli-born chief rabbi of Wrocław, has maintained that Jewish studies might be among the most effective factors in reviving Jewish life and the Jewish community in Poland. The strong ties that exist between academic centers of Jewish studies and Jewish communities in Poland indicate that this close coexistence is profitable for both.

The only group that has nearly disappeared in recent years are those who come to confront their anti-Jewish stereotypes. This certainly does not indicate the disappearance of such stereotypes. It is possible that, in the xenophobic climate of the current nationalist Polish government, fewer people feel the need to confront them. I suggest, however, that the real reasons lie elsewhere. Covertly critical comments do sometimes appear in what students write,[13] though only one student has openly admitted: "I grew up, I regret to say, in a home where the topic of Jews was rarely mentioned;

when it did appear in conversations, it boiled down to the reproduction of vile stereo-types." The quote is vividly descriptive and brave in admitting the limitations of one's own upbringing, but it is also illustrative of what has really happened to this group of students. What brings them to Jewish studies is not the anti-Jewish stereotypes them-selves, but their desire to confront—and also combat—them. They are self-aware of the xenophobic and destructive nature of these stereotypes, and they do not share them (or, at least, no longer share them). Twenty years ago, this group of students was far more diversified. Today, after several waves of public debate on antisemitism and Polish complicity in the Holocaust crimes, increasing numbers of our students explic-itly point to their shame upon encountering historical and contemporary antisemitism in Poland as the main motivation for their choice of Jewish studies. In other words, they have essentially merged with the last group of students, namely those highly critical of current trends in Polish national culture and desirous of restructuring it in a more liberal and tolerant vein. As one of the students explained: "The history of the Jews is my history, it is the story of every person who was once deprived of every-thing, of those whose very dignity was assaulted."

Alongside the other changes in student motivations outlined above, there are also two new groups of reasons that were not apparent ten or twenty years ago, or at least were never featured as prominently as they are today. One is the outcome of the dete-riorating status of the humanities. A number of students admit they had originally chosen economics, banking, or computer science simply out of a desire to avoid the stigma of being considered "losers," that is, people destined (as students of the humanities are often perceived to be) to become low-status and low-salaried employ-ees or professionals. One called it the outcome of the "humanities smear campaign." However, these "reasonable" choices sometimes led to frustration and consequently a swing in the opposite direction, toward "impractical" fields such as Jewish studies. (In several cases, students simultaneously pursue Jewish studies and computer science, biotechnology, or medicine.)

Another new and interesting factor is the transformative experience of visiting museums such as the Polin Museum of the History of Polish Jews in Warsaw. Perhaps even more interesting, a surprisingly high number of students now point to the influ-ence of one of their parents as the most important factor in their choice of studies: they cite such things as regular discussions or reading of Jewish publications, books rec-ommended by a mother, lectures attended with a father, interest in music, and visits to Jewish events. This development points to a certain maturation of the Jewish presence in contemporary Polish culture: parents who grew up in late Communist or early post-Communist Poland have successfully transferred to their children their own dreams of a more tolerant and open Polish society and their personal wrestling with the coun-try's historical legacies.

Research

Research conducted in Poland covers nearly all areas of Jewish studies, from the lin-guistics of ancient Israel to the sociology of contemporary American Jewry. But nat-urally there are areas of special interest as opposed to those that have developed more slowly, and the differences between the former and the latter tell us much about the field. What, then, are the main research interests in Jewish studies in Poland today?[14]

In order to trace the main characteristics of these research trends, I have conducted a bibliometric analysis of two datasets: 1) all the articles and review essays (though not single-book reviews) that appeared in all six of the Jewish studies journals published in Poland during the years 2010–2020;[15] and 2) all the research grants awarded in the same period by the two state-run grant institutions responsible for funding most of the academic research conducted in Poland.[16] To be sure, this is far from a complete list of all, or even all the important, publications in Jewish studies in Poland. It does not cover many excellent articles being published in periodicals not devoted specifically to Judaic studies, and, more importantly, it does not include publications appearing in collective volumes or monographs. Still, the two data sets seem to be sufficiently central to the field, sufficiently large in scope (907 articles and 140 grants), and cover a sufficiently long time period (a full decade) to give a fairly accurate indication of the dominant trends among Polish scholars in the past decade.

What is possibly the most striking tendency among both the journal articles and the research grants, and of the general field of Jewish studies in Poland, is its remarkable ethnocentrism. The field is heavily Polish in two senses. First, the vast majority of those publishing in Judaic journals in Poland are academically affiliated with Polish universities. It is noteworthy that all the journals make a laudable effort to reach an international audience, as they publish in English and other major languages. Their intention of reaching an international audience is augmented by the fact that their advisory boards are composed mostly of international scholars, many of high standing. Yet despite this declarative inclusiveness, all six journals are clearly and invariably limited in their pool of authors: between 65 and 87 percent of the authors (on average, 80 percent) are affiliated with Polish universities. Moreover, nearly all the journals are dominated by contributions from the faculty of their host institutions.[17] The same pattern appears in the lists of peer reviewers and book reviewers commissioned by the journals.[18] A similar tendency is apparent in other periodicals and collected volumes, as well as in the doctoral and promotion committees at virtually all Polish universities, where it is rare to meet a reader from outside of Poland.

A second, and equally significant indicator of ethnocentrism is that the articles and grants maintain a similar focus on Poland when it comes to their subject matter. Fig. 1 presents the results for both datasets, showing the geographic and topical focus of published articles and research grants. As it demonstrates, 71 percent of published articles in the six journals and 73 percent of grants on Jewish topics awarded to scholars in Poland focus on Poland. In addition, in some instances, Poland is researched together with one or two other areas (for instance, migration from Poland to Palestine, or the intelligentsia in Eastern Europe), such that the actual number of articles and grants in which Poland features prominently is actually greater. Less than 10 percent of the articles and grants are connected with Israel/Palestine and the Near East; all other country-values are negligible. This confirms the notion that Jewish studies in Poland is predominantly a matter of identity quest, directly linked to the national debates about Poland and Polish culture/society. An obvious advantage of such a focus is that many of the articles, by virtue of their focus on Poland, are perceived as relevant to the wider Polish arena. The danger is that the strong focus on Poland serves

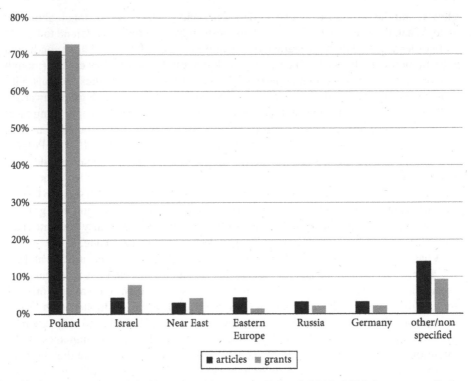

Fig. 1. Articles in Judaic journals and grants in Poland, 2010–2020, by area studied.

to distance Polish–Jewish studies from mainstream interests and developments in the broader field of Jewish studies, where Poland is far from being a central area of academic interest.[19]

A further indication of the connection between Jewish studies and identity quests in Poland can be gleaned from the distribution of research topics in published articles and research grants of 2010–2020 (Fig. 2).[20] The leading topic by far was the Holocaust, followed by articles and grants pertaining to relations between Jews and non-Jews. As noted, both subjects are strongly linked with current debates regarding identity politics. As in many other societies, Polish public debate has been informed by the clash between progressive-liberal and conservative worldviews. In the specific case of Poland, this has devolved into two fundamental areas of disagreement. One is the conflict between individual rights versus what is portrayed as the "rights of the community" (which recently has taken on an increasingly alarming form in "anti-gender" and anti-LGBT campaigns).[21] The other is between those who advocate the need to take account of Poland's historical failures as opposed to others who call for "defending the good name of the Polish nation."[22] This latter area of debate is historically oriented and, over the last twenty years, has been largely dominated by the topic of Jewish–Polish relations. The single most important event associated with this debate was the publication of Jan T. Gross's book *Neighbors* (2000), an account of the murder of the Jewish inhabitants of the small town of Jedwabne by their Polish neighbors in the summer of 1941. The book ignited an enormous controversy in Poland, sparking numerous articles and academic studies.[23] Subsequently, Holocaust-related topics were revived in the public arena by the appearance of a number of additional important publications on the Holocaust in Poland, as well as by the opening and startling success of the Polin Museum in Warsaw, and later, by the passage of the infamous "Holocaust law" of 2018, with which the Polish government attempted to curb freedom of debate on the subject of Polish complicity in the Holocaust.[24] As shown in Fig. 2, every third publication in the realm of Jewish studies deals with the Holocaust. Another 12 percent discuss relations between Jews and non-Jews, often involving its antisemitic expressions—not infrequently in direct relation to the time of the Shoah; in third place (in terms of research grants) is the topic of memory and commemoration, most often with regard to commemoration of the Holocaust and the memory practices of societies struggling with the heritage of the Second World War.

To be sure, the high visibility of Holocaust research is not limited to Poland. Indeed, it has become one of the main areas of international research in the humanities and social sciences.[25] It is also understandable that various aspects of the Holocaust—in particular, such topics as ghettos, death and concentration camps, *Judenräte*, and death marches—feature prominently in research in Poland, on whose territory most of the

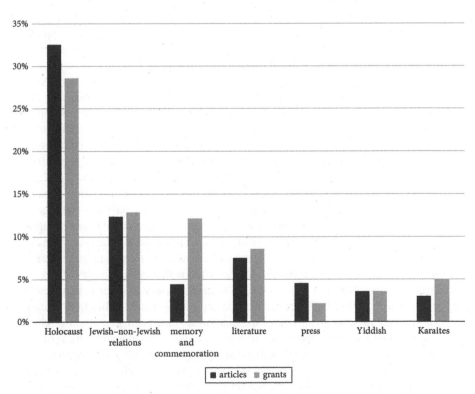

Fig. 2. Articles in Judaic journals and grants in Poland, 2010–2020, by topics studied.

atrocities actually happened. At the same time, it is striking that the number of articles on the Holocaust so clearly surpasses all other topics, including those that otherwise seem to be flourishing. Studies of Yiddish literature in Poland, for example, a subject that may justly be considered the pride of Jewish studies in Poland, are, quantitatively speaking, hardly visible. Women as a topic barely register: a mere 2 percent. Research on religion does not fare much better, as recently demonstrated by Wojciech Tworek.[26] On a macro scale, this might communicate the relative insignificance of these topics for Jewish studies in Poland.

There are two ways to understand this situation. One might conceivably reject quantitative data and their implications by arguing (with some justification) that in scholarship it is quality, not quantity, that counts. As noted, Polish Yiddish studies are blossoming even though they do not demonstrate significant quantitative strength; as proof, one may point to the major research grants, translation projects, and monumental monographs on the subject.[27] Several other subfields, such as the study of modern Jewish politics, liberal Judaism, or the religion and culture of the Karaites, have experienced similar development and growth, again without making a clear quantitative impression. Moreover, when seen in proper context, fields that might be considered "exotic" for Polish Jewish studies—for instance, Ladino literature or Balkan Jews—are surprisingly prominent, even though there were "only" several dozen published articles in these subfields over the past decade.

I am inclined, however, to follow a second approach that understands the quantitative data as reflective of certain general macro tendencies that might be less apparent in small, blossoming subfields, but which do inform the field in the longer run. Simply put, for research subfields to flourish, they need a sustained influx of students, doctoral candidates, and new scholars following in the footsteps of their teachers. As we shall see in the following section, some of the once well-established areas that until quite recently experienced their heydays are now, twenty years later, nearly on the verge of extinction. Rapid and radical changes in the proportions between various research interests should make us sensitive to the possible pitfalls or risks endangering a broad, intellectual agenda. Moreover, even though one might fully agree that the Holocaust or anti-Jewish violence are topics that do require extensive new research—which, therefore, cannot be deemed objectionable in itself—this certainly does not necessarily explain or excuse the neglect of other topics. Few would argue that development in the research on the Holocaust and antisemitism should take complete precedence over other subfields of Jewish studies. In other words, the problem is not the laudable development of the study of the Holocaust or antisemitism, but rather the decline of some other areas of research. The question is thus how to support both.

Therefore, some reflection and discussion seem necessary in order to consider the long-range effects of the heavy concentration on a few, clearly politicized research areas on the general transformation of the discipline. One such side effect might be a decreasing need for methodological innovation. Among the many hundreds of articles and research grants, there are few that display any engagement with the dominant methodological challenges of the current generation: postcolonial theory, gender, and digital humanities. While gender studies do gain some currency in the research on Jewish history and culture conducted recently in Poland (including important studies on the gendered structure of the Holocaust experience or of anti-Jewish violence), postcolonial theory and, especially, the digital humanities are almost completely absent.[28] Spatial analysis, visual anthropology, and cultural poetics, discourse analysis, and queer studies do not fare any better. Significant debates on the methodological challenges facing Jewish studies, such as in a recent series of publications on antisemitism, do not feature scholars from Poland and do not find significant reverberations in Polish publications.[29] That is not to say that the areas of especially high interest, the Holocaust and Jewish–non-Jewish relations, cannot be methodologically innovative—quite the contrary. A few of the methodological advances that have been developed in recent Polish historiography, such as post-anthropocentric, forensic, or environmental approaches, have been made precisely in the areas of the Holocaust and genocide studies.[30] Still, there seems to be little correlation between the directions taken in the mainstream development of those areas and methodological advances that more often than not occur on the peripheries of these mainstream studies.

Apart from ethnocentrism and a focus on the Holocaust and Jewish–non-Jewish relations, there is a third trend that may be discerned from the two datasets under analysis: a rapid shift of research interest toward contemporary issues. This is illustrated in Fig. 3.

Distribution of articles and research grants is highly disproportional. Studies on antiquity (weak among publications, but much stronger among research grants) might indicate a tendency to publish the results of these research grants elsewhere rather than in Polish Jewish periodicals, which are rightly perceived as obsessively focused on Polish Jewish history. Still, even with this correction, antiquity is very weakly represented. Medieval topics are barely visible among the published articles, and while early modern history is relatively strongly represented, this is not the case with regard to the research grants, which might well be an indication of future trends (more below). The most significant trend visible in Fig. 3 is a huge—and growing—interest in wartime and post-Holocaust topics. Every second grant and article deals with either the Second World War or the postwar period. This is a very significant change relative to the state of affairs ten or twenty years ago, when the very concept of post-Holocaust Jewish history in Europe was highly controversial. Today, studies of the Holocaust, and especially its aftermath, dominate the field. It seems this reflects a global turn from history to memory studies and cultural studies, visible in history departments and public venues worldwide, alongside an increasing focus on the 20th century and non-historical analyses of contemporary cultures and societies. This is not the place to discuss the long-lasting consequences of the decline of historical thinking for the intellectual condition of the modern world.[31] But it is worth noting that this tendency seems to have reached alarming proportions in Poland, especially when we consider that it is matched with a near-obsessive focus on things Polish; and when we take into account the extensive political interference of state authorities, executed under the rubric of "historical policy," that heavily promotes research on the Second World War and postwar topics. This is illustrated by, among other things, the history book awards (invariably about the history of 20th-century Poland), new museums (with the notable exception of the Polin Museum), public debates, and articles appearing in academic and popular periodicals.

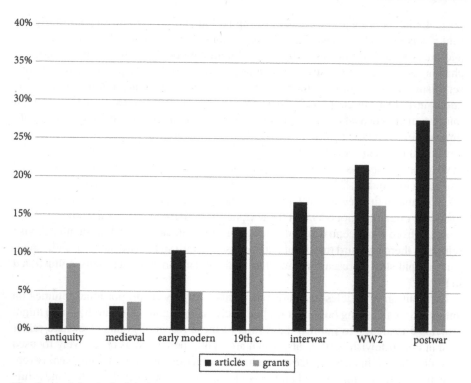

Fig. 3. Articles in Judaic journals and grants in Poland, 2010–2020, by period studied.

The Future: Doctoral Dissertations

When one wants to determine where a given academic field is likely to be in ten or twenty years from now, the most useful exercise is to look at doctoral dissertations. What fields or research topics are doctoral students choosing? Which areas have fallen out of favor?

The most convenient venue to examine the prospects for the field of Polish Jewish studies in Poland is the Polin Museum's Global Education Outreach Program (GEOP), a multi-year program of academic and semi-academic activities aimed at the global community of scholars researching Polish Jewish history and culture. Among its numerous activities is a monthly seminar for doctoral students writing their dissertations on aspects of Polish Jewish history and culture at Polish universities.[32] For the years 2015–2019 (the run available for inspection), there were 141 applications from all academic centers in Poland, and especially from Warsaw, Kraków, and Wrocław, accounting for the vast majority of doctoral candidates writing on Polish Jewish history and culture.[33] This is certainly a sufficiently broad and indicative sample.

The great variety of topics, methodologies, and approaches notwithstanding, a clear thematic-temporal pattern emerges from these lists. Of the total of 141 dissertations, not one deals with medieval Jewish history; only four dissertations

(3 percent of the total), are devoted to the early modern period. This is very troubling, especially given the central role of early modern studies for methodological innovations in historiography over the last two generations. Exacerbating the situation is the fact that the field of early modern Jewish history boasts a number of excellent senior and mid-career scholars active in Poland, and belongs to the central areas of Polish Jewish history cultivated abroad.[34] Despite this prominent position, and despite continuous efforts at raising interest in early modern history, the number of doctoral candidates interested in this period is very low and seems to be rapidly decreasing. The drop in interest in medieval or early modern topics seems to be reaching proportions that actually endanger the generational chain of scholarly transition, indicating a drastic loss of specific linguistic and technical skills cultivated through generations.

The long 19th century fares somewhat better, as it makes up 11 percent of the total, with the interbellum period comprising 22 percent of doctoral dissertations. In the Polish case, the preference for the period between the two world wars over the 19th century is not only an expression of a larger transfer of historical interest to "contemporary history," but also of a more prosaic expression of language preferences: because of the partitions and the non-existence of the Polish state in the 19th century, the vast majority of archival materials on 19th-century Polish (and Polish Jewish) history is not in Polish, but rather in Russian and German. In contrast, the vast majority of archival materials on the interwar Second Polish Republic is in Polish.

The remaining 60+ percent of doctoral students applying to the GEOP seminars decided to spend several years of their life studying the Holocaust or the post-Holocaust period. The distribution here is indicative and very close to what we have seen for the articles and research grants: 30 percent are working on the Shoah and 34 percent on the post-Holocaust period. Even if many or indeed the majority of the dissertations on the post-Holocaust period are in fact related to aspects of the Second World War and the destruction of European Jewry, this is a significant transfer of research interest, showing the possible direction of further scholarly engagement with Polish Jewish history and the Holocaust. On the one hand, the numbers confirm the centrality of the Holocaust as a research topic. On the other hand, for a sizable cohort of young scholars, it is not the Holocaust itself that captures their attention, but rather post-Holocaust memory, commemoration, and the use of Holocaust-related themes in the arts, literature, and popular culture. This seems to confirm the above observation concerning the shift to the study of contemporary topics. Suffice it to say that the majority of doctoral students gathered at Polin's historical seminars are moving toward contemporary topics, shunning history as their primary discipline.

Interestingly, all the tendencies outlined above find additional confirmation in a small collection of questionnaires filled out by BA students of history and Jewish studies at the University of Warsaw.[35] Only 2 of 27 students expressed any interest in periods prior to the 20th century. Among the topics they cited, antisemitism, postwar Poland, and Holocaust-related issues absolutely dominate. Unfortunately, I do not possess any comparative data for Polish Jewish studies in Europe, Israel, and North America. Hopefully, future research will show the extent to which the pattern discussed here is similar to, or dissimilar from, others.

The Future: Politics

These speculations about the future remain more or less relevant only if political factors do not interfere, or, indeed, do not clash with the wider cultural trends under discussion here. The 2022 Russian aggression against Ukraine is a good example of such an unexpected and radical factor that might easily turn the tables.

But even before, the interrelation between academic history and politics has been a hot topic in Poland, given the egregiously xenophobic and chauvinist-nationalist rhetoric promoted by government officials and the state-owned media (not to be confused with independent public media, which have ceased to exist in Poland). In the public sphere, political intervention has taken the form of the so-called historical policy, the state-sponsored program of promoting the picture of Poland's unblemished past.[36] Ethnic or religious minorities, social conflicts, or historical crimes committed by the representatives of the Polish nation certainly do not belong in this heroic picture. Possibly the best known and the most curious expression of this policy was the 2018 "Holocaust law" that sought to penalize anyone making assertions that Poland or Poles had any sort of complicity in the Holocaust or in Nazi war crimes.[37] Under the pressure of the United States, Israel, and the European Union, the reformulated and more objectionable parts of the law were soon revoked, but that does not mean the Polish authorities changed their long-term agendas. Government officials and state-owned media have, on a number of occasions, continued to express their dissatisfaction with academic research on sensitive issues such as Polish involvement in Holocaust-related crimes or Polish antisemitism. At times this has taken the form of incitement against institutions or individual scholars, most notably Jan Gross and leading figures of the excellent Polish school of Holocaust studies, including Jacek Leociak and Barbara Engelking. The academic promotion of Michał Bilewicz, a leading Polish social psychologist, has been frozen for more than two years because his research on antisemitism appeared unflattering in the opinion of some representatives of the Polish regime. Another grave expression of this policy was the minister of culture's refusal to nominate Dariusz Stola for the post of director of the Polin Museum, in violation of the decision of the search committee, the formal agreement with the museum's partners,[38] and his own promises. Similarly, the Jewish Historical Institute in Warsaw, for the first time since its establishment in Stalinist Poland, was given a director with no academic credentials.

Does this mean the official policy of the Polish regime might pose a real threat to Jewish studies in Poland? It might, but there is a chance this threat may be less harmful than it appears. I offer this position of reserved optimism based on three premises. First, the Polish authorities are not hostile to Jewish studies (in fact, they do quite a bit to avoid appearing as such) but rather to some areas and topics they consider harmful to the "good name of the Polish nation." While such political interference is deleterious both to those immediate areas and to the wider integrity of academic freedom, the damage is certainly not as extensive as many feared it might be. In effect, much of Polish–Jewish studies flourishes almost undisturbed.

Second, as with several other right-wing populist regimes, the Polish government is highly ineffective. The spectacular failure of the "Holocaust law" demonstrates its limited ability to implement a truly effective, long-term, strategic plan of action. This does not mean, of course, that the government cannot or does not attempt to micromanage individual cases of museum exhibitions, research grants, professorial nominations, or university promotions. But it is rather difficult to say whether or not this implies a high degree or an imminent risk of mounting a concerted form of political pressure on the academic community at large, which might have significant effects on future research planned and conducted in Poland.

Third, despite attempts to rein in the Polish academic community, it maintains a fair level of autonomy. Even if most of the funding to support research comes from the government and is subject to its agendas (surprisingly little comes from the EU or private foundations, which itself is highly problematic), the granting bodies themselves operate on peer-review processes. These committees are staffed not by ministerial officials but by university professors, who actually often take special care not to exert discrimination against individuals, topics, or projects publicly disfavored by the government. As a result, among the research projects funded by the two granting institutions, there is an impressively high number of studies concerning such subjects as Polish complicity in the crimes of the Holocaust, antisemitism and anti-Jewish violence, pogroms, wartime informing, failures of Polish culture to deal with the memory of the Holocaust, and the painful return of Holocaust survivors to their expropriated homes. The monumental publication of the complete set of 35 volumes of the Warsaw ghetto's *Oneg Shabes* archives, a four-volume series of books on pogroms in modern Poland, and a book on Polish whitewashing of Holocaust-era crimes conducted by Poles were all funded, or co-funded, by the Polish state-run granting institutions.[39] In a word, Jewish studies in Poland fare pretty well despite the politicized climate of discourse, and the topics researched certainly do not follow the expectations of the regime.

This does not guarantee, of course, that there will be no government interference, nor does it imply that politically disfavored areas of academic pursuit do not or will not experience any form of harassment. It is possible that the political line of the regime still poses a threat to the unfettered development of Jewish studies. The fact that the potential damage is not now particularly extensive does not necessarily mean it will remain so.[40]

But the real question is not the individual actions of this government, however annoying they might be, but rather to what extent they reflect a broader climate of public opinion and, conversely, how these actions shape and influence the public mood. How long will this unfavorable political climate continue to exist, and if it does continue into the foreseeable future, how might this reflect on longer-range trends in scholarly interests, choice of studies, distribution of human and financial resources, and public debates? In the short run, the pronounced polarization of Polish society and major public debates prompt quite a number of individuals to choose studies that are meant to provide them with the tools for pursuing identity quests, of combating antisemitism, and propagating a more diversified and liberal version of Polishness. In this sense, Jewish studies in Poland, as in several other East European countries, is the paradoxical beneficiary of right-wing populism and the rising wave of xenophobia.

In the longer run, however, we cannot be certain this will remain the case. Furthermore, we need to consider the possibility that these negative factors might continue even after the current populist government leaves the scene, since the more general socio-cultural trends that brought it to power are not going to disappear overnight. Likewise, it is hard to predict what the mid-term and long-lasting effect of the Russo-Ukrainian war on the regional identities and regional politics will be, but it is close to impossible to expect it will not harm fields of the humanities as vulnerable as East European Jewish studies. Together with the globally declining position of the humanities and the general challenges affecting the Polish academic system, this might negatively reflect on the position of Jewish studies among prospective students and researchers, in addition to harming its international academic standing. *Utinam falsus vates sim.*

Notes

1. On BA and MA programs in Jewish studies at universities in Wrocław, Warsaw, and Kraków, as well as Hebrew studies programs in Warsaw and Poznań, see Stefan Gąsiorowski, (ed.), *Studia żydowskie w Polsce—przeszłość, stan obecny, perspektywy* (Kraków: 2014), 139–291.

2. For more information on the Kotarbiński Award, see uni.lodz.pl/strona/szczegoly/nagroda-im-t-kotarbinskiego (accessed 13 December 2020).

3. See, for instance, the following articles appearing in *Journal of Modern Jewish Studies* 10, no. 1: Felicia Waldman and Michael Shafir, "Jewish Studies in Romania" (pp. 71–84); András Kovács and Michael L. Miller, "Jewish Studies in Contemporary Hungary" (pp. 85–92); Šarūnas Liekis, "Jewish Studies in Lithuania Since 1990" (pp. 93–100); Victoria Mochalova, "Jewish Studies in Russia in the Post-Communist Era" (pp. 119–133); Marie Crhová, "Jewish Studies in the Czech Republic" (pp. 135–143).

4. See Olga Gershenson and Barbara Kirshenblatt-Gimblett, "New Jewish Museums in Post-Communist Europe," *East European Jewish Affairs* 45, nos. 2–3 (2015), 153–157. On stages of the debate concerning the Polin Museum in Warsaw, and how these may be regarded as the best indicator of general opinions on the state of Polish–Jewish studies, see Moshe Rosman, "Categorically Jewish, Distinctly Polish: The Museum of the History of Polish Jews and the New Polish–Jewish Metahistory," *Jewish Studies Internet Journal* 10 (2012), 361–387; Irena Grudzińska-Gross (ed.), *Poland and Polin: New Interpretations in Polish–Jewish Studies* (Frankfurt: 2016); Barbara Kirshenblatt-Gimblett, "Inside the Museum: Curating Between Hope and Despair: Polin Museum of the History of Polish Jews," *East European Jewish Affairs* 45, nos. 2–3 (2015), 215–235. On the debate surrounding the Moscow Jewish Museum and Tolerance Center, see esp. Olga Gershenson, "The Jewish Museum and Tolerance Center in Moscow: Judaism for the Masses," in ibid., 158–173.

5. See esp. Moshe Rosman, "A New Scholarly Foundation: The Historiography of Polish Jewry Since 1945," in id., *Categorically Jewish, Distinctly Polish: Polish Jewish History Reflected and Refracted* (London: 2022), 41–64; id., "Między koniecznością a modą: Uwagi nad przeszłością i przyszłością badań nad dziejami Żydów w Polsce," in *Małżeństwo z rozsądku? Żydzi w społeczeństwie dawnej Rzeczypospolitej*, ed. Marcin Wodziński and Anna Michałowska-Mycielska (Wrocław: 2007), 131–134; Edyta Gawron, "Jewish Studies in Postwar Poland," *Scripta Judaica Cracoviensia* 11 (2013), 55–66; Adam Teller, "Polish–Jewish Relations: Historical Research and Social Significance. On the Legacy of Jacob Goldberg," *Studia Judaica* 15, nos. 1–2 (2012), 27–47; David Engel, "Some Observations on Recent Polish Writing about Polish Jewry during the Holocaust," *Studia Judaica* 7, no. 2 (2004), 249–256. For an overview of earlier developments (between 1945 and 1995), see Moshe Rosman, "Historiografiyah shel yahadut polin, 1945–1995," in *Kiyum veshever: yehudei polin ledorotehem*, ed. Israel Bartal and Israel Gutman, 2 vols. (Jerusalem: 2001), 2:697–724.

6. As a departure point I shall use my essay published ten years ago, which allows for a comparative perspective on where we were then and where the field of Jewish studies in Poland has moved since then; see my "Jewish Studies in Poland," *Journal of Modern Jewish Studies* 10, no. 1 (2011), 101–118.

7. For the best introduction, see Geneviève Zubrzycki, "The Politics of Jewish Absence in Contemporary Poland," *Journal of Contemporary History* 52, no. 2 (2017), 250–277; eadem, "Nationalism, 'Philosemitism,' and Symbolic Boundary-Making in Contemporary Poland," *Comparative Studies in Society and History* 58, no. 1 (2016), 66–98.

8. Ibid., 67; Katka Reszke, *Return of the Jew: Identity Narratives of the Third Post-Holocaust Generation of Jews in Poland* (Boston: 2013); Jan Lorenz, "Being and Becoming: Polish Conversions to Judaism and the Dynamics of Affiliation," *Polin* 33 (2021), 425–438.

9. For a full description of these groups see Wodziński, "Jewish Studies in Poland," 107–109.

10. For a fascinating, if at times controversial, analysis of the entanglement of philo- and antisemitic attitudes in Poland today, see Elżbieta Janicka and Tomasz Żukowski, *Przemoc filosemicka: Nowe polskie narracje o Żydach po roku 2000* (Warsaw: 2016). For an over-view of Orientalist perspectives on the Jews, see Ivan Davidson Kalmar and Derek J. Penslar, "Orientalism and the Jews: An Introduction," in *Orientalism and the Jews*, ed. Kalmar and Penslar (Boston: 2005), xiii–xl.

11. On the changing concept of virtually Jewish culture, see Ruth Ellen Gruber, *Virtually Jewish: Reinventing Jewish Culture in Europe* (Berkeley: 2002); eadem, "Beyond Virtually Jewish: New Authenticities and Real Imaginary Spaces in Europe," *Jewish Quarterly Review* 99, no. 4 (2009), 487–504. On Jewish culture in postwar Poland and its transformation from Jewish culture to culture about Jews, see Monika Adamczyk-Garbowska and Magdalena Ruta, "From Jewish Culture to Culture about Jews," in *Jewish Presence in Absence: The Aftermath of the Holocaust in Poland, 1944–2010*, ed. Feliks Tych and Monika Adamczyk-Garbowska (Jerusalem: 2014), 823–846.

12. See census data for 2018; online at: https://stat.gov.pl/obszary-tematyczne/inne-opra cowania/wyznania-religijne/wyznania-religijne-w-polsce-20152018,5,2.html (accessed 17 January 2021).

13. For instance: "Jews don't want to discuss their affairs in English, so I decided to learn Hebrew," which refers to a well-known antisemitic trope concerning the "hidden language" of the Jews. See Sander Gilman, *Jewish Self-Hatred: Anti-Semitism and the Hidden Language of the Jews* (Baltimore: 1986).

14. In order to avoid the bias of ethnic categories, I shall consider only institutional affilia-tions: "Polish scholar" refers to a scholar affiliated at a university in Poland, regardless of or-igin, ethnicity, or creed. This is also important to avoid any arbitrary attribution of identities to scholars who are no longer in Poland.

15. These are *Studia Judaica* (biannual), *Jewish History Quarterly* (quarterly), *Scripta Judaica Cracoviensia* (annual), *Studia Żydowskie. Almanach* (semi-annual), *Iudaica Russica* (semi-annual), *Zagłada Żydów. Studia i Materiały* (yearly) and its irregular English variant, *Holocaust Studies and Materials*. There is also the most recent, government-sponsored *Polish-Jewish Studies* (annual) which was not included in this analysis due to its appearance after the research had been completed. The database of all the articles and review essays (but not reviews) in those journals for the years 2010–2020 contains 907 records. Many thanks to Jerzy Mikołaj Wodziński for assisting me in collecting these data.

16. These are the National Programme for the Development of Humanities (Ministry of Science and Higher Education) and the National Science Centre. Together they awarded 140 research grants in the years 2010–2020 to projects dealing exclusively or predominantly with Jewish studies.

17. For instance, in Kraków-based *Scripta Judaica Cracoviensia*, every second article came from the faculty at the Jagiellonian University in Kraków.

18. *Scripta Judaica Cracoviensia* lists 17 reviewers for the years 2017–2018 (the only lists available for that journal), of whom 71 percent are faculty at the Jagiellonian University; on-line at: ejournals.eu/Scripta-Judaica-Cracoviensia/menu/211/ (accessed 13 March 2020). On

a parallel "list of permanent reviewers," that of the *Jewish History Quarterly*, 31 percent are employees or recent employees of the journal's sponsoring institution, the Jewish Historical Institute; online at: jhi.pl/ksiegarnia/kwartalnik-historii-zydow (accessed 15 September 2020).

19. See Wodziński, "Eastern European Jewish Studies: The Past Thirty Years," *Jewish Quarterly Review* 112, no. 2 (2022), 196–217.

20. All the articles and grants under analysis here were tagged with two topical categories, usually provided by the authors themselves in the titles or abstracts.

21. For a fine introduction to the so-called anti-gender movement, see David Paternotte and Roman Kuhar (eds.), *Anti-Gender Campaigns in Europe: Mobilizing against Equality* (London: 2017). On the divide within Polish society, see the penetrating analysis by Brian Porter-Szűcs, "Meritocracy and Community in Twenty-First-Century Poland," *Shofar: An Interdisciplinary Journal of Jewish Studies* 37, no. 1 (2019), 72–95.

22. On the broader ramifications of European debates between "glorification of the past or taking responsibility," see Aleida Assmann, "Europe's Divided Memory," in *Memory and Theory in Eastern Europe*, ed. Uilleam Blacker, Alexander Etkind, and Julie Fedor (New York: 2013), 25–43.

23. For the main overviews of the debate and its further repercussions, see Antony Polonsky and Joanna Michlic (eds.), *The Neighbors Respond: The Controversy over the Jedwabne Massacre in Poland* (Princeton: 2004); Paweł Machcewicz and Krzysztof Persak (eds.), *Wokół Jedwabnego* (Warsaw: 2002); Piotr Forecki, *Reconstructing Memory: The Holocaust in Polish Public Debates* (New York: 2013).

24. For more details regarding this law, see the essay by Jonathan Zisook in this volume, esp. pp. 26–28.

25. On Holocaust memory, see Daniel Levy and Natan Sznaider, *The Holocaust and Memory in the Global Age*, trans. Assenka Oksiloff (Philadelphia: 2006); for a useful overview of the development of Holocaust research and its wider ramifications, see Boaz Cohen, *Israeli Holocaust Research: Birth and Evolution* (London: 2013). For an attempt at a post-colonial deconstruction of Holocaust memory, see Michael Rothberg, *Multidirectional Memory: Remembering the Holocaust in the Age of Decolonization* (Stanford: 2009).

26. See Wojciech Tworek, "The Eastern European Problem of Hasidic Studies," *Jewish Quarterly Review* 112 no. 2 (2022), 256–259. For a recent account of the "booming" field of religious studies on Jewish Eastern Europe, see Ada Rapoport-Albert and Marcin Wodziński, "Jewish Religious Life in Poland since 1750: Introduction," *Polin* 33 (2021), 3–16.

27. On Yiddish studies in Poland, see Ewa Geller, "Yiddish for Academic Purposes: The Polish Perspective," *Jewish Studies Quarterly* (2006), 212–221; Monika Adamczyk-Garbowska and Joanna Lisek, "Polskie przekłady z literatury jidysz—projekty, serie, tendencje (2006–2021)," in *Jidyszland—nowe przestrzenie*, ed. Joanna Lisek, Monika Adamczyk-Garbowska, and Magdalena Ruta (Warsaw: 2022), 168–169.

28. For the most prominent examples of gender studies in Poland today, see esp. Joanna Lisek, *Kol isze—głos kobiety w poezji jidysz od XVI wieku do 1939* (Sejny: 2018); *Moja dzika koza: Antologia poetek jidysz* (Kraków: 2018). On the debates over the role of the digital humanities, see Jo Guldi and David Armitage, *The History Manifesto* (Cambridge: 2014), 88–116; Richard Grusin, "The Dark Side of Digital Humanities: Dispatches from Two Recent MLA Conventions," *Differences* 25, no. 1 (2014), 79–92. For an introduction concerning digital humanities in Jewish studies, see Heidi A. Campbell (ed.), *Digital Judaism: Jewish Negotiations with Digital Media and Culture* (New York: 2015); Yitzchok Adlerstein, "Digital Orthodoxy: The Making and Unmaking of a Lifestyle," in *Developing a Jewish Perspective on Culture*, ed. Yehuda Sarna (New York: 2014), 270–301; Michelle Chesner, "JS/DH: An Introduction to Jewish Studies/Digital Humanities Resources," *Judaica Librarianship* 20 (2017), 194–196.

29. See Scott Ury and Guy Miron (eds.), *Antishemiyut: beyn musag histori lesiaḥ tziburi* (special issue of *Zion* 85 [2020]); "AHR Roundtable: Rethinking Anti-Semitism," *American Historical Review* 123, no. 4 (2018), 1122–1245.

30. See, for instance, Roma Sendyka, "Sites That Haunt: Affects and Non-Sites of Memory," *East European Politics and Societies* 30, no. 4 (2016), 687–702; Jacek Małczyński,

Ewa Domańska, Mikołaj Smykowski, and Agnieszka Kłos, "The Environmental History of the Holocaust," *Journal of Genocide Studies* 22, no. 2 (2020), 183–196; Ewa Domańska, *Nekros. Wprowadzenie do ontologii martwego ciała* (Warsaw: 2017). See also Natalia Aleksiun, "Precarious Muse: Holocaust Studies and Polish Jewish Studies," *Jewish Quarterly Review* 112 no. 2 (2022), 245–250, which despite her argument to the contrary demonstrates rather limited methodological innovation of the Holocaust Studies in Poland.

31. See Guldi and Armitage, *The History Manifesto*, 81–85; Benjamin M. Schmidt, "The History BA since the Great Recession," *Perspectives on History* 56, no. 9 (December 2018), online at: historians.org/publications-and-directories/perspectives-on-history/december-2018/the-history-ba-since-the-great-recession-the-2018-aha-majors-report (accessed: 18 January 2021); see also Eric Alterman, "The Decline of Historical Thinking," *The New Yorker* (4 February 2019).

32. Online at: https://polin.pl/en/geop-doctoral-seminars (accessed 18 January 2021).

33. As the seminar is specifically "devoted to the history and culture of Polish Jews," it excludes dissertations focusing on other Jewish communities. In addition, the topics of ten of the dissertations did not easily fit into any chronological rubric, and were therefore excluded from this calculation.

34. See, for instance, Moshe Rosman, "An Intellectual Biography," in *Moshe Rosman: Doctor Honoris Causa of the University of Wrocław* (Wrocław: 2016), 49–50; Teller, "Polish–Jewish Relations."

35. This refers to 27 questionnaires from the years 2016–2020. Many thanks to Artur Markowski for generously sharing this material with me.

36. For a good overview of the extensive debates concerning Polish and European "historical policies," see Alexei Miller and Maria Lipman (eds.), *The Convolutions of Historical Politics* (New York: 2012); Nikolay Koposov, *Memory Laws, Memory Wars: The Politics of the Past in Europe and in Russia* (Cambridge: 2017).

37. On the "Holocaust law," see Jörg Hackmann, "Defending the 'Good Name' of the Polish Nation: Politics of History as a Battlefield in Poland, 2015–18," *Journal of Genocide Research* 20, no. 4 (2018), 587–606; Kornelia Kończal, "Mnemonic Populism: The Polish Holocaust Law and Its Afterlife," *European Review* (2020), 1–13; Katarzyna Liszka, "Articles 55a and 55b of the IPN Act and the Dialogue about the Holocaust in Poland," *Archiwum Filozofii Prawa i Filozofii Społecznej* 21, no. 3 (December 2019), 81–94.

38. Atypically for Poland, the Polin Museum was created by a partnership between the state (ministry of culture), the municipality of Warsaw, and the Association of the Jewish Historical Institute, the private foundation that effectively represents Jewish interests.

39. *Archiwum Ringelbluma*, 35 vols. (Warsaw: 1997–2020); Sławomir Buryła, Kamil Kijek, Artur Markowski, and Konrad Zieliński (eds.), *Pogromy Żydów na ziemiach polskich w XIX i XX wieku*, 4 vols. (Warsaw: 2018); Tomasz Żukowski, *Wielki retusz: Jak zapomnieliśmy, że Polacy zabijali Żydów* (Warsaw: 2018).

40. For a similar assessment, see Beth Holmgren, "Holocaust History and Jewish Heritage Preservation: Scholars and Stewards Working in PiS-Ruled Poland," *Shofar: An Interdisciplinary Journal of Jewish Studies* 37, no. 1 (2019), 96–107.

Jewish Cultural Heritage in the USSR and after Its Collapse

Vladimir Levin

(THE HEBREW UNIVERSITY)

It is commonly believed that Jewish material culture and its heritage were completely repressed in the USSR, and even deliberately destroyed. Indeed, in exploring cities and towns in areas that were once within the historical Pale of Jewish Settlement under Russian Imperial rule—where the largest part of the world's Jews lived until just a hundred years ago—one hears about hundreds of vanished synagogues and cemeteries, and it is frustrating to find only a paltry number of Jewish objects in local museums. Evidence of Jewish sites and monuments is easily overlooked, unless one searches intensively and with specific information.

The main task of this essay, therefore, is to account for the current situation with respect to Jewish material and visual heritage in countries that had been part of the Soviet Union. The discussion will focus on material testimonies of the Jewish past that are commonly perceived as "heritage"—that is, synagogue buildings, Jewish cemeteries, and objects created for Jewish worship and everyday life. Other forms of cultural heritage such as archives and libraries, as well as intangible heritage, lie beyond the scope of this discussion.

At the outset, I argue that, with some exceptions, Soviet policy toward Jewish heritage was generally in line with the regime's basic policies toward all other ethnic and religious groups' heritage. The state antisemitism of the postwar period marginalized the discourse about Jews and had a negative effect on the preservation of their heritage, but not in a totally systematic way, contrary to common perception. At least until the Russian invasion of Ukraine in February 2022, some post-Soviet states continue the Soviet approach, whereas others have adopted a completely opposite approach or have found something that is in-between.

In dealing with Jewish heritage in the Soviet Union, one has to keep in mind that, from the Jewish perspective, the territory of the USSR was not homogeneous. In the former Pale of Jewish Settlement that embraced the western areas of the Russian empire, populous Jewish communities existed in almost every town, and this implied the existence of numerous synagogues and cemeteries (from two or three synagogues in a small town to many dozens in large cities, plus at least one cemetery in each town).

Vladimir Levin, *Jewish Cultural Heritage in the USSR and after Its Collapse* In: *Becoming Post-Communist*. Edited by: Eli Lederhendler, Oxford University Press. © Oxford University Press 2023. DOI: 10.1093/oso/9780197687215.003.0006

Only the eastern parts of these territories were under Soviet control in the interwar period; the western and northwestern areas were incorporated into the Second Polish, Lithuanian, and Latvian Republics, and the Kingdom of Romania, respectively. In 1939–1940, however, almost the entire former Pale of Settlement as well as Eastern Galicia and Northern Bukovina (which had never been part of the Russian empire) were occupied and then annexed by the USSR. The majority of Jews in the former Pale of Settlement and Galicia perished in the Holocaust, most of them in mass shootings carried out not far from their place of residence.

Quite a different situation prevailed in the interior of Russia, "beyond the Pale," where, until the 1917 Revolution, only relatively small Jewish communities existed, mostly in the cities. Such communities, which after 1917 fell under Soviet rule, usually possessed one or two synagogues (with rare exceptions) and one cemetery. In addition, there were smaller Jewish communities in the Caucasus and Central Asia, comprising Georgian, Mountain, and Bukharan Jews, as well as Krymchaks, each of which possessed a significantly different heritage. Their fate contrasted with that of their Ashkenazi brethren, as many of them were not directly affected by the Holocaust.

Thus, four distinct areas (the interwar Soviet territory, the annexed western territories, the interior of Russia, and the areas of non-Ashkenazi communities) will be involved in our discussion, though the greatest attention will be devoted to Ashkenazi Jewry, since it was significantly larger in size and therefore produced a greater number of Jewish sites and objects.

The Soviet Union in the Interwar Period

Although Russian authorities began to pay attention to "ancient buildings" and to seek their conservation as early as 1826,[1] interest in the cultural heritage of East European Jews emerged much later, at the turn of the 20th century.[2] The most influential event signifying this "heritage turn" was the historical-ethnographical project identified with Solomon An-sky (Rapoport) and his team's fieldwork expeditions in 1912–1913,[3] but this was not the only such instance: many others at that time had begun to pay attention to monuments and objects of Jewish material culture.[4]

The First World War caused large-scale damage, including the destruction of Jewish sites and objects. Many wooden synagogues burned down and many valuable items were lost. As a result of the war, East European Jewry and its heritage became divided between several states that emerged on the ruins of the empires in the region.

In independent Poland, Lithuania, Latvia, and Romanian Bessarabia (today Moldova), Jewish communal life and activities continued without hindrance until the Second World War. Jewish, Polish, and Lithuanian scholars engaged in documenting and sometimes preserving evidence of the Jewish legacy. Among the initiatives were the establishment of the Lwów Jewish Community Commission for the Preservation of Jewish Monuments, commonly known as the Kuratorium, and the documentation of synagogues by the students of Adolf Szyszko-Bohusz (from Kraków), Oskar Sosnowski (from Warsaw), and Paulius Galaunė (from Kaunas).[5] In Soviet Russia, however, events took a different course.

The Bolsheviks, who came into power following the October Revolution of 1917, sought to create a completely new society. They came to regard monuments of the past, as they put it, as "the soil on which the new people's art will grow."[6] Since Jewish heritage was tied to an ethnic group and was strongly connected to the Jewish religion, it had to be considered in the appropriate revolutionary framework. The Bolsheviks defined the Jews as one of the Soviet nationalities, and Judaism as one of the existing religions. Therefore, Jews were entitled to the same treatment as other minorities, and until the end of the 1930s, approved aspects of Jewish culture, such as the Yiddish language, were supported by the Soviet state. In contrast, Judaism as a religion was persecuted in the same way as other religions.

As early as April 1918, the newly established Commissariat for Jewish National Affairs announced its intention to create a Central Jewish Archive, whereby "museums, libraries, archives and collections of manuscripts are hereby taken under the protection of the government of workers and peasants, as the national property of the Jewish people."[7] As it turned out, the Central Archive was not created, but the declaration illustrates the intended inclusion of Jewish heritage under the Soviet agenda. The decision referred to movable heritage items that underwent museification even before the Revolution: these were perceived as a treasury that would aid in creating a modern, revolutionary Jewish national culture. In general, the Soviet state in the interwar period supported both conservation and research on items of Jewish movable heritage in the same degree as it did regarding other groups in the Soviet population, re-contextualizing it and subjecting it to increasing ideological control.

Examples of this attitude are well known and have been thoroughly researched in the last decade. The Jewish Museum in Petrograd/Leningrad, first founded in 1915 to house objects brought by the An-sky expedition, existed until 1929, when it was closed as a bourgeois organization and its collections and archives were dispersed.[8] This, however, did not mean the concealing of Jewish heritage: five years later, a Jewish department was established in the State Museum of Ethnography in Leningrad, which housed a significant portion of the objects removed from the closed museum, and a large exhibition titled "Jews in Tsarist Russia and the USSR" was launched there in 1939.[9]

State institutions devoted to Jewish research also emerged in Kyiv and Minsk at the turn of the 1920s and existed until 1936, when a reduction of Jewish cultural and other activities took place.[10] These institutions, which were mainly "text-oriented," dealt with history, literature, and philology and collected libraries and archives. In their collecting activities they more or less followed the famous 1891 dictum of the historian Simon Dubnov with regard to the need to collect written documents of Jewish historical significance. They also implicitly continued the 19th-century Central European scholastic approach known as Wissenschaft des Judentums, which concentrated on texts and ignored the visual side of Jewish culture. Notwithstanding, recently discovered documents concerning the competition between the centers in Kyiv and Minsk in the wake of the closure of the Jewish Museum in Leningrad and the dispersal of its collections indicate that material culture was not completely absent from their agenda. When the Leningrad museum and the Jewish Historical-Ethnographical Society were closed in 1929, their archives, library, and collection of objects (apart from those given to the State Museum of Ethnography) were shipped to Kyiv, but pressure from

Belarus forced a transfer of the museum's holdings to Minsk, where they were kept in the Jewish department of the Belorussian State Museum.[11]

While there was no separate Jewish museum in Belarus, such museums were founded in Uzbekistan, Georgia, and Ukraine. A Jewish museum was established in Samarkand in 1921 and existed until 1937.[12] The Jewish museum in Tbilisi was established in 1933 and closed in 1951.[13] In Ukraine, under its first, short-lived, pre-Soviet socialist government (the Central Rada), a decision was made in April 1917 to create a Jewish museum.[14] A Jewish museum under Soviet auspices was established only in 1927 in Odesa, called the Mendele Moykher-Sforim All-Ukrainian Museum of Jewish Culture. The museum was closed in 1933 but reopened in 1940 and existed until the Romanian occupation of the city in 1941.[15] This museum not only strived to collect Jewish objects, but also conducted several scholarly expeditions, during the course of which the architects Usher Hiter and Eliakim Malz prepared numerous paintings of old synagogues and Jewish houses.[16] General Ukrainian museums also paid significant attention to Jewish monuments and objects, documenting and collecting them.[17] The most notable efforts to document historical synagogues (especially wooden ones), cemeteries, and Jewish houses were undertaken in the 1920s and early 1930s by Danylo Shcherbakivs'kyi, a professor at the Academy of Arts in Kyiv,[18] by museum curator Stefan Taranushenko and his assistant Pavlo Zholtovs'ky,[19] and by the director of the Art School in Kamianets-Podilskyi, Volodymyr Hagenmeister.[20] (In Belarus, several synagogues were photographed by Alexei Viner, a researcher of murals.[21]) As Sergey Kravtsov has demonstrated, these Ukrainian scholars perceived Jewish monuments as being integral parts of the Ukrainian national heritage, in line with the similarly "inclusive" attitudes of some Polish and Lithuanian researchers.[22]

Jewish heritage was also preserved in Soviet museums that were dedicated to propagating the struggle against religion. The Central Antireligious Museum of the League of Militant Atheists in Moscow, the State Antireligious Museum in the former St. Isaac's Cathedral in Leningrad, and the Museum of the History of Religion in the former Kazan Cathedral in Leningrad (founded in 1932) presented Judaism via Jewish objects and works of Jewish artists.[23]

Synagogues and Their Objects

While all heritage activities in the Soviet Union (in contrast to Poland and Lithuania) were funded by the state, the state also played the decisive role in the destruction of heritage sites and objects. On January 23, 1918, Soviet Russia nationalized all religious buildings and movable objects housed therein and rented them out to "religious congregations."[24] In claiming the ownership of all churches, mosques, and synagogues, the Bolsheviks asserted their complete control, and this became an effective weapon in their war against religion. Until 1929, however, the Soviet state persecuted mostly the Russian Orthodox Church and Roman Catholicism, which were perceived as dangerous political enemies, whereas the struggle against Judaism was almost totally vested in the hands of the Jewish sections of the Communist Party (Evsektsiia).[25]

The first massive attack on "clericalism" came in 1922, when the Soviet government organized the requisition of precious metals from churches, mosques, and synagogues, on the pretext of helping famine victims in the Volga area. While Russian Orthodox churches had many massive gold objects that could be confiscated, synagogues possessed only silver items, often of inferior quality, and not in very large amounts.[26] Ironically, the confiscation proved to be a decisive factor in the preservation of Jewish ritual objects: hundreds of silver objects, after being kept in the Odesa Jewish Museum, were sent to the Museum of Historical Treasures in Kyiv, where they constituted one of the largest Judaica collections in the Soviet Union.[27]

After the requisition of 1922, the central government in Moscow did not orchestrate further attacks on houses of worship until the end of the 1920s. On the local level, however, synagogues were often closed and converted into Soviet institutions mostly serving the Jewish population. For example, in Vitsebsk, the Uzgorskaia Synagogue and four prayer houses in its *shulhoyf* (courtyard) were closed as early as 1921 and transferred to the Jewish Communist University.[28] Arkadi Zeltser, who researched this event, states that "the seizure of synagogues became widespread" by 1923.[29] Indeed, the Choral Synagogue in Minsk was closed in 1923 and used as the Jewish Workers House of Culture (in 1928 the building was given to the Belorussian State Jewish Theater); by 1924, about half of the synagogues in Minsk had been confiscated.[30] In Homel, however, only one synagogue was closed at that time.[31] According to Zvi Gitelman, the number of functioning synagogues in Soviet Ukraine declined only by 10 percent in the 1920s: from 1,034 in 1917 to 934 in 1929.[32]

At this time, the intense struggle against all religions resumed in the USSR alongside the push for massive industrialization and collectivization, known as Stalin's revolution.[33] A wave of church, mosque, and synagogue closures began in January 1929, following a secret directive from Moscow, and continued in 1930 and 1931.[34] In Belorussia, 59 percent of the synagogues were closed in these years.[35] It seems that the authorities intended to keep only one "cult building" for each religion per town; since the number of synagogues was usually much greater than the number of churches, especially in small towns, more synagogues were shut down. The last blow to religion in the Soviet Union was dealt in 1938–1939, when an absolute majority of all churches and synagogues were officially closed.[36]

The fate of most movable objects from these synagogues is unclear.[37] While precious metals were confiscated back in 1922, by 1929 the most important objects remaining in the synagogues were Torah scrolls and items made of textiles. Such objects from the Choral Synagogue in Leningrad were transferred in 1930 to special storage in the State Russian Museum; similar objects from the Poliakov Synagogue in Moscow were given to the Central Antireligious Museum.[38] In addition, many local museums across the Russian Federation still retain one or several Torah scrolls and/or some other synagogue items.[39] It is plausible that synagogue furniture usually remained in the building to serve the new tenants. For example, a photograph of the former synagogue in Kazan, which served as the House of Jewish Culture and later as the House of Pioneers (Communist youth club), shows typical synagogue pews and two Hanukah menorahs, while the former Torah ark is decorated with the portraits of Communist leaders (Fig. 1). In other instances, however, Jewish objects were known

Fig. 1. Interior of the former synagogue in Kazan, Tatarstan, Russia. Photo c. 1930. The National Museum of the Republic of Tatarstan, HMPT KK-35972/248.

to have been destroyed, as was the case in Nasovichy, near Homel, where the local Pioneers "broke pews, tore books and burned them in a stove."[40]

In many cases, the closure of houses of prayer was followed by their immediate demolition. As Catriona Kelly has demonstrated in the case of Leningrad, even churches that were listed as protected monuments were razed in order to make Leningrad an "exemplary socialist city."[41] The policies of preservation in the 1920s and 1930s were not clearly defined; lists of protected sites were constantly being revised, and the preservationists did not attribute value to buildings constructed after 1850. In practice, this meant that the majority of existing synagogues were not deemed worthy of protection.[42]

The demolition of churches was a symbolic act that eliminated religion from the socialist cityscape, creating a place for new, decidedly Soviet buildings. Suffice it here to mention the Cathedral of Christ the Savior in Moscow, blown up in 1931 to be replaced by the Palace of the Soviets (slated for the Supreme Soviet, the USSR's parliament), and St. Michael's Golden-Domed Monastery in Kyiv, demolished in 1937 to make way for a new administrative quarter. Kelly points out that Leningrad churches without "ecclesiastical appearance" were more likely to remain intact.[43] Synagogues usually had no "ecclesiastical appearance" and generally had a very modest role, if at all, in the cityscape of towns and cities.[44] Former synagogues were also more suitable than churches for conversion to secular purposes, especially taking into account that new construction in the Soviet Union was never adequate to satisfy the demand for apartments, offices, warehouses, and factories. Nonetheless, many synagogues were destroyed. It appears that the best-known synagogue demolished in the 1920s was the Shiv'a Kru'im Kloyz in Minsk.[45] In this case, however, its visual prominence played a role, since it was the only synagogue in the city crowned by a dome.

Subject to verification by future research, it is possible to estimate the scale of synagogue destruction by comparing the territories that were divided between the USSR and Poland in the interwar period: fully two-thirds of the preserved synagogues in today's Belarus are situated in its western regions, annexed from the territory of the interwar Polish Republic.[46] Similarly, the percentage of still-extant synagogues in the former Volhynian Governorate in Ukraine is significantly higher in the territory that had been under Polish rule between the wars than in its eastern, Soviet parts.[47]

Cemeteries

The Bolsheviks regarded old cemeteries as inherently connected to religion and religious superstitions and therefore irrelevant to the new society that was to be constructed. Cemeteries in the Soviet Union were declared property of the state in 1918, with municipalities given the authority to deal with them as they wished. As a result, numerous cemeteries were liquidated; their grounds became parks or were built over; and tombstones and metal fences were sold as building material.[48] Usually, only graves of prominent cultural figures and monuments of high artistic value were singled out and transferred to new locations (the best example of this approach is the creation of the Necropolis of the Masters of Art / the Museum of Urban Sculpture in Leningrad in the 1930s).

As was the case with synagogues, Jewish cemeteries were not singled out for special treatment. Old Jewish cemeteries that were situated in city centers, together with monastery cemeteries, were the first to be cleared away for new, socialist urban developments. For example, the First Jewish Cemetery in Odesa, together with the adjacent Christian, Muslim, and Karaite cemeteries, was demolished in 1937; these were replaced by a park, a zoo, and a stadium.[49] Similarly, the Old Jewish Cemetery in Minsk was destroyed in 1931 to allow for the construction of a stadium.[50] The authorities, however, permitted the relatives of the deceased to relocate graves and tombstones to other cemeteries. Moreover, cemeteries that were still in use and which were situated far from city centers usually were not demolished. For example, the Preobrazhenskoe Jewish Cemetery at the southeast end of Leningrad was not damaged even when two neighboring cemeteries (one Catholic, the other Lutheran), were demolished in 1936 in order to afford space for a factory. As it happened, the factory was never built, and the land of both former Christian cemeteries became part of the Jewish cemetery in the 1950s.[51]

Thus, during two decades between the Revolution and the Second World War, the entire structure of Jewish heritage profoundly changed. Buildings, ceremonial objects, and cemeteries that were in the hands of private persons and congregations became state property. In addition, buildings and objects were requisitioned to fulfil new functions. Finally, the destruction of cemeteries, former synagogues, and objects of Judaica was greatly accelerated. At the current stage of research, it is hard to gauge precisely the total scale of losses, but evidently they were very extensive.

The Second World War

The Second World War had a decisive influence on the remaining forms of Jewish heritage in the Soviet Union. On the one hand, large territories with old Jewish communities and rich heritage were annexed to the USSR in 1939 and 1940. On the other hand, both the German–Soviet war, which commenced in June 1941, and the Shoah caused widespread destruction of Jewish heritage sites in the western areas of the Soviet Union.

In contrast to Germany, where the Nazis torched the majority of synagogues during the Kristallnacht pogrom of 1938, synagogues in the occupied Soviet territories were not slated by the Nazis for systematic destruction. The murder of the entire Jewish population in these areas began in June 1941,[52] and German forces apparently felt there was no need for symbolic murder in the form of desecration of Jewish places of worship. In some cities, nonetheless, synagogues were deliberately burned down, as was the case with the Great Synagogue in Kremenets. The rest of the synagogues in Kremenets were burned when a group of Jewish fighters set fire to the ghetto during its "liquidation" on August 10, 1942; only one synagogue building, relatively far from the town center, remained standing and is still extant.[53] In many towns, synagogues that were situated inside the ghettos were heavily damaged or completely destroyed, while those outside had a better chance to remain intact.

Synagogues were also affected by the general destruction caused by the war.[54] The majority of synagogues in Eastern Europe were built of wood and thus destroyed by fire. All splendid wooden synagogues of the 17th and 18th centuries that had remained after the First World War were consumed by fire during the Second World War. At the same time, wartime destruction should not be overexaggerated. For example, in Stalingrad, where fierce house-to-house fighting continued for several months, two former synagogues withstood the battle.[55] In contrast, the great masonry synagogues of Novogrudok, Mir, Nesvizh, and Pinsk (located today in Belarus) were severely damaged during the war: in 1946, all four of them were roofless structures with completely destroyed interiors.[56] The building in Mir was renovated, while the older synagogues in Navahrudak, Niasvizh, and Pinsk were razed to the ground. Arbitrary postwar decisions dictated whether such buildings were reconstructed or demolished.

As was the case with synagogues, the Nazis had no special interest in destroying Jewish cemeteries, although they did use tombstones as building material. In some towns, tombstones from the cemeteries were used as pavement—as in Lviv, where the Old Cemetery was demolished in 1943, or in Kolomyia, where Jewish tombstones were used to pave the courtyard of the Gestapo headquarters.[57] There is still no serious research on the fate of Jewish cemeteries in the Soviet Union during the war. In many places (as, for instance, in Hlybokaye, Belarus), the destruction of the cemetery is attributed to the Nazis.[58] However, as Krzysztof Bielawski's new study on the destruction of cemeteries in Poland shows, local populations were no less eager than Nazi authorities to use tombstones for building purposes, and wooden fences for firewood.[59]

The war also had an impact on collections of Jewish objects in museums. For example, Jewish objects from the Belorussian State Museum, as Anatol Sinila has demonstrated, were taken to Germany; only a portion of them returned to the USSR after 1945, with the remainder disseminated around the world.[60] It seems that very few religious objects remained in former synagogues in the pre-1939 territory of the USSR. In the annexed western territories, such objects were still in use in 1939–1940. Later, however, the synagogues were plundered by the local population.

According to Arkadi Zeltser, Soviet Jews in the postwar years erected approximately 700 monuments to commemorate sites of mass murder.[61] Those monuments became in essence a new type of Jewish heritage and deserve a special place in the discourse of Jewish heritage, especially for the years of *perestroika* and thereafter, in the period following dissolution of the Soviet Union.

The Postwar Years

The Second World War was a turning point in the attitude taken by the Soviet state toward its Jewish citizens. State antisemitism intensified in the late 1940s and early 1950s, reaching its climax during the so-called "Doctors' Plot" of 1953 (just prior to Stalin's death), which marked the de facto exclusion of Jews from the "fraternal family of the Soviet peoples." Although the anti-Jewish campaign ceased forthwith after Stalin's death, Jews never again reverted to the status of equal Soviet citizens. Jewish topics were completely marginalized, and Jews were rarely mentioned in the Soviet press and books.

Museums

Together with the Jews, Jewish heritage almost totally disappeared from the public space. Jewish collections and archives became inaccessible, and Jewish items were not exhibited in general museums. In addition, specifically Jewish institutions were eliminated: the Jewish Museum organized by Holocaust survivors in Vilnius in 1944 was closed in 1949 and its collection dispersed among Lithuanian museums;[62] the Jewish exhibition in the local museum in Birobidzhan was dismantled in 1949;[63] and the Jewish Museum in Tbilisi was shut down in 1951. The only context in which Jewish objects were exhibited was that of atheism and anti-religion: thus, the Museums of the History of Religion and Atheism in Leningrad and Lviv continued to present Judaism among other religions. A small showcase in the Leningrad museum, for instance, contained a Torah scroll and a photograph titled "Pioneer girl convincing an old man to remove a prayer shawl,"[64] whereas the museum's very rich collection of Judaica was kept from view.[65] In the Lviv museum, opened in 1973, the exhibition was larger and much more diverse, including objects from the Golden Rose Synagogue, the oldest synagogue of the city.[66] However, it paid special attention to the "inseparable connection" between Judaism and Zionism and included a set of photographs demonstrating the "barbaric deeds of Israeli aggressors."[67] Thus, under the pretext of presenting a "reactionary and nationalistic" religion, Jewish ritual objects were not only preserved but also exhibited, although in a highly politicized context. In general, antireligious activities in the late Soviet Union were the main channel of transmitting knowledge about religions.

While it was easy to hide collections of Jewish objects, synagogue buildings and Jewish cemeteries could not be concealed so simply.

Cemeteries

In the aftermath of the Second World War, Soviet policy vis-à-vis Jewish cemeteries remained as before. It is possible to speak about destruction on two levels—official and private. In terms of the latter, private individuals pilfered tombstones to be used as building material for their houses, especially for foundations. In such cases, the cemetery as a designated place remained, but the tombstones partially or entirely disappeared. One of the most marked examples is the New Jewish Cemetery in Horodenka, Ukraine, where only "stumps" are left from grave markers made of sandstone, while markers made of concrete remain intact, since they could not as easily be reused for construction (Fig. 2).[68]

At the official level, entire Jewish cemeteries were razed, with their land designated for new purposes, and tombstones reused in buildings. Thus, by 1948, the Jewish Dorogomilovo Cemetery in Moscow had been demolished together with the adjacent Christian cemetery to make room for a new neighborhood for high-status residents.[69] The Old Jewish Cemetery in Vilnius was destroyed in 1950–1955 in order to construct a stadium and a pool, and the same fate awaited the city's Užupis Cemetery in 1961–1965, whose tombstones were used as construction materials in the city.[70] The cemetery in Ostroh, Ukraine, and the second cemetery in Minsk were demolished in 1968 and in 1970–1972, respectively, to become parks.[71] As during the interwar period, it was possible to transfer some graves to other cemeteries. Thus, the remains of the Vilna Gaon and several people buried around his grave in the Old Cemetery were reinterred in the Šeškinė Jewish Cemetery in Vilnius, as was true for the remains of several prominent personalities buried in the Užupis Cemetery. Rabbi Yeruham Yehuda Leib Perelman, the Gadol of Minsk, and his family were reinterred in the cemetery in Barysaŭ in 1972.[72]

While the theft of tombstones for private buildings characterized mostly small towns in which people lived in private houses, the demolition of entire cemeteries was usually practiced in cities and was part of urban development. According to information gathered by Maceva, the Lithuanian cemetery-conservation society, out of 200 Jewish cemeteries in Lithuania, about 40 were totally demolished.[73] It seems that the general Soviet disrespect for historical heritage, and the real need for land in the city centers, were often combined with both anti-Jewish feelings and the desire, although not always articulated, to erase the memory of the Jewish past.

Fig. 2. New Jewish Cemetery in Horodenka, Ukraine, "stumps" of stone grave markers and preserved concrete grave markers. Photo by Vladimir Levin, 2010.

A factor that could sometimes prevent the reuse of a cemetery for a different purpose was public hygiene regulations, which stipulated a mandatory 20-year moratorium, after the last burial, in order to assign a former cemetery to new uses. For example, in 1946, the local soviets (municipalities) of Solotvyn and Kalush (two small towns in Western Ukraine), requested permission to "liquidate" Jewish cemeteries but were refused, since 20 years had not passed and the higher authorities saw in their application only "the tendency . . . to use monuments and headstones for construction needs."[74]

There were a few attempts to save historic cemeteries. The commission that initiated the demolition of the above-mentioned cemetery in Ostroh in 1968 stated that "we recommend the transfer of monuments having architectural value to the regional museum." The final decision on the demolition, however, did not include this clause.[75] The workers of the regional museum in Medzhybizh, Ukraine, wishing to preserve the most valuable and richly carved 18th-century tombstones, removed them from the old cemetery and placed them in the local museum in 1988. After protests, the tombstones were returned to the cemetery the following year.[76]

Not all Jewish graves were marked by masonry gravestones: a considerable number had wooden markers.[77] To the best of my knowledge, only two cemeteries still have wooden grave markers, in Lenin, Belarus,[78] and in Yakutsk, Siberia,[79] while in all other cemeteries in the USSR, such markers disappeared during the postwar period.

Synagogues

The fate of former synagogues in the USSR was very similar to the fate of the cemeteries. As noted, many synagogues in the pre-1939 Soviet territories had been already reassigned for new functions. In the "new" (annexed) western territories, local authorities were eager to utilize former synagogues in like manner. During the war and its aftermath, two population groups in those territories disappeared: Jews were murdered, and Poles were expelled to the new territorial borders of Poland. There were many local soviets that applied for permission to use former synagogues and Catholic churches for secular needs.[80] Like the churches, great synagogues were buildings with large prayer halls: many of these were transformed into sport facilities, movie theaters, or Houses of Culture, where a hall for theater and concerts was needed. Other former synagogues, however, housed offices, apartments, factories, workshops, and warehouses.[81]

Of these transformations, warehouses were the least destructive, as such use entailed minimal damage to the former synagogue's exterior and interior decorations (including murals); in addition, the owner of the storage space cared for the upkeep of the roof. Several gems of Jewish architecture survived into the post-Soviet period as warehouses. These include the Maharsha Synagogue in Ostroh, the Tsori Gilad Synagogue in Lviv (both in Ukraine), the Great Synagogue in Slonim, and the Great Synagogue in Ashmiany (in Belarus).

Notwithstanding the new usages assigned to former synagogues, many of them were demolished in the postwar period. Probably the most dramatic example is that of the Great (City) Synagogue and the *shulhoyf* in Vilnius, which survived the "liquidation" of the ghetto. In 1946, the short-lived Jewish Museum listed the Great Synagogue as a historic monument, but the following year, the synagogue was blasted; its ruins were pulled down in 1955–1957 to enable the enlargement of Vokiečių Street.[82] It seems that the demolition of the synagogue was a step in the Lithuanization of Vilnius, as it removed the most important building associated with Vilna Jewry. Similarly, the Great (Cold) Synagogue in Minsk, which had also been listed as a protected monument, was demolished in 1965 by order of the leader of Soviet Belorussia, Petr Masherov.[83] The examples of Vilnius and Minsk demonstrate that the initiative for destroying synagogues was taken by local authorities, not by the central government in Moscow. The policies of state antisemitism and marginalization of Jewish topics facilitated such decisions, but in general the disrespect of historic buildings and their demolition were not exceptional in the 1950s and 1960s.

There are, however, examples of a different approach. One of the ten members of the commission that decided on the demolition of the Great Synagogue in Vilnius, architect Eduardas Budreika, contested the plan and proposed the preservation of the building as a historic site.[84] When the authorities planned to dynamite the magnificent Great Synagogue in Lutsk in the early 1970s, only the intervention of the chief architect of the province, Lev Sanzharov, saved the building. The synagogue was listed as a protected monument, though its Jewish identity was blurred by naming it "the Low Castle or synagogue" and presenting it as part of the Lutsk fortifications. In 1976–1977, the synagogue became an athletic gymnasium. The architect responsible for the renovation, Rostyslav Metel'nyts'kyi, did not succeed in preventing the destruction of the interior. In the end, the unique building was preserved, but completely lost its interior structure and decorations.[85]

Other heritage workers also paid attention to synagogues. In Belarus, for example, the survey and documentation of architectural monuments in 1945–1949 included many synagogues.[86] In the early 1980s, nine prominent former synagogues (those of Minsk, Kletsk, Stolin, Pruzhany, Kobryn, Bykhaŭ, Shkloŭ, Hrodna, and Slonim) were included in a book series titled *Collection of Monuments of the History and Culture of Belarus*. Some of those synagogue entries were accompanied with floor plans and photographs.[87] A similar publication listing all architectural monuments in Ukraine in the early 1980s included only six former synagogues (those of Lutsk, Sharhorod, Zhovkva, Sataniv, Pidhaitsi, and Husiatyn), also with floor plans and photographs.[88] The restoration of the Great Sobieski Synagogue in Zhovkva took place in 1955–1956,[89] and the restoration project of the Old Synagogue in Brody was implemented in 1960.[90] Publications on architectural monuments and restoration projects demonstrate that Jewish heritage in the Soviet Union was not totally concealed and that its inclusion into the local heritage in Ukraine and Belarus, which began in the 1920s, was not completely ignored in the postwar era. However, this inclusion was marginal.

Table 1. Estimated number of synagogues in the western territories of the USSR

	Synagogues, early 20th c.	Extant synagogues, early 21st century	Percentage of extant synagogues
Latvia	338	38	11
Lithuania	933	106	11
Belarus	at least 1,685	121	7
Ukraine	at least 3,662	474	13
Moldova	306	29	9

The situation of the Jewish built heritage at the end of the Soviet period can be estimated numerically. Table 1, based on research by the Center for Jewish Art at the Hebrew University of Jerusalem, shows that during the 20th century, about 90 percent of synagogue buildings disappeared in the westernmost areas of the USSR. The numbers in the table are not exact, but the situation it depicts is very clear.

A comparison of this data with that on synagogues in Siberia—which were not affected by wartime destruction—enables us to differentiate between the losses caused by the Second World War and losses inflicted during peacetime. Of course, the overall number of synagogues in Siberia was very small in comparison to the corresponding number in the areas of the former Pale of Settlement. Nonetheless, the loss of about 60 percent of Siberian synagogues enables us to assume that the level of peacetime destruction in the west was not significantly smaller.[91]

Postwar Jewish Attitudes toward Jewish Heritage

Most discussions of the postwar fate of former synagogues and Jewish cemeteries in this essay concentrate on the attitudes and approaches of Soviet authorities. Among the many examples described above, Jewish actors were involved in only three cases: the unsuccessful attempt of the Jewish Museum in Vilnius to protect the Great (City) Synagogue just after the war, and the reinterment of the remains of the Vilna Gaon and of the Gadol of Minsk.

Soviet Jews who were interested in things Jewish were mostly busy with trying to support active synagogues, which did not always occupy historical buildings. Active synagogues situated in historical buildings only rarely had enough financial backing to fund renovations, and quite often buildings were preserved in the same state as before the 1917 Revolution. There were cases in the mid-1940s when the local authorities were allegedly willing to transfer former synagogues to Jewish communities, on condition that the communities would renovate them. But these communities, composed of impoverished Holocaust survivors, did not have the means to renovate the Great Synagogues in Vilnius or Lutsk.[92] Jews had no effective ways to preserve former synagogues and cemeteries, apart from the transfer of several of the most important graves, under the guise of caring for deceased relatives. A rare case of explicitly expressed Jewish concern about a former synagogue occurred in Dubno, Ukraine. A Jew, the head of the local Voluntary Society for Support of Army, Air Force, and Navy (DOSAAF) branch that occupied the former Great Synagogue in the 1980s, reportedly vowed to preserve the building to the best of his abilities.[93]

In several regions of the USSR, Jews continued to occupy the houses that belonged to their families prior to the 1917 Revolution. One such region is Uzbekistan, where the late 19th- and early 20th-century houses in the traditional Jewish quarters of Bukhara and Samarkand contained extensively decorated main halls, often with Hebrew inscriptions and Jewish symbols.[94] Another such region is eastern Podolia in Ukraine (also known as Transnistria), which fell under Romanian occupation during the Second World War.[95] Many Jewish homes there, remaining in Jewish hands, preserved their original structure, which significantly differed from that of Christian houses and reflected the urban occupations of the Jews in small trade and artisanship.[96] It is impossible to state that Jewish families consciously preserved traditional Jewish dwellings, but they undoubtedly would have shown more respect to their Jewish features than did non-Jewish residents.

The Jewish national movement, which emerged starting in the early 1970s, was oriented toward emigration, and therefore Jewish heritage in the Soviet Union was of little to no interest to its activists. The disregard of Jewish heritage by the Soviet authorities was only one (relatively minor) part of the large picture of official negative attitudes toward the Jews that fueled the movement. This could be seen, for example, in the oeuvre of Shimon Yantovsky, who traveled throughout the USSR from 1976 to 1987 in order to see "the life of Jews who preserved their traditional religious way of life."[97] Yantovsky visited active synagogues and Jewish cemeteries in hundreds of cities and towns; although he was interested in religious Jews, he also paid attention to former synagogues and photographed them. For him, however, the existence of former synagogues used for secular purposes only stressed the miserable conditions in which Jewish religious life was conducted in the USSR. Hence the title of his book, published in Israel in 1987 under the pen name Israel Tayar, was *Synagogue Devastated, but Unsubdued*.[98]

Only in the early 1980s did some of the Jewish activists begin to develop an interest in local culture and heritage. In 1982–1986, a Historical-Ethnographic Commission began to meet in Moscow, while an illegal seminar on Jewish history was established by Michael Beizer in Leningrad in 1982.[99] Beizer also researched the history of Jews in the city and organized illegal guided tours, which he later published as a book.[100] The most significant group of Jewish activists dealing with Jewish heritage emerged in the mid-1980s in Leningrad and was institutionalized in 1989 as the Jewish University of Leningrad. Under the leadership of Ilya Dvorkin, this group conducted expeditions to former shtetls in Ukraine and Belarus as well as to Uzbekistan, aiming to create a "collection of Jewish Monuments" similar to the Belorussian and Ukrainian "Collections of Monuments." The Jewish identity of this group was shaped inter alia by direct contact with Jewish heritage.[101]

The Post-Soviet Period

The disappearance of a state-controlled narrative about the past during the years of *perestroika* in 1985–1991 and the emergence of independent states on the ruins of the USSR in 1991–1992 created a situation in which the place of Jewish heritage and its visibility had to be reconsidered and renegotiated. The almost total silencing of Jewish topics that characterized the late Soviet Union ceased, and Jews and non-Jews alike had to develop new approaches to the Jewish heritage that survived the Soviet era or was created during it. This process went hand in hand with nation-building in the new states, the mass emigration of Jews, and the entry to the local scene of Israeli and American Jewish organizations. It was also interwoven with the reconsideration of the Shoah, which could not be detached from the fate of Jewish heritage in the western regions of the USSR.

Museums

Museums with Jewish collections had the easiest entry into the new reality. During *perestroika*, several state museums "discovered" their collections of Jewish objects and began to study, publish, and exhibit them, first and foremost as temporary exhibitions shown abroad.[102] Three of the major museums were the State Museum of Ethnography in St. Petersburg, with a significant part of the An-sky collection;[103] the Museum of Historical Treasures in Kyiv, with a collection of ceremonial objects from the 1922 confiscations,[104] and the Museum of Ethnography and Crafts in Lviv, where the collection of Maximilian Goldstein is housed.[105] In 2000, the Museum of the History of Religion in St. Petersburg established an impressive Judaica room in its permanent exhibition;[106] the above-mentioned Museum of Ethnography created a permanent exhibition in 2007;[107] and the Bukharan-Jewish Museum—a department of the Samarkand Museum of Regional Studies—opened its exhibition in 2008.[108] Sometimes the appearance of Jewish exhibitions in the state museums was triggered by accidental factors. For example, the Jewish exhibition in the National Museum of the Republic of Buryatia in Ulan Ude was created in 2016, following the visit of the research expedition of the Center for Jewish Art in 2015, which documented the Jewish objects that reached the museum from the closed local synagogue.[109]

Most of the state museums in Russia, Belarus, Ukraine, and Moldova, however, did not change their permanent exhibitions to include Jews in their narrative, even in those cities and towns where Jews had constituted about half of the population before the Shoah. Moreover, many regional museums were forced to return some of their Jewish objects to revived Jewish communities. In contrast, as demonstrated by Milda Jakulytė, museums in Lithuania reconstructed their exhibitions in the 2010s and included Jews in the image of history that they sought to present.[110] The same process, according to Ilya Lensky, took place in Latvia.[111]

The revitalization of Jewish identity among former Soviet Jews included an interest in Jewish history and culture. Numerous Jewish organizations and religious communities that were established in the late 1980s and 1990s began collecting historical materials, and by the early 2000s, small Jewish museums had been founded in several cities. For example, the Jewish museum in Riga was founded in 1988, together with the Society for Jewish Culture, though its permanent exhibition was opened in the community building only in 1996.[112] Only the Vilna Gaon Museum of Jewish History in Vilnius (the successor of the Jewish museum of 1944–1949, reestablished in 1988–1989) and the David Baazov Museum of History of Jews of Georgia in Tbilisi (the successor of the Jewish museum of 1933–1951, reestablished in 1992, whose permanent exhibition opened in 2014) were created as state institutions and are funded by the state.[113] These museums were also the recipients of objects that originally belonged to the museums that had been closed in 1949 and 1951, which had been transferred to other state museums and archives.

All other Jewish museums remained communal institutions. The majority of them are situated in the buildings of synagogues and community centers and occupy one or two rooms. Their "narrative" exhibitions are devoted to local Jewish history and the modest collections contain mostly objects, documents, and photographs donated by local Jews.[114] According to Anastasia Felcher, who researched the museums in Chișinău (Kishinev), Odesa, Lviv, and Minsk, "the personality of the museum director is of exceptional importance in designing" the messages that the museum transmits.[115]

A similar museum of the "communal type" was created in the Holocaust Memorial Synagogue in Moscow in 1998. However, Moscow has two other important museums. The Jewish Museum and Tolerance Center, opened in 2012, tells the story of Russian and Soviet Jews through an impressive multimedia exhibition. The museum belongs to the Chabad-dominated Federation of Jewish Communities of Russia, and it is supported by the highest authorities of the Russian Federation: President Vladimir Putin was reported to have made a donation of one month's salary for the building of the museum.[116] In contrast, the Museum of Jewish History in Russia (MIEVR), opened in 2011, is owned by a private person. It has succeeded in gathering an extremely valuable collection of artifacts of Jewish daily life from all areas of the former Russian empire and the USSR.[117]

Cemeteries

With the initiation of *perestroika* in 1985 and the growing attention to issues of heritage, the destruction of cemeteries almost ceased. Probably one of the last damaged cemeteries is the New Cemetery in Pinsk, Belarus, demolished in 1990–1992.[118] By this point, however, many old and unused cemeteries were in very poor condition. In Lithuania, the Society for Jewish Culture and the Jewish Museum initiated a proposal that was later approved by the Lithuanian government regarding preservation of cemeteries and mass graves of Holocaust victims. During 1991 and 1992, many cemeteries were cleaned and fenced, and memorial signs indicating their former function were installed.[119] During the same years, plaques commemorating the Vilnius ghetto were placed around the city and Jewish tombstones that had been used as building materials began to be returned to the Užupis Cemetery.[120]

In the last two decades, tombstones removed from cemeteries and used for construction have often been brought to the existing cemeteries or their sites, as has occurred in Lviv, Minsk, Vilnius, and elsewhere.[121] As far as I know, only in Vilnius has there been a systematic removal of tombstones from Soviet-era buildings, and broken stones are gathered at the Užupis Cemetery, where some of them were used in the design of a memorial in 2004.[122] Only in rare cases has there been partial restoration of cemeteries that were demolished in the Soviet era. For example, Mikhail Evtushenko, the (non-Jewish) director of the Agricultural Lyceum, which occupies part of the former Jewish cemetery in Dubroŭna, Belarus, gathered about 40 preserved tombstones in one place in 2001 and then fenced this area (Fig. 3).[123] In Ostroh, Ukraine, the local Jewish activist Hryhoryi Arshynov collected tombstones found in various parts of the town and placed them in an upright position in the cemetery.[124]

Jewish initiatives concerning the historical cemeteries are often driven by rabbis and religious bodies. From the religious point of view, it is important to protect old burial grounds and to preserve the graves from desecration, whereas tombstones as such have no inherent religious value. Therefore, such organizations mainly invest in fencing the cemeteries. Construction of roofed structures (*ohalim*) over the graves of hasidic leaders took place in Ukraine in the 1990s and 2000s, in close connection with the rise of hasidic pilgrimage to those sites. Adherents of the non-hasidic (or "Lithuanian") current in Orthodox Judaism have erected new tombstones for famous heads of historic Lithuanian yeshivas. The single most important and best-known pilgrimage activity that has taken place in the last decades revolves around the grave of R. Nahman in Uman, where the cemetery was demolished in the Soviet era, but the case of Medzhybizh, the town of the founder of Hasidism, R. Israel Ba'al Shem-Tov (Besht), is instructive. The grave of the Besht never had an *ohel*.[125] In the early 2000s, however, a large *ohel* was erected there, which includes as well the nearby graves of his disciples;[126] a synagogue and a pilgrims' hostel were built nearby.[127] Thus, the redevelopment of meaningful gravesites is made not in the framework of heritagization, but rather to serve the needs of contemporary religious groups. In 2021, Agudas ohalei tzadikim, led by Isroel Meir Gabay, uprooted tombstones in one of the most impressive cemeteries in Ukraine, that of Sataniv, reset them in concrete bases, and artificially arranged them in straight rows, thus completely destroying the authenticity of that cemetery.[128]

Fig. 3. Tombstones in the former Jewish cemetery in Dubroŭna, Belarus, concentrated in one corner and fenced by the director of the Agricultural Lyceum. Photo by Vladimir Levin, 2010.

In contrast, non-religious organizations and volunteer groups are mostly interested in tombstones, their documentation and, in recent years, digitization. The cemeteries mostly belong to city authorities, which manage them, sometimes in cooperation with the local communities. The emigration of the majority of Jews caused the emergence of a new way of providing grave-cleaning service: in order to enable potential customers from abroad to order the cleaning, many active cemeteries were completely inventoried, with photographs of the graves made accessible online.

Thus, Jewish cemeteries stand today at the intersection of considerable scholarly attention, on the one hand, and the economic interests of local administrations, cleaning services, and pilgrimage organizers, on the other. Their heritagization is usually accepted and understood by the local population, which sometimes supports such initiatives.

Synagogues

The collapse of the USSR created the issue of private ownership of real estate. In the Soviet Union, all buildings other than private houses were the property of the state, but after 1991, ownership by private persons and legal entities became possible. While in

Fig. 4. Great Maharsha Synagogue in Ostroh, Ukraine, after 15 years of being abandoned and before its recent restoration. Photo by Vladimir Levin/Center for Jewish Art, 2011.

Lithuania and Latvia many former synagogues were transferred to the ownership of the umbrella Jewish communal organizations, in other post-Soviet states only local religious communities were allowed to "repossess" the houses of worship nationalized in Soviet times.[129] In effect, some former synagogues in those countries became the property of communities, whereas others remained the property of the state. With the development of the market economy in the 1990s, Soviet organizations that had used former synagogues often disappeared, leaving the buildings without even minimal care, as in the case of the Great Maharsha Synagogue in Ostroh, Ukraine (Fig. 4).

The return of former synagogues to Jewish religious communities created a number of new problems. Many of the synagogues had been heavily reconstructed during the Soviet era and were often without their original interior (or sometimes, even exterior) features. Moreover, the size of some extant historic synagogues much exceeded the needs of small contemporary communities. In many localities in Lithuania and Latvia, where the former synagogues were returned to the umbrella Jewish organizations, no Jews remained and no Jewish religious—or other—activities were taking place. In light of this reality, three approaches to historic synagogues owned by religious communities could be observed in the last 30 years.

The first approach concerns those synagogues that functioned during the Soviet period or else were well preserved, having fulfilled other functions during the Soviet period. These had to be repaired and maintained. While the general tendency is to preserve them as they are, renovations are often made without regard to heritage considerations. Thus, while the Choral Synagogue in St. Petersburg was repaired in 2000–2003, the wooden floor of the prayer hall was replaced with ceramic tiles, the *bimah* was moved to the center of the hall, and part of the original pews was removed. In Lviv, the 1936 murals by Maksymilian Kugel in the Tsori Gilad Synagogue were covered up by new paint in 2009. Although the painters followed the original outline of the murals, details and palette were altered, and the authentic murals no longer exist.[130]

The second approach to synagogues returned to the communities is to reconstruct the facades to conform to their supposedly original form, while completely redesigning the interior. The problem is that the original appearance of the facades is often known only from one or two photographs.[131] A similar approach characterized the restoration of the dome of the Choral Synagogue in Moscow in 2000–2001. Although originally part of the synagogue design, the dome was never in use; it was removed in 1888 (before the inauguration of the synagogue), on demand of the Russian Orthodox Church.[132] The restoration of synagogue exteriors and the cupola in Moscow is part of a general trend vis-à-vis historical churches that were demolished during the Soviet era. Suffice it to mention the Cathedral of Christ the Savior in Moscow and St. Michael's Golden-Domed Monastery in Kyiv, built anew in 1994–1999 and 1997–1998. Thus, the "restored" historical appearance in functioning synagogues fits very well into the general tendency, and in that sense the rebuilding of the 18th-century wooden *kloyz* of the Besht in Medzhybizh that was burned down during the Second World War is not very exceptional.[133]

The third approach is observed in Lithuania and Latvia, where the former synagogues belonging to the Jewish umbrella organizations are physically restored, but are used as cultural venues for the local non-Jewish population. Public interest in the Jewish heritage of Lithuania began to emerge in the 1990s, and in the 2000s it found its expression in the increasing number of publications about Lithuanian synagogues.[134] As of 2021, there is a long list of former synagogues, restored in the last two decades, that are now serving as cultural centers, museums, exhibition or concert halls.[135] The most outstanding example is the restoration of the wooden synagogue in Pakruojis in 2015–2017 as a children's library: its interior and wall paintings were remade according to detailed photographs from the 1930s and a computer model that was prepared by Sergey Kravtsov of the Center for Jewish Art (Fig. 5).[136] The same process is taking place in Latvia.[137]

The list of restored or renovated synagogues in Latvia and especially in Lithuania is very impressive, although there are still former synagogues that await repair and there are some losses, such as three synagogues in Plungė, Lithuania, that were demolished by the local Jewish community in 2008,[138] or the wooden synagogue in Subate, Latvia, which was razed to the ground by the municipality in 2009.[139] An important role in the restoration of synagogues belongs to local authorities who are eager to incorporate former synagogues into the contemporary life of their cities and town as cultural venues—both representing the Jewish past of those localities and serving their residents in the present. There also exists a strong desire to eliminate traces of the Soviet past. Restoration efforts have intensified in the last decade, as the awareness of Jewish heritage has grown and funding from the European Union and other European

Fig. 5. Interior of the wooden synagogue in Pakruojis, restored as children's library. Photo by Sergey Kravtsov/Center for Jewish Art, 2017.

organizations has become more readily available. The movement toward restoration of former synagogues and their incorporation into local life signify the adaptation of Jewish monuments by parts of the local society and their inclusion into a new cultural-historical narrative.

The situation and approach in Belarus is completely different.[140] Here, synagogues that were listed in the *Collection of Monuments* in the 1980s are still in the same physical state or else have significantly deteriorated.[141] There are also losses, such as the wooden Great Synagogue in Liuban, which was demolished in 2009 (Fig. 6).[142] Several former synagogues were transferred to Jewish communities, but only one of them, the Great Synagogue in Hrodna, preserves its original interior.[143] In 2020–2021, a new mode of dealing with Jewish heritage emerged: municipalities now auction former synagogues, conditioning the sale upon the buyer's commitment to restore the building.[144] An important case of dealing with Jewish built heritage—led by Belarusian ICOMOS (The International Council on Monuments and Sites)—is the Great Synagogue in Ashmiany, which, as of 2012, had become part of the regional museum.[145] Although this has not yet resulted in its restoration, its inclusion in the local cultural framework is a significant step. Another important case is the conservation of the ruined synagogue on Chanharskaia St. in Babruisk and the creation there of "the Jewish courtyard" in 2019.[146]

Fig. 6. Demolition of the wooden Great Synagogue in Liuban, Belarus. Photo by Alexander Astraukh, 2009. Courtesy of the photographer.

In contrast to Lithuania and Latvia, Belarus is not oriented toward Europe; European values and Jewish history are almost absent from its official narrative. The same attitude characterizes a significant part of Belarusian society. As a leader of Belarusian ICOMOS, Stsiapan Stureika, formulated it, "synagogues are not perceived as our own."[147] Only small groups of Jewish activists and non-Jewish, European-minded young professionals are interested in the preservation of Jewish heritage in Belarus and its inclusion into the cultural-historical narrative of the country. A growing number of publications about synagogues in Belarus in the last few years testifies that some interest in this topic indeed exists.[148]

The situation in Ukraine partially resembles Belarus, notwithstanding the difference in official discourse, which declaratively rejects the Soviet past. On the one hand, according to the research project "Historical Synagogues of Europe" conducted by the Center for Jewish Art and the Foundation of Jewish Heritage, about 50 important former synagogues in Ukraine are (even before Putin's invasion) in a state of ruin or in very bad disrepair—a significantly greater number than in any other country of Europe (Belarus is in second place in this regard).[149] Among them are the Great Synagogues in Brody (which partially collapsed around 1980), Zholkva, Pidhaitsi, Sharhorod, and Husiatyn, which were listed as protected monuments even in the Soviet era. On the other hand, several projects for restoring former synagogues have begun or have been completed in recent years. The most significant of those projects is the Space of Synagogues project in Lviv, which created a well-designed memorial space around the conserved ruin of the 16th-century Golden Rose Synagogue and the foundations of the Great City Synagogue and Beit Hamidrash.

Initiated by the Center for Urban History of East Central Europe, the project was adopted by the Lviv municipality and inaugurated in 2016. As Ruth Ellen Gruber, the editor of *Jewish Heritage Europe*, wrote: "The project is believed to mark the first time in Ukraine that a memorial commemorating Jews was initiated by city authorities and represents a public recognition of Jewish history as local history."[150]

Most other projects involving the rescue of synagogue ruins are initiated by Jewish actors. Thus, Hryhoryi Arshynov led the restoration of the Great Maharsha Synagogue in Ostroh from 2016, which saved the building (which had stood abandoned from the time of the 1990s) from impending collapse (Fig. 4).[151] The Great Synagogue in Sataniv was restored by Arthur Friedman in 2012–2015,[152] and the Ceremonial Hall at the Chernivtsi Cemetery was renovated in 2017–2018.[153] Renovation works have been taking place in the Jakób Glanzer Shul in Lviv and in the Great Synagogue of Sharhorod since 2017,[154] and the restoration of the synagogue in Vil'khivtsi (Irhócz in Hungarian) began in 2021; this building is slated to become a Jewish heritage museum and Holocaust memorial.[155] The Rebbe's Kloyz in Sadhora was returned to the hasidic community and renovated in 2013–2016;[156] a similar future awaits the synagogues in Chechelnyk[157] and Lutsk.[158] In contrast to hasidic renovation works that usually show little respect for modern heritage approaches, the "secular" projects are expected to be more careful with regard to the preservation of authenticity. To be sure, lack of funds can get in the way of good intentions. For example, the unique murals in the synagogue in Novoselytsia, Ukraine, discovered in 2008 and cleaned up in 2009, are in real danger of vanishing, owing to the deteriorating state of the building.[159]

The common feature of all of these projects (apart from the Spaces of Synagogues in Lviv) is that they are undertaken by Jews and Jewish organizations, with the funding for their implementation coming from Jewish sources. With the exception of Lviv, there is, to the best of my knowledge, no involvement of state or city authorities in rescuing Jewish heritage buildings, and Ukrainian society shows only minor interest in these initiatives.

The situation in Moldova is very similar, both in the "mainland" and in the unrecognized Republic of Transnistria. Apart from the Jewish cemetery in Chişinău that was proclaimed an "open air museum," the few other initiatives to preserve Jewish heritage have all originated in Jewish circles.[160]

The Russian Federation—the largest of the post-Soviet states—presents an ambiguous picture. Many synagogue buildings were returned to the Jewish communities and restored along the principles described above. However, former synagogues that were *not* claimed remain in the ownership of city authorities, which are not interested in their heritagization. For example, the former wooden synagogue in Kansk, Siberia, which served as an apartment house until 2014, was dismantled for firewood in 2016.[161]

In Georgia, the preservation and renovation of synagogues was the lifework of the architect Shota Bostanashvili. More than two dozen synagogues exist in the country, some of them serving active communities and others abandoned. Functioning synagogues underwent repairs, which sometimes resulted in the loss of original interiors (as happened, for instance, at the Ashkenazi Synagogue in Tbilisi in 2007 and the synagogue in Surami in 2012), but in other cases (for instance, the Akhaltsikhe Synagogue in Tbilisi), the interiors were preserved. The synagogue in Oni was restored after the earthquake of 1991.[162]

In Azerbaijan, the Mountain Jews lived mostly in three places: Baku, Quba, and Oguz. Historical synagogues in Quba and Oguz were returned to the communities and renovated, while in Baku, new buildings for synagogues were constructed.

The situation in Uzbekistan is different. The functioning Gumbaz Synagogue in Samarkand was extensively renovated in 1980, and two functioning synagogues in Bukhara were likewise refurbished in the early 1990s. There are also several functioning synagogues in provincial cities, some of them built in the Soviet era. All other synagogues were closed by the Soviets and none of them was returned to the community or restored.[163] Essentially, synagogues are not a heritage issue in Uzbekistan. In addition, houses once belonging to Bukharan Jews have passed to new owners, who renovate them without regard for their historical features and specific decorations.

Soviet-Jewish Heritage

The attitude toward Soviet-era Jewish buildings and items is rarely discussed or even noted. The buildings of synagogues opened after the Second World War were usually nondescript, located in residential buildings that were purchased by the congregations and converted for Jewish worship; ritual objects produced for those synagogues were not numerous, since the congregations were extremely small and usually had enough pre-revolutionary objects for their modest needs. The quality of Soviet-era objects is far inferior to the pre-revolutionary items, and many of them are unsuitable for the religious needs of contemporary communities.

Notwithstanding, there exists a certain respect for the buildings and objects produced during Soviet times. Some items are exhibited in communal museums, while others are still in use. For example, the Soviet-era synagogue (today called Beit Teshuva) in Birobidzhan still uses two Torah arks and the *'amud* made in 1957; while another *'amud* is exhibited in the communal museum in the modern Chabad synagogue in that city.[164] The small Soviet-era synagogue in Saratov was turned into a Jewish museum in 2019, although it lost the majority of its architectural features, apart from the street facade.[165]

In contrast, Soviet-era tombstones usually do not attract attention of heritage-minded activists. Moreover, many Holocaust monuments erected by the Soviet Jews in the 1940s–1980s were significantly altered in the 1990s and 2000s in order to replace the original Soviet-style inscriptions about murdered "noncombatant Soviet citizens" with new texts and Jewish symbols.[166] In other words, the Jewish buildings, objects, tombstones, and memorials from the Soviet period do not possess the same symbolic value as similar items from the earlier periods. Their heritagization has taken place only to a minimal degree.

Conclusion

The beginning of the 21st century in Europe was marked by growing attention to Jewish heritage, understood now not as the culture of a foreign people, but as part and parcel of a common European heritage. Many Jewish museums and Jewish

exhibitions in general museums were created, dozens if not hundreds of former synagogues were restored, and Jewish cemeteries were fenced and cleaned. A significant
factor underlying this turn to Jewish heritage is memories of the Holocaust and its
reconceptualization. In the countries of the former Soviet Union, the attitude toward
Jewish heritage is derived from the dominant attitude toward contemporary European
ideas and the comprehension of the Shoah, but equally from each country's perspective vis-à-vis its Soviet past.

In the interwar period, the Soviet leadership perceived Soviet Jews as belonging
to one of many Soviet peoples; consequently, their cultural heritage was allocated a
place in many state museums and other institutions, and like other heritages, it was
under strict and constantly intensifying ideological control. Synagogues and Jewish
cemeteries were often closed or mercilessly demolished together with churches,
mosques, and Christian and Muslim cemeteries. In general, the Jewish heritage in the
interwar USSR experienced the same fate as the heritage of other Soviet peoples.

The turn to state antisemitism in the late 1940s singled Jews out from other Soviet
nationalities. Jewish topics, aside from anti-Zionism, were marginalized and often
silenced. Museum collections almost totally disappeared from display, while synagogues and cemeteries were razed. Although the issue of museum collections is relatively easy to understand, that of demolition of synagogues and cemeteries is much
more complicated. Regarding the latter issue, there was no consistent governmental
policy dictated from Moscow that stipulated the destruction of Jewish material culture. All decisions were taken locally by city or republic-level authorities, and a
good deal of research remains to be done in order to clarify which considerations
stood behind each decision to demolish a former synagogue or to convert a cemetery
into a park. To what extent did anti-Jewish feelings on the part of local leaders influence the urban planning that involved destruction of Jewish monuments? To what
degree did the attitude toward Jewish monuments differ from that toward the heritage of other groups, both the "titular" nations of each republic and other minority
groups (for instance, Poles in the western areas of the USSR, whose "invisibility"
very much approximates that of the Jews)? While in some cases, as in Vilnius and
Minsk, it seems relatively clear that the desire to erase prominent Jewish sites from
the urban fabric was a factor, other cases need to be explored. Many synagogues were
demolished, whereas some were listed as protected monuments or even restored, such
that a case-by-case examination may produce unexpected conclusions. Moreover, the
general perception of what is heritage and which buildings are worthy of conservation
is changing with the times. With some exceptions, the architecture of the second half
of the 19th and the first half of the 20th centuries was not considered valuable in the
Soviet era, even among preservationists. Thus, the majority of former synagogues had
no chance to be regarded as heritage, and consequently protected.

In the post-Soviet geographical region, the division in approaches is obvious. In
those countries that tended to overcome their Soviet experience and sought to join the
European Union (Lithuania, Latvia, Estonia), Jewish heritage gradually became part
of the local heritage and has been absorbed into the local cultural-historical narrative.
Usually this has happened in the context of coping with the Shoah and its implications.
In those states, national heritage authorities and municipalities, along with Jewish organizations, have taken an active role in restoring and memorializing historic monuments.

The situation is different in other post-Soviet countries. Although in some of those states the rejection of the Soviet past has been solemnly proclaimed, the *Weltanschauung* of most of the people has not changed significantly, and has not been replaced by European values. In addition, Georgia, Azerbaijan, and Uzbekistan were not touched by the Shoah, while the Holocaust experience in Russia, Belarus, Ukraine, and Moldova holds only a marginal place—if at all—in the national, state-supported historical narrative. The basis for dealing with former synagogues in those countries is religious: that is, religious communities are entitled to claim those buildings and to use them for performing religious ceremonies. The communities are relatively free to rebuild those monuments with minimal or superficial involvement of heritage authorities. The dominating discourse in those cases is not the memorialization of a monument, but the restoration of its religious value. Therefore, those former synagogues that are not claimed by communities are left to deteriorate and collapse without intervention by local authorities and society. Jewish monuments are perceived as "theirs," belonging to Jews, who are entitled to deal with them, and not as an integral part of local history and culture that should be preserved for the benefit of the entire population. Only small circles of relatively young people have absorbed the European ideas of tolerance and inclusion, but in most cases (the notable exception being the Space of Synagogues in Lviv) these individuals are not influential enough to change the dominant discourse. Jewish heritage remains a Jewish matter, to be dealt with by the Jews.

Notes

I am very grateful to Anna Berezin, Milda Jakulytė, Ekaterina Oleshkevich, and Arkadi Zeltser, who read the first versions of this article. Their feedback was crucial for its completion.

1. M.A. Poliakova, *Okhrana kul'turnogo naslediia Rossii* (Moscow: 2005), 28–30.
2. See, for instance, Mirjam Rajner, "The Awakening of Jewish National Art in Russia," *Jewish Art* 16–17 (1990/1991), 98–121; Grigory (Hillel) Kazovskii, *Artists from Vitebsk: Yehuda Pen and His Pupils* (Moscow: 1991); idem, *Khudozhniki Kul'tur-Ligi* (Moscow and Jerusalem: 2003).
3. On An-sky and his expeditions see, for instance, Gabriella Safran and Steven J. Zipperstein (eds.), *The Worlds of S. An-Sky: A Russian Jewish Intellectual at the Turn of the Century* (Stanford: 2006); Gabriella Safran, *Wandering Soul: The Dybbuk's Creator, S. An-Sky* (Cambridge, Mass: 2010).
4. See, for instance, Mathias Bersohn, *Kilka słów o dawniejszych bóżnicach drewnianych w Polsce*, vol. 1 (Kraków: 1895); Majer Balaban, *Dzielnica Żydowska, jej dzieje i zabytku* (Lwów: 1909); Rachel Bernstein-Wischnitzer, "Iskusstvo u evreev v Pol'she i na Litve," in *Istoriia evreev v Rossii*, ed. A.I. Braudo et al., vol. 11 (1), *Istoriia evreiskogo naroda* (Moscow: 1914), 390–405; Alfred Grotte, *Deutsche, böhmische und polnische Synagogentypen vom XI. bis Anfang des XIX. Jahrhunderts* (Leipzig: 1915).
5. Sergey Kravtsov, "Studies of Jewish Architecture in Central-Eastern Europe in Historical Perspective," in *The History of Art History in Central, Eastern and South-Eastern Europe*, ed. Jerzy Malinowski, vol. 1 (Toruń: 2012), 183–189.
6. An appeal of the Soviet of Workers' and Soldiers' Deputies, 1917, in T.L. Karpova, N.A. Potapova, and T.P. Sukhman, *Okhrana kul'turnogo naslediia Rossii, XVII–XX vv. Khrestomatiia*, vol. 1 (Moscow: 2000).
7. Beniamin Lukin, "K stoletiiu obrazovaniia peterburgskoi nauchnoi shkoly evreiskoi istorii," in *Istoriia evreev v Rossii: problemy istochnikovedeniia i istoriograsii*, ed. Dmitrii

Elyashevich, vol. 1, *Trudy po iudaike Peterburgskogo evreiskogo universiteta* (St. Petersburg: 1993), 20.

8. Ibid., 23.

9. Liudmila Uritskaia and Semion Yakerson, *Evreiskie sokrovishcha Peterburga: Ashkenazskie kollektsii Rossiiskogo etnograficheskogo muzeia* (St. Petersburg: 2009), 144–150; Alexander Ivanov, "'Evrei v tsarskoi Rossii i v SSSR'–vystavka dostizhenii evreiskogo khoziaisvennogo i kul'turnogo stroitel'stva v Strane Sovetov," *Novoe literaturnoe obozrenie* 102 (2010), 158–182; idem, "Vystavka 'Evrei v tsarskoi Rossii i v SSSR' v kontekste sovetskogo muzeinogo stroitel'stvva v 1930-e gg.," in *Sovetskaia iudaika: istoria, problematika, personalii*, ed. Mark Kupovetskii (Jerusalem/Moscow: 2017), 157–200; idem, "'V poiskakh novogo cheloveka na beregakh rek Biry i Bidzhana': Evreiskaia sektsiia Gosudarstvennogo museia etnografii v Leningrade (1937–1941)," in *Sovetskaia geniza: novye arkhivnye razyskaniia po istorii evreev v SSSR*, ed. Gennady Estraikh and Alexander Frenkel, vol. 1 (Boston/St. Petersburg: 2020), 171–292.

10. In Kyiv, the Office for Jewish Culture, a low-status institution, existed until the late 1940s. See Efim Melamed, "Iz istorii nezavisimykh issledovanii v oblasti iudaiki v Ukraine: sud'ba Evreiskoi istoriko-arkheograficheskoi komissii (1919–1929)," *Arkhiv evreiskoi istorii* 5 (2008), 77–98; idem, "Iz istorii sobiraniia i izucheniia evreiskogo pis'mennogo nasledia na Ukraine v 20–30-e gody XX v. (O popytke sozdaniia Tsentral'nogo evreiskogo istoricheskogo arkhiva v Kieve)," *Judaica Rossica* 4 (2006), 51–77; idem, "The Fate of the Archives of the Kiev Institute of Jewish Proletarian Culture: Puzzles and Discoveries," *East European Jewish Affairs* 42 (2012), 99–110; idem, "Kak byl unichtozhen 'venets evreiskoi kul'tury': Evreiskie uchionye Kieva nakanune i vo vremia Bol'shogo terrora," in Estraikh and Frenkel (eds.), *Sovetskaia geniza*, 109–170; Ella Tsyhankova, *Skhodoznavchi ustanovy v Ukraini (radians'kyi period)* (Kyiv: 2007); Inna Gerasimova, "K istorii evreiskogo otdela Instituta belorusskoi kul'tury (Inbelkul'ta) i evreiskogo sektora Belorusskoi akademii nauk v 20-30-kh godakh," *Vestnik Evreiskogo universiteta v Moskve* no. 2(12) (1996), 144–167; Dmitrii Shevelev, "Evreiskie issledovaniia v Belorusskoi SSR v 1933–1941 gg. (po dokumentam Tsentral'nogo nauchnogo arkhiva Natsional'noi akademii nauk Belarusi)," in *Materialy 16-oi Ezhegodnoi mezhdunarodnoi mezhdistsiplinarnoi konferentsii po iudaike*, vol. 2 (Moscow: 2009), 483–489; idem, "Iz istorii evreiskikh akademicheskikh podrazdelenii v Belorusskoi Sovetskoi Sotsialisticheskoi Respublike v 1920-kh – nachale 1940-kh gg." in Kupovetskii (ed.), *Sovetskaia iudaika*, 72–81; Elissa Bemporad, "'What Should We Collect?' Ethnography, Local Studies, and the Formation of a Belorussian Jewish Identity," in *Going to the People: Jews and the Ethnographic Impulse*, ed. Jeffrey Veidlinger (Bloomington: 2016), 85–99.

11. Efim Melamed, "Istochniki dlia istorii evreiskikh nauchnykh i kul'turno prosvetitel'skikh uchrezhdenii 1920–1940-kh godov v arkhivakh Ukrainy," in *Idish: yazyk i kul'tura v Sovetskom Soiuze*, ed. Leonid Katsis, Maria Kaspina, and David Fishman (Moscow: 2009), 232. On the Jewish Department, see Bemporad, "What Should We Collect?" 91. On the fate of the objects in Belarus, see Anatolii Sinilo, "Eksponaty iz Muzeia Evreiskogo istoriko-etnograficheskogo obshchestva v sobraniiakh belorusskikh muzeev," *Trudy po evreiskoi istorii i kul'ture. Materialy XXII Mezhdunarodnoi ezhegodnoi konferentsii po iudaike* 52 (2016), 346–394; idem, "Zbory iaureiskaha addzela Belaruskaha dziarzhaunaha muzeia u 1920–1940-kh hh.," *Belaruski historychny chasopis*, no. 3 (2021), 24–34. See also Darya Sialitskaya (ed.), *The Second Birth: The Reconstruction of the Jewish Collection of the Belarusian State Museum in the 1920s–1930s* (Minsk: 2021).

12. Zeev Levin, *Collectivization and Social Engineering: Soviet Administration and the Jews of Uzbekistan, 1917–1939* (Leiden: 2015), 222–225; Michael Nosonovsky, "Isaak Lurie i evreiskii muzei v Samarkande," in *Elena Korovai: inoi vzgliad: Bukharskie evrei v russkoi kul'ture*, ed. Rafael Nektalov (Moscow: 2020), 266–273.

13. Shota Bostanashvili, "Sinagogi Gruzii," in *Stranitsy istorii evreev Gruzii (po sledam ekspeditsii 2013 g.)*, ed. Mikhail Chlenov (Moscow: 2014), 50. The history of the museum was researched by Marina Shcherbakova and presented in her unpublished paper, "The Museum of the Jews of Georgia (1933–1952) in the Context of Soviet Ethnography" at the 17th World Congress of Jewish Studies, Jerusalem, 6–10 August 2017.

14. Marina Shcherbakova, "K voprosu o kontseptual'nom razvitii evreiskogo muzeia i etnografii evreev na territorii Ukrainy v 1917–1941 gg.," *Judaic-Slavic Journal* no. 1(2) (2019), 49.

15. Vera Solodova, "Odesskii Muzei Evreiskoi Kul'tury (1927–1941)," online at: http://ju.org.ua/ru/publicism/210.html (accessed 14 September 2021); Yakov Bruk, *Yakov Kagan-Shabshai i ego Evreiskaia khudozhestvennaia galereia* (Moscow: 2015), 53–56; Shcherbakova, "K voprosy o kontseptual'nom razvitii," 59–62.

16. Eugeny Kotlyar, "Tvorcheskoe nasledie Ushera Hitera i Elyukima Maltsa v kontekste razvitiia evreiskoi etnografii i muzeinoi praktiki mezhvoennogo vremeni," *Judaic-Slavic Journal* no. 1(2) (2019), 81–118.

17. Shcherbakova, "K voprosu o kontseptual'nom razvitii," 62–67. For example, on the initiative of Feodosii Molchanovkii, the founder of the Social-Historical Museum in Berdychiv, part of the Berdychiv Jewish cemetery and the wooden synagogue in Pohrebyshche were listed as protected monuments. See Eugeny Kotlyar, "Evreiskie muzei pervoi treti XX veka (L'vov – Sankt-Peterburg–Odessa–Kiev)," *Visnik KhDADM* 12 (2009), 126.

18. Eugeny Kotlyar, "Danylo Shcherbakivs'kyi: naukovi rozvidki ta vidkryttia evreis'koho mystetstva," *Narodoznavchi zoshyty* no. 5(119) (2014), 884–913.

19. Eugeny Kotlyar, "Ukraïns'ka yudaïka Pavla Zholtovs'koho," *Narodoznavchi zoshyty*, no. 2(128) (2016), 418–50.

20. Eugeny Kotlyar, "Vyrvannye evreiskie stranitsy: po sledam izdanii po iudaike Vladimira Gagenmeistera," *Tsaytshrift* 2 (2012), 64–81; idem, "Pam'iatky evreis'koho mystetstva Kam'ianechchyny u vydanniakh shkoly Hahenmeistera: poshuky i vidkryttia," *Narodoznavchi zoshyty* 6 (2014), 1474–1487.

21. Vol'ga Kukunia, "Sinahohi Belarusi: inventaryzatsyinyia materyialy, 1945–1949 hh.," in *Sinahohi Belarusi: biuleten' manitorynhu histarychnai prastory* (Warsaw: 2017), 95.

22. Kravtsov, "Studies of Jewish Architecture," 186.

23. Alla Sokolova, "Grafika i fotografii Solomona Yudovina iz sobraniia Gosudarstvennogo muzeia istorii religii: mezhdu etnografiei i antireligioznoi propagandoi 1930-kh gg.," *Trudy Gosydarstvennogo muzeia istorii religii* 18 (2016), 68–94; 316–26; idem, "Between Ethnography of Religion and Anti-Religious Propaganda: Jewish Graphics in the Leningrad and Moscow Museums in 1930s," in *Three Cities of Yiddish: St Petersburg, Warsaw and Moscow*, ed. Gennady Estraikh and Mikhail Krutikov (Cambridge: 2017), 158–193.

24. Arie Yodfat, "Hadat hayehudit bemisgeret hama'amad haḥuki shel hadat bevrit hamoa-tzot," *Beḥinot* 1 (1970), 132–134; Joshua Rothenberg, "The Legal Status of Religion in the Soviet Union," in *Aspects of Religion in the Soviet Union, 1917–1967*, ed. Richard H. Marshall (Chicago: 1971), 63–66.

25. Arkadii Zeltser, *Evrei sovetskoi provintsii: Vitebsk i mestechki* (Moscow: 2003), 229.

26. On the number of objects in synagogues see Vladimir Levin, "The Social Function of Synagogue Ceremonial Objects in Volhynia," in Sergey Kravtsov and Vladimir Levin, *Synagogues in Ukraine: Volhynia* (Jerusalem: 2017), 139–173.

27. Tatiana Romanovskaya, "'Sovershenno sekretno . . .': istoriia kollektsii iudaiki Muzeia istoricheskikh dragotsennostei Ukrainy," *Egupets* 8 (2001), 398–406.

28. The Jewish Communist University in Vitsebsk was created in autumn of 1921; by the end of the year it was renamed the Jewish Provincial Party School. See Zeltser, *Evrei sovetskoi provintsii*, 146.

29. Ibid., 237–241. Cf. Konstantin Karpekin, *Iudeiskie obshchiny v Belorusskoi SSR (ianvar' 1919 – sentiabr' 1939 g.)* (Vitebsk: 2016), 63.

30. Bemporad, *Becoming Soviet Jews*, 114–115.

31. A. Lebedev and V. Pichukov, "Politika sovetskoi vlasti v otnoshenii iudeiskoi religii na Gomel'shchine v 1920–1930-kh gg.," *Tsaytshrift* 2 (2012), 30.

32. Zvi Y. Gitelman, *Jewish Nationality and Soviet Politics: The Jewish Sections of the CPSU, 1917–1930* (Princeton: 1972), 314.

33. Sheila Fitzpatrick, *The Russian Revolution*, 2nd ed. (Oxford: 1994), 120–147.

34. Zeltser, *Evrei sovetskoi provintsii*, 253–254; Jeffrey Veidlinger, *In the Shadow of the Shtetl: Small-Town Jewish Life in Soviet Ukraine* (Bloomington: 2013), 117.

35. Zeltser, *Evrei sovetskoi provintsii*, 257. According to official data quoted by Leonid Smilovitsky, 633 out of 704 synagogues were closed in Belorussia by 1937; see idem, *Jewish Life in Belarus: The Final Decade of the Stalin Regime (1944–53)* (Budapest: 2014), 50.

36. Michael Beizer, *Evrei Leningrada, 1917–1939: natsional'naia zhizn' i sovetizatsiia* (Moscow/Jerusalem: 1999), 218–235; idem, *Our Legacy: The CIS Synagogues, Past and Present* (Moscow/Jerusalem: 2002), 29–36; Zeltser, *Evrei sovetskoi provintsii*, 253–257, 264; Veidlinger, *In the Shadow of the Shtetl*, 113–120; Bemporad, *Becoming Soviet Jews*, 117–119; Vladimir Levin, "The Legal History of Synagogues of Volhynia," in Kravtsov and Levin, *Synagogues in Ukraine: Volhynia*, 41–43; Karpekin, *Iudeiskie obshchiny*, 66–71, 140–142.

37. To the best of my knowledge, Karpekin's is the only work that asks the question about the fate of objects from the closed synagogues; see *Iudeiskie obshchiny*, 82–85.

38. Sokolova, "Grafika i fotografii," 75, 83.

39. This is a conclusion from the 2015 and 2021 research trips by the Center for Jewish Art at the Hebrew University of Jerusalem to Siberia and to the Volga.

40. Lebedev and Pichukov, "Politika sovetskoi vlasti," 30.

41. Catriona Kelly, "Socialist Churches: Heritage Preservation and 'Cultic Buildings' in Leningrad, 1924–1940," *Slavic Review* 71, no. 4 (Winter 2012), 792–823.

42. Ibid., 820. See also Poliakova, *Okhrana kul'turnogo naslediia Rossii*, 55–73.

43. Kelly, "Socialist Churches," 816, 821.

44. Vladimir Levin, "Maps, Synagogues, the City of Vilne, and Zalmen Szyk," *Colloquia* 48 (2022): 98–112.

45. Bemporad, *Becoming Soviet Jews*, 117.

46. Vladimir Levin, "Sinagogi Belarusi: issledovanie, sokhranenie, pamiat'," *Tsaytshrift* 7 (2020), 9–10.

47. Kravtsov and Levin, *Volhynia*.

48. Svetlana Malysheva, *"Na miru krasna": instrumentalizatsiia smerti v Sovetskoi Rossii* (Moscow: 2019), 269–282; Mordechai Altshuler, "Jewish Burial Rites and Cemeteries in the USSR in the Interwar Period," *Jews in Eastern Europe* no. 1–2(47–48) (2002), 85–104. On the closing of Jewish cemeteries in Belarus in the interwar period see Karpekin, *Iudeiskie obshchiny*, 72–75.

49. Anastasia Felcher, "Beyond the Trauma: New Perspectives for Preservation, Management and Museum Representation of Jewish Cultural Heritage in Post-Soviet Cities" (Ph.D. thesis, IMT School for Advanced Studies Lucca, 2016), 142–143.

50. Ibid., 148.

51. Beniamin Lukin, "Evreiskoe kladbishche (Prospekt Aleksandrovskoi Fermy 66a)," in *Istoricheskie kladbishcha Peterburga: spravochnik-putevoditel'*, ed. A.V. Kobak and Yu.M. Piriutko (St. Petersburg: 1993), 455, 457.

52. On the Shoah in the USSR, see Mordechai Altshuler, "The Unique Features of the Holocaust in the Soviet Union," in *Jews and Jewish Life in Russia and the Soviet Union*, ed. Yaacov Ro'i (Ilford: 1995), 171–188; Yitzhak Arad, *The Holocaust in the Soviet Union* (Lincoln/Jerusalem: 2009).

53. Kravtsov and Levin, *Volhynia*, 339, 349, 354–358.

54. A document of 1945 states that 532 synagogues were destroyed in the occupied territories. A document of 1958 concerning Belarus notes that 91 synagogues were destroyed. In Vinnytsia, 22 synagogues were destroyed. Mordechai Altshuler, *Yahadut bamakhbesh hasovyeti: bein dat lezehut yehudit bevrit hamoatzot, 1941–1964* (Jerusalem: 2008), 56 (n. 67).

55. The Bezalel Narkiss Index of Jewish Art (hereafter IJA, accessible at cja.huji.ac.il/browser.php?mode = main), ID 24043; ID 24171.

56. Kukunia, "Sinahohi Belarusi," 106–109, 111–113, 115–119.

57. IJA, ID 14955.

58. Michael Nosonovsky, "Evreiskie nadgrobnye nadpisi iz Glubokogo kak istoricheskii istochnik i iavlenie kul'tury," in *Glubokoe: pamiat'o evreiskom mestechke*, ed. Olga Belova (Moscow: 2017), 289.

59. Krzysztof Bielawski, *Zagłada cmentarzy żydowskich* (Warsaw: 2020).

60. Sinila, "Zbory iaureiskaha addzela," 28–30.

61. Arkadi Zeltser, *Unwelcome Memory: Holocaust Monuments in the Soviet Union*, trans. Avram S. Brown (Jerusalem: 2018).

62. On the museum, see David E. Fishman, *The Book Smugglers: Partisans, Poets, and the Race to Save Jewish Treasures from the Nazis* (Lebanon, N.H.: 2017), 137–235; idem, "Evreiskii muzei v Vilniuse, 1944–1949 gg.," in Kupovetskii (ed.), *Sovetskaia iudaika*, 242–260.

63. Robert Weinberg, "Jewish Revival in Birobidzhan in the Mirror of *Birobidzhanskaya Zvezda*, 1946–49," *East European Jewish Affairs* 26, no. 1 (June 1996), 51.

64. M.S. Butinova and N.P. Krasnikov, *Muzei istorii religii i ateizma: spravochnik-putevoditel'* (Moscow/Leningrad: 1965), 186.

65. A more developed showcase appeared in the museum in the late 1970s. I thank Alla Sokolova for this information.

66. P.M. Avramenko, M.V. Kosiv, and Yu.M. Matiukhin, *L'vivs'kyi muzei istoriï relihiï ta ateïzmu: putivnyk* (Lviv: 1975), 52, 150–167.

67. V.M. Vikhot', M.V. Kosiv, and Yu.M. Matiukhin, *L'vivs'kyi muzei istoriï relihiï ta ateïzmu: narys-putivnyk* (Lviv: 1974), 35.

68. IJA, ID 11537.

69. E.N. Ulitskii, *Istoriia moskovskoi evreiskoi obshchiny: dokumenty i materialy* (Moscow: 2006), 50.

70. Genrikh Agranovskii and Irina Guzenberg, *Vilnius: po sledam Litovskogo Ierusalima. pamiatnye mesta ereiskoi istorii i kul'tury*, 2nd ed. (Vilnius: 2016), 673–676.

71. Michael Nosonovsky and Alexandra Fishel, "Ob unichtozhennom stareishem v Vostochnoi Evrope (1520 g.) ashkenazskom nadgrobii iz Ostroga," *Tirosh: Trudy po iudaike, slavistike, orientalistike* 20 (2020), 184–187; Felcher, "Beyond the Trauma," 148.

72. Agranovskii and Guzenberg, *Vilnius*, 685–691; for Barysaŭ, see IJA, ID 65658.

73. Interview with Sandra Petrukonytė (19 July 2021).

74. The State Archives of Ivano-Frankivsk Region (hereafter: DAIFO), coll. 388sch, inv. 2, file 63, fol. 1; file 64, fol. 31. Copies in the Central Archives of the History of the Jewish People in Jerusalem (hereafter: CAHJP), HM2/9129.3 and HM2/9129.4, available also at jgaliciabu-kovina.net/uk/133667/document/closing-jewish-cemeteries-kalusz-and-solotvin and jgali-ciabukovina.net/133683/document/closing-jewish-cemeteries-kalusz-and-solotvin-response, (accessed 11 July 2021).

75. Nosonovsky and Fishel, "Ob unichtozhennom," 184, 186.

76. Ilya Dvorkin, "Staroe evreiskoe kladbishche v g. Medzhibozhe," in *Istoriia evreev na Ukraine i v Belorussii. Ekspeditsii, pamiatniki, nakhodki*, vol. 2, *Trudy po iudaike*, ed. Valery Dymshyts (St. Petersburg: 1994), 191. For photographs of the removed tombstones, see IJA, ID 33245.

77. IJA, ID 38488. For wooden tombstones in Romania, see IJA, ID 10117; ID 10118; ID 22009; ID 22007.

78. IJA, ID 9354.

79. IJA, ID 30706.

80. For example, the commissioner for religious cults of the Ukrainian SSR dealt with the closing of the synagogue in Rozhniativ and Catholic churches in Lysets and Nadvorna in the same letter in 1948. See DAIFO, coll. 388sch, inv. 2, file 63, fol. 13; copy in CAHJP, HM2/9129.3; jgaliciabukovina.net/133671/document/about-closing-synagogue-rozhniatovo (accessed 14 September 2021).

81. For an overview of the postwar usage of former synagogues in Belarus, see Smilovitsky, *Jewish Life in Belarus*, 50–54.

82. Vladimir Levin, "Synagogues, Batei Midrash and Kloyzn in Vilnius," in *Synagogues in Lithuania: A Catalogue*, ed. Aliza Cohen-Mushlin, Sergey Kravtsov, Vladimir Levin, Giedrė Mickūnaitė, and Jurgita Šiaučiūnaitė-Verbickienė, vol. 2 (Vilnius: 2012), 289; Agranovskii and Guzenberg, *Vilnius*, 84–88.

83. Uladzimir Dzianisau, "Minskaia halounaia sinahoha, XVII—pachatak XX st.," in *Sinahohi Belarusi: Biuleten' manitorynhu histarychnai prastory*, 10.

84. Agranovskii and Guzenberg, *Vilnius*, 85; Fishman, *The Book Smugglers*, 236–237.

85.   Kravtsov and Levin, *Volhynia*, 411.

86.   Kukunia, "Sinahohi Belarusi."

87.   All of the following were edited by S.V. Martseleu: *Zbor pomnikau historyi i kul'tury Belarusi: Hrodzenskaia voblasts'* (Minsk: 1986), 77–78, 304; *Zbor pomnikau historyi i kul'tury Belarusi: Mahiliouskaia voblasts'* (Minsk: 1986), 132, 382; *Zbor pomnikau historyi i kul'tury Belarusi: Minskaia voblasts'*, vol. 1 (Minsk: 1987), 211–12; *Zbor pomnikau historyi i kul'tury Belarusi: Minsk* (Minsk: 1988), 58; *Svod pamiatnikov istorii i kul'tury Belorussii: Brestskaia oblast'* (Minsk: 1990), 248, 370, 382. The *Collection of Monuments* also includes some memorials on the mass graves of Jews killed in the Holocaust.

88.   I.A. Ignatkin (ed.), *Pamiatniki gradostroitel'stva i arkhitektury Ukrainskoi SSR: illiustrirovannyi spravochnik-katalog*, vol. 2 (Kiev: 1985), 37, 53; G.N. Logvin (ed.), *Pamiatniki gradostroitel'stva i arkhitektury Ukrainskoi SSR: illiustrirovannyi spravochnik-katalog*, vol. 3 (Kiev: 1985), 104, 154–155; idem (ed.), *Pamiatniki gradostroitel'stva i arkhitektury Ukrainskoi SSR: illiustrirovannyi spravochnik-katalog*, vol. 4 (Kiev: 1986), 43, 61–62, 199.

89.   Logvin (ed.), *Pamiatniki gradostroitel'stva*, 3:155.

90.   Sergey Kravtsov, "Na ratunek Wielkiej Synagodze w Brodach," *Sztuka i Krytyka / Art and Criticism* no. 10(85) (2019), 30.

91.   On the synagogues in Siberia, see the forthcoming book on Jewish material culture in Siberia by Anna Berezin and myself.

92.   Kravtsov and Levin, *Volhynia*, 368; Agranovskii and Guzenberg, *Vilnius*, 85.

93.   Kravtsov and Levin, *Volhynia*, 237.

94.   Zoya Arshavsky and Ruth Jacoby, *Beniyah yehudit besamarkand: beito shel Rafael Abramov* (Jerusalem: 2015); Zoya Arshavsky, "Batei hamegurim," in *Merkaz asiyah: bukhara veafganistan*, ed. Zeev Levin (Jerusalem: 2018), 297–306.

95.   On Jewish life in Transnistria, see Veidlinger, *In the Shadow of the Shtetl*, 186–231.

96.   In the last two decades, the majority of these houses were reconstructed beyond recognition or razed to give way to new buildings. On the traditional Jewish dwellings in Podolia, see Alla Sokolova, "Architectural Space of the Shtetl—Street—House: Jewish Homes in the Shtetls of Eastern Podolia," *Trumah: Zeitschrift der Hochschule für Jüdische Studien* 7 (1998), 35–85; idem, "Arkhitektura shtetla v kontekste traditsionnoi kul'tury," in Beniamin Lukin, Boris Khaimovich, and Alla Sokolova, *100 evreiskikh mestechek Ukrainy: istoricheskii putevoditel'*, vol. 2 (St. Petersburg: 2000), 53–84; idem, "Brick as an Instrument of Innovative Assault: The Transformation of the House-Building Tradition in the Shtetls of Podolia in the Late 19th and Early 20th Centuries," in *Central and East European Jews at the Crossroads of Tradition and Modernity*, ed. Jurgita Šiaučiūnaitė-Verbickienė and Larisa Lempertienė (Vilnius: 2006), 188–219; idem, "Shtetl Houses and Synagogues: From the History of Architecture to Stories about Architectural Monuments," in *Jewish Architecture in Europe*, ed. Aliza Cohen-Mushlin and Harmen H. Thies (Petersberg: 2010), 159–173.

97.   Shimon Yantovskii, *Sud'by evreiskikh obshchin i ikh sinagog, SSSR, 1976–1987* (Jerusalem: 2003), 16.

98.   Israel Tayar, *Sinagoga razgromlennaia, no nepokorionnaia* (Jerusalem: 1987).

99.   Igor Krupnik, "Kak my zanimalis' istoriei... i etnografiei. K 35-letiiu Evreiskoi istoriko-etnograficheskoi komissii, 1981–1990 gg.," in Kupovetskii (ed.), *Sovetskaia iudaika*, 286–360; Michael Beizer, "Podpol'naia iudaika v Leningrade v 1980-kh godakh," in ibid., 361–378. On the activities of groups studying the Holocaust in those years, see Zeltser, *Unwelcome Memory*, 323–336.

100.   Mikhail Beizer, *The Jews of St. Petersburg: Excursions through a Noble Past*, ed. Martin Gilbert (Philadelphia: 1989); idem, *Evrei v Peterburge* (Jerusalem: 1989).

101.   On this group, see Semion Goldin's essay "Becoming Jews: The Petersburg Jewish University in the 1990s," in this volume. The name of the city was changed in 1991.

102.   For an overview of Jewish museums in the post-Soviet space, see Boris Khaimovich, "Evreiskie muzei na postsovetskom prostranstve: evreiskii i neevreiskii obshchepoliticheskii kontekst," in *Ezhegodnik EAEK 2020–2021* (Herzliya: 2021), 119–132.

103. Mariëlla P. Beukers and Renée Waale (eds.), *Tracing An-Sky: Jewish Collections from the State Ethnographic Museum in St. Petersburg* (exhibition catalog, Joods Historisch Museum, Amsterdam) (Zwolle: 1992); Rivka Gonen (ed.), *Back to the Shtetl: An-Sky and the Jewish Ethnographic Expedition, 1912–1914. From the Collections of the State Ethnographic Museum in St. Petersburg* (Jerusalem: 1994); Uritskaia and Yakerson, *Evreiskie sokrovishcha Peterburga.*

104. Alexander Kantsedikas, Yelena Volkovinskaya, and Tatiana Romanovskaya, *Silver* (Moscow: 1991); Alexander Kantsedikas, *Bronze* (Moscow: 1991).

105. Sarah Harel Hoshen (ed.), *Treasures of Jewish Galicia: Judaica from the Museum of Ethnography and Crafts in Lvov, Ukraine* (Tel Aviv: 1994).

106. Interview with Alla Sokolova (7 July 2021).

107. Shimon Iakerson and Marina Shcherbakova, "A Museum in a Museum—the Experience of Exhibiting Jewish Collections in the Russian Museum of Ethnography, St. Petersburg," *East European Jewish Affairs* 45, no. 2–3 (2015), 326–329.

108. Zeev Levin, "The Bukharan-Jewish Museum in Samarkand: Memory Preservation of a Rapidly-Diminishing Community," *East European Jewish Affairs* 45, no. 2–3 (2015), 305–311.

109. Interview with the curator of the museum, Liudmila Tsyrempilova, https://burunen.ru/news/culture/49226-buryatiya-multikulturnaya-polutoravekovaya-istoriya-iudaizma-v-res publike (accessed 10 July 2021).

110. Milda Jakulytė-Vasil, "Art-yudaïka u muzeiakh Lytvy," *Ehupets* 26 (2016), 289–298.

111. Ilya Lensky, "Representing the Jews in Regional Museums of Latvia: Absence – Presence – Exhibition," unpublished paper given at the GEOP Interdisciplinary Research Workshop "Representations of Jewish-Slavic Relations in Museums and Internet Databases," Polin Museum, Warsaw, 13–15 June 2018.

112. Interview with Ilya Lensky (5 July 2021).

113. Rachel Margolis, "Nachalo," in *Žydų muziejus. Evreiskii muzei. The Jewish Museum*, ed. Evsey Ceitlin (Vilnius: 1994), 16–17; information online at: https://en.wikipedia.org/wiki/David_Baazov_Museum_of_History_of_Jews_of_Georgia.

114. On the Jewish History and Culture Museum of Belarus, in Minsk (founded 2002), the Museum of Jewish Heritage of Moldova, in Chişinău (founded 2005, closed 2018), the Museum of the History of the Odesa Jews "Migdal Shorashim" (founded 2002), and the museum room "Tracing Galician Jews" at the Hesed-Arieh Jewish Home in Lviv (founded c. 2001), see Anastasia Felcher, "Small Exhibits, Major Steps: Four Post-Soviet Jewish Museums," *East European Jewish Affairs* 45, no. 2–3 (2015), 312–320; idem, "Beyond the Trauma," 185–189, 193–196, 210–216; Magdalena Waligórska, "Jewish Heritage and the New Belarusian National Identity Project," *East European Politics and Societies* 20, no. 10 (2015), 4–5. See also online sites for the Jewish Memory and Holocaust in Ukraine Museum in Dnipro (opened in 2012), at: jmhum.org/en; the Jews in Latgale Museum in Daugavpils, at: www.jewishlatgale.lv/en; the Estonian Jewish Museum in Tallinn, at: museum.jewish.ee. For the communal museums in Tver, Yaroslavl (established in 1997 by Miron Sterin), Kostroma (founded 2021), Nizhnii Novgorod, Kazan, and Saratov, see IJA, ID 33674; ID 40076; ID 39992; ID 39986; ID 40072; ID 40078. For the Museum of Mountain Jews that opened in Quba, Azerbaijan, in 2020, see, for instance, www.thej.ca/2020/08/26/azerbaijans-mountain-jews-a-model-for-jewish-muslim-coexistence.

115. Felcher, "Small Exhibits, Major Steps," 319.

116. Olga Gershenson, "The Jewish Museum and Tolerance Center in Moscow: Judaism for the Masses," *East European Jewish Affairs* 45, nos. 2–3 (2015), 158–173; Benjamin Nathans, "Torahs, Tanks, and Tech: Moscow's Jewish Museum and Tolerance Center," ibid., 190–199. Putin's donation was reported online: https://novayagazeta.ru/news/2007/06/06/14128-putin-perechislit-v-fond-stroitelstva-evreyskogo-muzeya-tolerantnosti-svoyu-mesyachnuyu-zarpl atu (accessed 1 November 2021).

117. Boris Khaimovich and Hillel (Grigory) Kazovsky, "The History and Collections of the Museum," in *Museum of Jewish History in Russia*, ed. Hillel (Grigory) Kazovsky, Maria

Kaspina, and Boris Khaimovich, vol. 1 (Moscow: 2015), 8–14; Maria Kaspina and Hillel Kazovsky, "The Museum of Jewish History in Russia, Moscow," *East European Jewish Affairs* 45, no. 2–3 (2015), 323–325.

118. Olga Goleta, "Spuren jüdischen Lebens in Belarus – Die Geschichte der Zerstörung jüdischer Friedhöfe nach 1945," in *Jüdisches Kulturerbe (re-)präsentieren*, ed. Katrin Kessler et al. (Braunschweig: 2019), 75–76.

119. Iosif Levinson, "Chto by ne kanulo v nebytie," in Ceitlin (ed.), *Žydų muziejus*, 254–267.

120. Genrikh Agranovskii, "Vekhi istorii," in ibid., 268–270.

121. Felcher, "Beyond the Trauma," 146, 148. For the uncovering of fragments in Brest, Rohatyn, and Husiatyn see *Jewish Heritage Europe*, online at: jewish-heritage-europe.eu (hereafter JHE), (3 June 2014), (2 July 2021), (9 November 2014), (22 March 2017); see also vice.com/en/article/av4qkp/jewish-graves-in-brest-belarussia-kate-samuelson-333 (accessed 19 September 2021).

122. Online at: samgrubersjewishartmonuments.blogspot.com/2011/12/lithuania-vilnius-middle-school-has.html; see also: defendinghistory.com/when-old-stones-speak-to-middle-school-pupils-jewish-gravestones-in-a-vilnius-school-yard/26651 (accessed 17 October 2021); see also JHE (12 December 2011), (24 June 2016), (16 November 2016), (22 January 2019).

123. Interview with M.D. Evtushenko by Vladimir Levin and Arkadi Zeltser (17 May 2010). See also IJA, ID 8344.

124. JHE (20 August 2017); IJA, ID 7917.

125. Avrom Rekhtman, *Di yidishe etnografie un folklor* (Buenos Aires: 1958), 115–118, 179. Cf. Vladimir Levin, "Material Culture," in *Studying Hasidism: Sources, Methods, Perspectives*, ed. Marcin Wodziński (New Brunswick: 2019), 241.

126. IJA, ID 26932.

127. IJA, ID 14076.

128. JHE (17 August 2021).

129. On the legal aspects of the return of synagogues, see Beizer, *Our Legacy*, 49–64.

130. Ilia Rodov, "Ars Brevis, Vita Longa: On Preservation of Synagogue Art," *Studia Hebraica* 9–10 (2009/2010), 96–98. During the postwar period, the Tsori Gilead synagogue was used as a warehouse and thus its murals were not damaged; it was returned to the community in 1989.

131. For example, the Golden Rose Synagogue in Dnipro, the Brodsky Synagogue in Kyiv, the Main Synagogue and the Chabad (former Tailors') Synagogue in Odesa, the synagogues in Nizhnii Novgorod, Tver', Yaroslavl, Tiumen, Tomsk, Irkutsk and Vladivostok.

132. Yvonne Kleinmann, *Neue Orte – neue Menschen: Jüdische Lebensformen in St. Petersburg und Moskau im 19. Jahrhundert* (Göttingen: 2006), 340–344.

133. IJA, ID 10220.

134. On the history of the research of synagogues, see Vilma Gradinskaite, "Lithuanian Synagogues: From the First Descriptions to Systematic Research," *Arts* 9, no. 2 (21 May 2020), 13–14. On the synagogues, see Marija Rupeikienė, *Nykstantis kultūros paveldas: Lietuvos sinagogų architektūra* (Vilnius: 2003); in English (trans. Kamilė Rupeikaitė, ed. Joseph Everatt), *A Disappearing Heritage: The Synagogue Architecture of Lithuania* (Vilnius: 2008); Alfredas Jomantas (ed.), *Jewish Cultural Heritage in Lithuania* (Vilnius: 2006); Aliza Cohen-Mushlin, Sergey Kravtsov, Vladimir Levin, Giedrė Mickūnaitė and Jurgita Šiaučiūnaitė-Verbickienė (eds.), *Synagogues in Lithuania: A Catalogue*, 2 vols. (Vilnius: 2010–2012); Aistė Niunkaitė Račiūnienė, *Lietuvos žydų tradicinio meno ir simbolių pasaulis: Atvaizdai, vaizdiniai ir tekstai* (Vilnius: 2011). To date, the only full-length publication about the synagogues of Latvia is that of Rita Bogdanova, *Latvia: Synagogues and Rabbis, 1918–1940* (Riga: 2004).

135. The Great Beit Midrash (2002), the Great Synagogue (2003–2004), and the Great Kloyz (1993 and 2020–2021) in Kėdainiai; the White and Red Synagogues in Joniškis (2002–2017 and 2007–2014); the Beit Midrash (2001–2007) and the Great Synagogue (began in

2021) in Kalvarija; Hakhnasat Orḥim Synagogue in Marijampolė (2000); Zavl's Kloyz on Gėlių St. in Vilnius (since 2015); masonry synagogue in Alytus (2017–2021), Žemaičių Naumiestis (since 2019), and Švėkšna; the wooden synagogues in Žiežmariai (2016–2020), Alanta, and Kurkliai (both since 2019). See Cohen-Mushlin et al. (eds.), *Synagogues in Lithuania* and JHE.

136. JHE (4 October 2015), (24 May 2017).

137. The synagogue in Sabile (1990s, 2021), the synagogue and the beit midrash in Kuldīga (2000s), the wooden synagogues in Ludza and Rēzekne (both 2016). The information derives from the interview with Ilya Lensky (5 July 2021), and JHE.

138. Cohen-Mushlin et al. (eds.), *Synagogues in Lithuania*, 2:40.

139. IJA, ID 9490.

140. For a detailed presentation of the present state of synagogues in Belarus, see I. Romanova and I. Shenderovich, "Istoriia sinagog posle sinagog," *Tsaytshrift* 6 (2019), 22–45; Aleksei Eremenko and Mordechai Raikhinshtein, *Sinagogi Belarusi: katalog sushchestvuiushchikh zdanii* (Minsk: 2019).

141. As of 2021, the Great Synagogues in Bykhaŭ and Slonim still have roofs, while the Great Synagogue in Stolin stands roofless, and the roof of the Great Synagogue in Ruzhany collapsed in 2018 or 2019. See IJA, ID 8337; ID 33716; ID 31422; ID 34207.

142. IJA, ID 9361.

143. The synagogue was returned in 1991 and renovated in 2013. See IJA, ID 33202; Romanova and Shenderovich, "Istoriia sinagog posle sinagog," 40. Historic synagogues in Babruisk, Homel, and Pinsk were also returned to the local Jewish communities, but their interiors are completely new; see Eremenko and Raikhinshtein, *Sinagogi Belarusi*, 21, 47, 117.

144. The Great Synagogue in Slonim, after three unsuccessful auctions, was purchased by a private person in January 2021; as of September 2021, the Great Synagogue in Astryna, the Beit Midrash in Vasilishki, and the Great Lubavich Synagogue in Vitsebsk are for sale. See JHE (7 January 2021), (2, 25, and 26 February 2021).

145. Stepan Stureiko, "Sokhranenie byvshikh sinagog v Belarusi: kommunikativnoe izmerenie problemy," *Tsaytshrift* 6 (2019), 14; Romanova and Shenderovich, "Istoriia sinagog posle sinagog," 35–36.

146. Romanova and Shenderovich, "Istoriia sinagog posle sinagog," 39.

147. Stureiko, "Sokhranenie byvshikh sinagog," 13. See also Levin, "Sinagogi Belarusi."

148. See, for instance, *Sinahohi Belarusi: Biuleten' manitorynhu histarychnai prastory*; Eremenko and Raikhinshtein, *Sinagogi Belarusi*; see also volumes 6 (2019) and 7 (2020) of the periodical *Tsaytshrif*, which are devoted to the topic of heritage and synagogues.

149. Online information at: historicsynagogueseurope.org (and also cja.huji.ac.il/mhs/browser.php?mode = home_page).

150. JHE (5 September 2016). On the project, see Sergey Kravtsov, "Prostranstvo sinagog vo L'vove: istoriia, vyzovy i problemy rekonstruktsii," in *Ezhegodnik EAEK 2020–2021*, 133–144.

151. Sergey R. Kravtsov, "The Great Maharsha Synagogue in Ostroh: Memory and Oblivion: Have We Reached the Point of No Return?" JHE (17 December 2015); see also later posts (12 March 2017), (26 August 2018), (2 November 2020).

152. JHE (5 December 2012); interview with Arthur Friedman (9 September 2014).

153. JHE (30 March 2017), (12 February 2018).

154. JHE (4 May 2018), (9 September 2020), (3 December 2018).

155. JHE (17 January 2021).

156. JHE (6 November 2016).

157. JHE (25 February 2018).

158. JHE (19 April 2021).

159. Boris Khaimovich, *The Murals in the Novoselitsia Synagogue* (Kyiv: 2016), 57.

160. Interview with Irina Shikhova (20 July 2021).

161. IJA, ID 22238.

162. Bostanashvili, "Sinagogi Gruzii." See also IJA.

163. Zoya Arshavsky, "Batei hakneset," in *Merkaz asiayah*, 191–200.

164. IJA, ID 23700; ID 23698; ID 23706; ID 23694. On the Soviet-era objects in Birobidzhan, see the forthcoming book on Jewish material culture in Siberia by Anna Berezin and myself.

165. IJA, ID 40014.

166. Zeltser, *Unwelcome Memory*, 330, 336.

Russian Jewry in the Post-Soviet Era: Socio-Demographic Transformation

Mark Tolts

(THE HEBREW UNIVERSITY)

The post-Soviet period has been a time of dramatic socio-demographic transformation in Russia. The transition of Russian society to life under capitalism inevitably influenced the country's Jewish population, and the aim of this article is to study the effects of this great shift on Russian Jewry. The significant topics to be explored include the increase of mixed marriage among the Russian Jewish population, as well as the rising prominence of Hebrew and the demise of Yiddish, changes in adult Jews' educational attainments by area, the differentiation in the attained levels of higher education between Jewish females and males, and transformations in the occupational profile of Moscow's Jews.

Sources of the Study

For this study, I used indicators that were computed based on data from the last Soviet census of 1989 and the two Russian censuses of 2002 and 2010.[1] The 1989 Soviet census, which covered the entire Russian Jewish population, gave us a good starting point for evaluation of post-Soviet dynamics. However, the post-Soviet Russian censuses do not provide full coverage of the Jewish population. The Jewish population of Russia at the time of each census has been estimated at 254,000 in 2002 and 200,000 in 2010.[2] These estimates are higher than the Jewish census figures for which we have socio-demographic data that were used in our study: 229,900 and 156,800, respectively (see Table 1). Thus, the census data supplied us with ample detailed information that covers most of Russian Jewry in the post-Soviet period: 90.5 percent in 2002, and 78.4 percent in 2010.

Only a very small fraction of each gap between my estimates and the above-noted census figures may be accounted for by the numbers of Jews separately recorded as Georgian Jews, Mountain Jews, Central Asian (Bukharan Jews), and Krymchaks. The 2002 Russian census reported only 3,394 Mountain Jews, 53 Georgian Jews, 54 Central Asian (Bukharan) Jews, and 157 Krymchaks. The next Russian census

Mark Tolts, *Russian Jewry in the Post-Soviet Era: Socio-Demographic Transformation* In: *Becoming Post-Communist.* Edited by: Eli Lederhendler, Oxford University Press. © Oxford University Press 2023. DOI: 10.1093/oso/9780197687215.003.0007

Table 1. Distribution of the Jewish Population in the Russian Federation, by Area, 1989, 2002, and 2010

Census	Total	Moscow city	St. Petersburg city	Provinces
Thousands				
1989[a]	551.0	175.7	106.5	268.8
2002	229.9	79.4	36.6	113.9
2010	156.8	53.1	24.1	79.6
Percent				
1989[a]	100	32	19	49
2002	100	34	16	50
2010	100	34	15	51

[a] Including those recorded as Georgian Jews, Mountain Jews, Central Asian (Bukharan Jews), and Krymchaks.
Sources: 1989 Soviet census; 2002 and 2010 Russian censuses.

of 2010 reported even lower numbers: 762 Mountain Jews, 78 Georgian Jews, 32 Central Asian (Bukharan) Jews, and 90 Krymchaks. Therefore, the gaps between the census figures for Jews and the estimates presented above may be mostly attributed to people included in my estimates as Jews but who, in the censuses, belong to the group of people whose ethnicity was not stated/known.[3]

For the purposes of this study, the Russian Jewish population will be divided, wherever possible, into three groups by area: the Jews of Moscow, St. Petersburg, and those of the provinces (outside those two major cities). Almost all Jews in contemporary Russia are urban dwellers. Therefore, urban ethnic Russians will be used as a group for comparison.

Sex Imbalance and Mixed Marriage

The observed increase in mixed marriages is not merely attributable to trends toward assimilation but also stems from certain demographic realities. The primary demographic factor in the rise of intermarriage rates in the former Soviet Union (FSU) before the start of the mass emigration of recent decades was the relative shortage of Jewish marriage partners for Jewish males. According to the 1989 census, the number of Jewish males in the Russian Federation was higher than that of Jewish females in all ages up to 60 (Table 2). Analysis reveals that the analogous age-sex structure[4] in the total Soviet Jewish population (according to this census, the male surplus occurred up to age 55) was a consequence of the small sex difference in the level of mortality.[5]

In part, this dearth of potential Jewish brides in Russia stems from the earlier migration to this republic of predominantly male Jews from Ukraine and Belarus,[6] where the sex imbalance was much more moderate. According to the 1989 census, the only age groups with more males than females were under age 40 in Ukraine and under age

Table 2. Sex Ratio and Mixed Marriage among Jews in the Russian Federation, 1989–2010

Age and sex	1989	1994	2002	2010
Number of females per 100 males				
Age group				
20–24	87	86	89	91
25–29	87	83	83	89
30–34	87	80	72	84
35–39	88	86	75	79
40–44	88	85	74	77
45–49	92	85	79	77
50–54	89	74	80	82
55–59	94	95	87	83
60–64	114	85	87	88
65–69	141	115	88	92
Percentage of mixed married among all currently married				
Females	40	44	53	54
Males	58	63	72	72

Sources: 1989 Soviet census; 1994 Russian microcensus; 2002 and 2010 Russian censuses (Mark Tolts, "Contemporary Trends in Family Formation among the Jews in Russia," *Jews in Russia and Eastern Europe* 57, no. 2 [2006], 7 and 18; Evgeny L. Soroko, "Etnicheski smeshannye supruzheskie pary v Rossiiskoi Federatsii," *Demograficheskoe obozrenie* 1, no. 4 [2014], 101–105).

45 in Belarus. Corresponding to the higher sex imbalance, the percentage of mixed marriages was highest in Russia.

An examination of census data on the ratio of females to males in the relevant age groups shows that the mass emigration between 1989 and 2002 seriously increased the severe age-sex imbalance that had already existed among adult Jews. According to the 2002 Russian census, this imbalance in the sex ratio expanded up to ages 65–69. There must be reasons for these developments, but they cannot be explained by the difference in mortality rates between the sexes, as male mortality rates are usually higher than those of females. A more plausible explanation is that in this period of mass emigration, Jewish females were more prone than Jewish males to leave the country.[7] Alternative interpretations, such as higher rates of ethnic assimilation of Jewish females in mixed marriages and/or higher rates of ethnic reaffiliation with the Jewish people among males of mixed parentage, appear less plausible given available data, especially for the older age groups in which the Jewish sex imbalance grew as well.

As a result of this rising imbalance, there was a further increase in mixed marriages. According to the estimate based on the data of the 1989 Soviet census, by the start of the great emigration, among all then-currently married Jews in the Russian Federation, 58 percent of the males and 40 percent of the females had spouses from another ethnic group. On the basis of the 1994 Russian microcensus data, after five years of the most intensive mass emigration, the mixed marriage indicator was estimated at 63 percent for Jewish males and 44 percent for Jewish females; an increase of 5 and 4 percentage points, respectively (Table 2).

An estimate based on data from the 2002 Russian census suggests that the mixed marriage indicator continued to increase: by that time, 72 percent of the males and 53 percent of the females had spouses from another ethnic group. Accordingly, between the 1994 Russian microcensus and the 2002 Russian census, the estimated increase was 9 percentage points both for married Jewish males and married Jewish females. These figures clearly show a continuing increase in the incidence of mixed marriage during this period of continuing mass emigration. Moreover, it should be noted that the change in the mixed marriage indicator has been somewhat restrained by the aging of the Russian Jewish population, since the incidence of mixed marriage in older age groups is lower than in younger ones. However, the level of mixed marriage among Russian Jewry had apparently become especially high in comparison with other Jewish communities around the world.[8]

Yet, perhaps surprisingly, according to the 2010 Russian census data, the increase of the mixed marriage indicator seems to have stalled: for females it increased by only one percentage point, to 54 percent, and for males it remained at the same level as in 2002 (72 percent). Simultaneously, the sex ratio improved somewhat at all ages under 45; that is, the numbers of females per 100 males increased. The period between 2002 and 2010 saw much lower Jewish emigration than previously.[9] Inevitably, the role of emigration in demographic processes among Russian Jewry also decreased. At the same time, mortality may have played a greater role in producing changes in demographic processes, leading to alterations in the sex ratios. Unfortunately, there is no data on the dynamics of Jewish mortality in Russia for the post-Soviet period. However, something might be inferred indirectly by examining educational attainment. Since 1989, the gap in educational attainment between Jewish males and females in Russia has become wider, while the level of higher education of Jewish males in some age cohorts has even decreased (see below). Here, we should bear in mind that persons with higher educational attainments have a relatively lower mortality level.[10] If that is the case, the rising educational gap might be a partial explanation for the decreased deficit of females per males and, in consequence, the recent alterations in Jewish marriage patterns.

Rising Prominence of Hebrew and Demise of Yiddish

The last Soviet census of 1989 recorded both native and second languages claimed by respondents. According to that census, 36,888 Jews (7.1 percent) in the Russian Federation (not including Dagestan, Checheno-Ingush, Kabardino-Balkar, and North Ossetian autonomous republics) declared Yiddish as their native language while another 19,453 Jews (3.7 percent) named Yiddish as their second language.[11] At the same time, Hebrew was not listed in the *Dictionary of Nationalities and Languages* in that census as it was in previous Soviet censuses.[12] Therefore, there is no information about Hebrew in the results of the 1989 Soviet census.

It should be noted that, in the Soviet censuses, the question on "native language" (*rodnoi iazyk*) was not clearly defined in the instructions to census takers, so answers to this question are a problematic linguistic indicator.[13] "Native language" cannot necessarily be regarded as equivalent to "language of early childhood" or "mother tongue." During the late Soviet period, Yiddish was regarded by some Russian Jews as an ethnic symbol, so that answers to the question on native language were sometimes performative, and therefore unrelated to respondents' actual linguistic behavior. In the post-Soviet period, Yiddish seems to have lost this perceived function (see below).

Only in the month following the conclusion of the 2002 Russian census did the Russian State Committee for Statistics (Goskomstat) include Hebrew—for the first time—in its listing of languages.[14] That led, unfortunately, to the result that in the 2002 census there is an aggregate number of Yiddish and Hebrew speakers—30,019, of whom about 20,000 were Jews[15] and 8,165 were ethnic Russians. Consequently, these figures are not suitable for our analysis here.

The 2010 Russian census recorded 18,822 people who noted a knowledge of Hebrew (Table 3). Among these were more ethnic Russians (48.6 percent) than Jews (41.9 percent). Among Jews tabulated in this census (156,800; Table 1) the share of those noting a knowledge of Hebrew was rather considerable: 5.0 percent. In post-Soviet Russia, in striking contrast to the Soviet era, Hebrew is taught in Jewish schools.[16] Therefore, we cannot attribute knowledge of Hebrew in contemporary Russia solely to return migration from Israel,[17] even for ethnic Russians. Moreover, it is a well-known fact that many ostensibly Jewish schools also enroll non-Jewish children who fulfill the criteria of the Israeli Law of Return[18]—which gives the right of immigration to Israel to children and grandchildren of Jews—although these may have no intention of migrating to Israel. All these factors led to the appearance of a sizable number of ethnic Russians among Hebrew speakers.

The distribution of Jews and Russians who noted a knowledge of Hebrew in the census was noticeably different. Among the Jews, 45.6 percent lived in Moscow, 13.2 percent in St. Petersburg, and 41.2 percent in the provinces; that is, a sizably higher share of Jews with knowledge of Hebrew lived in Moscow than the share of Moscow residents among the total Jewish population of Russia (34 percent; Table 1). At the same time, only 26.2 percent of Russians with knowledge of Hebrew lived in Moscow, with another 12.2 percent in St. Petersburg. The majority, 61.6 percent, lived in the provinces. Only in Moscow was the number of Jews with knowledge of Hebrew higher than that of Russians.

The 2010 Russian census recorded only 1,683 people with knowledge of Yiddish, whereas 5,820 were listed as having knowledge of an unspecified Jewish language (Table 3). Unlike the case of Hebrew, most people who claimed a knowledge of Yiddish and an unspecified Jewish language are recorded as Jews: 68.2 and 65.8 percent, respectively. There were 1,147 Jews who noted a knowledge of Yiddish and 3,828 an unspecified Jewish language; that is, 0.7 and 2.4 percent, respectively, of the total Jewish population in Russia (excluding those recorded as Georgian Jews, Mountain Jews, Central Asian [Bukharan Jews] and Krymchaks).

Table 3. Number of People Noting Jewish Languages as Known and Native Tongue in the Russian Federation, by Area, 2010

Area	Known language			Native language		
	Hebrew	Yiddish	Jewish language (unspecified)	Hebrew	Yiddish	Jewish language (unspecified)
Total	18,822	1,683	5,820	3,011	469	5,222
of which:						
Jews	7,885	1,147	3,828	2,666	425	4,883
Russians	9,145	433	1,235	120	13	72
Others[a]	1,792	103	757	225	31	267
Moscow city	6,644	599	1,330	1,635	220	1,567
of which:						
Jews	3,595	410	995	1,471	196	1,492
Russians	2,399	137	227	50	7	24
Others[a]	650	52	108	114	17	51
St. Petersburg city	2,343	247	326	315	54	200
of which:						
Jews	1,042	189	228	261	52	190
Russians	1,117	51	69	18	1	1
Others[a]	184	7	29	36	1	9
Provinces	9,835	837	4,164	1,061	195	3,455
of which:						
Jews	3,248	548	2,605	934	177	3,201
Russians	5,629	245	939	52	5	47
Others[a]	958	44	620	75	13	207

[a] Including those whose ethnicity was unknown.
Source: 2010 Russian census.

In the official instructions to the Soviet censuses, all persons who might note an unspecified Jewish language were traditionally portrayed as Yiddish-speakers, and were included as such in the census results. However, in the post-Soviet period, there were many instances in which non-Ashkenazi Jews in the Russian Federation started calling themselves "Jews," without specification.[19] This inevitably led to a situation wherein, among those people for whom an unspecified Jewish language was recorded, there was a sizable number of non-Ashkenazi Jews who had their own Jewish languages (for instance, Judeo-Tat). Two-thirds (68.1 percent) of the Jews with an unspecified Jewish language lived in the provinces, whereas among those Jews who noted a knowledge of Yiddish, the share of provincial Jewry was less than half (47.8 percent), which is slightly lower than their share in the total Jewish population of

Russia (51 percent; see Table 1). The 2010 Russian census additionally provided information on a native language.[20]

Naturally, less knowledge of Jewish languages among Jews is coupled with almost universal Russian language proficiency. According to the data of the 2010 Russian census, 99.3 percent of Jews knew Russian, and 93.4 percent—the highest share among all non-Russians in the country—noted this language as native.[21] Contemporary Jews in Russia are Russian Jews by their language.

Dynamics of General Educational Levels

During the Soviet era, the high profile of educational achievement among Jews was the main factor determining their socioeconomic positions in Soviet society.[22] Within the Soviet Jewish population, the educational attainment level of Russian Jewry per se was highest, relative to Jews living in the other Soviet republics. According to the last Soviet census of 1989, 53.8 percent of Jews in the Russian Federation, aged 20 and over, had attained higher education (Table 4). In Ukraine, only 37.3 percent of the Jews had attained this level, and in Belarus the percentage was even lower (34.9 percent);[23] that is, for Russian Jewry, this percentage was higher by a factor of 1.4 and 1.5 than was recorded for those in Ukraine and Belarus, respectively. It is notable that even among Russian provincial Jewry, the level of higher educational attainment was higher (46.7 percent; Table 5) than that among Jews in Ukraine and Belarus.

The educational level among urban ethnic Russians aged 20 and over was much lower (Table 4). According to the 1989 Soviet census, only 14.9 percent of them had attained higher education; thus, by comparison, the educational attainment level of Russian Jews was 3.6 times higher than the figure for urban Russians. Accordingly, among adult urban Russians, the attainment of a general secondary education (that is, a high school diploma without higher educational degrees) was the most common (27.1 percent); among Russian Jews, in contrast, those who had only completed a general secondary education accounted for just 12.3 percent, while Jews who had had a secondary vocational level of education (17.9 percent) were somewhat more common, coming second after those holding a higher educational degree. If we consider that 3.3 percent of the Jews in Russia also had incomplete higher education (partial completion of requirements for a degree), we may conclude from the above-noted figures that the great majority of them (87.3 percent) had a secondary general or higher level of education. At the same time, only two-thirds (67.3 percent) of urban Russians had attained this level of education. Lower levels of education were held by only 12.7 percent of Russian Jews and a third (32.7 percent) of urban Russians.

In the post-Soviet period, the incidence of higher education increased among Russian Jews, as well as among urban Russians. The share of Jews aged 20 and over with higher education reached 61.5 percent in 2002 and 67.7 percent in 2010. Among urban Russians, the increase was steeper: the share of people with higher education rose to 21.7 percent in 2002 and 30.1 percent in 2010. However, despite doubling the relevant percentage as of 1989, the incidence of higher education among urban Russians in 2010 was still 2.2 times lower than that of Jews in Russia. According to

Table 4. Distribution of Jews and Urban Russians in the Russian Federation Aged 20 and Over, by Educational Level, 1989, 2002 and 2010 (percent)

Educational level	1989	2002	2010
Jews[a]			
Higher	53.8	61.5[b]	67.7[b]
Incomplete higher	3.3	4.1	3.6
Secondary vocational	17.9	17.7	17.6
Secondary general	12.3	7.5	6.1
Incomplete secondary	7.4	3.6	2.5
Primary vocational		3.4	1.1
Primary general	3.9	1.9	1.2
Less than primary	1.4	0.3	0.2
Total	100.0	100.0	100.0
Urban Russians			
Higher	14.9	21.7[b]	30.1[b]
Incomplete higher	2.1	3.7	5.0
Secondary vocational	23.2	32.8	35.3
Secondary general	27.1	14.7	14.4
Incomplete secondary	16.9	8.5	6.5
Primary vocational		12.5	4.8
Primary general	10.8	5.6	3.6
Less than primary	5.0	0.5	0.3
Total	100.0	100.0	100.0

[a] For 1989, including those recorded as Georgian Jews, Mountain Jews, Central Asian (Bukharan Jews), and Krymchaks.
[b] Including postgraduate degrees presented separately in the census results.
Sources: 1989 Soviet census; 2002 and 2010 Russian censuses.

the census data, among urban Russians in 2002 and 2010, the most frequently attained level of education became secondary vocational, which increased steadily (32.8 and 35.3 percent, respectively). Among Russian Jews, this level of education continued to take second place; its share was practically unchanged (17.7 percent in 2002 and 17.6 percent in 2010). The incidence of all lower levels of education decreased among Russian Jews, and in this, Russian Jews were similar to urban Russians.

Looking further into the percentages of Russian Jews and urban Russians aged 20 and over possessing a higher education, we can analyze the differentiation of educational levels and their dynamics by area. According to the 1989 census, there were substantial educational differences between the Jews of Moscow, St. Petersburg, and those of the provinces.[24] The percentage of Jews aged 20 and over who had obtained a higher education varied: 62.4 percent in Moscow, 57.1 percent in St. Petersburg, but only 46.7 percent in the Russian provinces (Table 5). Some of my previous research showed that the majority of Moscow and St. Petersburg Jews under the age of 40

Table 5. Percentage of Jews and Urban Russians Aged 20 and Over with Higher Education in the Russian Federation, by Area, 1989, 2002, and 2010

Area	1989[a]	2002[b]	2010[b]
Jews			
Total	53.8	61.5	67.7
Moscow city	62.4	67.5	74.9
St. Petersburg city	57.1	64.3	69.6
Provinces	46.7	56.4	62.2
Urban Russians			
Total	14.9	21.7	30.1
Moscow city	27.6	34.4	45.3
St. Petersburg city	...	30.9	39.2
Provinces	...	19.6	27.4

[a] Including those recorded as Georgian Jews, Mountain Jews, Central Asian (Bukharan Jews), and Krymchaks.
[b] Including postgraduate degrees presented separately in the census results.
Sources: 1989 Soviet census; 2002 and 2010 Russian censuses.

consisted of *intelligentsia*[25] with higher education, as was true of their parents before them. This was not true of provincial Jewry.[26] However, according to the 1989 census, among Russian provincial Jewry, the share with higher education (as noted, 46.7 percent) was 1.7 times higher than among Russians in Moscow (27.6 percent).

The post-Soviet censuses showed that sizable differences by area of residence persisted. According to the 2002 Russian census, the percentages of Jews aged 20 and over who had attained higher education increased everywhere: it reached 67.5 percent in Moscow, 64.3 percent in St. Petersburg, and 56.4 percent in the Russian provinces. By 2010, this indicator had increased further, to 74.9 percent in Moscow, 69.6 percent in St. Petersburg, and 62.2 percent in the Russian provinces. The educational gap between Moscow Jews and provincial Jews narrowed from 15.7 percentage points in 1989 to 11.1 percentage points in 2002 and then widened again to 12.7 percentage points in 2010. These dynamics were coupled with a Moscow-oriented trend of internal migration among the general population of Russia and its highly educated segment, in particular.[27]

At the same time, it should be noted that, in 2010, the educational indicator of Jews of the provinces reached the 1989 level of Moscow Jews. From this we may surmise that the majority of provincial Jewry under the age of 40 in 2010 consisted of *intelligentsia* with higher education, as was true of their parents before them. The census data showed that the educational gap between Russian Jewry and urban Russians persisted in each area. In 2010, even the 45.3 percent level of higher education of the Russians in Moscow was slightly lower than that of provincial Jewry in 1989 (46.7 percent).

The post-Soviet census data show that sizable differences also persisted between Russian Jewry and Jews in Ukraine and Belarus after the dissolution of the Soviet

Union. Unlike in the Russian Federation, according to the 2001 Ukrainian census, the percentage of Jews aged 20 and over who attained a higher education and who lived in the country's capital, Kyiv (50.7 percent) was almost the same as the average for Jews of all regions for which we have data (49.2 percent). However, in Belarus we see a pattern that bore greater similarity to the Russian Federation in this respect. According to the 1999 Belorussian census, in Minsk, the capital of Belarus, the share of Jews aged 20 and over who attained higher education was 55.4 percent; that is, much higher than that country's average for Jews (41.7 percent).[28]

However, general data cannot provide us with enough knowledge about the direction of changes or differentiation in educational levels between Jews and urban Russians. For a better understanding of these, we must analyze data on educational levels by age and sex among both Russian Jews and urban Russians.

Differentiation in Levels of Higher Education by Age and Sex

An analysis of the differences between females and males provides us with a much more nuanced picture of post-Soviet dynamics. The 1989 Soviet census data show that only among Jews under age 30 were there more females than males with higher education. In 2002, such a pattern was observed for those under age 40, and in 2010, for those under age 45 (Table 6). This coincides with a similar development among the total urban population, where this female–male crossover happened earlier and was more pronounced. According to the 1989 Soviet census data, among the total urban population, under age 45 the percentage of females with higher education exceeded that of males.

According to the 2002 Russian census, the percentage of male Jews with higher education decreased for those under 45 years of age. For Jewish females, the respective decrease occurred only at age 30–34, and this was much less pronounced (3.9 percentage points) than for Jewish males of the same age group (11.3 percentage points). For Jewish males at age 40–44, this dynamic was especially unfavorable. In this age group, the share with higher education decreased from 69.4 percent in 1989 to 66.6 percent in 2002 and to 65.8 percent in 2010. Thus, the post-Soviet dynamics of higher education for Jewish males was rather unfavorable, especially between 1989 and 2002. At the same time, in the post-Soviet period among urban Russians, the percentage with higher education grew steadily at all ages for both females and males.

Census data also give us the possibility to gauge the influence of migration, another important factor of post-Soviet Jewish population dynamics, on the educational level of Russian Jews.[29] Dynamics of cohort data between 1989 and 2002, the time of the highest emigration, show a very moderate increase in the percentage of Jews with higher education. This was especially negligible for females (less than one percentage point); however, even for males, this increase did not exceed two percentage points in these years (Table 7). In the following intercensal period, between 2002 and 2010, when the birth cohorts were older, the increase was more pronounced for both females and males, but it still did not exceed 3–4 percentage points.

Table 6. Percentage of Females and Males among Jews and Urban Russians in the Russian Federation with Higher Education, by Age, 1989, 2002, and 2010

Age group	Jews			Urban Russians		
	1989	2002[a]	2010[a]	1989[b]	2002[a]	2010[a]
Females						
25–29	61.2	62.3	73.1	20.2	28.8	51.0
30–34	65.4	61.5	73.1	20.6	29.2	46.4
35–39	64.1	66.2	70.9	19.7	29.9	40.6
40–44	63.7	66.6	70.8	22.8	27.6	37.6
45–49	59.9	66.0	71.5	17.5	25.2	33.8
50–54	60.0	64.3	69.4	15.0	23.2	29.0
55–59	59.3	63.8	68.1	10.6	25.5	25.7
60–64	48.9	60.1	65.9	7.9	18.3	24.7
65–69	49.6	63.2	64.2	7.7	15.6	23.1
70 and over	29.3	51.0	61.0	3.6	9.4	15.1
Males						
25–29	59.5	56.5	69.1	15.0	22.5	35.8
30–34	67.2	55.9	69.5	17.4	22.6	34.5
35–39	68.4	62.5	70.0	18.7	24.4	31.5
40–44	69.4	66.6	65.8	22.0	23.4	29.6
45–49	68.0	69.3	72.5	20.0	23.2	28.9
50–54	69.0	70.4	73.7	19.2	23.8	26.5
55–59	64.2	71.5	73.7	13.1	26.4	26.4
60–64	57.2	69.7	74.2	11.8	23.5	27.8
65–69	57.1	70.5	72.9	15.3	21.4	28.0
70 and over	47.2	62.4	71.4	11.2	15.9	24.1

[a] Including postgraduate degrees presented separately in the census results.
[b] Total urban females and males.
Sources: 1989 Soviet census; 2002 and 2010 Russian censuses.

Thus, from the data presented, we see that the post-Soviet-period emigration did not lead to a decrease in the level of education for birth cohorts of either females or males who had reached the age of 30 in 1989; that is, these data provide no proof that more educated Jews were more prone to leave Russia. At the same time, a good explanation for the moderate increase in the level of education of these birth cohorts, which rose with their aging, may be found in the above-noted fact that persons with higher education have a lower mortality level. Therefore, this moderate increase in the percentage of Jews with higher education probably correlated with their extended longevity.

Table 7. Percentage of Jews in the Russian Federation with Higher Education in Selected Birth Cohorts, 1989, 2002, and 2010

Years of birth	1989 census data		Years of birth	2002 census data[a]		Years of birth	2010 census data[a]	
	Age in the census	Percentage with higher education		Age in the census	Percentage with higher education		Age in the census	Percentage with higher education
Females			Females			Females		
1954–1958	30–34	65.4	1953–1957	45–49	66.0	1956–1960	50–54	69.4
1949–1953	35–39	64.1	1948–1952	50–54	64.3	1951–1955	55–59	68.1
1944–1948	40–44	63.7	1943–1947	55–59	63.8	1946–1950	60–64	65.9
1939–1943	45–49	59.9	1938–1942	60–64	60.1	1941–1945	65–69	64.2
Males			Males			Males		
1954–1958	30–34	67.2	1953–1957	45–49	69.3	1956–1960	50–54	73.7
1949–1953	35–39	68.4	1948–1952	50–54	70.4	1951–1955	55–59	73.7
1944–1948	40–44	69.4	1943–1947	55–59	71.5	1946–1950	60–64	74.2
1939–1943	45–49	68.0	1938–1942	60–64	69.7	1941–1945	65–69	72.9

[a] Including postgraduate degrees presented separately in the census results.
Sources: 1989 Soviet census; 2002 and 2010 Russian censuses.

Changes in Occupational Profile: The Case of Moscow Jewry

A comparison of the data from the Soviet 1989 census and the 2002 Russian census allows us to study changes in the occupational profile of the largest and most advanced sector of Jews in Russia—Moscow Jewry. According to the 1989 census, there were important differences between employed Moscow Jews and their counterparts outside of Moscow, as seen by economic sector.[30] In Moscow, the largest share of Jews (28.7 percent) was employed in science,[31] whereas for non-Moscow Jews in Russia, the main employment sector was industry (manufacturing activity; 30.2 percent).[32] In Moscow, the share of Jews employed in industry was about half that (16.8 percent). At the same time, the largest share of Russians in Moscow was comprised of those employed in industry (25.2 percent).

Since 1989, the situation has changed dramatically. In the post-Soviet period, employment in many economic sectors and professions decreased, whereas the prominence of others grew.[33] According to the 2002 census data, the largest share of Moscow Jews was employed in a combined group of financial activities that includes real estate, rental and business activities, as well as research and computer-related activities—17.0 percent—whereas for Russians in Moscow, the main sector was the combined group of wholesale and retail sales; hotels and restaurants; repair of motor vehicles, motorcycles, and personal and household goods—18.2 percent.[34] According to the data from this census, the shares of Moscow Jews and Russians employed in industry were the same—about 13 percent—which points to a decrease of less than 4 percentage points for Jews from that of the 1989 Soviet census. At the same time, science lost its prominence as the largest sector of employment for Moscow Jews in the post-Soviet period.

According to the census data, in Moscow between 1989 and 2002, the share of Jews both among the total number of employed and in all the occupation groups presented dropped sizably (Table 8), a fact that corresponds to the large numerical decrease of the Jewish population in the city during this period (see Table 1). However, in some occupation groups, there was a particularly dramatic decline. For example, in 1989, the highest share of Jews was among physicians (7.5 percent), whereas in 2002, the corresponding share dropped as low as 1.0 percent. The share of Jews among researchers decreased from 6.7 percent in 1989 to 2.3 percent in 2002 (Table 8).

According to the 1989 Soviet census data, in Moscow among both employed Jews and employed Russians, the largest shares worked in engineering and technical fields: 28.7 percent and 20.9 percent, respectively (Table 9).[35] According to the 2002 Russian census data, this share among employed Jews (5.7 percent) had dropped dramatically by about four-fifths, whereas it decreased by less than half among Russians (to 11.3 percent).

Between the 1989 and 2002 censuses, both among employed Jews and employed Russians, the share of researchers dropped dramatically, from 10.1 to 2.9 and from 2.8 to 0.9 percent, respectively. This corresponds to the general decline of employment in science in the post-Soviet period.[36] At the same time, we note that the share of researchers among employed Jews, even in 2002, was slightly higher than it had been that among Russians in 1989 (2.9 and 2.8 percent, respectively).

Table 8. Percentage of Jews among All Employed in Some Occupational Groups in Moscow City, 1989 and 2002

Occupational groups[a]	1989	2002
Total	2.0	0.6
Physicians	7.5	1.0
Researchers	6.7	2.3
Heads/top managers of enterprises	5.6	1.9
Literary and press personnel, artists, producers, composers, conductors	5.0	2.3
Primary and secondary school teachers	4.8	1.3
Engineering and technical personnel	2.7	0.4
Heads/top managers of governmental bodies, including economic sectors	2.2	1.5
Sales workers	1.0	0.3
Machine-building and metalworkers	0.6	0.2
Drivers	0.3	0.2

[a] Arranged in descending order according to the percentage of Jews among all employed in 1989.
Sources: 1989 Soviet census and 2002 Russian census (Mosgorstat, *Itogi Vsesoiuznoi perepisi naseleniia 1989 g. po gorodu Moskve: Natsional'nyi sostav naseleniia goroda Moskva* [Moscow: 1991], 60-62; Liubov' V. Ostapenko and Irina A. Subbotina, *Moskva mnogonatsional'naia. Starozhily i migranty: smeste ili riadom* [Moscow: 2007], 77–78).

According to the 2002 Russian census data, among employed Jews in Moscow, there were more sales workers (3.7 percent, not including managerial positions in sales enterprises) than researchers (2.9 percent). Heads/top managers of enterprises had become the prime occupation group of employed Jews (25.8 percent).

According to the 2002 Russian census data, 91.5 percent of employed Jews in Moscow were salaried employees, whereas among employed Russians the share was even higher: 95.0 percent (Table 10). Correspondingly, the share of self-employed (7.9 percent) was higher among economically active Jews than among economically active Russians (4.2 percent), and the share of self-employed with employees was more than 3 times higher among Jews (4.1 percent) than among Russians (1.3 percent). In 2002, the share of Jews in the total number of self-employed with employees in Moscow was only 2.0 percent. Thus, the share of Jews among Moscow's "capitalists" as a whole was very moderate.

Occupational and employment data analyzed by ethnicity for Moscow from the 2002 Russian census are unique. Such data were not processed at that time for Russia as a whole, nor for any other individual parts of the country outside Moscow. Moreover, the 2010 Russian census, as well as the most recent one of 2021, included no corresponding questions and provide no occupational data by ethnicity. Thus, our examination of changes in the occupational profile of Moscow Jewry from 1989 to 2002 cannot be repeated based on new material. Its unique character underlines the importance of its results for an understanding of the post-Soviet transformation of Jews in Russia.

Table 9. Employment of Jews and Russians in Moscow City, by Some Occupational Groups, 1989 and 2002 (percent)

Occupational groups[a]	Jews		Russians	
	1989	2002	1989	2002
Total	100.0	100.0	100.0	100.0
Engineering and technical personnel	28.7	5.7	20.9	11.3
Heads/top managers of enterprises	18.6	25.8	9.9	14.6
Researchers	10.1	2.9	2.8	0.9
Physicians	7.8	6.9	3.7	4.5
Literary and press personnel, artists, producers, composers, conductors	4.9	4.2	1.8	1.2
Primary and secondary school teachers	4.4	4.9	1.7	3.1
Machine-building and metalworkers	4.1	1.2	14.1	4.5
Sales workers	1.1	3.7	2.2	6.4
Drivers	1.0	1.9	5.2	6.5
Heads/top managers of governmental bodies, including economic sectors	0.5	0.6	0.4	0.3

[a] Arranged in descending order according to the percent for Jews in 1989.
Sources: 1989 Soviet census and 2002 Russian census (Mosgorstat, *Itogi Vsesoiuznoi perepisi naseleniia1989 g. po gorodu Moskve: Natsional'nyi sostav naseleniia goroda Moskva* [Moscow: 1991], 60-62; Liubov' V. Ostapenko and Irina A. Subbotina, *Moskva mnogonatsional'naia. Starozhily i migranty: smeste ili riadom* [Moscow: 2007], 80-81).

Table 10. Employed Jews and Russians in Moscow City, by Status of Employment, 2002 (percent)

Status of employment	Jews	Russians
Total	100.0	100.0
Employees	91.5	95.0
Self-employed	7.9	4.2
of whom:		
With employees	4.1	1.3
Without employees	2.0	2.0
Employees not stated/unknown	1.8	0.9
Status of employment not stated	0.6	0.8
Percentage of noted ethnic group in the total number of self-employed with employees	2.0	76.7

Source: 2002 Russian census (Liubov' V. Ostapenko and Irina A. Subbotina, *Moskva mnogonatsional'naia. Starozhily i migranty: smeste ili riadom* [Moscow: 2007], 112 and 116; Marina L. Bell, *Etnicheskie moskvichi* [Moscow: 2009], 137).

Conclusion

Our analysis suggests that in the post-Soviet period, the rising sex imbalance was a major cause for the increase of mixed marriage among Russian Jewry. However, some subsequent improvements in the sex ratios led to a stabilization in the mixed marriage indicator for females and males. Somewhat counterintuitively, the 2010 Russian census data show that there were more Russians than Jews who claim a knowledge of Hebrew. Results of the recent Russian censuses clearly demonstrate that sizable differences in educational attainments persisted among the different parts of Russian Jewry, and Moscow Jews fortified their lead in this regard. Yet, while Russian Jewry has kept its position as the most educated group in the country, the gap in higher educational attainment between Jewish females and males has widened in favor of females, and the level of higher education among Jewish males in some age cohorts decreased during the post-Soviet transformation. The study did not find that levels of educational attainment led to differing propensities to emigrate.

Much effort has been devoted to studying the dramatic labor transformation (changes of profession and branch of economic activity) among FSU immigrants in Israel.[37] Our analysis based on Moscow data shows clearly that Jews remaining in Russia underwent an analogous transformation. These transformations among both groups were caused by the new socioeconomic realities that Jews who remained in the Russian Federation experienced in the course of the post-Soviet transition to the new capitalist economy, whereas FSU immigrants in Israel experienced an inevitable transformation in their new home.

Notes

1. The results of the 2002 and 2010 Russian censuses are available at the site of the Federal State Statistics Service (Rosstat), online at: rosstat.gov.ru/vpn_popul (accessed 7 December 2021). The data of the 1989 Soviet census were drawn from the two main publications: Goskomstat Rossii, *Nekotorye pokazateli, kharakterizuiushchie natsional'nyi sostav naseleniia Rossiiskoi Federatsii*, vols. 2; 3, part 1 (Moscow: 1992–1993); Interstate Statistical Committee of the CIS, *1989 USSR Population Census*, CD-ROM ed. (Minneapolis: 1996). Additionally, certain unpublished materials of this Soviet census were kindly provided by Dmitry D. Bogoyavlensky, for which the author is deeply grateful. Other sources used in the study are noted in the text.

2. Mark Tolts, "Post-Soviet Jewish Demographic Dynamics: An Analysis of Recent Data," in *Jewish Population and Identity: Concept and Reality*, ed. Sergio DellaPergola and Uzi Rebhun (Dordrecht: 2018), 215.

3. Ibid., 214–215.

4. In this article, standard demographic terminology has been used for the terms related to age-sex structure; see, for instance, Population Reference Bureau, *Glossary of Demographic Terms*; online at: prb.org/resources/glossary (accessed 6 December 2021).

5. Mark Tolts, "Jewish Marriages in the USSR: A Demographic Analysis," *East European Jewish Affairs* 22, no. 2 (1992), 4–5.

6. Mark Tolts, "Demographic Trends among the Jews in the Three Slavic Republics of the Former USSR: A Comparative Analysis," in *Papers in Jewish Demography 1993*, ed. Sergio DellaPergola and Judith Even (Jerusalem: 1997), 147–175.

7. Mark Tolts, "Recent Jewish Emigration and Population Decline in Russia," *Jews in Eastern Europe* 35, no. 1 (1998), 10–13.

8. See Sergio DellaPergola, "Jewish Out-Marriage: A Global Perspective," in *Jewish Intermarriage around the World*, ed. Shula Reinharz and Sergio DellaPergola (London: 2009), 13–39.

9. See Mark Tolts, "A Half Century of Jewish Emigration from the Former Soviet Union," in *Migration from the Newly Independent States*, ed. Mikhail Denisenko, Salvatore Strozza, and Matthew Light (Cham: 2020), 323–344.

10. On the differentiation of mortality in Russia by educational level, see, for instance, Tatyana L. Khar'kova, Svetlana Yu. Nikitina, and Evgueni M. Andreev, "Zavisimost' prodolzhitel'nosti zhizni ot urovnia obrazovaniia v Rossii," *Voprosy statistiki*, no. 8 (2017), 61–69; on Jewish mortality, in particular, in the post-Soviet period, see Vladimir M. Shkolnikov, Evgueni M. Andreev, Jon Anson, and France Meslé, "The Peculiar Pattern of Mortality of Jews in Moscow, 1993–95," *Population Studies* 58, no. 3 (2004), 311–329.

11. Mark Tolts, "Yiddish in the Former Soviet Union since 1989: A Statistical-Demographic Analysis," in *Yiddish in the Contemporary World*, ed. Gennady Estraikh and Mikhail Krutikov (Oxford: 1999), 133–146.

12. See Goskomstat SSSR, *Slovari natsional'nostei i iazykov* (Moscow: 1988).

13. See, for example, Brian D. Silver, "The Ethnic and Language Dimensions in Russian and Soviet Censuses," in *Research Guide to the Russian and Soviet Censuses*, ed. Ralph S. Clem (Ithaca: 1986), 88–89.

14. Goskomstat Rossii, *Dopolneniia k dokumentam Vserossiiskoi perepisi naseleniia 2002 goda k avtomatizirovannoi obrabotke* (signed by Chairperson of Goskomstat, 12 November 2002), 2.

15. Boris N. Mironov, "Krizis evreiskoi diaspory v Rossii," *Noveishaia istoriia Rossii*, no. 1 (2017), 186.

16. See, for instance, Alexandra L. Polian, "Prepodavanie i izuchenie ivrita v SSSR i sovremennoi Rossii," in *Sovremennyi Izrail': iazyki, obshchestvo, kul'tura*, ed. Elena E. Nosenko-Shtein and Denis Sobolev (Moscow: 2020), 48–94.

17. On return migration, see Mark Tolts, "Demography of the Contemporary Russian-Speaking Jewish Diaspora," in *The New Jewish Diaspora: Russian-Speaking Immigrants in the United States, Israel, and Germany*, ed. Zvi Gitelman (New Brunswick: 2016), 28–32.

18. Zvi Gitelman, "Do Jewish Schools Make a Difference in the Former Soviet Union?" *East European Jewish Affairs* 37, no. 4 (2007), 385–386.

19. Tolts, "Post-Soviet Jewish Demographic Dynamics," 215–216.

20. According to the data of the 2010 census, 1.8 times more Jews were recorded with an unspecified native Jewish language (4,883, or 3.1 percent) than was true of those claiming Hebrew as their native language (2,666, or 1.7 percent); the number of those claiming Yiddish was much lower—425 (0.3 percent). Distribution by area of Jews who noted Hebrew and an unspecified Jewish language as their native tongue in the census was noticeably different. Among those who noted Hebrew, 55.2 percent lived in Moscow, 9.8 percent in St. Petersburg and 35.0 percent in the provinces, whereas among those who noted an unspecified Jewish language the majority lived in the provinces—65.6 percent. The number of non-Jews who opted to claim a Jewish language as their native tongue was very low (Table 3).

21. See Dmitry D. Bogoyavlensky, "Etnicheskii sostav naseleniia i vladenie iazykami," in *Naselenie Rossii 2010-2011*, ed. Anatoly G. Vishnevsky (Moscow: 2013), 128–130 and 139–141.

22. See, for instance, Igor Krupnik, "Soviet Cultural and Ethnic Policies toward Jews: A Legacy Reassessed," in *Jews and Jewish Life in Russia and the Soviet Union*, ed. Yaacov Ro'i (Ilford: 1995), 67–86; Samuel Barnai, "Social Trends among Jews in the Post-Stalin Years," in *Revolution, Repression and Revival: The Soviet Jewish Experience*, ed. Zvi Gitelman and Yaacov Ro'i (Lanham: 2007), 131–152.

23. Viacheslav Konstantinov, *Evreiskoe naselenie byvshego SSSR v XX veke* (Jerusalem: 2007), 100.

24. For detailed educational characteristics of these three groups of Russian Jews in the late Soviet period, see Mordechai Altshuler, "Socio-Demographic Profile of Moscow Jews," *Jews and Jewish Topics in the Soviet Union and Eastern Europe* 16, no. 3 (1991), 32–34; Marina Kogan, "Jews of Leningrad According to the Census of 1989," *Jews in Eastern Europe* 25, no. 3 (1994), 46–47; Mark Tolts, "The Interrelationship between Emigration and the Socio-Demographic Profile of Russian Jewry," in *Russian Jews on Three Continents*, ed. Noah Lewin-Epstein, Yaacov Ro'i, and Paul Ritterband (London: 1997), 166–168.

25. In Russian usage the term *intelligentsia* extends to nearly all certified professionals—a white-collar professional class at large—and is not limited to the cultural-scholarly elite.

26. Tolts, "The Interrelationship between Emigration and the Socio-Demographic Profile of Russian Jewry," 167.

27. See Nikita V. Mkrtchyan, "Rol' moskovskogo stolichnogo regiona kak krupneishego tsentra vnutrirossiiskoi migratsii," *Nauchnye trudy Instituta narodnokhoziaistvennogo prognozirovaniia RAN* 17 (2019), 252–268; Stepan P. Zemtsov and Vera M. Kidyaeva, "Faktory privlekatel'nosti regionov Rossii dlia migrantov s vysshim obrazovaniem," *Regional'nye issledovaniia* 67, no. 1 (2020), 39–52.

28. Mark Tolts, "The Jews in the Three Post-Soviet Slavic Countries: Selected Population Trends," in *Jews and Slavs*, vol. 19, ed. Wolf Moskovich and Leonid Finberg (Jerusalem: 2008), 205.

29. A starting point for this study may be found based on a very close correspondence between age data from the 1989 Soviet census, which was organized at the very beginning of the year (January), and cohort data by years of birth, which is necessary for this analysis. At the same time, cohort data by years of birth from the following Russian censuses of 2002 and 2010 can be approximated more roughly considering that both censuses were executed near the end of the year (October). Though these latter data do not give us a full overlap in birth years for the cohorts from the 1989 Soviet census, they do provide a rather good possibility to trace higher educational dynamics (see Table 7).

30. For a comprehensive analysis of the labor profile of Moscow Jews based on the 1989 Soviet census, see Mordechai Altshuler, "Socio-Demographic Profile of Moscow Jews," 35–39.

31. This figure includes people employed in research activity in all fields of science.

32. Based on the 1989 Soviet census data, a comparison of some characteristics of Moscow Jewry with those of other parts of Russian Jewry are presented in Mark Tolts, "The Interrelationship between Emigration and the Socio-Demographic Profile of Russian Jewry," 168–171.

33. On general changes in the Russian labor market in the 1990s, see, for instance, Vladimir Gimpelson and Douglas Lippoldt, *The Russian Labour Market: Between Transition and Turmoil* (Lanham: 2001).

34. Liubov' V. Ostapenko and Irina A. Subbotina, *Moskva mnogonatsional'naia. Starozhily i migranty: smeste ili riadom* (Moscow: 2007), 75.

35. For a comprehensive comparative analysis of the occupations of Jews and Russians in the entire Russian Federation based on the data of the 1989 Soviet census, see Michael P. Sacks, "Privilege and Prejudice: The Occupations of Jews in Russia in 1989," *Slavic Review* 57, no. 2 (1998), 247–266.

36. See, for instance, Frants E. Sheregi and Mikhail N. Strikhanov, *Nauka v Rossii: sotsiologicheskii analiz* (Moscow: 2006).

37. See, for instance, Sarit Cohen Goldner, Zvi Eckstein, and Yoram Weiss, *Immigration and Labor Market Mobility in Israel, 1990-2009* (Cambridge: 2012); Viacheslav Konstantinov, "The Professional Mobility of FSU Immigrants in Israel, 1990-2010," in *Research in Jewish Demography and Identity*, ed. Eli Lederhendler and Uzi Rebhun (Boston: 2015), 169–196.

Becoming Jews: The Petersburg Jewish University in the 1990s

Semion Goldin

(THE HEBREW UNIVERSITY)

"The Jews of Silence," the phrase that headlined Elie Wiesel's popular 1960s-vintage book about Soviet Jewry, became embedded in public consciousness and helped to foster a particular image of Soviet Jews after the Holocaust.[1] Wiesel's literary talents and his role as a formidable chronicler of the Jewish struggle for survival in the 20th century undoubtedly reinforced his approach (and that of many others) in depicting a stark opposition between the Jews and the Soviet regime: two clearly defined entities, as it were, one of them "good" and the other "bad." This approach, which Alexei Yurchak has termed a model of binary categories, divides everything that occurred in the USSR into neat "Soviet–anti-Soviet," or "conformist–nonconformist" conceptual boxes.[2] Because of their reputed "silence"—that is, to continue Wiesel's parable, their stifled voice under the Soviet regime—the Jews were seen primarily (and justifiably so, to a considerable degree) as a collective opponent and victim of the Soviet system.[3]

The end of the Jews' "silence," that is, their recovered "voice" revealed during the revival in the USSR of legal Jewish activity, independent of the regime, was inextricably connected to the *perestroika* (restructuring) initiated by Mikhail Gorbachev, the last Soviet leader, in 1985.[4] As a result of foreign policy considerations and in the context of a policy of *glasnost* (openness) inside the country and a broad concern for the nationality question and the status of ethnic groups in Soviet society, Gorbachev rejected the state antisemitism that was characteristic of the late Soviet period and permitted the mass emigration of Jews from the USSR.[5] Gorbachev's reforms, ostensibly aimed at reinforcing the Communist Party and stimulating the socioeconomic development of the USSR, led fairly quickly, however, to structural erosion and deep political crisis in the Soviet system, which culminated in the collapse of the Soviet Union at the end of 1991.[6]

What was the nature of the renaissance of Jewish activity in those last years of the Soviet Union, which manifested itself in the energetic creation of new structures (sometimes termed the rebuilding of old ones destroyed by the Soviet regime)? The

Semion Goldin, *Becoming Jews: The Petersburg Jewish University in the 1990s* In: *Becoming Post-Communist*. Edited by: Eli Lederhendler, Oxford University Press. © Oxford University Press 2023. DOI: 10.1093/oso/9780197687215.003.0008 revival occurred in the context of an ideological and moral revolution that engulfed the USSR toward the end of the 1980s, and the dramatic weakening and rapid collapse of the Soviet system against the background of economic crisis.[7] Possibly, these factors were not merely the background but also a causal step in the emergence of a renewed Jewish identity; in which case that development ought "to be understood as a construct in response to the circumstances."[8] Was there a certain ideology or long-term vision underlying the newly appearing Jewish structures, particularly if we address ourselves to a number of new Jewish activities of a non-Zionist and nonreligious nature? Finally, can one see the new structures that the Jews created as successors of Soviet reality that retained in their very form and character a symbiosis of "Sovietness" and "Jewishness"?[9]

I shall try to elucidate these questions through an examination of the history of the St. Petersburg Jewish University (PJU), an independent Jewish academic body that existed from 1989 to 1998.[10] To my knowledge, this is the first time that PJU's history has been examined in an academic publication.

From Expeditions to Shtetls to the Establishment of PJU (1980s)

The pre-history of the establishment of PJU is inextricably connected to the intellectual and spiritual atmosphere of the late USSR, on the one hand, and to the history of underground Jewish activity in Leningrad, on the other. The figure and personal history of the university's founder and rector, Ilya Dvorkin (b. 1954), unites these two lines.

Born into a family belonging to the successful Soviet technological elite, Dvorkin "until a certain time, did not see himself" as a Jew.[11] As a young man he was interested in theoretical physics, but he was unable to study in Leningrad University's physics department because Soviet state antisemitism restricted Jews' enrollment in such programs. As he later put it, "I did not attribute any particular significance to this other than that it was unpleasant."[12] Graduating from the Leningrad Polytechnic Institute, Dvorkin did not become an ordinary Soviet engineer: he participated actively in informal scientific seminars and wrote scientific papers, studying in various doctoral programs without completing a Ph.D. degree.[13] In the course of his ongoing intellectual development, he recalled, "I went from physics to philosophy, from philosophy to religion: in religion, *I came up with Judaism,* and I began to study Hebrew and Jewish texts."[14] Dvorkin turned to Judaism following an initial attraction to Christianity and to Islamic mysticism (Sufism).[15] The timing of this "turn," in the early 1980s, was not fortuitous: precisely in that period, emigration to Israel was almost completely halted, thus leading to the flourishing of underground refusenik circles in Leningrad.[16] At the same time, Dvorkin realized that there was no hope of succeeding in the official sphere or of engaging in science. In addition, the rapid succession of funerals of Soviet leaders (Brezhnev, Andropov, and Chernenko) convinced him that the USSR was coming to an end; he sensed an imminent apocalypse. He saw Jewish underground activity as a way out of this dead end.[17] Accordingly, Dvorkin set up underground Jewish schools that operated in refuseniks' apartments, and seminars to study Jewish texts in his own home (Fig. 1). "I have an organizational flair; therefore, all the time I was organizing

Fig. 1 *Dvorkin in the 1980s* from personal archive of Ilya Dvorkin.

something, bringing people together," Dvorkin reported in my interview with him. He also noted, in characterizing that time: "I was a nobody, and the repression at official levels did not affect me."[18]

In his account, what animated all this activity was a universal "utopian idea": Judaism as a great civilization could be the basis of any contemporary science, physics, or philosophy.[19] "I saw that I had sources on which it was possible to build a new language of the sciences, including the natural sciences," he reflected. "I arrived intuitively at the idea of Jewish science, at some kind of Haskalah [enlightenment] that in no way contradicted traditional Judaism."[20] Dvorkin differed from others in the circle of Jewish activists in Leningrad in two respects: "I did not plan to leave; it seemed utterly unimportant where one lived, and I did not see why I had to leave such a city. And my Judaism was very different from that of the *baalei teshuvah* [newly observant Jews] in Leningrad. I approached Judaism as a civilization, with the philosophy of Maimonides. It was not a personal religion in the sense of searching for one's roots; it was an intellectual system, a civilization in its entirety."[21]

Dvorkin's initial interest in the historic shtetls of the former Pale of Settlement was also intellectual in nature: in 1982, in the context of taking an interest in Hasidism and upon reading Martin Buber's hasidic tales and Elie Wiesel's *Somewhere a Master: Hasidic Portraits and Legends*, he traveled to Ukraine. "I took a bicycle, rode a train until Khmel'nyts'kyy, got on my bicycle there, and arrived in Medzhybizh," the town where Israel Ba'al Shem-tov, the hasidic founder, had lived.[22] Dvorkin was struck by "these cities and[their]monuments" (meaning, their historic sites), and he also experienced a shock upon encountering the history of the Holocaust: "Until then I knew nothing about it, and here people began to weep in relating what had happened."[23] After that experience, Dvorkin was unable to travel to Ukraine for several years, but in 1983, he set out for Belarus. Initially, he did not want to take pictures, as he felt

"I should experience the trip personally, not document it for someone."[24] In 1986, however, upon returning to Ukraine, he "realized what treasures are hidden there,"[25] and he began to document them, keeping a diary, photographing, and later, recording videos. In this manner, his trips turned into "expeditions." To be sure, "I knew nothing about An-sky [Shlomo Zanvil Rapoport (1863-1920), a.k.a. S. An-sky, who had led Jewish ethnographic expeditions in the area early in the 20th century]; I did not understand what I should record."[26] Yet even though he was unskilled in the science of documentation, Dvorkin saw value in recording his impressions. The following is a description of a Jewish cemetery from his expedition diary of 1986 (published several years later in a newspaper article): "We crawl over a low stone wall. Here you don't feel at all the breath of death; there are no gravestones or photographs of people who lived at some time [a common phenomenon in Soviet times]. You feel a lightness. At times it even seems that our ancestors are smiling at us . . . they are watching with their kind eyes. 'You came? Shalom Aleichem!' "[27]

In the summer of 1988, several friends joined Dvorkin on a trip to Medzhybizh: Veniamin Lukin (b. 1950) with his family; Katia (now Hava-Brokha) Korzakova (b. 1969); and Vladimir (Yehudah) Gorenshtein (b. 1958). Lukin, both an engineer by training and a freelance researcher, described the existing Jewish cemetery of Leningrad for a collective project titled "Petersburg Historical Cemeteries."[28] In his words, "Dvorkin aroused us with his stories," and for this reason, he and his family decided to spend their vacation in Medzhybizh. Korzakova, a student of classical philology at Leningrad State University, was interested in Hebrew and Jewish culture. Gorenshtein, a participant in Jewish circles who had graduated as a camera operator from the VGIK (Gerasimov Institute of Cinematography), took a Panasonic video camera with him (it had been brought in from the West by Jewish "tourists" for sale in the USSR to fund the needs of the Jewish movement).[29] Lukin remembers Medzhybizh in 1988 as "an ordinary, dusty Ukrainian village . . ., and at the cemetery, something wondrous—magnificent white carved gravestones with interesting symbolism, amazing bas reliefs." All the participants in the expedition felt that they had "encountered something genuine and incomprehensible,"[30] which deeply influenced them.

In Dvorkin's words: "We did not notice the start of perestroika; only around 1988 did we comprehend that something was changing."[31] However, in Leningrad in 1988, a legal society of Jewish culture had already been formed,[32] and its organizers invited Dvorkin to give a lecture on Jewish culture in the Karl Marx (!) House of Culture. To his amazement: "I go there to deliver my first lecture on biblical literature and my eyes pop out of my head because there are approximately 300 people there!"[33] Mikhail Nosonovskii (b. 1970), a member of the audience and a student at the Polytechnical Institute at the time, provides the following recollection: "The lectures made an unforgettable impression on me. I was then somewhat familiar with Jewish history . . . however, from Dvorkin I learned a mass of new words dealing with concepts and names that I had not heard before, such as 'musar,' 'Medzhybizh,' the 'magid of Mezerich.' "[34]

In the summer of 1989, a Jewish expedition again set out to Medzhybizh and other historic Ukrainian shtetls. Dvorkin's friends were there, and they met up as well with a number of other students. Dvorkin had come upon Leningrad students in Vilnius, where he had gone to persuade participants of the first and last USSR "Jewish student construction brigade" to join his expedition.[35] Among those who arrived from Vilnius was a student of the Leningrad Polytechnical Institute, Leonid Maksimov (Aryeh Ol'man, b. 1969), who recalls: "Dvorkin invited us to clear the area of the Jewish cemetery, where there were amazing works of art. We arrived in Medzhybizh, and Ilya led us literally into the forest! We took saws and axes and began to clear [the area]" (Fig. 2).[36] The expedition participants paid their own way, although they received food and lodging. "Refuseniks provided me with money," recalls Dvorkin. "I had no need of money because, thank God, my parents made a good living and I did not need anything, and I spent this money on expeditions to shtetls."[37]

Among the participants of the 1989 expedition were Dvorkin's old friends, the chemist Valery Dymshits (b. 1959) and his wife, Olga. In Dymshits' recollection: "We are talking about young people from a subculture of the Soviet intelligentsia. For them, travel and summer trips were part of the usual way of life; after all, one had to spend the vacation somehow! In these trips, people saw amazing gravestones, incomprehensible inscriptions, which had to be understood, deciphered, studied. That's how the stimulus to study came about."[38] In the evenings, after working at the cemetery, the participants gave lectures and studied Hebrew. "Ilya had a brilliant idea: in

Fig. 2 *Dvorkin at Jewish cemetery, Ukraine 1989* from personal archive of Ilya Dvorkin.

order to work successfully in the expeditions, one needed trained people, specialists. He returned with the idea of opening a university."[39] According to Dvorkin, he did not actually plan to establish a university, but it turned out that one needed to prepare people for the expeditions, to teach them to read inscriptions.[40] Ol'man remarks astutely: "The year 1989 was the best time in Russian history over the last hundred years: the economy and the system were still working, but the country was already free. A year later, the system was already destroyed, and a year before then, we did not have freedom. It was, therefore, entirely natural to think of opening a university precisely in 1989; it was a period when the unthinkable was possible."[41]

The idea for a Jewish university had two other, unexpected, co-authors. At that time, Dvorkin began to work with Yuri Ruppo, a Jewish intellectual who had established a cosmetics cooperative in Leningrad. Dvorkin proposed organizing Jewish tourism, that is, bringing "people from all over the world" to visit the Jewish shtetls of Ukraine and Belarus.[42] The plan to earn "big money" from large-scale foreign Jewish tourism in the USSR became the pragmatic basis for founding the university. Dvorkin and Ruppo felt that in order to succeed in developing the tourist business, it was necessary to establish documentation of Jewish communities and to train knowledgeable guides and tour leaders. This required "preparatory courses," which Ruppo was willing to finance.[43] In addition, in the fall of 1989, the director of the Kirov House of Culture, "Comrade Rodzevich," as Dvorkin referred to him, made an offer. In this House of Culture, a large venue for cultural activities, "in one room sat the Pamiat' Society [devoted to cultivating Russian national historical heritage],[44] in another some other nationalists, nearby were Tatars, and they gave the Jews a little room." Rodzevich suggested that Dvorkin establish a Jewish people's university and become its rector. "And then they wrote me down as the rector of this Jewish evening university. Frankly speaking, I did not even establish it; it arose on its own in the fall of 1989," recalls Dvorkin.[45]

Formally, the university was founded in affiliation with the Leningrad Society of Jewish Culture (LSJC). According to Dymshits, two factions conducted a struggle within the society—Soviet Jewish veterans who wanted to return to the 1930s-model of Soviet culture in Yiddish, and "underground youth in jeans," namely, Zionists promoting Hebrew and Israel. Dvorkin's model of an apolitical university avoided this generational conflict and suited all sides.[46]

The University Opens

"In 1988," Dvorkin recalls, "I was 34 years old. I had publications, academic experience, friends—scientific notables. I was part of the academic milieu but did not have a formal status. I understood the structure of academic science very well; in that sense, I was not an imposter."[47]

Dvorkin's friend Veniamin Lukin felt that the university was continuing the tradition of the early 20th-century Petersburg school of Jewish academic science under new conditions: "We had heard about An-sky and the Jewish museum [that contained his collections] and we felt that we were reviving [that] tradition."[48] Dvorkin, for his part, recalls that Lukin was "very excited over the continuity with the turn of the century; it did not excite me that much."[49] Nonetheless, in his contacts with various official bodies, Dvorkin raised the issue of succession to the Leningrad Jewish university that had been closed by authorities in 1925—in particular, with regard to obtaining a permanent building from municipal authorities (this, however, never came about).[50] In a newspaper article from 1992, Dvorkin is identified as the rector "of the educational institution that had existed on the banks of the Neva until the end of the 1920s, was destroyed at the time and restored three years ago."[51]

In order to attract students, a publicity campaign was launched in the fall of 1989. "We called people, we organized evenings with lectures in the synagogue, and we left our telephone numbers so they could call us. I rang up an enormous number of people from my home," recalls Hava-Brokha Korzakova. "We left notices about enrollment. Various kinds of people came, some more serious, others less so; people came who intended to emigrate. People would come to one lecture and then not appear again. Non-Jews also came; we did not drive anyone away."[52] At one student gathering, there was an exhibition of photographs from the previous summer's expedition. Vladimir Levin (b. 1971), at that time a student at the Herzen Pedagogical Institute in Leningrad, recalls: "I was amazed by the photographs of Medzhibozh, not so much the Jewish headstones but that there are such castles in the USSR! It was clear that I ought to go to the lectures."[53]

As Dvorkin admits, the structure set up in 1989 hardly deserved the title of "university"; in reality, it was "courses in Judaic studies," with evening classes conducted two or three times a week in rented quarters.[54] "It was not really on the level of a genuine university, of course, but we did not feel like merely a study group," remarks Korzakova.[55] In fact, this framework ideally suited the interests of many Leningrad Jews who, as a result of Soviet antisemitism, were unable to enroll in humanities departments and so became chemists, engineers, or mathematicians. "People retrained: engineers became historians and students of the humanities."[56]

Dymshits, for instance, was working at the time on a doctoral dissertation in chemistry:

> All the PJU students were working somewhere and studying at some primary institution, and in the evenings and during days off, they studied [in the Jewish courses] seriously. As I did not plan to make a living from this or to engage in it professionally, I studied for pleasure; there were no exams or report cards. . . . This was also a Soviet model—the evening university of Marxism-Leninism, that is, the right thing you do for self-education: you go there; sometimes it's boring, sometimes not, sometimes you play hooky.[57]

As Vladimir Levin recalls his studies: "There were evening lectures; I did not always attend them, and I was not always paying attention when I went. In the end, Dvorkin gave me a piece of paper certifying that I had studied at his place."[58]

Instructors at PJU included the following Leningrad humanities professors: Aleksander Zaitsev (classical antiquity), Leonard Gertsenberg (Indo-European studies), and Natal'ia Iukhneva (ethnography). The main "discovery" was Isidor Levin, who had studied Judaica in Tartu (Estonia) in the interwar period and who considered himself a follower of Wissenschaft des Judentums.[59] More than thirty years later, his students remember Levin's lectures: "The Temple was like a slaughterhouse, columns of smoke, blood, and the odor of burnt meat."[60] As Dymshits recalls: "The brilliant humanistic scholars did not always know a lot about the Jews, but they gave the audience a notion of how an academic looks, how he thinks, how science is done; this was very important. . . . I studied Hebrew and Yiddish; there was a heap of strange lectures on Jewish history, linguistics, and so forth."[61] The abundance of subjects was related to Dvorkin's approach that "it is impossible in principle to have Judaic studies without Hebrew texts . . . a person who is incapable of reading any Hebrew text is not a specialist in Judaic studies."[62]

The popularity of the self-styled "university" for evening courses grew. "In 1990, we received 450 applications. . . . Everyone wanted to study Judaic studies, although no one knew what it was."[63] The university's organizers announced in 1990 that 30 people had completed the first year of courses; in 1990, they planned to enroll a new cohort of 120 students. In the 1989–1990 academic year, a total of about 200 people participated in studies, and the plan was for 400–500 for the following year.[64] Semyon Parizhskii (b. 1968) decided to join PJU in 1992, when it started to offer classes on a regular basis, not only in the evening: "I was studying in the philosophy department of St. Petersburg State University and I wanted to study in tandem with my other degree program; I was seeking a lively and serious intellectual life."[65]

Around 1992, PJU turned into a major project. It now had three departments: historical-ethnographic, philological, and a faculty of Judaic studies, along with two institutes—one devoted to research on the East European diaspora (which was responsible for the expeditions); and a methodological center for Jewish education, which dealt with educational projects. Alongside this was a beit midrash—an attempt to create an academic yeshiva[66] —which played an important role in the project: "Dvorkin, when he saw how a beit midrash operates, also began to operate one. Activity included not only the discussion of texts; in addition, artists sketched what we constructed in our heads in the beit midrash. Then musicians joined in and began to form a 'creative beit midrash'—pre-prepared texts were discussed and transformed into sketches and theatrical studies" (Fig. 3).[67]

Initially, all instructors worked as volunteers.[68] In the fall of 1989, Ruppo arranged salaried positions for three people under the aegis of his cosmetics cooperative: Dvorkin, Lukin, and Boris Khaimovich (b. 1955, an astronomer, who became dean of the historical faculty and head of the institute for the study of the East European diaspora). "But money was procured also by other means. From the West, people sent computers and cameras, which Ilya would sell, and we worked," recalls Khaimovich.[69] Eventually, Ruppo also began to pay the instructors out of his own pocket. Dvorkin recalls that in 1990, during a visit to Jerusalem, executives at the Joint Distribution Committee (JDC) asked him, "Why don't you request money from us?" A grant was received and then "we had plenty of money, we began to pay a normal salary."[70] At the time, the university benefited from the very high exchange rate of the dollar and the low cost of living in the USSR, as measured in dollars. In the early 1990s, ten dollars was considered a substantial sum, and a hundred dollars was equivalent to a monthly salary.[71] At the beginning of the 1990s, Khaimovich and Dymshits were consultants for the production of a French film about Soviet Jews; with the money they received for two weeks of consultations, 50 students at PJU traveled around Ukrainian shtetls

Fig. 3 *Beyt midrash at PJU, about 1990* from personal archive of Aryeh Ol'man.

for three months on expeditions, with fully subsidized transportation and housing. Afterwards, however, "when life in Russia improved, the money [we had available] was incompatible with our needs, and this harmed our projects," recalls Dymshits.[72]

Evidently, it was not large salaries that attracted the instructors. Dvorkin himself reflects about that time: "I did not earn much money at that university. I received a salary just like everyone else, rather modest. But my father had a good salary and I had no material problems in those years. . . . The important thing was the feeling that you were somewhere on top of social and academic life, associated and meeting with each prominent foreign Jewish figure arriving in Russia, from Yitzhak Shamir to Shlomo Carlebach and Rabbi [Adin] Steinsaltz."[73]

"It Was Like a Family"

Everyone who remembers PJU of the early 1990s invariably notes the special atmosphere that prevailed there. "In the first year or two it was very much like a family, we were continually meeting, we would celebrate holidays together and meet on Shabbat."[74] "There was the feeling of a family, of closeness. Expeditions possessed the atmosphere of a Soviet tourist excursion. And at the university, they would organize a seder for all the students, instructors, and members of their families, Jews and non-Jews—everyone." There was no feeling of any hierarchy: the prevailing favorite term of the perestroika period, informality, was considered "a particular virtue . . .

This was the spirit of the time."[75] Vladimir Levin, studying in parallel at a state institution of higher education, notes that "there was nothing [PJU had] in common with the strict Soviet hierarchical academic system"; particularly striking, of course, in PJU was "the rector, at whose home half the students could always be found."[76]

Semyon Parizhskii, who also came to PJU from the state university, recalled being astonished by "strange people who combined the figure of a yeshiva *bokher* and university student. There was a domestic situation there: they cooked soup; people would walk around with cooking pots, and study the Talmud."[77] Efim Levertov decided to become a student in the fall of 1992. This is what he recalls about his first visit to the university:

A group of mainly bearded men were sitting under a lattice-like awning—it was Sukkot, and they were celebrating the Jewish holiday. At the head of the table sat the rector himself, Ilya Dvorkin. That's how we met. We drank kosher Israeli vodka and they served refreshments. After two or three glasses, Ilya asked me what particularly interested me; what did I want to study. I was prepared for the question and answered that I was interested in the philosophy of Spinoza. Ilya paused for a second to think and raised his eyes to the latticed roof. "In Russia," he said, "no one studies this. So, for now, you'll be an evening auditor."[78]

Dmitrii El'iashevich (b. 1964), who came to work at the university in 1990 (among the staff, he was the sole possessor of a "genuine" advanced degree in the humanities [Russ. – *kandidat nauk*, the equivalent of a Ph.D.]), recalls PJU not as "an academic structure but rather a club of friends with a mass of interesting interaction." El'iashevich was teaching in a state institute of higher education, and initially his work at PJU was essentially a hobby, a place for friendly socializing. He agrees that the very division into an official sphere (regular work) and an intimate one—friendly, Jewish—reflected a norm on the part of the Soviet intelligentsia.[79] Dymshits notes: "Ninety percent of the students did not need the PJU diploma, which did not offer anything; they did not need a "piece of paper"; it was interesting for them to find out about something and to be in good company and spend time in an interesting way" (Fig. 4).[80]

It is possible to speak of a generation of autodidacts who established Jewish studies in Russia.[81] Vladimir Levin recalls: "In my third year of study at PJU, I myself conducted a seminar about the Jews of Petersburg. A lack of knowledge did not bother us: after ten Hebrew lessons, I began to lead tours in Hebrew. It was not dilettantism; there were other criteria. In those lectures that I attended at the state university, not everything was profound science, one cannot say that in PJU the level of teaching was worse."[82] Aryeh Ol'man adds: "You can say that instruction followed the 'Lancaster system': today I teach what I learned yesterday. What was studied yesterday passed through the personality; it was not the sum of knowledge, but transmission of one's self. It was the method of instruction of the first European universities, as with Abelard."[83] El'iashevich agrees: "Everyone both taught and studied. I began to deliver a course about the history of the Jews of Russia, and knew little more than the students, but it was very interesting to prepare. We all were simultaneously students and teachers."[84]

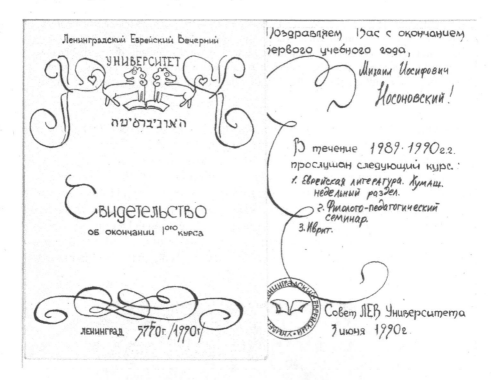

Fig. 4 *Diploma of M. Nosonovskii, first year of PJU, 1990.*

Parizhskii recalls that many foreigners came to teach at the university: "Russia was fashionable; people would travel." For example, Prof. Haggai Ben Shammai came from the Hebrew University, and it turned out there was no one to translate for him. "Dvorkin summoned me, [saying], you'll translate. And I was just beginning to study Hebrew. From the second year, I was already teaching Hebrew."[85] Parizhskii thinks that Dvorkin "purposely brought" religiously Orthodox professors from Israel who "not so much imparted knowledge through their lectures as served as role models, showing that such a combination in general was possible, that it was possible to be an intellectual, an Orthodox Jew, and a university professor."[86]

PJU and the Shtetl Expeditions

As we have seen, the very establishment of the university was closely tied to the need to train professional cadres for expeditions to former Jewish shtetls. Mikhail Nosonovskii recalls:

The linchpin uniting the informal life of this strange institution was the summer trips to Ukraine and other places. Dvorkin set very general and vague objectives for the trips: questioning and recording (without a specific goal) local residents about their prewar life and about the Holocaust; simultaneously photographing gravestones, Jewish homes, and the buildings of former synagogues, and in general, anything of interest that turned up. I think that for Ilya, pedagogical tasks were foremost: participants of the trip became imbued with the spirit of Jewish history; they saw with their own eyes where their grandmothers and grandfathers came from; and at the same time, they read suitable Jewish texts.[87]

Boris Khaimovich was in charge of the expeditions (Fig. 5). An old acquaintance of Dvorkin, he happened to meet him in 1989 after the latter's return from a summer expedition. Shaken by the material from the Medzhybizh cemetery that Dvorkin showed him, Khaimovich left his work in the Pulkovskii observatory: "I understood that I had to change my destiny."[88] A broad work plan for expeditions and follow-up for the coming years was drawn up, which was meant to culminate in the creation of a catalog of Jewish "monuments" (historical and commemorative sites) in Ukraine, though this project did not come to fruition.[89] In the beginning, some of the work of the expeditions reflected the original plan to organize mass Jewish tourism (tours, guides, and so

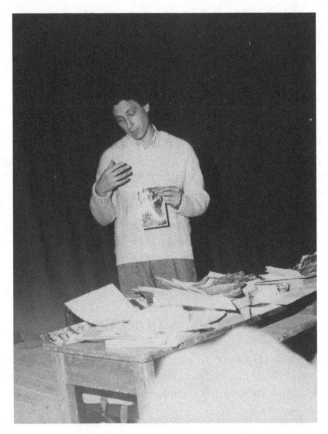

Fig. 5 *Khaimovich with materials of expeditions, 1990s* from personal archive of Aryeh Ol'man.

forth were prepared); later, this part of the program was dropped. However, these initial ideas produced many years of fruitful cooperation with the Center for Jewish Art of the Hebrew University of Jerusalem (Lukin, who immigrated to Israel at that time, was able to arrange the contact between PJU and the center). Between 1992 and 1997, the university and center conducted dozens of joint expeditions, not only to Ukraine but also to Belarus, Lithuania, the Caucasus, and Central Asia (Fig. 6).

In hindsight, Khaimovich analyzes the grandiosely ambitious expedition project as follows:

> We did not have much experience: for example, we devoted less attention to people and more to buildings and cemeteries. We did not have an ethnographer, we did not have professionally prepared questionnaires, and we let people talk about what they wanted to say. And they talked about the Holocaust. Rites, local customs, language—this was hardly discussed, unfortunately. . . . I understood that we were operating unprofessionally but it was impossible to act otherwise. It was on a mass scale; all the students went; it was part of the educational process.[90]

Valery Dymshits also participated regularly in the expeditions: "It was a kind of spiritual meat grinder from which people emerged somehow different. Along with this, Dvorkin regenerated all of us nationally."[91] Dymshits felt that, in the expeditions, "knowledge was not a goal but an instrument"; expedition participants "understood what Jewishness was, that it meant something more than an entry in a passport [i.e., the "nationality" entry in Soviet identity cards]."[92] Khaimovich agrees: "He [Dvorkin] *made Jews*, conscious ones at that, out of an enormous number of people."[93]

Fig. 6 *Dvorkin at the Bukhara expedition, 1990s* from personal archive of Ilya Dvorkin.

Today, however, Vladimir Levin regards these expeditions as a failure, certainly in
the scientific sense:

These expeditions were not about science; it was the quintessence of a search for identity,
an excursion around Jewish places. I would ask where the graves of murdered Jews were
located and I would say kaddish over the graves. It was important to me. Today I understand that our expeditions were a complete failure, that the [academic] level was very low,
that we missed out on a lot of information that was then still possible to obtain [but is no
longer available]. The studies in classes in Petersburg were not a sham, but the expeditions were a sham; we missed the most important things. It did not occur to us to invite
professionals, especially ethnographers, to teach us. The primary result of the expeditions
was, however, that we formed our identity, and that is very good.[94]

In a personal conversation, Dvorkin explained the importance of the trips around
the shtetls in one sentence: "There, it was simpler to imagine ourselves as Jews." It
seems one could not better formulate the purpose and content of the PJU-organized
expeditions.

Crisis and Termination of the University's Operation

The crisis that unfolded at the university in the mid-1990s had several causes. "In the
mid-1990s, after everyone who wanted to immigrate to Israel had already departed,
the exchange rate of the dollar [against the ruble] stabilized and the former scope of
activity became impossible. The staff was reduced, PJU accumulated debts, salaries
were paid three months late."[95] Indeed, many of my interviewees, formerly students
and instructors at PJU, immigrated to Israel: Hava-Brokha Korzakova and Veniamin
Lukin in 1990; Boris Khaimovich, Vladimir Levin, and Aryeh Ol'man in 1992. All of
them, however, continued to participate in PJU activities, to join expeditions, and to
remain part of that society.[96]

By the mid-1990s, in addition to the emigration of a significant portion of the
founders and the impossibility of continuing such broad activity on relatively small
grants, internal conflicts hindered the work of the university. One of the disputes between the directors of the two institutes (education and the diaspora) and the rector,
Dvorkin, concerned financial allocations. According to Dvorkin: "My colleagues
wanted to divide the funds themselves, directly for projects, not through the university. When sponsors gave money for education, I took grants for the university and
utilized those grants for teaching. The same thing with the expeditions—they gave
money for expeditions, I transferred it to university seminars. My colleagues thought
that I was taking "their" money—all with the best intentions.[97]

PJU's fundamental problem, however, was deeper than personnel or financial disagreements. Valery Dymshits speculates:

In the mid-1990s, I already understood that our activity had to take on a professional
configuration, [that we needed] to establish a faculty or center like everywhere else in
the world. The active participation and investment of various international Jewish studies

institutions in our university showed that we were not doing the right thing. Our inter-action with them indicated that we were a very amateur outfit, lacking professionalism. Dvorkin's conception did not correspond to the generally accepted notion of a university, faculty, and so forth. In sum, we seemed like ridiculous dilettantes, with ideas about the new Jew, but without following the rules of the game of the professional academic world.[98]

Vladimir Levin agrees. "As long as Dvorkin was operating an open university, that is, evening classes, it worked. But if one looks seriously at a university in which there is 'a rector without a degree,' as one Israeli professor said to me with a laugh, it no longer works. From the viewpoint of a normal Western academy, Dvorkin and his activity could not be considered academic activity."[99] Dvorkin, in turn, believes that by 1994–1995, it became clear that "Jewish academic work was not taking place in Russia . . . we were not producing any *Wissenschaft* in Russian, and in any case, I was not the person who should be dealing with this."[100]

The professional who attempted to carry out the necessary reforms was Dmitrii El'iashevich:

> Having become a deputy rector and dean, I quickly understood that if we wanted to be something serious, we had to reform this interest club into something much more serious. I began to require documentation for the courses (at least, a syllabus) and to invite professionals. People wanted to preserve the atmosphere of the early 1990s, but this was impossible. Toward the end of the 1990s, the government began to introduce stricter requirements and criteria of a formal nature. The notion of free-wheelers and a club could not survive, and Ilya was well aware of this. The reason for his departure was precisely because of this understanding that the university could not exist in the form that he had conceived it.[101]

In the summer of 1998, in the context of these conflicts, Dvorkin decided to immigrate to Israel, study in the Mandel School for Educational Leadership (whose program he completed in two years), and to write a doctoral dissertation (which he did not complete). Currently, he lives in Jerusalem and is engaged in educational projects (mostly involving the post-Soviet geographic space). Dmitrii El'iashevich won the election for rector that was arranged by the academic council of PJU (he was the only candidate), but he did not continue the work of PJU. On the basis of the university's faculties, he created a different institute of higher education, the Petersburg Institute of Judaic Studies, which was accredited and exists to this day.[102] Thus ended the saga of the Petersburg Jewish University.

Looking Back at the PJU Project: Achievements and Limitations

PJU arose in the context of enormous interest in everything that seemed "Jewish" in the USSR of the late 1980s.[103] "The very word 'Jew' in the USSR was taboo, devoid of any positive content. It was something that prevented you from being accepted into an institute."[104] The combination of the words "Jewish" and "university" was, therefore, very attractive to many. "Some, genuinely interested, made it their profession, their life's work. For others, it was important to impart some content to the word 'Jew.'. . . . [The latter] were people who studied intensively, went on expeditions, but at some point went away, 'surfeited' by this."[105]

For Ilya Dvorkin, the founder and rector of the university, things were different: his tasks were more universal. Utopia, he says, was "the chief motor that drove me," just as it "evidently motivated the people two hundred years ago who founded Wissenschaft des Judentums, the utopia of Jewish science."[106] Dvorkin saw in the university "an attempt to revive Jewry via the academy, via research, and the discovery of new facts, Jewish intellectualism." Thus, he understood Judaism "not through mitzvot, ritual, and prayer, but as an intellectual tradition, Jewish thought, and so forth."[107]

Armed with his utopian vision, Dvorkin—this "vessel with charisma,"[108] as Vladimir Levin characterized him—was able to attract his students. "Dvorkin, of course, was a person with a messianic bent; he instilled this messianic idea into others; he had his hasidim. Formally, he was the rector, but in reality, he was a hasidic tzadik. This undoubtedly pleased him; he frequently spoke about it."[109] Aryeh Ol'man notes:

> We were ordinary Russian people, absolutely ignorant in the Jewish sense . . . and behold, in our midst arose a great project to create a new culture uniting the Soviet intelligentsia and Jewish knowledge. I was most influenced by the novel of Chingiz Aitmatov, *And the Day Lasts More than a Hundred Years*; it had the image of a *mankurt* [the author's term for an unthinking slave], beings who had lost their memory and roots. And I strove to stop being a *mankurt*.[110]

He adds: "The main idea of the university was *Bildung*, building oneself within the project. . . . We did not speak then of "creating a civilization," because we were unfamiliar with such words. But there was a sense of universality and generality of the project."[111] Semyon Parizhskii goes further in his thoughts:

> For me it was an important moment: I saw Jewish culture, texts, and thought as an alternative to Western science and culture. A different view of European science and thought. There was the illusion that this was an alternative philosophical teaching, one of the means of overcoming European metaphysics, as later on, people began to perceive, for example, postcolonialism and other trends. In that sense I was a true "hasid" of Ilya Dvorkin. It was viewed as a philosophical-anthropological project, that is, the creation of a new type of thinking, based on both European science and Jewish texts, on a particular approach to them.[112]

Dvorkin understood very well that not everyone shared his majestic utopian vision. Dymshits, for instance, treated it ironically:

> Dvorkin presented it as if in our midst there would be a new Jew; in order to create him/her, we needed all of world culture: Greek, Latin, Persian. From Dvorkin's point of view, the Jew was some sort of cultural superman, practically Nietzschean, who must master all world knowledge. It's similar to Lenin's remark that one could become a communist only by mastering all human knowledge.[113]

El'iashevich completely agrees with this: "With regard to the utopia of creating a civilization, a new Jew, a new culture—this was heard and discussed, but I did not believe in it. If it is incommensurate with one's possibilities, it turns into farce."[114]

An alternative approach that united Lukin, Khaimovich, and Dymshits was an interest in the history of Jewish culture "without the religious underpinnings."[115] For Lukin, the main thing was "history as a principle uniting the people." He explains:

> There was the feeling of a desert, the absence of Jewish content in Petersburg, and behold, the city was filled with people and movement. Then, on a more romantic level, it seemed as though awareness of the past is what makes us Jews. Jews are not born but become, thanks to received knowledge, said Isidor Levin. *Many, indeed, became such*, thanks to the university.[116]

For Khaimovich, "the main thing was attaining civilization." He adds:

> Dvorkin wanted to establish a *new* civilization. I did not believe in this; I did not even believe in the creation of a new culture. This is not [something that is] created artificially; I did not believe that certain people, even super-talented, could create a civilization. I wanted to restore civilization; it was important to attain and present it, to show what kind of civilization we had had. Achieving this was constructive for me.[117]

There are various ways of judging the success of PJU. Parizhskii believes that, initially, it offered an alternative to the "colonization" of Jewish life in the post-USSR by the Jewish Agency, the "Joint" (JDC), and Habad, all of which "import Jewish content" without enabling "anything authentic to grow." As opposed to this: "Academic Judaica could just have been the substratum from which . . . Russian Jews could have acquired their voice, found for themselves their usable past, selected cultural codes for expressing their world view. . . . I saw the task as the decolonization of Russian Jewish life, wherein academic Judaica . . . would remain the sole enclave where . . . foreign models did not dominate."[118]

These hopes were not realized, however, as post-Soviet Jewry produced "not one writer, not one philosopher, not one book that would become a fact of Jewish culture."[119] Parizhskii's harsh conclusion is that: "Russian Jewry again became 'the Jews of silence,' because it had nothing to say. Colonial, imported Jewish cultural projects completely drowned out any attempts to think independently, to understand on our own how Jewish culture in Russia could or ought to appear. The idea of basing a new Jewish culture on academic Judaic studies failed."[120]

A more positive assessment is offered by El'iashevich:

> This nongovernmental activity later led to the establishment of two departments in state higher educational institutions. They revived Jewish academic life, which was very important. It was by no means a failure. To obtain a successful outcome, one needed a long-standing tradition, which had been severed. It is naive to expect us to produce a new Dubnov. Something developed, and in this I see the merit of the generation of the 1990s. In the 1980s, it seemed that everything would be different; today it is understandable that it could not have been otherwise.[121]

In the view of Valery Dymshits: "Broadly speaking, yes, it was an all-round failure. But from the viewpoint of individual careers of people who decided that this was important and their life's work, it's fine. Everything worked out for those who wanted it. Great Russian Judaica did not appear out of this. Nothing came of the great ideas, but nevertheless, something developed."[122] In fact, the overwhelming majority of my informants built successful careers in various spheres of Judaic studies (Lukin, Khaimovich, Levin, and Ol'man, in Israel; El'iashevich, Parizhskii, and Dymshits, in Russia). Thus, unquestionably, PJU played an important positive role in the lives of many people.

The Significance of PJU in the History of Soviet and Post-Soviet Jewry

Among the active participants of the PJU project, only Ilya Dvorkin was involved in the Jewish underground of the 1980s, and even he could not be considered a "fighter against the regime." Others of his generation (Khaimovich, Lukin, Dymshits) were recognized and established Soviet professionals. None of them, of course, was active in the Communist Party, but neither were they political dissidents or refuseniks. One could apply to all of them (including Dvorkin) Alexei Yurchak's notion of "ideology inside out"—that is, a negation of both of the major contending positions—which applied to a large group of Soviet people who identified neither with the regime nor with the struggle against it.[123] In that sense, and in light of the case we have discussed here, the image of an oppressed mass of Soviet Jews silently opposing the Soviet regime requires refinement and further nuancing. Moreover, the common view that Soviet Jews faced three options in 1991—reviving Jewish life and rebuilding Jewish communities; disappearing as Jews and living in the newly established post-Soviet states; or abandoning their homelands to emigrate[124]—is oversimplified. In fact, it was possible to choose more than one of these options, which, indeed, many of the leading figures of this article did.

Evidently a surfeit of vision in creating new Jewish structures was common, at least in Leningrad. Ilya Dvorkin saw himself as the founder of an innovative form of Jewish identity, if not Jewish civilization.[125] In a less grandiose form, other founders of PJU also envisioned a universal idea (if not of building, then "attaining" or "recovering" civilization).

As evidenced in the recollections of eyewitnesses, late Soviet and post-Soviet Jewish activity inevitably was a continuation under new conditions of Soviet experiences and Soviet forms of life, from summer vacations to the "university of Marxism-Leninism." PJU's form of socializing the project's participants very much recalls the youth movements in the late USSR, "where it did not matter in which direction they moved, only that they were moving; these were informal organizations in which the most important thing was associating together, people who create a social milieu and live in it. The content itself was unimportant."[126]

Dvorkin, of course, would not agree with such a definition; for him content played a most important role. In Dvorkin's success in playing the role of a "hasidic tzadik," however, one truly could see the legacy of something quintessentially Soviet, namely, a culture in which dissidents thrived as intellectual gurus of the Soviet period, always elaborating universal intellectual theories and surrounded by young followers/ disciples. Dvorkin associated closely with some of those gurus (for instance, Georgii Shchedrovitskii and Yuri Lotman).[127] Undoubtedly (as Dvorkin himself mentions), he broadly followed the outline of a late Soviet intellectual milieu centered around a "fantastic academic leader" surrounded by a "heap of youth."[128] Moreover, the transformation of PJU (and other Jewish structures) into flourishing institutes in the late Soviet period recalls the experience of other movements that emerged from the underground and successfully integrated into Soviet reality of the late 1980s.[129]

The epoch of genuine revolution in the USSR in the late 1980s–early 1990s was a unique context for Dvorkin's utopian ideas. "There was a lot of revolutionism in the endeavor to establish some kind of unfamiliar separate Jewish university, a feeling that this would be a new earth and a new sky and a new person. There was a lot of madness in this but also pragmatism, because if you seek a lot, there is a chance to obtain something. It was similar to the first years after the 1917 revolution."[130] According to Dvorkin: "Had we not tried to develop Judaic studies from 1989 to 1994, it is not certain that they would have arisen later."[131] All those whom I interviewed agreed that "this was a time of a certain intoxication, a euphoric sense that suddenly everything was possible, of great hope that it would be better. It was if we were following a path toward a bright future, along the model of the West, which, it seemed, was comprehensible and toward which we should strive. It was not even utopia but a clear plan."[132] Perestroika, thus, to a decisive degree, was the reason for the establishment of PJU, as for all independent Jewish activity in the last years of the USSR. Outside of this revolutionary context, Dvorkin would have remained semi-marginal, working officially as a tutor, and Valery Dymshits would have continued his work as an academic chemist. Moreover, PJU was part of an ecosystem of Jewish organizations in Petersburg and the USSR/Russia that emerged in the general context of mass aliyah and exuberant societal activity. The university was not "standing alone in an empty field": it was in contact with other Jewish organizations in Petersburg. "After all, everyone knew everyone else and interacted with each other."[133]

My informants' recollections of a happy epoch of freedom and fulfilled hopes in the 1990s contrasts sharply with the image in the mass consciousness of today's Russia of the "wild" 1990s, a time of economic decline and rampant criminality.[134] Evidently, this dissonance reflects the contrast between the experience, on the one hand, of young Jewish intellectuals who received a chance to realize their dreams, and, on the other, that of the "ordinary" Soviet citizen who barely survived the difficult reality of a country undergoing transformation. This topic is worthy of further examination. In the meantime, this essay offers a preliminary sketch in the research regarding Jewish academic activity as part of the post-Soviet cultural renaissance of the 1990s. My description, based on the story of PJU, requires further study—foremost, a comparison with occurrences at that time in Moscow, Ukraine, and other centers of Jewish life.[135]

Glancing at the past, Ilya Dvorkin gave an embittered evaluation (possibly in the wake of the collapse of global plans and personal ambitions): "Russian Jewry, like Soviet Jewry, is a very weak society; it lacks brains . . . it has very deep roots but a burdensome fate . . . it is a very weak thing, unable to reach internal agreement, and incapable of uniting efforts."[136] The brief history presented here indicates that Dvorkin's assessment may be overly pessimistic. The fantasies of a new civilization or great scientific school indeed disintegrated, but the successful professional careers in Judaic studies of some two dozen scholars, and the experience of hundreds of people connected to the university who acquired content for their nominal Jewishness, indicates the importance of the PJU project.

Notes

Stefani Hoffman translated this essay. I am grateful to her, as well as to Vladimir Levin, and Hillel Kazovskii, for their useful remarks.

1. Elie Wiesel, *The Jews of Silence: A Personal Report on Soviet Jewry*, trans. Neal Kozodoy (Philadelphia: 1967).

2. Alexei Yurchak, *Everything Was Forever, Until It Was No More: The Last Soviet Generation* (Princeton: 2005), 5–6.

3. Yaacov Ro'i, "Soviet Jewry from Identification to Identity," in *Contemporary Jewries: Convergence and Divergence*, ed. Eliezer Ben-Rafael, Yosef Gorny, and Yaacov Ro'i (Leiden: 2003), 183–193; Benjamin Pinkus, *The Jews of the Soviet Union: The History of a National Minority* (Cambridge: 1988), 216–232.

4. Benjamin Pinkus, *Sofah shel tekufah: yehudei brit hamoatzot be'idan Gorbachev, 1985–1991* (Beersheva: 1999), 257–275. For a survey of events related to the Gorbachev epoch, see Archie Brown, *Seven Years that Changed the World: Perestroika in Perspective* (Oxford: 2007); Anthony D'Agostino, *Gorbachev's Revolution, 1985–1991* (Basingstoke: 1998).

5. Zvi Gitelman, *A Century of Ambivalence: The Jews of Russia and the Soviet Union, 1881 to the Present*, 2nd expanded ed. (Bloomington: 2001), 193–194. On the direct link between the late Soviet regime's growing economic dependence on the West and liberalization in the policy toward East European countries and toward national minorities inside the USSR, see Yegor Gaidar, *Collapse of Empire: Lessons for Modern Russia*, trans. Antonina W. Bouis (Washington, D.C.: 2007), 167–175.

6. Among the authors writing about perestroika who adhere to this approach, see, in particular, Steven Kotkin, *Armageddon Averted: The Soviet Collapse, 1970–2000* (Oxford: 2001); Mark Kramer, "The Demise of the Soviet Bloc," *Journal of Modern History* 83 (2011), 788–854.

7. On perestroika as a moral and idea-driven revolution, see Leon Aron, *Roads to the Temple: Truth, Memory, Ideas, and Ideals in the Making of the Russian Revolution, 1987–1991* (New Haven: 2012).

8. Zvi Gitelman, "The Meanings of Jewishness in Russia and Ukraine," in Ben Rafael, Gorny, and Ro'i (eds.), *Contemporary Jewries*, 212.

9. One sees the clear imprint of this mixture of styles, for example, in the video recording of the opening of the International Mikhoels Center of Jewish Culture in the Jewish Chamber Music Theater on February 12, 1989, online at: youtube.com/watch?v = Y3X6MCK3nC0&ab_channel = MosheHemain (accessed 6 October 2021). We see hundreds of people gathering in a very Soviet setting (the Moscow Taganka movie theater); some of them look and act like "normal" members of the Soviet intelligentsia at an official event. Others look more informal, some wear "Jewish" headgear—a *kipah* or cap—and they try hard to act as relaxed as possible, demonstrating their newly acquired freedom. On the establishment of the Mikhoels Center, see Gitelman, *A Century of Ambivalence*, 224; also see online site at: http://mikhoelscenter.ru/.

10. This article is based on interviews that I conducted between March and May 2021. Additional support for my analysis comes from a volume of interviews with figures in the current Russian Jewish academic milieu: see Galina Zelenina, *Iudaika dva: renessans v litsakh*

(Moscow: 2015). See also Zvi Gitelman, "The Phoenix? Jewish Studies in Post-Communist Europe," *Journal of Modern Jewish Studies* 10, no. 1 (March 2011), 65–69.

11. Zelenina, *Iudaika dva,* 307.

12. Ibid.

13. Ibid., 313–315. "My brilliance was always a bit strange, part genius and part not" (ibid.), 310.

14. Ibid., 312 (emphasis added). Dvorkin also noted: "I began to observe Shabbat independently, but I observed it very strangely, I did not know that it begins on Friday evening. I simply devoted the Sabbath itself to studying Hebrew and Jewish books" (ibid., 308).

15. Ibid., 307–308. Dvorkin's search was typical of a trend among the intelligentsia of the late Soviet period. On Soviet Jews' turn to ecumenicism and Christianity, see Stefani Hoffman, "Sovetskaia evreiskaia intelligentsia: ee rol' i poiski identichnosti," in *Istoriia evreiskogo naroda v Rossii, t.3: Ot revolutsii 1917 goda do raspada Sovetskogo Soiusza,* ed. Michael Beizer (Jerusalem: 2017), 306–308.

16. Gitelman, *A Century of Ambivalence,* 184–186; Michael Beizer, "Jewish Studies Underground in Leningrad in the 1980s," *East European Jewish Affairs* 48, no. 1 (2018), 56–77.

17. Interview with Ilya Dvorkin (1 March 2021).

18. Ibid.

19. On the utopian ideas of opposition Jewish intellectuals at that time, see Hoffman, "Sovetskaia evreiskaia intelligentsia," 300–301.

20. Interview with Dvorkin.

21. Ibid.

22. Zelenina, *Iudaika dva,* 320. The distance between Khmelnitsky and Medzhibozh is 40 kilometers.

23. Ibid.

24. Ibid.

25. Ibid.

26. Ibid.

27. B. Usviatsova, "Shalom aleikhem!" *Vechernii Peterburg* 188 (1992), 3.

28. *Istoricheskie kladbischa Sankt-Peterburga,* eds. A. Kobak and Ju. Piriutko (St. Petersburg: 1993).

29. Interview with Veniamin Lukin (20 May 2021); "Leto v Slavute 1988: Ilya Dvorkin and Vladimir Gorenshtein," online at: youtube.com/watch?v = VMPMGs55O10. For part of the video filmed by Gorenshtein in 1988, see: youtube.com/playlist?list=PLDA25AF3C28922D17 (both accessed 6 October 2021). This kind of model was common as a means of financing Jewish activity in the USSR; cf. Mikhail Beizer, "Evreiskoe natsional'noe dvizhenie v SSSR, 1960–1989 gg.: prichiny, istoki i suchnost," in Beizer, *Istoriia evreiskogo naroda v Rossii, t.3,* 343–345.

30. Interview with Lukin.

31. Interview with Ilya Dvorkin (3 March 2021).

32. On the organization of Jewish cultural associations in the USSR beginning in 1988, see Pinkus, *Sofah shel tekufah,* 266–270.

33. Zelenina, *Iudaika dva,* 325.

34. Mikhail Nosonovskii, "K 30 letiiu Peterburgskogo evreiskogo universiteta," online at: https://blogs.7iskusstv.com/?p=77389 (accessed 6 October 2021).

35. In the late Soviet period, a "construction brigade" was a group of students operating under the aegis of the Komsomol, the youth wing of the Communist Party. During their summer vacations, these students would go to work at construction sites, combining vacation with work. The authorities officially recognized the Komsomol construction brigade movement; participants frequently were given a uniform. It is significant to note the use of this purely Soviet term (*stroiotriad*) with regard to the trips of Jewish students for excavations in the old city of Vilnius.

36. Interview with Aryeh Ol'man (7 May 2021).

37. Zelenina, *Iudaika dva,* 322.

38. Interview with Valery Dymshits (20 April 1921).

39. Ibid.

40. Interview with Dvorkin (1 March 2021).

41. Interview with Ol'man.

42. Zelenina, *Iudaika dva*, 323.

43. Interview with Dvorkin (1 March 2021).

44. The Pamiat' Society was a Russian nationalist organization that arose in the 1980s, initially to oppose the destruction of Russian national monuments, but which later became notorious for its antisemitism. See William Korey, *Russian Antisemitism, Pamyat, and the Demonology of Zionism* (Chur: 1995).

45. Zelenina, *Iudaika dva*, 325.

46. Interview with Dymshits (4 April 2021).

47. Interview with Dvorkin (10 March 2021).

48. Interview with Lukin. See also idem, "K stoletiiu obrazovaniia peterburgskoi nauchnoi shkoly evreiskoi istorii," in *Istoriia evreev v Rossii: problemy istochnikovedeniia i istoriografii,* ed. Dmitri A. El'iashevich (St. Petersburg: 1993), 1:13–26. On the An-sky collection, see the essay by Vladimir Levin in this issue, pp. 86, 98.

49. Interview with Dvorkin (1 March 2021).

50. For example, see the appeal written by Israeli professor Bezalel Narkiss to Petersburg mayor Anatolii Sobchak from November 6, 1991. Clearly written for Narkiss by someone in PJU (in Russian), it contains an emphatic request to return the university "to its former building or to another one that suits the needs of the educational process" (from the personal archive of Veniamin Lukin).

51. "Istoriiu obmanut' nevozmozhno," *Smena* (31 July 1992), 3. One might mistakenly conclude from the article that Dvorkin himself was the rector back in the 1920s, especially as "in his lectures . . . other epochs are present. . . . He recalls a medieval individual immersed in comprehending the secrets of being." (However, "the racing bike leaning against the bookcase returns one to the twentieth century" [ibid.].)

52. Interview with Hava Korzakova (14 April 2021).

53. Interview with Vladimir Levin (22 April 2021). Levin is referring to the restored remains of the Medzhybizh Castle, built in the 16th century.

54. Zelenina, *Iudaika dva*, 326. Lukin recalls: "I was skeptical about the university, as that appellation did not correspond to what, in fact, was a lecture hall" (interview with Lukin).

55. Interview with Korzakova.

56. Ibid.

57. Interview with Dymshits (20 April 2021).

58. Interview with Levin (20 April 2021).

59. Zelenina, *Iudaika dva*, 327–329.

60. Interview with Levin (22 April 2021).

61. Interview with Dymshits (20 April 2021).

62. Zelenina, *Iudaika dva*, 333.

63. Ibid., 326.

64. "Leningradskii evreiskii otkrytyi universitet" (from the personal archive of Veniamin Lukin), 1.

65. Interview with Semyon Parizhskii (21 April 2021).

66. Zelenina, *Iudaika dva*, 332.

67. Interview with Aryeh Ol'man (9 May 2021).

68. Interview with Dvorkin (10 March 2021).

69. Interview with Boris Khaimovich (11 May 2021). On this model of financing Jewish activities in the USSR, see n. 29.

70. Zelenina, *Iudaika dva*, 326. The Joint Distribution Committee grant was for $50,000, which in the USSR at the time was a fabulous sum (interview with Dvorkin [1 March 2021]).

71. Interview with Dymshits (20 April 2021). Cf.: "In 1991, a dollar was worth over one hundred rubles, and a wage of around one thousand rubles per month was considered respectable. On the basis of several hundred dollars received from sponsors, one could organize an expedition and not worry about money" (Mikhail Nosonovskii, "K 30 letiiu

Peterburgskogo evreiskogo universiteta," https://blogs.7iskusstv.com/?p=77389 [accessed 13 October 2021]).

72. Interview with Dymshits (20 April 2021).
73. Zelenina, *Iudaika dva,* 334. Ruppo also financed a professional film of Shlomo Carlebach's trip to the USSR (interview with Dvorkin [10 April 2021]).
74. Interview with Khaimovich.
75. Interview with Dymshits (20 April 2021).
76. Interview with Levin (22 April 2021).
77. Zelenina, *Iudaika dva,* 343.
78. See Levertov's recollections: https://blogs.7iskusstv.com/?p=77389 (accessed 6 November 2021). The informal gathering characteristic of Dvorkin and his circle, which was the essence of the university, has its roots in the Soviet intelligentsia tradition of "get-togethers," with alcohol as an important part of intellectual life.
79. Interview with Dmitrii El'iashevich (23 April 2021). On the division of spheres in the USSR, see Yurchak, *Everything Was Forever,* 116–118, 131–133.
80. Interview with Dymshits (20 April 2021).
81. Zelenina, *Iudaika dva,* 518, 521.
82. Interview with Levin (22 April 2021).
83. Interview with Ol'man (7 May 2021).
84. Interview with El'iashevich.
85. Interview with Parizhskii.
86. Zelenina, *Iudaika dva,* 348.
87. Mikhail Nosonovskii, "K 30 letiiu Peterburgskogo evreiskogo universiteta."
88. Interview with Khaimovich.
89. Nosonovskii, "K 30 letiiu Peterburgskogo evreiskogo universiteta."
90. Interview with Khaimovich.
91. Zelenina, *Iudaika dva,* 508.
92. Ibid., 509.
93. Interview with Khaimovich (emphasis added).
94. Interview with Levin (22 April 2021).
95. Nosonovskii, "K 30 letiiu Peterburgskogo evreiskogo universiteta."
96. Interview with Aryeh Ol'man (5 May 2021); interview with Khaimovich.
97. Interview with Ilya Dvorkin (14 April 2021).
98. Interview with Dymshits (20 April 2021).
99. Interview with Levin (22 April 2021).
100. Zelenina, *Iudaika dva,* 334.
101. Interview with El'iashevich.
102. Zelenina, *Iudaika dva,* 336.
103. Pinkus, *Sofah shel tekufah,* 199–205.
104. Interview with Dymshits (20 April 2021). This attitude toward one's Jewishness is a "passive identity," that is, an attribute "conferred upon them willy-nilly by genetics, history, accident of birth, and state-imposed ethnic identification" (Ro'i, "Soviet Jewry from Identification to Identity," 191).
105. Interview with Dymshits (20 April 2021).
106. Zelenina, *Iudaika dva,* 334.
107. Interview with Dvorkin (14 April 2021).
108. Interview with Levin (22 April 2021).
109. Interview with Khaimovich. Vladimir Levin thinks that Hava-Brokha Korzakova came up with this definition of Dvorkin as a tzadik in one of the first expeditions.
110. Interview with Ol'man (7 May 2021).
111. Ibid. (9 May 2021).
112. Interview with Parizhskii.
113. Interview with Dymshits (20 April 2021). Dymshits' irony relates to a well-known statement by Lenin that appeared on a poster usually displayed in Soviet schools and institutions of higher education.

114. Interview with El'iashevich.

115. Interview with Dvorkin (14 April 2021).

116. Interview with Lukin (emphasis added).

117. Interview with Khaimovich.

118. Zelenina, *Iudaika dva,* 360.

119. Ibid., 368. See also Simon Parizhsky, "Jewish Studies in the FSU: From Scholarship to Social, Cultural and Educational Construction, Regeneration and Growth," *Educational Eclectics: Essays in Memory of Shlomo (Seymour) Fox by Graduates of the Mandel Leadership Institute*, ed. Shmuel Wygoda and Israel Sorek (Jerusalem: 2009), 49–97.

120. Interview with Parizhskii.

121. Interview with El'iashevich.

122. Interview with Dymshits (20 April 2021).

123. Yurchak, *Everything Was Forever*, 102–108.

124. Zvi Gitelman, "Introduction," in *Jewish Life after the USSR*, 1.

125. See the description of PJU (on the basis on an interview with Dvorkin) as the cradle of a new type of Jewish spirituality: Elena Ostrovskaya, "Religious Identity of Modern Orthodox and Hasidic Jewry in St. Petersburg," *Transcultural Studies* 12 (2016), 167–169.

126. Interview with Ol'man (9 May 2021). On informal organizations and youth circles in the USSR, see Yurchak, *Everything Was Forever*, 134–138.

127. On this association, see Zelenina, *Iudaika dva,* 313–315. On Yuri Lotman and the theory of semiotic culture, see Aleksei Semenenko, *The Texture of Culture: An Introduction to Yuri Lotman's Semiotic Theory* (Basingstoke: 2012); on the "methodological theory" of Georgii Shchedrovitskii, see *Georgi Petrovich Shchedrovitskii*, ed. P.G. Shchedrovitskii and V.L. Danilova (Moscow: 2010).

128. Zelenina, *Iudaika dva*, 315.

129. For example, rock music clubs, associations of bodybuilders or eastern martial arts (see A.V. Golubev, "V poiskakh vnenakhodimosti," *Istoricheskaia ekspertiza* 1, no. 2 [2015], 21–22).

130. Interview with Dymshits (20 April 2021).

131. Zelenina, *Iudaika dva,* 333.

132. Interview with Levin (22 April 2021).

133. Ibid.

134. Mikhail Gorshkov, "Twenty Years that Shook Russia: Public Opinion on the Reforms," in *The Social History of Post-Communist Russia,* ed. Piotr Dutkiewicz, Richard Sakwa, and Vladimir Kulikov (London: 2016), 95–129.

135. See, for example, Semyon Charnyi, "Evreiskii Universitet v Moskve (1991–2009)," in *Proceedings of the Sixteenth Annual International Conference on Jewish Studies*, Part 2 (Moscow: 2009), 490–522; Yohanan Petrovsky-Shtern, "The Revival of Academic Studies of Judaica in Independent Ukraine," in *Jewish Life after the USSR*, 152–172.

136. Zelenina, *Iudaika dva*, 337, 339.

Essay

Bridging the Divide: Philanthropy as an Intersection Point in Belgian Jewish Society during the Interwar Period

Janiv Stamberger

(UNIVERSITY OF ANTWERP)

At the end of the 1920s, when Belgium's population was getting ready to celebrate a century since the nation's founding, the country's Jewish community was still relatively young—yet already characterized by great demographic changes and upheavals. It consisted of a small group of acculturated "Belgian Jews," immigrants from Western and Central Europe who had arrived in the country during the 19th century, and a large group of immigrants, most of them East European, who began arriving at the end of that century.[1] Up until the Second World War, Belgium's Jewish population was marked by sustained growth: from some 2,000 individuals (in 1830) to 4,000 (in 1880), after which the numbers accelerated in the wake of the East European Jewish immigration. By 1914, an estimated 40,000 Jews were living in Belgium; a number that increased to 50,000 by 1930 and to some 70,000 in 1940.[2]

During the interwar period, Belgium's Jewish community was marked by enormous diversity. About 40 percent of its Jewish population were Polish citizens, most of them Yiddish-speaking immigrants who arrived in the 1920s. A small Russian Jewish colony; Magyar-speaking Jews (Romanian or Hungarian nationals); a tiny "Turkish" and "Algerian" Sephardic community; a relatively large Dutch Jewish minority; and, at the end of the 1930s, German Jewish refugees, comprised Belgium's Jewish melting pot.[3] Set apart from these "foreigners" was a small community of native-born Belgian Jews. Of the approximately 70,000 Jews living in Belgium on the eve of the Second World War, only one in ten were Belgian citizens.[4] This diversification of Belgium's Jewish population based on language,[5] nationality, and culture was further compounded by differences in political ideology, degree of religiosity, and socioeconomic class.

A distinctive feature of Belgian Jewish society from the late 19th century is that its historical development can be described as "a tale of two cities." Unlike other Jewish communities in Western Europe, where cities such as Paris, London, Berlin, or Amsterdam developed into the principal centers of Jewish life, Belgium's Jewish

Janiv Stamberger, *Bridging the Divide: Philanthropy as an Intersection Point in Belgian Jewish Society during the Interwar Period* In: *Becoming Post-Communist.* Edited by: Eli Lederhendler, Oxford University Press. © Oxford University Press 2023. DOI: 10.1093/oso/9780197687215.003.0009 communal life was roughly equally concentrated in two cities: Brussels and Antwerp. Together, they accounted for 90 percent of Belgium's Jewish population.[6] By the late 1920s, the two Jewish communities had developed clearly distinct characters. In Brussels, a small group of "acculturationist" Belgian Jews who were organized around the local Communauté Israélite de Bruxelles remained relatively isolated from the large East European Jewish immigrant community, and relations between the groups were tense and defined by mutual distrust. In Antwerp, by contrast, the influence of East European Jews could be observed in all aspects of Jewish communal life. Due to the enormous wealth generated by the diamond industry, a new East European Jewish economic elite had been co-opted into leadership positions in the community in the first decade of the 20th century. By the mid-1920s, almost all of the highest functions in the Jewish welfare and religious organizations in the city were in the hands of Jews of East European descent, and Jewish religious Orthodoxy and Zionism became the defining features of Jewish life in the city.

With this bipolar concentration of Jewish life, enormous internal diversity, and the demographic dominance of East European Jews, conflicts inevitably arose within Belgian Jewish society over communal authority. These conflicts were predicated on competing views of religious practice, forms of political and cultural activism and, more generally, the question of which attitudes and positions Jews ought to adopt vis-à-vis Belgian society. In this essay, I examine the debates and different visions within Belgian Jewish society with regard to a very specific form of Jewish communal organization—namely, Jewish philanthropic work.

Based on the religious precept of *tzedakah* (lit. justice), philanthropic activity had long since been a cornerstone of Jewish communal life. After Jewish emancipation and the dismantling of Jewish communal autonomy, Jewish philanthropy had become a voluntaristic endeavor.[7] In Belgium in the 19th century, Jewish philanthropic initiatives came almost entirely from wealthy benefactors closely connected to the Consistoire central israélite de Belgique, the official body of Belgian Jewry in its relations with the state, or the local Communautés israélites. With the arrival of East European Jewish immigrants at the turn of the century, Jewish philanthropy became a much more diversified field as immigrant actors became involved.[8] During the interwar period, Jewish philanthropy, like many other aspects of Jewish life, was affected by processes of increased politicization. However, in contrast to other areas of Belgian Jewish life in which conflicts and debates reflected existing fault lines, philanthropic work allowed Jews from different ethnocultural, ideological, and socioeconomic backgrounds to work together in support of the poor, thus creating the possibility of bridging divides and allowing for new political and communal frameworks. As will be seen, local realities in Brussels and Antwerp worked in different ways either to advance or block these efforts at cohesion.

Brussels: Tentative Convergence in Jewish Philanthropic Work

In Brussels, a network of philanthropic institutions had been created around the Consistoire in the course of the 19th and early 20th century. Institutions such as the

Société israélite de bienfaisance (1833), Société de secours efficaces (1852), Société des mères israélites (1869), Orphélinat israélite (1870), Comité des apprentis et de la jeunesse israélite (1870), Maison de retraite pour les vieillards (1875), Villa Johanna (1901), Société israélite d'assistance antituberculeuse (1911), and La mutuelle israélite (1913) provided a broad spectrum of philanthropic support.[9] In many ways, Jewish philanthropy followed the example of the Catholic and (tiny) Protestant religious institutions (parallel to Liberal and Socialist initiatives) as Belgian society from the end of the 19th century became increasingly subdivided according to parallel confessional or political lines (a process known in Belgium and the Netherlands as pillarization).[10] While in principle Belgian non-Jewish institutions were accessible to the Jewish population, most Jews preferred recourse to their intracommunal associations. Rumors reported in the Jewish press in the 1920s and early 1930s—according to which Jews who had been placed in Belgian Catholic institutions were baptized "in extremis" (for instance, when they were dying), or forced to recite Christian prayers or to eat non-kosher food—made many Jews reluctant to turn to Belgian facilities, and this mobilized the Jewish community into establishing institutions of its own.[11] Being able to look for aid in one's own language from people who were familiar and responsive toward specific Jewish needs somewhat lessened the shock of immigration. Combining elements of both the "old" and the "new" world, Jewish philanthropic societies often formed a first link and contact with the specific conditions of Belgian (Jewish) society.

The ideological foundation of this network, which was financially supported and run by notables closely connected to the Communauté israélite de Bruxelles, the oldest Jewish religious community in Brussels, was motivated by religious precepts as well as by a keen sense of solidarity with less fortunate (immigrant) co-religionists.[12] Alongside these more altruistic motivations, the responsibility of taking care of the Jewish poor also served as an important means of ethnic identification for the acculturated Belgian Jewish establishment.[13] Patriotism and considerations of civic duty further underlined the attitude of Belgian Jewish elites in Brussels viv-à-vis charitable work. In 1936, for instance, Jules Philippson, vice president of the Consistoire and president of the Oeuvre central israélite de secours, proudly proclaimed (at a function honoring the 10th anniversary of the latter organization): "We are thus fulfilling not only a duty of religious solidarity, but also a duty of gratitude toward our dear liberal and tolerant country."[14] Fearing that the Jewish poor might become a burden on the Belgian welfare institutions—and, consequently, reinforce negative stereotypes about Jews—Belgian Jewry supported institutions of its own. Hiding the "shameful poor" (*pauvres honteux*) from the public eye was a means of self-preservation, expressing Belgian Jewry's own insecurity as a minority community.[15] As elsewhere, elite Jewish philanthropy was not intended solely to aid the poor in a material sense: it also served a regenerative purpose.[16] By creating educational frameworks for vocational training, and by organizing French classes, the Jewish establishment aimed to "moralize" the poor and turn them into "productive citizens."[17]

Beginning in the first decade of the 20th century, recently arrived East European Jewish immigrants in Brussels began creating their own Jewish philanthropic associations. Although these institutions often paralleled the existing philanthropic associations of Belgian Jewry in their goals and methods, there were also significant differences. Unlike the Belgian Jewish philanthropic institutions, the character of these associations was decidedly East European, with an emphasis on traditions of Jewish charity in Eastern Europe. The distinction made in "native" philanthropic institutions between *pauvres honteux* and foreign-born poor (*pauvres étrangers*), the latter being excluded from benefiting from some of the services available for those who had been living in Brussels at least for several years, was not applied in the East European associations; these emphasized notions of hospitality (*hakhnasat orkhim*) rather than welfare.[18] Jewish East European philanthropic associations in general were more considerate (at least on the symbolic level) to the sensitivities of the poor Jewish immigrant arrivals, their founders having been immigrants themselves.

The first association established by East European Jewish immigrants in Brussels of which we have a historical record was created in 1909; known as Ezrat yoledot 'aniyot, it was run by and for Jewish women, at first offering aid to poor pregnant women and later becoming active more broadly in women's causes.[19] The association was closely connected to the recently established East European Orthodox religious community in the capital, Shomrei das.[20] The next significant East European Jewish initiative came during the First World War, when East European Jews, independently from the relief efforts of Belgian Jewry's philanthropic organizations, established Ezrah to support the Jewish poor during the course of the harsh German occupation. In the early 1920s, the association was totally reorganized and refocused on the many Jewish (trans)migrants traveling to and through the city—in the aftermath of the First World War, Belgium had once again become a major transit country for Jews (and others) fleeing Eastern Europe, many of whom passed through cities such as Liège and Brussels on their way to the port city of Antwerp. Seeking to address their needs, Ezrah opened a small night shelter, supplied train tickets, clothes, showers, and vouchers for cheap kosher meals, and also organized a labor office for those who wound up remaining (for either a temporary or a more extended period of time) in Brussels.[21]

In the 1920s and especially toward the end of that decade (which marked the peak of East European Jewish immigration to Belgium), East European Jewish philanthropic and hometown associations proliferated independently from one another. The onset of the Great Depression, marked by large-scale unemployment and economic destitution, accelerated this process. While most philanthropic institutions of Brussels' Belgian Jewish elites were located at the rue Joseph Dupont in the city center, in the same building as the administrative offices of the Communauté israélite de Bruxelles and the Consistoire (right next to the majestic Grande synagogue de Bruxelles), the bulk of new immigrant associations were situated in the poor, crowded, and heavily Jewish (immigrant) neighborhoods around Brussels' South Train Station. In December 1928, for instance, Linath hatsedek was established, providing medical care at sharply reduced prices at its premises on the rue George Moreau in Cureghem.[22] The same year, two separate credit unions providing low-cost credit loans for their members, the Gemilut khesed kase and the Société coopérative de crédit mutuel "Ivriah," were created by immigrant Jews.[23] Early in 1930, the Folkskikh (popular kitchen; in French: Cuisine populaire) was opened to provide inexpensive hot kosher meals.[24] This initiative was taken by a few prominent members of the new Jewish immigrant bourgeoisie in the capital with the support of Rabbi David Bermann of the Communauté israélite de Bruxelles.[25] In 1932, another association with a similar goal, called Beth lechem, was established by recently arrived immigrants. This association delivered food packages once a week in a "discrete" manner (in French, the society was sometimes referred to as Assistance discrète) to the homes of poor Jewish families. The creation of Beth lechem, however, led to fierce discussions in Jewish immigrant society, the argument being that such a "rival association" dangerously undermined the work of the Cuisine populaire.[26]

Indeed, the proliferation of Jewish philanthropic organization in Brussels in the 1920s, many of which had similar (or even identical) goals, gave rise to attempts to "rationalize" and centralize Jewish charity. This need was most urgently felt by the Belgian Jewish establishment and by the immigrant Jewish bourgeoisie and middle classes who predominantly carried the financial burden to support philanthropic work. A commentator in *Di yidishe prese*, one of the main and longest-running Yiddish weeklies of the interwar period in Belgium,[27] argued against the absurd situation of some 25 philanthropic associations existing independently from each other, serving the same beneficiaries and wasting valuable funds.[28] The creation of a strong central institution, so he argued, would manage resources more efficiently, maintain public order, and allow a more thorough investigation into the worthiness of the recipients (many "professional beggars," he noted, were able to go from one organization to the next without any form of control). Fears both of "profiteering" on the part of beggars and of diminishing budgets underlined many of the arguments of those who made the case for centralization, and such concerns were not without merit.

The first centralization attempt occurred in the spring of 1926. One of the oldest Jewish philanthropic associations in Belgium, the Société israélite de bienfaisance (run by Jewish notables of the Communauté israélite de Bruxelles), merged with Ezrah, the association established by Jewish immigrants during the First World War, to become the Oeuvre central israélite de secours (OCIS). Its committee was composed in equal parts of members of its two constituent associations.[29] Among its 450 members in the late 1920s, both Belgian and East European Jews could be found, and the association was warmly supported by the Communauté israélite de Bruxelles and the East European Communauté israélite orthodoxe (the former Shomrei das). In terms of philanthropic work, OCIS inherited the wide array of responsibilities of both its predecessor associations. This included aid to (trans)migrants in the form of medical assistance, pharmaceuticals, coal, and meals for the poor on Pesach. In addition, the association subsidized other philanthropic institutions in the capital.[30] Located (as of 1931) on the rue Joseph Claes in Saint Gilles, the association was at the center of the East European Jewish immigrant neighborhoods.[31] From the start, OCIS had the ambition of becoming the central charitable association of the capital, following the example of the Centrale in Antwerp, as will be described. To this end, it both established and assisted in setting up new philanthropic associations that did not compete with its own work. In October 1931, for instance, it founded the Oeuvre de la protection de l'enfance et d'assistance médicale (OPEAM) to improve the hygienic and medical situation of poor Jewish children in the capital. In 1934, it opened a modern pediatric clinic in its offices where prenatal care, regular medical exams, and dental care were given to pregnant women and poor Jewish children.[32] Later it would also host the offices of the Hilfswerk der Arbeitsgemeinschaft (HIDAG), the Jewish refugee aid committee run by German Jews in Belgium.[33]

The unification of Société israélite de bienfaisance and Ezrah into OCIS was positively received. *Di yidishe prese* reported with satisfaction that, during its first fundraising Hanukah ball—attended by a host of Jewish and non-Jewish dignitaries, among them the Polish consul of Brussels—"it is noticeable that it is the first time that an event is organized with Belgian, Polish, and Russian Jews together and is also the first time that the results are so splendid, these are the fruits of unification."[34]

Notwithstanding, the goal of centralizing Jewish philanthropic organizations in Brussels proved to be elusive. As previously seen, philanthropic associations such as Linath hatsedek, the Folkskikh, and Beth lechem, all of which came into being after 1926, remained independent from OCIS. Newly arrived immigrants often preferred associations that conformed more closely to their particular religious or sociocultural sensibilities. There was also no shortage of what were known as *klal tuers,* potential voluntary communal activists, in the Belgian capital. Presiding over or serving as a committee member of a philanthropic association brought with it social prestige and heightened some benefactors' sense of self-importance. Similarly, Jewish organizations and political parties recognized the usefulness of philanthropic activity as a way to bind individuals to their cause and to serve the needs of their own members. All these aspects presented serious obstacles to any centralizing effort.

From the mid-1930s, a grassroots expansion of Jewish relief associations could be observed in Brussels, as Jewish *landsmanshaftn*, religious societies, political movements, and trade associations established philanthropic committees and other benevolent associations (for instance, burial societies) of their own. The immigrant character of the vast majority of Belgium's Jewish population and the limited time most had spent in Belgium (many arrived during the second half of the 1920s) added to the institutional fluidity, disorganization, and at times even anarchistic character of Jewish institutional life in general, including Jewish philanthropic organizations. At the end of the 1930s, Meir Sagalovitsh, rabbi of the Communauté israélite orthodoxe, estimated that some 70 separate Jewish philanthropic institutions were operating in the larger Brussels area.[35] Elsewhere, a figure of 80 associations was cited.[36] This represents an astounding number, given that the entire Jewish population of Brussels at the time consisted of some 25,000 to 30,000 individuals.

This extreme decentralization led to consternation among the Jewish economic elites. In the first years of the depression of the 1930s, massive unemployment and economic distress greatly increased the burdens on Jewish charity. Once again, an initiative was launched to centralize Jewish philanthropic work in Brussels. In early 1932, members of OCIS and the Consistoire took the initiative to create a joint committee, the Comité d'entente des oeuvres philantropiques juives, uniting immigrant and "native" philanthropic organizations to address "the anarchy" raging in Jewish philanthropy in the capital.[37] This effort, in effect, represented a first substantive overture by the Brussels-based Belgian Jewish establishment toward the immigrant Jewish arrivals of the 1920s. Their abject poverty, which risked reinforcing Belgians' xenophobic sentiments, forced the Jewish establishment to abandon its previously passive and (at times) antipathetic attitudes toward Jewish immigrant society. In the course of 1932, the newly established committee organized a series of meetings in which the different philanthropic associations of the capital were represented. While it succeeded in creating an emergency fund (Fonds de ressources extraordinaire) to relieve some of the pressures on the Jewish philanthropic associations, it failed to establish a strong centralized Jewish philanthropic federation. Eventually the project fizzled out and was abandoned.[38]

The failure of this project reflected deeper disagreements on how Jewish philanthropy should be organized, whom it should serve, and what its goals ought to be. Brussels-based Jewish left-wing associations, for instance, held very different notions on Jewish philanthropic work. In the course of the 1920s, in the wake of the immigration of politicized Jewish immigrants and political refugees, East European Jewish parties such as the Bund, Poale Zion (Linke and Rechte), as well as Jewish Communists, were transplanted to Belgium, where they became active in cultural activism (*kultur faraynen* and various other cultural associations), unionization efforts of Jewish immigrant laborers, and various forms of political activism and fundraising. They retained close ties with their East European (and Soviet and Palestinian) counterparts while acting as the local auxiliaries on the "Jewish immigrant street" of Belgium's political parties on the Left (Parti ouvrière Belge, Parti Communiste de Belgique) with whom they were aligned, either in the Labor and Socialist International or in the Third International (Comintern)[39]—in Belgium, the Jewish Communists were incorporated in the Main d' oeuvre étrangère (MOE), the foreign immigrant sections of the Belgian Communist Party (Parti Communiste de Belgique).[40]

The Jewish Left (especially its more radical revolutionary factions) generally regarded traditional Jewish philanthropy with extreme suspicion. The central role of Jewish economic elites in philanthropic work vindicated the Left's belief that philanthropy constituted "class institutions" that were far removed from the people; they were undemocratic, overly bureaucratic, and open to corruption.[41] Moreover, the Left harbored no sympathy for the ways in which traditional philanthropy catered to the religious sensitivities of Jewish donors and immigrant receivers. "A conscious laborer does not eat kosher and does not concern himself with bourgeois principles,"[42] was the stern verdict of one of the organizers of a Jewish proletarian soup kitchen in the early 1930s. Instead, Jewish left-wing parties advocated the integration of Jewish "working masses" into the social network of the Belgian labor movement. In time, however, the Jewish proletarian parties were forced to reevaluate some of their previous principles. The massive unemployment of Jewish non-unionized workers and, after 1933, the Belgian government's legal measures depriving foreign workers from receiving unemployment benefits, forced Jewish proletarian parties in Brussels to establish societies of their own to come to the aid of the large number of Jewish unemployed.[43] Having to explain their revised ideological position against Jewish philanthropy, the Linke Poale Zion, somewhat gratuitously, stated in its periodical: "We consider philanthropy to be a social action undertaken by civil [i.e., bourgeois] society. From the moment, however, when the organized representative of the Jewish working-class undertakes to perform these activities, they are no longer to be referred to as philanthropy but rather as proletarian self-help."[44]

Although, during 1932, calls were made in Jewish left-wing party periodicals for "cross-party efforts," the different Jewish proletarian parties were unable to overcome their mutual animosity and ideological rigidity. When the Linke Poale Zion in

Brussels wrote to the Jewish Communists, suggesting that they might establish a joint unemployment committee, its request was rebuffed.[45] Rigorously following the official line of the Comintern, with its politics of class warfare and non-fraternization (1928–1935), the Communists resolutely opposed any cooperation with *sotsyal fashister* (social fascists): that is, with "Zionists" and "reformist" elements. Instead, following the example of their comrades in Paris, they established an independent Arbetslozer-komitet (unemployment commission) as a Jewish section within the unemployment committee of the Belgian Communist Party.[46] Somewhat later, the small Bundist circle in Brussels also became active in relief efforts and in the autumn of 1933 established the Arbeter-ring (Workmen's circle).[47]

Thus, whereas the economic crisis had propelled Jewish proletarian parties in Brussels into the field of philanthropy in order to supply immediate relief to the poor, their efforts only achieved modest results, which in substance consisted mainly of the non-kosher soup kitchens set up independently by each party. The internecine struggles of the Jewish Left, alongside a lack of resources, prevented it from creating a strong philanthropic network. The fact that the Linke Poale Zion, for instance, did not shy away from turning to Jewish "bourgeois institutions" for financial support of its institution, justifying this by regarding it as a form of repayment for all the goods that came from "the sweat and blood of the laboring masses"[48] (a position that left it open to harsh criticism from political opponents), further attests to this. For the most part, the proletarian relief committees served the needs of the party's own members and were never able to reach a broader segment of the Jewish unemployed, most of whom still looked toward the "traditional" Jewish philanthropic associations for support.

The attempt of the Jewish proletarian parties to go it alone and establish their own social and philanthropic networks is emblematic of the general situation of Jewish philanthropy in Brussels. Even though in the mid-1930s the philanthropic associations established by the immigrant Jewish bourgeoisie and Belgian Jewry saw a further convergence—Beth lechem, for instance, became part of the network of OCIS[49] — this ran counter to the process of fragmentation of Jewish philanthropic work. Only among this small group of "economic elites" in Brussels' Jewish society did joint philanthropic activity serve as a cohesive force, reflecting and further reinforcing a general trend of rapprochement between Belgian Jewry and the immigrant East European upper class taking place in the mid-1930s. Among the rest of Jewish immigrant society, the strong political fault lines and cultural differences between them and Belgian Jewry, and among themselves, thwarted any attempts at the consolidation of Jewish philanthropy within a strong centralized institution.

At the very end of the 1930s, even the joint philanthropic work of the East European Jewish economic elites and Belgian Jewry risked falling victim to internal political disputes. The question of how to combat antisemitism and defend specific Jewish interests vis-à-vis Belgian authorities had decisively pitted the small group of Belgian-born Jews against a broad coalition of immigrant Jewish associations. The established Belgian Jewish groups advocated a "quietist" approach in the form of low-key intercession with the authorities and influential political figures, in the tradition of personal lobbying (Hebrew: *shtadlanut*). They regarded the publicity-based tactics of immigrant associations, such as the boycott against Nazi Germany, their "noisy" political demonstrations held together with progressive (and left-wing) Belgian allies, and the creation of Jewish "representative" organizations (both internationally in support of the World Jewish Congress and locally in the form of *Conseils*, "councils," that united the different organizations in Jewish society), as ill-conceived and potentially dangerous.

During the late 1930s, tens of thousands of German Jewish refugees and East European Jewish immigrants were targeted by government legislation; the former were banned from entering the labor market, and certain economic activities such as peddling and market trading were subject to increasingly strict regulations.[50] While the government never specifically categorized "Jews" as the target of these measures, their introduction—following intense pressure on the part of professional and middle-class organizations, which railed against the "invasion" of Jewish refugees and the unfair competition from "disloyal" and "tax-evading" small-scale Jewish manufacturers—leaves little doubt as to their intended targets.[51] For German and Austrian Jewish refugees as well as the East European Jewish immigrants who were affected by these measures, this meant a life in poverty or taking recourse to being employed "under the counter," which left them at the mercy of their employers, vulnerable to exploitation.

The concomitant rising tide of dependent persons threatened to surpass the capacity of Jewish philanthropies to provide for their needs. Once again, attempts were launched to centralize Jewish philanthropy in Brussels. However, two separate organizations sponsored rival initiatives. In early 1940, the Conseil des associations juives de Bruxelles, the Jewish "representative" association uniting immigrant Jewish society (ranging from bourgeois, ultra-Orthodox, to Communist-dominated organizations) established a liaison office (Service social) representing all immigrant philanthropic associations. At the same time, a rival liaison office operated by the Foyer israélite, Belgian Jewry's counterpart to the immigrants' Conseil des associations, united the philanthropic associations under its control.[52] Philanthropic work, despite its promise to act as a more cohesive force, ultimately failed to overcome the political turbulence and resulting fragmentation of Brussels' Jewish society.

Antwerp: Toward an Integrated Jewish Philanthropy

The oldest philanthropic association in Antwerp was a burial society, Chewra gemiloet gassadim, established by Dutch Jews in 1828. Although additional philanthropic associations were likely created in the mid-19th century, the patchy historical record during this period prevents us from forming a clear picture. Towards the end of the 19th century, there was a rapid expansion of Jewish philanthropic associations, coinciding with East European migration and the demographic growth of Antwerp's Jewish community. The Joodsche Liefdadigheidsvereeniging voor Weduwen en Weezen (Association of Jewish Widows and Orphans) was established in 1880, followed in 1891 by the Vereniging tot steun aan de Russisch Uitgewekene, later known as the Israëlietische Hulpkas, which provided food aid and financial support to the poor and to (trans)migrants. Five years later, in 1896, Bikur Cholim, offering medical assistance, was established. In 1902, a new organization, the Kurlaendischer

Frauenverein, began to take care of poor women and children, among them pregnant women and brides in need of dowries. Charitas (first known as the Vereeniging van Israëlietische Jonge Dames), run by Jewish women, supplied clothing for poor schoolchildren. A year later, the society Ezra was created, which provided transport tickets along with financial and legal assistance to Jewish transmigrants. In 1907, at the height of Jewish transmigration through Antwerp, the newly founded Israëlietisch Kledingswerk collected clothes and shoes for the poor.[53] Some of these organizations, especially the earliest among them, were run by the "old" Dutch/German elites together with the new East European Jewish bourgeoisie. Others were initiated solely by the new East European "diamond aristocracy." All, however, worked independently from one another.

In the years immediately after the First World War, a new chapter of Jewish philanthropy in the city began. The war had affected Antwerp's Jewish community in a particularly harsh manner.[54] In the years following the armistice, Antwerp's Jewish philanthropic organizations were overwhelmed by the growing number of local dependents: returning wartime refugees and Jewish transmigrants passing en masse through the city. To reduce financial costs and provide more effective aid, the preexisting Jewish charity organizations (as well as some charities established in the immediate postwar period) were centralized in a single organization. In 1920, after extensive discussions, prominent members of the community managed to unify seven associations: Bikur Cholim, Israëlietische Hulpkas, Kas voor Werkelijke Hulp (Leenkas), Charitas, Ezra, Arbeitsheim, and Hachnosas orchim within a central association called the Centraal Beheer voor Joodse Weldadigheid (General Administration for Jewish Charity), commonly known as De Centrale.[55] This politically neutral federative association, while leaving its affiliated associations with a degree of autonomy, coordinated philanthropic work in the city and allocated financial resources from a central fund.

In the early 1920s, the network of the Centrale was expanded. Other preexisting associations such as the Israëlietisch Kledingswerk (1921) and the Association of Jewish Widows and Orphans (1922) joined the institution. Entirely new associations, or subcommittees in existing associations, were created to provide additional care. Within Bikur Cholim, committees such as Beth Hacholim (fund for the creation of a Jewish hospital), Kraamvrouwenvereniging (care for pregnant and nursing women), a kosher food service for patients in Flemish hospitals, and a Linath hacholim (bedside vigil) were created. In 1922, the Centrale Keuken (Popular Kitchen) was established to provide kosher meals both for the poor and for transmigrants. In 1923, the Vereniging voor Openluchtwerk en Kinderbescherming was created to provide care for poor and mentally challenged children; it later opened a children's colony known as Villa Altol in a rural area outside Antwerp. Two years later, in 1925, the Edouard Kirschen Fonds was established to support Jewish immigrants looking for work and to direct them and Jewish youth to "useful occupations" outside of the diamond industry. Finally, in 1931, the Centrale opened an old age home located on the Generaal Drubbelstraat.

In the course of the 1920s, the Centrale developed into a broad and popular philanthropic institution. Its offices, located at the edge of the Jewish quarter in the Lange Leemstraat, became the central address for the Jewish poor seeking assistance, as well as for migrants and, later on, German Jewish refugees. By the end of the 1920s, the Centrale was being funded by more than 2,000 regular donors. These were mostly middle- and upper-class East European Jews who had arrived in Antwerp prior to the First World War, and who were associated with the diamond exchanges (*Diamantkringen*) at which polished and rough diamonds were traded.[56] Yet the entire community supported its philanthropic work. In Jewish homes and shops throughout the city, traditional *pushkes* (tin charity boxes) provided an added source of small contributions to the funds of the association. To keep the wider Jewish public engaged, the Centrale published a bi-weekly, *La Centrale*, in which French- and Dutch-language articles detailed the latest developments in the different organizations or discussed issues in philanthropic work.[57]

As in Brussels, the Centrale and its middle- and upper-class base often held opinions about Jewish philanthropic work that conflicted with those of the more recent Jewish immigrant arrivals of the 1920s. Notwithstanding their mutual common background and their sense of solidarity with poor East European Jewish immigrants, more veteran members of the community felt considerable anxiety when they considered how the influx of poor Jewish immigrants might threaten the prestige and hard-earned positions of the more established *antverpener*.[58] The many Jewish poor roaming the streets or begging on the pavements next to the diamond exchanges were often regarded as a source of embarrassment. Such sentiments were reflected in the pages of *La Centrale*, where the "psychological abnormalities" of "Eastern Jews" were analyzed in terms of the specific political conditions under which they had lived; these were sometimes cited as a cause for their precarious social condition and alleged moral dysfunctionality. Such notions highlighted the significant acculturation process of East European Jewish elites in the Centrale's committees, who dichotomized the notion of "Eastern psychology" with the "Western psychology" they ascribed to themselves.[59] Like native Belgian Jewry in the capital, the Centrale aimed to "moralize" the poor, fight against *shnoreray* (professional beggary), and integrate Jewish immigrants into Belgian society through language courses and education. This integrationist program reflected the elites' paternalistic attitude toward recently arrived East European Jewish immigrants.

If committee members of the Centrale sometimes treated the recipients of Jewish charity with a certain aloofness and expressed disappointment at their perceived shortcomings, such negative sentiments were reciprocal. Although there are far fewer sources focusing on the perspective of those who were the recipients of Jewish charity, some indications of their views nonetheless seep through the existing material. In the pages of *La Centrale*, for instance, one could find indignant descriptions of the *chutspe* (impertinence) of recently arrived immigrants and their unreasonable demands. Some, it was reported, even reviled the staff with comments such as: "A goy iz beser fun a yid" [Even a Gentile would be better than such a Jew]. Such outbursts highlighted the tense relations that at times defined the interaction between receivers and benefactors of Jewish charity.[60] The expectations of recently arrived immigrants often clashed with those of their benefactors. Some felt that the support they received was their due rather than a gesture of compassion; having arrived in Belgium after a long and arduous journey, they often expected to be helped and viewed the assistance they received as a self-evident form of interethnic solidarity. Thus, when a Jewish immigrant who had settled in Brussels failed to receive further help from the local charitable organizations, he saw no problem in turning to the Centrale in Antwerp for help, confidently asserting that "there [real] Jews live."[61] (His request for aid was turned down, as the Centrale felt strongly that each city ought to take responsibility of its own poor.) Naturally, more positive interactions also transpired and most likely far outweighed the antagonistic relations between recipients and benefactors. The more benign aspects of Jewish philanthropic work underscored common attitudes, a shared sense of responsibility, and a mutual willingness to work for the welfare of the entire community.

Criticism by individual recipients was only one issue with which the Centrale had to contend. From the middle of the 1920s, a new immigrant intelligentsia, consisting predominantly of political and cultural activists who arrived after the First World War, did not shy away from stating its opposition to some of the Centrale's methods and particularities. Especially in the Belgian Yiddish press of the 1920s and 1930s, the Centrale did not escape the critical gaze and sharp pen of the (mostly) progressive and left-wing authors. One of the most important points of criticism was that the Centrale focused too narrowly on superficial "philanthropy" that did no more than alleviate the immediate needs of the poor, whereas far too few resources were allocated to "productive" social work that would lead to significant structural improvements. Philanthropy, according to members of the immigrant intelligentsia, created dependency and encouraged *shnorers*.[62] Another point of criticism repeatedly directed against the Centrale was its bourgeois nature and the "snobbism" that allegedly characterized Jewish philanthropic work in Antwerp. In a scathing article published on the occasion of the annual charity ball of the Centrale in 1930, the editor of *Di yidishe prese*, H. Tsvir (the penname of Herman Jacubowitz), spoke out strongly against both the "aristocratic" nature of the ball with its formally attired men and women and the prominence accorded to the Belgian (non-Jewish) press covering the event. Year after year, Tsvir wrote, the Centrale had prevented journalists of the Yiddish immigrant press from attending its activities, lest they embarrass the guests with their lack of "fine manners"—it had even neglected to send them a press release.[63] Further irritating the Jewish immigrant intelligentsia was the fact that the articles in *La Centrale* were written only in French or Dutch, thus preventing many of the Yiddish-speaking Jewish immigrants from reading about developments in the associations. This, they claimed, was further proof of the Centrale's *folksfremdkayt* (alienation from the real people) and undemocratic character.[64] In sum, it was imperative that the Centrale reorient itself to social work and commit to democratizing its institutions.

This call for "democratization"[65] must be placed within the context of wider efforts by Jewish progressive circles—as opposed to more openly revolutionary Jewish groups that advocated separate organizations along class lines—for the reconstitution of all official institutions of Belgian Jewish society into representative institutions. The creation of such democratic institutions, which would be able to transcend class barriers and unite the entire Jewish community, was underlined by the ideological concept of *klal yisrael* (all Jews as one united community) and more national perceptions of Jewish identification. The argument ran as follows: if Belgian Jewry in its entirety constituted part of the Jewish people, and if Jewish politics were meant to work toward the benefit of the entire *klal* (community), then Belgian Jewish institutions ought to reflect this position. Jewish philanthropy was to be no exception to this idea; it needed to be placed within a larger, representative framework. This said, advocates of democratization never formulated a clearly defined program detailing how "democratic" philanthropic institutions should function.

Moreover, such discussions on the role of Jewish philanthropy and mutual self-help were nothing new. Frequent debates on the issue had taken place elsewhere in Europe, including the Russian empire, from the late 19th century, and the tension between "progressive" and "establishment" forces was often more rhetorical than real.[66] To a degree, Jewish philanthropists were prepared to expand their activities along the lines advocated by members of the left-wing (immigrant) intelligentsia; the latter, in turn, remained entirely dependent on the financial means and influence of the Jewish economic elite to realize the social policies they advocated. The progressive intelligentsia's call for democratization was ill-suited to the socioeconomic realities underpinning Jewish philanthropic organization in Belgian society. As such, it can be seen more as an expression of Jewish left-wing ideological aspirations than as a feasible political project.

Yet even if the political concepts of progressive Jewish opinion-makers were somewhat unrealistic, the Centrale was willing to address some of the most stinging criticisms—although it was not always motivated by the same ideological considerations. Many of its prominent members were conscious of the need to consolidate wide segments of Jewish society around its work and further expand its base of potential donors. While the association assiduously countered any criticism in its press organ, the Centrale nonetheless introduced some of the demanded changes by taking both practical and symbolic measures. In the late 1920s, it began reevaluating the role of social work as a preventive, structural, and long-term method to ameliorate social conditions afflicting parts of Jewish society.[67] This "social turn" was recognized symbolically at the Centrale's annual assembly in 1930, when the words "Maatschappelijke Hulpbetoon" (Social Work) were added to its official name. Henceforth the association was known as the Centraal Beheer van Joodse Weldadigheid en Maatschappelijke Hulpbetoon (General Administration for Jewish Charity and Social Work).[68] Additionally, the late 1920s marked a shift in policy at *La Centrale*, as the paper began to publish articles in Yiddish. While this remained the exception rather than the rule—for the most part, the bi-weekly retained its bilingual Dutch-French identity—it nonetheless indicated a willingness to engage with the recently arrived immigrants. Furthermore, the Centrale made a concerted effort to disseminate its activities in the Jewish immigrant press.[69] This more open and inclusive approach familiarized the Centrale among the city's Jewish population.

Leaving aside ideological differences, the views of the progressive immigrant intelligentsia and of members of the board of the Centrale were not all that different. While the more established board members of the Centrale aimed to "moralize" the Jewish poor in order to integrate them into Belgian (Jewish) society, the Jewish immigrant intelligentsia held similar notions of "elevating the Jewish masses" on economic, moral, social, and cultural levels. The immigrant intelligentsia's ideological notions were underlined by concepts of national regeneration or the foundation of a healthy Jewish working class. In practice, however, the proposed methods for achieving these goals were similar to those advocated by the Centrale. If institutions such as the labor office of the Edouard Kirschen Fonds of the Centrale were sometimes accused of not doing enough, the immigrant intelligentsia nonetheless strongly supported such initiatives to wean Jewish immigrants away from work in the diamond industry to more "productive" occupations.[70] Similarly, the establishment of a foundation in the Centrale in 1930 to improve hygienic conditions in squalid, crowded sections of the Jewish quarter could count on broad support.[71] Established in 1930, the Zilberblat Fund distributed financial prizes to those immigrants who kept the tidiest and cleanest homes, and this endeavor received positive coverage in the immigrant Jewish press.[72] To be sure, such projects were not launched merely to ameliorate the plight of the Jewish poor: both the Jewish establishment and immigrant opinion-makers feared that negative perceptions of the Jewish presence in Belgian society could be exploited by antisemites, further impelling them to take steps to remedy "social ills" such as crowded, unsanitary living conditions.

The social turn of the Centrale in the early 1930s led to a more cordial relationship with the immigrant intelligentsia. The harsh critical polemics in the Yiddish press of late 1920s were toned down significantly. *Di yidishe prese* for instance, became one of the Centrale's most vocal supporters, even taking up its defense against other, more critical immigrant periodicals.[73] The Great Depression and the need to form a united front in order to aid the many new poor and unemployed certainly contributed to this change in tone. In many ways, the question of social work versus philanthropy became irrelevant as the first priority now was to take care of the immediate needs of the many who were destitute. The Centrale's more open engagement with immigrant Jewish society, in part necessitated by this new situation, abetted this process and led to a more civil dialogue. Ironically, during these turbulent economic years, the Centrale relied more than ever on the shrinking base of the Jewish middle and upper class for its financial survival (at one point its membership dropped to 700).[74] At the same time, thanks to its more inclusive policy and its outreach to immigrant society, it gained in legitimacy as a democratic institution widely recognized by almost all elements in Antwerp's Jewish society. This process went hand in hand with a more active positioning of the Centrale in matters which, strictly speaking, lay outside the domain of Jewish philanthropy—as, for instance, its intervention against the ban against foreign street traders in the city of Merksem. During this period, the Centrale not only managed to consolidate its position in East European Jewish immigrant society of the 1920s, but also to lay bridges to Antwerp's strong Dutch Jewish minority, which traditionally had felt alienated from this "East European-dominated" organization.[75] As in Brussels, a (more limited) proliferation of new Jewish philanthropic associations or committees took place in Antwerp from the 1930s onwards.[76] The Centrale waged a tireless propaganda campaign in the Jewish press and for the most part managed to keep a measure of control over these developments, thus ensuring its primacy in Jewish philanthropy in the city.[77]

Conclusion

During the decades preceding the Second World War, Jewish philanthropy in Antwerp became organized on a more rational basis than was the case in Brussels. The latter city had no real counterpart to the Centrale. To be sure, certain factors outside of its control aided the Antwerp-based organization. For one thing, the majority of the Jewish community was concentrated in a relatively small area, which focused the Centrale's field of operation. In addition, the presence and influence of revolutionary Jewish parties was weaker in Antwerp than in Belgium's capital.

In both cities, Jewish philanthropy served as an intersection point between recent immigrants and "natives," new and old economic elites, and Jews from different backgrounds. Only in Antwerp, however, was Jewish organized philanthropic activity able to overcome the fault lines that crisscrossed Jewish society and to succeed in finding some degree of consensus. The primary reasons were the Centrale's strong organizational structure and its willingness to engage with more recent immigrant Jewish arrivals, thereby enabling the consolidation of large parts of Antwerp's Jewish population regardless of political affiliation, socioeconomic position, degree of religiosity, or national background. In Brussels, a far more limited process of convergence occurred. There, joint philanthropic work was restricted to immigrant economic elites and "established" Belgian Jewry, and even then, remained incomplete and fragile.

To a large degree, Jewish philanthropic organization reflected the distinct characteristics of Jewish communal life in both cities during the interwar period. In Brussels, the gap between the native Jewish establishment and immigrant Jewish society always remained more profound than in Antwerp, where common East European origins and shared worldviews (Zionism, Jewish Orthodoxy) among a majority of the Jewish population to some extent mitigated social divisions. This influenced the willingness of establishment figures and immigrants to work together toward common goals. Moreover, joint philanthropic work helped facilitate and consolidate new communal realities, thus acting as a cohesive force pushing forward integration of the Jewish community. While many differences remained, the joint philanthropic work in Antwerp contributed to bridging the gap between immigrants and establishment figures. In Brussels, by contrast, Jewish philanthropy became an extension of internal political disputes and the struggle for communal authority prior to the Second World War.

Only belatedly, in the aftermath of the Holocaust and following establishment of the state of Israel, did joint philanthropic work in Brussels transform into a launching pad, a bridge, on which "natives" and "immigrants" could come together. By this point, many of the old conflicts and debates had been rendered obsolete—in particular, those relating to Zionism, which was now fully accepted by the Jewish mainstream. In 1952, the Centrale d'oeuvres sociales juives (Central office for Jewish social work) was set up as the first major coordination effort between natives and immigrants in the Belgian capital in the postwar era.[78] Finally, the long-held goal of putting together a centralized and rationalized Jewish philanthropic network had been realized, which in turn paved the way for the creation of a new, more cohesive, Jewish community leadership, underpinned by novel (Belgian) Jewish identities.

By zooming in and analyzing the conditions through which Jewish philanthropy developed on the local communal level and from a comparative perspective, this essay has sought to go beyond more traditional conceptions and views of Jewish philanthropy as an elitist tool for the "moral civilization" or integration of newly arrived immigrants, or for the "socialization" of the poor. Instead, it has placed Jewish philanthropic organization within the wider political and ideological debates between different groups in Belgian Jewish society during the interwar period—as one aspect of a complex, intracommunal dialogue. Paying close attention to the local conditions driving Jewish philanthropic organization, and viewing these factors through a comparative lens, allows for greater understanding of the often contested nature of Jewish philanthropy, alongside its ability to emerge as a cohesive force in the Belgian Jewish community. Such analysis may well prove fruitful for other Jewish communities as well.

Notes

1. On Jewish immigration to Belgium in the 19th century and the development of Jewish life, see Jean-Philippe Schreiber, *L'immigration juive en Belgique du moyen âge à la première guerre mondiale* (Brussels: 1996). On East European Jewish (transit)migration, see Frank Caestecker and Torsten Feys, "East European Jewish Migrants and Settlers in Belgium, 1880–1914: A Transatlantic Perspective," *East European Jewish Affairs* 40, no. 3 (2010), 261–284; Frank Caestecker, "A Lasting Transit in Antwerp: Eastern European Jewish Migrants on Their Way to the New World, 1900–1925," in *Tales of Transit: Narrative Migrant Spaces in Atlantic Perspective, 1850–1950*, ed. Michael Boyden, Hans Krabbendam, and Liselotte Vandenbussche (Amsterdam: 2013), 59–79.

2. Schreiber, *L'immigration juive en Belgique*, 200–209; Willy Bok, "Considérations sur les estimations quantitatives de la population juive en Belgique," in (n.a.), *La Vie Juive dans l'Europe contemporaine* (Brussels: 1965), 90–104; Lieven Saerens, *Vreemdelingen in een wereldstad. Een geschiedenis van Antwerpen en zijn Joodse bevolking (1880-1944)* (Tielt: 2000), 18–23, 194–202.

3. Janiv Stamberger, "Jewish Migration and the Making of a Belgian Jewry: Immigration, Consolidation, and Transformation of Jewish Life in Belgium before 1940" (Ph.D. diss., University of Antwerp/Université Libre de Bruxelles, 2020), 125.

4. Ahlrich Meyer and Insa Meinen, "Immigrés juifs dans l'économie belge (de 1918 à 1942)," *Les Cahiers de la Mémoire Contemporaine* 14 (2020), 25. Among these Belgian Jewish citizens, many were former immigrants who had only recently been naturalized or else were the children of immigrants born in Belgium who, upon reaching the legal age of majority (16 at the time), opted for Belgian nationality.

5. An explanation is in order concerning the spelling of French and Dutch-language names and toponyms in this article (for the spelling of Hebrew and Yiddish, see n. 19). In Brussels, which, by the 20th century, was almost totally "Frenchified," matters were fairly straightforward, as French became the dominant language. Antwerp, however, was charaterized by a complex linguistic reality. Many among the upper classes, or those aspiring to be upper-class, continued to use French as their cultural language, whereas Dutch (Flemish), considered "lowbrow," was used by a majority of the Flemish population. Jewish elites in Antwerp generally shared this "bourgeois" proclivity for French rather than Dutch, and for this reason, many Jewish organizations in Antwerp were known by both a French and Dutch name (and often had a Hebrew name as well). To simplify matters, I have chosen to use French for organizations and places in Brussels, and Dutch for organizations and places in Antwerp.

6. The rest lived in what was referred to as "the provinces," in cities such as Liège, Charleroi, Ghent, Oostende, Seraing, Arlon, and a few other small towns.

7. For a general overview of its historical development, see Jay R. Berkovitz, "Jewish Philanthropy in Early Modern and Modern Europe: Theory and Practice in Historical Perspective," in *Toward a Renewed Ethic of Jewish Philanthropy*, ed. Yossi Prager (New York: 2010), 93–122.

8. Nancy Green's article has been an inspiration for this article, given the similarities between the Belgian and French cases. See "To Give and to Receive: Philanthropy and Collective Responsibility among Jews in Paris, 1880–1914," in *The Uses of Charity: The Poor on Relief in the Nineteenth-Century Metropolis*, ed. Peter Mandler (Philadelphia: 1990), 197–226.

9. Thomas Gergely, "La bienfaissance à Bruxelles, hier et de nos jours," in (n.a.), *La grande synagogue de Bruxelles: Contributions à l'histoire des Juifs de Bruxelles 1878–1978* (Brussels: 1978), 149–158.

10. Jewish society, however, never constituted a separate "pillar" in Belgian society because of its small size and internal political and ideological diversity.

11. See, for instance, "Une affaire de baptême," *Hatikwah* 12 (11 June 1926), 215; "A shreklikhe tsushtand," *Di yidishe prese* (2 September 1927), 5; "Frisher pruv tsu smadn a yid. froy," *Di yidishe prese* (28 September 1928), 5; "In gojim's handen," *La Centrale* (29 April 1927), 1–2. Such concerns had existed since the 19th century (see Schreiber, *L'immigration juive en Belgique*, 269), and the rumors may in fact have had a factual basis, given that in Catholic society (and among smaller Protestant missions) there was a tendency to convert ("save the souls of") Jews on their deathbeds or Jewish orphans placed in Catholic institutions. Little to no research has been done on this topic in Belgium, apart from a recent book on Protestant missions; see Jan Maes, *De ster en het kruis. De Gereformeerde Jodenzending in Antwerpen en Brussel (1931-1948)* (Brussels: 2020).

12. In the 1880s, a few smaller Jewish philanthropic institutions such as the Cercle des amis israélites, l'Egalité, Vooruitgang, and Menachem avelim, remained outside of the network of the Communauté israélite de Bruxelles. Many of them were run by (and for) Dutch Jews in the Belgian capital. See Louis Frank, "La bienfaisance israélite à Bruxelles," in *Revue Belge*, 58 (1888), 285; YIVO Archives, Territorial Collection (Vilna Online Archives), RG 33, box 3, folder 17 (Belgium–Israelite Friends Circle, 1889–1900).

13. In this respect Belgian (consistorial) Jewry followed an approach similar to that of the Jewish elites in France; see Lee Shai Weissbach, "The Nature of Jewish Philanthropy in France and the Mentalité of the Jewish Elite," *Jewish History* 8, no. 1–2 (1994), 191–204.

14. Archives de Consistoire central israélite de Belgique (henceforth: CCIB), Fonds oeuvres sociales communautaires, 23.45 (OCIS), "Rapport de l'O.C.I.S. 1936," 7.

15. This follows the same pattern of the French Jewish elites in Paris; see Green, "To Give and to Receive," 207.

16. For France, see ibid.; for Germany, see Derek Penslar, "Philanthropy, the 'Social Question' and Jewish Identity in Imperial Germany," *Leo Baeck Institute Yearbook* 38 (1993), 51–73; on England, see Mordechai Rozin, *The Rich and the Poor: Jewish Philanthropy and Social Control in Nineteenth-century London* (Brighton: 1999); Haim Sperber, "Philanthropy and Social Control in the Anglo-Jewish Community during the Mid-19th century (1850–1880)," *Journal of Modern Jewish Studies* 11, no. 1 (2012), 85–101; Eugene Charlton Black, *The Social Politics of Anglo-Jewry, 1880-1920* (Oxford: 1988).

17. Jean-Philippe Schreiber, *Politique et religion: Le consistoire central israélite de Belgique aux XIX siècle* (Bruxelles: 1995), 262–271.

18. Ibid., 267–268.

19. I have systematically used the original Latin alphabet spelling of Hebrew and Yiddish names of organizations as they appeared in the sources at the time. There was a great variety in the way Hebrew and Yiddish names were transcribed to the Latin alphabet, depending on the national and cultural origins (East European Ashkenazi, Sephardi, Dutch Jewish institutions) of the Jewish groups in question. For Yiddish titles of articles; I have used the YIVO system for transliteration but have maintained the original spelling even when inconsistent with the modern YIVO standard.

20. Many of the women serving in its committees were the spouses or relatives of prominent members of the community. See "Froyen-farayn ezrat yoledot 'aniyot," *Di yidishe prese* (15 January 1926), 6; "A yidishe klal-tuerin bakumt a riter-ordn," *Di yidishe prese* (5 July 1935), 5; "Fraye tribune," *Di yidishe prese* (6 November 1925), 2. See also YIVO Archives, David Trotsky Papers, RG 235/48.

21. Janiv Stamberger, "The 'Belgian' Jewish Experience of World War One," *Les cahiers de la mémoire contemporaine* 13 (2018), 109. As used in this essay, "(trans)migrants" refers both to those migrants who left Europe and those who, for various reasons, stayed in Belgium.

22. CCIB, Fonds oeuvres sociales communautaires, 23.6. (Linath Hatsedek), "Lettre au grand rabbin Wiener, Février 9 1932"; "Linath hatsedek," *Di yidishe prese* (4 January 1929), 6; "Algemeyne farzamlung bey linath hatsedek," *Di yidishe prese* (24 January 1930), 6.

23. Stamberger, "Jewish Migration and the Making of a Belgian Jewry," 168–169.

24. The *Folkskikh* was first located on the rue Sergent de Bruyne, subsequently the rue de la Buandarie, and from 1938 on the rue de Vautour. See "Di grindung fun a folks-kikh," *Di yidishe prese* (21 March 1930), 9; "Bay der folkskikh," *Di yidishe prese* (30 October 1931), 6; "Khanukes haba' is fun der yidisher biliker kikh," *Di yidishe prese* (14 January 1938), 5.

25. This initiative was taken by Abraham Kubowitzki, Rogowski, Opal, and Gruman (apart from Kubowitzki, first names were not noted); see "Tsu der erefnung fun di yidishe populere kikh," *Di yidishe prese* (18 April 1930), 6.

26. "A brif in redaktsiye," *Di yidishe prese* (26 February 1932), 7; YIVO Archives, David Trotsky Papers, RG 235, folder 42.

27. Belgium had a lively Jewish press during the interwar period. Many weeklies were published. A few, such as *Di yidishe prese* (1925–1940), *Der kuriyer* (1929–1940), *Di vokh/Di yidishe vokh* (1933–1939), *Gaol* (1931–1939), *Hatikwah* (1905–1918, 1920–1932) and *L'Avenir Juif* (1936–1940), appeared for a long period of time; others had a shorter life span. Even a few dailies (*Letste nayes, Belgisher tog, Belgishe nayes, Unzer togblad*) were published in the 1930s, although these appeared for only a short period of time. For an overview of the Jewish periodicals and bulletins published in Belgium, see Maurice Krajzman, *La presse juive en Belgique et aux Pays-Bas: Histoire et analyse quantitative de contenu*, 2nd ed. (Brussels: 1975); Daniel Dratwa, *Répertoire des périodiques juifs parus en Belgique de 1841 à 1986* (Brussels: 1987).

28. "M'darf grindn a 'tsentrale,'" *Di yidishe prese* (8 January 1932), 7. See also "Ver darf fartretn dem bruseler yidentum?" *Di yidishe prese* (19 November 1931), 9.

29. "Ezrah," *Di yidishe prese* (5 February 1926), 5; "Di general-farzamlung bay der ezrah in brusel," *Di yidishe prese* (5 March 1926), 5; "Bay der ezrah," *Di yidishe prese* (4 June 1926), 5; see also CCIB, Fonds oeuvres sociales communautaires, file: Demandes de secours transmises par la Sté des Secours Efficiaces [Armoire], "Oeuvres Centrale israélite de Secours de Bruxelles, Association sans but lucratif [statuts]."

30. Oeuvre central israélite de secours, *Rapport des années 1927–1928–1929* (Brussels: 1929).

31. Archives du Musée Juif de Belgique, Fonds C.C.I.B. 1/101, "Oeuvre Central israélite de Secours, Rapport de l'exercice 1930," 7; "Der banayung fun der tetikeyt fun der ezrah (OCIS)," *Di yidishe prese* (2 October 1931), 6.

32. "Une Oeuvre intéressante: l'O.P.E.A.M," *La Tribune Juif* 5–6 (27 September 1935), 75–76; "Di tetikeyt fun der gezelshaft fun kinder-farzorgung un meditsinishe hilf, A sheyner initiativ," *Di yidishe prese* (6 June 1933), 6.

33. The Arbeitsgemeinschaft von Juden aus Deutschland was created in 1935 as a socio-cultural organization of German Jewish refugees in Belgium. Its aid organization, HIDAG, created in 1937, provided aid to German Jewish refugees who had obtained temporary residency permits in Belgium.

34. "Der ezrah-bal," *Di yidishe prese* (17 December 1926), 5.

35. "Vi halt es in brisl mit der hilfs-arbet?" *Unzer yishev* (15 January 1935), 4.

36. CCIB, Archives de Moscou, box 160/2 (1–18), no. 7, "Service sociale du foyer israélite, 1-er décembre 1937–15 janvier 1938."

37. "Le Comité d'entente des oeuvres et institutions juives de Bruxelles," *L'Alliance habrith* (20 February 1932), 8. The following associations were included: Société de secours efficaces; Société des mères israélites; Société israélite d'assistance antituberculeuse; OCIS; Société cult. sépharadite; Ouvroir; Association Sioniste; Cuisine populaire juive; Association des etudiants juifs; Linath hatsedek; Club des juifs russes; Ezrat yoledot 'aniyot; OCIS later

backed out of the project. See CCIB, Fonds oeuvres sociales communautaires, 23/41 (Comité d'entente des oeuvres et institutions juives de Bruxelles.)

38. CCIB, Fonds Oeuvres sociales communautaires, 23/41 (Comité d'entente des oeuvres et institutions juives de Bruxelles); "'Filanthropiye oder sotsialer hilf'? Oyf der farzamlung fun dem komitet d'antant," *Letste nayes* (25 April 1932), 3; "Di faraynikung fun di institutsyes," *Di yidishe prese* (23 December 1932), 3.

39. Only the Linke poale zion remained unaffiliated to any International after its request to join the Comintern was rejected.

40. On the history of the Jewish Communists in Belgium, see Rudi Van Doorslaer, *Kinderen van het getto. Joodse revolutionairen in Belgie 1925–1940* (Antwerp: 1995). For a general overview of the Jewish Left prior to the Second World War, see Stamberger, "Jewish Migration and the Making of a Belgian Jewry," 175–274.

41. "Filantropiye oder prolet. zelbst-hilf?" *Arbeter-vort* (20 February 1932), 2.

42. "Vider a kikh," *Di yidishe prese* (18 March 1932), 9.

43. Frank Caestecker, *Alien Policy in Belgium, 1840–1940: The Creation of Guest Workers, Refugees, and Illegal Aliens* (New York: 2000), 168–169.

44. "Filantropiye oder prolet. zelbst-hilf?"

45. "Proklamirt di arbetloze-aktsiye in belgye," *Arbeter-vort* (23 January 1932); "Shediker," *Arbeter-vort* (6 February 1932), 3; "Di arbetsloze-aktsiye, muz oysgebreytert vern," *Arbeter-vort* (27 February 1932), 3.

46. "Grindung arbetsloze-komitetn," *Arbeter-shtime* (March 1932), 6; "Di arbetsloze aktsiye in brisl," *Arbeter-shtime* (April 1932), 7. For France, see Paula Hyman, *From Dreyfus to Vichy: The Remaking of French Jewry, 1906–1939* (New York: 1979), 110–111.

47. YIVO Archives, David Trotsky Papers RG 235/18, 139, 149, 152; "Gegrindet a arbeter ring," *Di vokh* (15 September 1933), 4.

48. "Filantropiye oder prolet. zelbst-hilf?"

49. From 1933, Beth lechem was given subsidies by OCIS. See CCIB, Fonds Oeuvres sociales communautaires, 23/45 (OCIS), "Rapport de l'O.C.I.S. 1936," 5–6; "Di gezelshaft beth lekhem," *Di yidishe prese* 10 (6 March 1936), 5. The Cuisine populaire likewise developed ever closer ties to the Communauté israélite de Bruxelles; see *Annuaire de la communauté israélite de Bruxelles* (Brussels: 1937), 71.

50. Frank Caestecker, *Ongewenste gasten, Joodse vluchtelingen en migranten in de dertiger jaren* (Brussels: 1993), 136–144, 149; idem, *Alien Policy in Belgium, 1840–1940*, 182–184, 250–251.

51. Peter Heyrman, *Middenstandsbeweging en beleid in België. Tussen vrijheid en regulering* (Leuven: 1998), 332–335. This situation is similar to the events occuring in France. See Vicki Caron, "The Antisemitic Revival in France in the 1930s: The Socioeconomic Dimension Reconsidered," *Journal of Modern History* 70, no. 1 (1998), 24–73.

52. Stamberger, "Jewish Migration and the Making of a Belgian Jewry," 540–541, 543.

53. "Brief uit Antwerpen," *Nieuw Israëlietisch Weekblad* (20 June 1913), 10; "Kort overzicht van de geschiedenis van ons weeshuis," *La Centrale* (21 February 1930), 3–4; *Liefdadig Antwerpen* (Antwerp: 1935), 52–56; *Jaarboek der Israëlietische Gemeente te Antwerpen* (Antwerp: 1912), 52–60.

54. Stamberger, "The 'Belgian' Jewish Experience of World War One," 105–107.

55. On the history and institutions of the Centrale, see Michèle Frey, "Een Joodse solidariteitsbeweging te Antwerpen: De Centrale, 1920–1940" (Master's thesis, University of Ghent, 1975); Andrée Katz, *75 jaar Centrale: Armoede en uitsluiting . . . een uitdaging!* (Antwerp: 1995).

56. *La Centrale* (7 March 1930), 3; Frey, "Een Joodse solidariteitsbeweging te Antwerpen," 146.

57. Its circulation consisted of some 2,000 copies per issue; see Frey, "Een Joodse solidariteitsbeweging te Antwerpen," 141–142.

58. "Antverpener glikn," *Di yidishe tsaytung* (10 August 1928), 2.

59. "Methode," *La Centrale* (22 September 1926), 2.

60. "Methode," *La Centrale* (9 July 1927), 2–3.

61. "Typische gevallen," *La Centrale* (25 May 1928), 1

62. "Di tsentrale un ire institutsyes, unzer sakh-hakol," *Di yidishe tsaytung* (10 January 1930), 3; "Tsu der general-farzamlung fun der tsentrale," *Di yidishe prese* (10 February 1928), 2.

63. "Le bal de la Centrale," *Di yidishe prese* (28 November 1930), 2; "Yidishe beler u[n] a[zoy] v[ayter] . . . ," *Di yidishe prese* (9 March 1928), 2.

64. "Di tsentrale un ire institutsyes, unzer sakh-hakol," *Di yidishe tsaytung* (10 January 1930), 3.

65. Such calls were repeated elsewhere. At the first Party Congress of the United Jewish Socialist Party, Poale Zion–Zeire Zion in Belgium, for instance, Léon Kubowitzki, one of its leaders, argued for the re-organization of Jewish philanthropy as "democratic institutions of social work and self-care." See "Unzer ershter partey-tog," *Folk un arbet* (13 May 1932), 1.

66. Heinz-Dietrich Löwe, "From Charity to Social Policy: The Emergence of Jewish 'Self-help' Organizations in Imperial Russia, 1800–1914," *East European Jewish Affairs* 27, no. 2 (1997), 53–75.

67. "Charité ou Oeuvre Sociale," *La Centrale* (24 May 1929), 1.

68. *La Centrale* (7 March 1930), 5,7; "Help u Zelve!" *La Centrale* (April 1937), 1.

69. "Der bal fun der tsentrale," *Di yidishe prese* (1 January 1932), 6; "Der yerlekher bal in der tsentrale," *Di yidishe prese* (8 December 1933), 9.

70. "Di tsentrale un ire institutsyes. Der kirshn-fond," *Di yidishe tsaytung* (17 January 1930), 5.

71. "A sheyner oyftu in antverpn," *Di yidishe tsaytung* 22 (23 November 1928), 3; Stadsarchief Antwerpen, MA#27418 ("Bijzonder onderzoek in het Jodenkwartier").

72. "Lokale fragn," *Di yidishe prese* (27 June 1930), 2; "Grindet a 'toz,' gezelshaft tsu farhitn dos yudishe gezund," *Der Belgisher tog* (27 June 1930), 4.

73. "Vegen reynkeyt funm yidishn gedruktn vort," *Di yidishe prese* (16 January 1931), 5; "Tsu der general farzamlung fun der 'tsentrale,'" *Di yidishe prese* (30 January 1931), 2.

74. Frey, "Een Joodse solidariteitsbeweging te Antwerpen," 146.

75. On the interactions between the Centrale and Dutch Jews living in Antwerp, see Janiv Stamberger, "Dutch Jews and the Dutch Jewish colony in Antwerp during the heydays of Eastern European Jewish immigration to Belgium, 1900–1940," Studia Rosenthaliana, 47, no. 2 (2021), 159–161.

76. The Centrale supported a few associations outside of its direct control, such as the Joodsche Vrouwenraad (Jewish Women's Council), and it tolerated organizations with more religious concerns (which it regarded to be outside the scope of its responsibilities).

77. "Lommer grinden," *La Centrale* (January 1931) 2; "Avis important, " *La Centrale* (February 1935), 4; "Aan onze leden!" *La Centrale* (May 1938), 1; "Dringnde varnung," *Di yidishe prese* (1 June 1934), 7.

78. Catherine Massange, *Bâtir le lendemain: L'Aide aux Israélites victimes de la guerre et le Service social Juif de 1944 à nos jours* (Brussels: 2002), 104–107.

Review Essay

Antisemitism in Context:
Three Recent Volumes

Abigail Green and Simon Levis Sullam (eds.), *Jews, Liberalism, Antisemitism: A Global History*. London: Palgrave 2021. 429 pp.

Sol Goldberg, Scott Ury, and Kalman Weiser (eds.), *Key Concepts in the Study of Antisemitism*. London: Palgrave, 2021. 336 pp.

Scott Ury and Guy Miron (eds.), *Antishemiyut: bein musag histori lesiaḥ tziburi* (Antisemitism: Historical Concept, Public Discourse). Jerusalem: The Historical Society of Israel and the Zalman Shazar Center, 2020. 443 pp.

The literature on the history of antisemitism, together with its various social, cultural, or psychological sources, is by now so vast that it can no longer be surveyed. Still, the expansion of this field of research during the last decade has been truly extraordinary. Among the new publications are the three collections of essays under review.

The volume in Hebrew, edited by Scott Ury and Guy Miron, was published in lieu of four quarterly issues that constitute Volume 85 of the Israeli historical periodical *Zion*. The book contains 19 essays, all written as responses—some more direct than others—to David Engel's article of 2009, "Away from a Definition of Antisemitism: An Essay in the Semantics of Historical Description."[1] Engel's piece has been somewhat refreshed for this occasion and translated for the Hebrew reader as "On the Evolution of the Concept 'Antisemitism' and Its Use as an Aggregate Category." In it, Engel recapitulates his lingering frustration with the unclear nature of the term "antisemitism," which has never had an agreed-upon definition, he claims, a situation that repeatedly causes confusion and misunderstanding, in scholarly as well as in public debates. As a solution, Engel suggests to simply stop using the term. As far as he himself is concerned, he tells us, doing without it has proven easy and productive.

The contributors to this volume, mainly but not exclusively from Israel, were invited to react to this suggestion and their responses, divided into five sections, make up this sizable volume. The first part deals with some historiographical and theoretical sides of the issue; the following three provide a rough historical overview; and the last section consists of three additional theoretical essays directly responding to Engel's claims and suggestion, followed by Engel's own final rejoinder.

All of this is fascinating, readable, and instructive. The collection includes essays on the semantics of the term antisemitism, its changing meaning especially since the latter decades of the 19th century, and arguments that either justify its continued

Shulamit Volkov, *Antisemitism in Context: Three Recent Volumes* In: *Becoming Post-Communist*. Edited by: Eli Lederhendler, Oxford University Press. © Oxford University Press 2023. DOI: 10.1093/oso/9780197687215.003.0010 application or support the idea of stopping it altogether. Personally, I found particularly instructive the essays that are, in fact, either not directly or only partly related to the core of the controversy. Adi Ophir and Ishai Rosen-Zvi, for instance, expound upon the link between what most historians of the ancient world prefer to call "Judophobia," on the one hand, and "Jewish separatism," on the other. Both of these are exemplified by Ophir and Rosen-Zvi in a variety of Hellenistic and Roman texts. The authors stress the link between rejection of the Jews by non-Jews and the Jews' practice of self-separation in this context, and, in addition, describe how Jews repeatedly imagined acts of extermination planned and carried out against themselves, usually in response to their presumed loyalty to alien rulers. They thus offer an interesting background to Judophobia in the ancient world, if not a full explanation for it. To be sure, the theme of mutual hostility has been dealt with before in Jewish historiography. In his *Two Nations in Your Womb* (2008), for instance, Israel Yuval made the same point with a focus on the Middle Ages. Still, it is always useful, I think, to bring this duality back to our attention in discussing the various chapters in the history of antisemitism.

Moving on to modern times, Ofri Ilani likewise widens our approach to antisemitism by discussing problems that arise in the study of *philo*semitism. In a fine and learned analysis, he makes the distinction between *philo*-semitism and *anti*-antisemitism by recounting the case of Gotthold Ephraim Lessing in the latter half of the 18th century. Interestingly, while this is fairly far back in time, it proves to be relevant for present controversies with regard to antisemitism. Equally interesting are the following essays dealing with either the useful or disruptive effects of the main term in question, namely antisemitism, in more limited *national* contexts, such as in Poland (Gershon Bacon), the United States (Eli Lederhendler), and Britain (Arie Dubnov). Finally, two essays on Holocaust research present two contradictory positions. Going somewhat beyond Engel's argument, Havi Dreifuss makes the case that, despite the fact that Jewish victims of the Nazi so-called Final Solution varied considerably among themselves, their murder had much in common, justifying the use of a single term—antisemitism. Generalizations may indeed sometimes lead to false conclusions, she acknowledges, but they are indispensable for making fruitful comparisons and for not losing sight of the overall picture. Against her, Amos Goldberg and Raz Segal argue for exchanging this term with something more "concrete" that would enable us to distinguish among various reasons to discriminate, expel, or murder the Jews in the various regions of Europe. They make this point by observing the joint case of Romania and Bulgaria, where local eruptions of violent state nationalism combined with Nazi imperialist designs normally worked *against* the Jews, but occasionally also *for* them. On this background, they seem to agree with Engel that using a single term covers up too much and illuminates too little. Reading between the lines, however, I feel that in their case studies too, antisemitism—simply meaning a compound of anti-Jewish sentiments and action—always played at least some role in the run of events and often, indeed, a very central role.

Finally, Goldberg and Segal manage to interweave in their essay a discussion of the political use of the term antisemitism not only during the Nazi era but also today. They begin with the present debate on "global Holocaust memory" and end with a critique of the recent definition of antisemitism offered by the International Holocaust

Remembrance Alliance (IHRA). Reading them, one feels that finally, "the elephant in the room" has been addressed. To be sure, an earlier article by Arie Dubnov on the complexities of antisemitism in Great Britain between 1830 and 1982 likewise criticizes the separation of Jewish history from that of other minorities and claims that overuse of the term has only served to obscure the ambivalence typical of attitudes toward Jews in Great Britain for long periods of time. It also tends to obliterate the unique *imperial* context and minimize the degree to which Jews were themselves "active players" in processes of excluding others. In another essay, also based on the British case and titled "Antisemitism and Islamophobia," David Feldman briefly reviews the literature on the linkage between the two and the political changes that recently deepened the rift between them. He argues that both Jews and Muslims now tend to abandon the universalism that previously constituted the foundation of their arguments, so that while the gap between the two groups continues to grow, the alliance between each of them and the anti-immigration and islamophobic—or antisemitic—milieu in Britain as well as in Western Europe becomes ever stronger and ever more self-evident.

But it is, no doubt, with Goldberg and Segal that one faces the principled dilemma head on. They claim that efforts to prevent critiques of Israel, in general, and its policies against the Palestinians in the occupied territories, in particular, have damaged the validity of previous anti-antisemitic arguments. Under these circumstances, many scholars find it necessary to distance themselves from the very term and perhaps even to drop it entirely. Certainly, greater care and more precision are now required in applying the term antisemitism; this is clearly agreed upon by Engel and his critical colleagues. On balance, however, I find the latter's voice more convincing, especially after reading the closing section, including Maurice Kriegel's repudiation of Engel's semantic and historical analysis and Dan Michman's vehement rejection of his overall thesis.

In the end, the debate has produced a rare and interesting exchange among scholars. Individual researchers may now be encouraged to apply greater care in their terminology, though presumably they will continue to use conventional terms such as antisemitism. And in any event, public discourse is generally oblivious to scholarly disputes, and we as historians have only limited influence over its content. As conscientious citizens, we may well press for less political manipulation of terms we use in research in the service of particular interests. I, for one, feel that our scholarship and academic standing hardly affect, justifiably perhaps, such public matters.

In their introduction to the edited collection *Jews, Liberalism, Antisemitism: A Global History,* Abigail Green and Simon Levis Sullam note that, in post-imperial England, "we seek to reimagine a field shaped by European experiences and paradigms," and in which the spotlight is on "issues of race, discrimination and hybrid identities in colonial and post-colonial settings . . ." In such global settings, they add, "neither Jews nor the Holocaust play a very central role" (p. 2). Hence, the present volume of 17 essays, based on a seminar and a conference in Oxford, deal with the complex links among Jews, antisemites, and liberals, not only—though also—in Italy, Spain, and Vienna, but also in the United States (or "America," as it is here called), Turkey, the Middle East, and even the Caribbean.

In what she terms "a reassessment from the peripheries," Lisa Moses Leff selects examples from Romania and Algeria to show the possible alliance between antisemitism and liberal democracy. At first, according to her, the antisemitism of Romanian liberals was an added aspect of fierce nationalism, always mixed with general xenophobia. Later, however, in response to the intervention of Jewish organizations under the umbrella of the Alliance israélite universelle, which had pressed the Western Great Powers to introduce Jewish emancipation in Romania during the late 1870s, the same liberals embraced a full-fledged conspiracy theory. They apparently came to believe in the presumed threat of a "Jewish International," as was increasingly the case among antisemites in other parts of Europe. Still, Romanian liberals believed *theirs* was a more successful model of a national-state than that prevalent in the West and they continued to champion the principles of freedom, equality, and national self-determination. This, Leff claims, is reminiscent of postcolonial nationalists in Africa and Asia, such as in Algeria, where antisemitism emerged together with the quest for democracy, particularly among European settlers, who upheld their own brand of re-publicanism that was typically *antijuif.* In fact, the possible linkage between liberalism and anti-Jewish sentiment is known from some of the classic cases of European liberalism, even in Germany as early as the 1820s, or in Russia somewhat later during the 19th century. The postcolonial context manifests additional strands of the same alliance and ought to be integrated in our overall view of liberalism, which, Leff indicates, was exclusionist from the start and easily forged alliances with antisemitism.

The book offers other fascinating studies, most outstandingly Laura Arnold Leibman's piece about the clothing habits of Jewish men in the colonial Caribbean. "Clothing became a battleground on which the war over Jewish equality was waged," she writes, and where "Jews used clothes to stage their whiteness and political capabilities" or even their "right capacities" (p. 98). Coining the term "language of dress," she also offers a fine analysis of Delacroix's *Liberty Leading the People* of 1830, painted when everywhere in Europe "men's apparel signaled their readiness for citizenship" (p. 101). While this point may have been apparent to all at the time, it has generally been lost to historians. Portraits of Sephardic men from 1790 to 1830, known only to specialists, further illustrate her argument, and she claims that since Jews were often considered "swarthy" or "black" in the Caribbean, and since race was by then increasingly defined "by a person's physical form," Jews were preoccupied by male fashion perhaps even more than others. Moreover, all of this preceded similar developments on the continent and in England, where body and dress were eventually key sites of the Jewish struggle for equality. In fact, while the Jewish *body* has received some attention of historians, especially with regard to the second half of the 19th century and increasingly towards its end, *clothing* seems to be overlooked. Leibman's essay brings this theme back to our attention. It is original and refreshing, and the relatively long bibliography at the end invites further study of both texts and visual material.

There are also a number of biographical essays in this volume. Jonathan Kwann treats the life of Heinrich Jaque (1831–1894), a Jewish liberal parliamentarian in Vienna; Ozan Ozavsci reminds us of the lost liberalism of the so-called Revisionists in the Zionist movement through the figure of Vladimir (Ze'ev) Jabotinsky; and Arie Dubnov, treading somewhat more familiar terrain, examines the "independent voice" of historian Lewis Namier. In the final section, Malachi Haim Hacohen turns to the

"Jewishness" of what he calls "Cold War Liberalism," but though it is in itself a fascinating essay, it seems somewhat out of place at this point. Together with Abigail Green's contribution, reevaluating liberalism among Jews in the wake of the 1848 revolution, they both pull us back, as it were, to the familiar European context. Despite the fact that Hacohen treats European and American liberals together, and Green uses, indeed, what she calls "a transnational perspective," these essays, I feel, let down those readers who were, like me, fascinated by the volume's previous focus on the "periphery."

In its overall search for new conceptual approaches, the Green/Sullam volume leads us almost naturally to the last collection under review—in fact a small encyclopedia—edited by Sol Goldberg, Scott Ury, and Kalman Weiser. As befits such a volume, the list of contributors to *Key Concepts in the Study of Antisemitism* includes not only historians but also philosophers, psychologists, literary scholars, political scientists, jurists, and an anthropologist. In this alphabetic compendium, properly beginning with anti-Judaism and ending with Zionism, we go through some well-known stations in the form of essays on emancipation, the Catholic church, and nationalism, but then encounter essays on less expected terms, such as gender, orientalism and postcolonialism. Here, too, I found these latter essays particularly intriguing.

Antisemitism, writes Ivan Kalmar, "was not only *related* to orientalism; it was one of its central aspects" (p. 187). He begins by reminding us of the way biblical Jews were visualized as Orientals in European Art. Depicted as "Turks," they projected not only "Ottoman costume," but also the "authoritarianism of the Ottoman government" with regard to both Islam and Judaism. Having added the visual arts to our arsenal of historical sources (like Leibman in her essay in the Green/Sullam collection), Kalmar moves to literary texts, reviewing the philological and philosophical discourse on "Arabs" in Europe, beginning in the early 19th century and peaking finally with Ernest Renan. A theological debate concerning the "racial" origins of Jesus soon became part of this discourses as well, he tells us, showing how this half-hidden thread of associations going back to biblical times eventually led all the way to the Balfour Declaration of 1917. The entire Zionist project—perhaps especially as it was seen by non-Jews, one may add—is explained by Kalmar in the light of that long tradition, in which Jews too were considered "Semites," an integral part of the Orient. Only later, he adds, were they gradually transformed into proper Europeans who were not only foreign to the Near Eastern environment, but turned out to be active settlers and colonizers. The link between Arabs and Jews was thus severed, bringing about a changed image of both, the author claims, so that today's antisemitism no longer has much to do with the previous "oriental provenance of the Jews" (p. 197).

This is a forgotten, or at least long neglected, chapter in the modern history of antisemitism, though surely it has always played a part in some Jewish history books. After all, scholarship dealing with Sabbatai Zevi and Sabbateanism, not mentioned in Kalmar's essay, aimed at reformulating the links between Jews and Muslims, and for the 19th century, one recalls the work of historian Ismar Schorsch, who in some of his exemplary essays reminded us of the attraction felt by German Jews to all things Sephardic, especially to the unique Arabic-Muslim style of architecture known as the "Moorish" style.[2] Schorsch himself doubted that this style was chosen because it referred to the Oriental origins of the Jews, but in view of what we now know, perhaps this assumption ought to be revised. In fact, the affinity of even Western Jewry with the Orient or with Islam has been often enough noticed, even by scholars of the Wissenschaft des Judentums as far back as mid-19th century. In any case, this topic now requires our renewed attention, theoretically and methodologically, as yet another aspect in the study of antisemitism.

Another side of the same issue is taken up by Bryan Cheyette in his article on "Postcolonialism," which relies in the main (as with his previous books) on artistic, and even more so, *literary* representations of "the Jew." Following the Second World War, Cheyette explains, a number of authors "made connections" between genocidal antisemitism and European colonialism. Among them was Hannah Arendt, whose *Origins of Totalitarianism* he characterizes as "an intersectional analysis of colonial racism and antisemitism *avant la lettre*" (p. 232). This work, he argues, became "a common reference-point" for those within colonial studies who sought to explore interconnections between colonialism and antisemitism soon after the war. Later on, however, postcolonial authors shifted their attention away from what they sometimes called "the globalized Jewish Question" and took care to differentiate between postcolonial and Holocaust studies. This division, Cheyette adds, was deepened after 1967, as postcolonial studies increasingly stressed the plight of the Palestinians, whereas Jewish studies focused on "the plight of the Jews in pre-war Europe." Despite the fact that the two fields could have enriched each other and that their mutual affinities might have enabled both "to move beyond exceptionalist histories of victimization [to] adopt a more open-minded sense of historical connectedness" (p. 240), this step has not yet been taken, according to Cheyette. In fact, a growing number of studies mostly by German historians, among them most prominently Jürgen Zimmerer, deal with the extermination of the Herero and Nama tribes at the hands of German colonists and troops in South-Western Africa, and sometimes make the link, controversial, to be sure, between these atrocities and the later—but after all not *so* much later—Holocaust.

In any case, the choice of articles in this volume, including expected ones on "Nazism" (Doris Bergen), "Conspiracy Theory" (Jovan Byford), "The Ghetto" (Daniel Schwartz), or "Antizionism" (James Loeffler), but also extended entries on "Secularism" (Lena Salaymeh and Shai Lavi), "Gender" (Sara Horowitz), and—for me, especially interesting—"Orientalism" and "Postcolonialism," brings us up to date and makes for useful and interesting reading.

In the end, all three volumes help move the historiography of antisemitism forward in a way that has long been needed, presenting a panorama of new and interesting perspectives about an old but still important, relevant, and hotly debated theme.

SHULAMIT VOLKOV
Tel Aviv University

Notes

1. David Engel, "Away from a Definition of Antisemitism: An Essay in the Semantics of Historical Description," in *Rethinking European Jewish History*, ed. Jeremy Cohen and Moshe Rosman (Oxford: 2009), 30–53.

2. Ismar Schorsch, "The Myth of Sephardic Supremacy," in *Leo Baeck Institute Yearbook* 34 (1989), 47–66.

Book Reviews

Antisemitism, Holocaust, and Genocide

Kiril Feferman, *If we had wings we would fly to you: A Soviet Jewish Family Faces Destruction, 1941–42*. Boston: Academic Studies Press, 2020. xxvi + 322 pp.

As anyone who has worked with family letters can attest, most are filled with bland statements of affection, unsurprising news of people referred to only by nicknames, and discussions of health and the weather. Only very rarely does one find lyrical writing or important revelations. Like most of our day-to-day conversation, letters tend to be prosaic and personal. It is thus a challenge to turn a collection of letters into a compelling narrative.

In *If we had wings we would fly to you*, Kiril Feferman has the advantage of having discovered a trove of family letters composed at a particularly crucial juncture of the Second World War and the Holocaust. Yet the letters themselves are still mostly newsy and repetitive. Additionally, the reader knows from the start that most of the correspondents will not survive the war. It is thus a great credit to his scholarly and compositional skills that Feferman manages to draw the reader into the Ginzburg family's slowly unfolding tragedy.

Feferman originally came across the letter collection at Yad Vashem while researching an earlier project, and, as he explains in the preface, "it took me some time to realize the unprecedented value of the letters and to figure out what could be done with them" (p. ix). The letters were saved by Efim Ginzburg, a Soviet Jew who evacuated from Moscow to Omsk (in southwest Siberia) in 1941. Subsequently, he moved to Alma-Ata (today known as Almaty), in the then-Kazakh Soviet Socialist Republic, where he, along with many evacuated Soviet and foreign Jews, survived the war. Throughout this period of upheaval and deprivation, he remained in close contact with his three sisters and their adult children, all of whom lived in the family's hometown of Rostov-on-Don, in the North Caucasus. Efim was the only survivor of the family, and his widow later donated the collection to Yad Vashem.

The Ginzburg letters offer an intimate approach to the Holocaust in the USSR. As Feferman writes: "This communication revolves around one main issue that permeates the letters—evacuation: that is, if, when, and how the family should leave their home city, in order to evade capture by the Germans" (p. xvi). With the speed and success of the German invasion, evacuation was a major aspect of the war for the entire Soviet population. Over 16 million civilians and tons of industrial capacity were moved eastward ahead of the front. The population movement included both formal and organized evacuations and the flight of individuals such as Efim. Because of their location, the Ginzburg family faced a particular set of circumstances: two German

Book Reviews In: *Becoming Post-Communist.* Edited by: Eli Lederhendler, Oxford University Press. © Oxford University Press 2023. DOI: 10.1093/oso/9780197687215.003.0011

invasions in close succession. Feferman, whose previous book was *The Holocaust in the Crimea and the North Caucasus* (2016), does an excellent job of explaining the intricacies of the war, evacuation policies, and the Holocaust in this region. The book also includes a useful timeline.

Although in some ways this is a uniquely Soviet story, the letters also highlight the struggles and dilemmas many Jews encountered elsewhere during the Holocaust. Efim's choice to leave his home and work in Moscow left him vulnerable and alone. His sisters and nieces worried about him, often encouraging him to join them in Rostov, which was in fact an evacuation center. At times they sent him money to help him get by. Although Efim's letters did not survive, it is clear from the other side of the correspondence that he was simultaneously trying to convince the rest of the family to join him in the safety of Alma-Ata, and he was sending money for passage whenever he could afford to do so. None of the family knew how far the German advance would extend or what, exactly, were their plans for the Jewish population. Like other Jews across Europe who relied on intuition, rumors, and the limited information available in the press, they continually weighed their options and made and remade decisions within the fractured spheres of action available to them.

Although the letters themselves rarely directly reference press coverage, Feferman contextualizes them within research about what information was available in the national and local media outlets. After chapters introducing the family, the evacuation process, and the Holocaust in the North Caucasus, the book is organized chronologically, month-by-month. Each month includes either excerpts or complete letters, embedded within Feferman's account of the progress of the war, based on archival research in German and Soviet sources, and citations of any media that might possibly have reached the relatives in and around Rostov.

Tragically, although most of the Rostov family evacuated to a distant town within the region during the first German incursion in November 1941, they were unable to get sufficiently far away when the Germans returned in July 1942. The only survivor was the husband of one of Efim's nieces, who later died fighting in the Red Army. At several points in the book, including most strongly in the conclusion, Feferman refers to this failure to evacuate earlier and further as a "fatal mistake" (p. 263). Given his sensitive portrayal of the severe lack of information about either troop movements or mass murder, this is jarring. The text would seem to belie such a judgment.

One frustration with this powerful book, which Feferman seems to share, is how little can be pieced together about the individual members of the Ginzburg family. Although his research yielded beautiful photographs, and of course the letters in different hands and voices, the correspondents remain largely out of reach. This is understandable for the children, young mothers, and even middle-aged women whose lives were cut short by the Holocaust. It is harder to understand how Efim, who survived the war, married, and eventually moved to Israel, left so little trace. On a minor note, I expect that the publisher will fix some of the inexplicable gray highlighting of certain passages of text in later printings.

In June of 1942, just a month before the German takeover of Rostov and two months before her death, Liza Ginzburg wrote to her brother Efim: "Of course, it looks like something terrible is about to happen, but it may be that nothing bad will occur. Then the dark clouds will be scattered and nice bright days will come again"

(p. 239). Ultimately, it is this very human drive toward hope—and the desire to shield loved ones from worry—that comes across in the letters. As such, they provide us with a critically important window into the daily lives and concerns of Jews during the Holocaust. Through his careful translation and presentation of these letters, Feferman offers readers invaluable insight into ordinary lives under excruciating circumstances.

ELIYANA R. ADLER
Pennsylvania State University

Erin McGlothlin, Brad Prager, and Markus Zisselberger (eds.), *The Construction of Testimony: Claude Lanzmann's Shoah and Its Outtakes*. Detroit: Wayne State University Press, 2020. 504 pp.

It should be said right from the outset: *The Construction of Testimony: Claude Lanzmann's* Shoah *and Its Outtakes* is an outstanding contribution equally to film studies and to Holocaust studies. In order to better understand why this powerful anthology is so important, I would first like to mention an incident that took place in March 2004 at the Pompidou Center in Paris, during the final day of the Cinéma du Réel documentary film festival. According to the schedule, a second screening of a film titled *Route 181: Fragments of a Voyage to Israel–Palestine*,[1] a collaborative effort of Israel's Eyal Sivan and Palestinian director Michel Khleifi, was to be shown, but the screening was canceled, "for security reasons, and out of concern for public order."

Several weeks prior to the festival, a letter signed by leading French intellectuals and filmmakers that was published in the French newspaper *Libération* charged that "*Route 181* presents controversial historic truths and contributes to a poisoning of the political discussion of the Israeli–Palestinian conflict." The four-and-a-half-hour-long film, documenting a journey of the two directors along the 1947 partition plan border, featured interviews with Israeli Jews and Palestinian Arabs along the seam between Israel and the would-be state of Palestine, and it included several painful accounts about the roots of the conflict. The letter's signatories (among them, directors Arnaud Desplechin and Noemie Lvovsky, philosophers Bernard-Henri Lévy and Elisabeth de Fontenay, and author Philippe Sollers) made particular reference to a scene in which a Palestinian barber living in Lod, while cutting Khleifi's hair, describes the massacre of unarmed Palestinians at the Dahmash mosque in Lod during the 1948 war. The scene lasts 12 minutes and ends with images of train tracks in Lod; according to the signatories, this was a clear reference to one of the scenes in Claude Lanzmann's *Shoah*, in which a Jewish barber named Abraham Bomba speaks of how he was persecuted by the Nazis during the Holocaust. In the opinion of the letter writers, the similarities linking the two scenes generated a comparison between Jews and Nazis, or, more specifically, between the Palestinian victims of the *Nakba* (the catastrophe, that is, Israel's War of Independence) and the Jewish victims of the Holocaust.

The decision to cancel the second screening of the film led to another public letter published in *Libération* and signed by 300 French intellectuals (including director Jean-Luc Godard). It criticized the decision of the festival directors, "which looks like unspoken censorship," arguing that allegations that *Route 181* was "an anti-Semitic or Judeophobic film" were ridiculous: "The film takes part in an intellectual discussion in which everyone has the freedom to criticize." This incident marked a turning point in the attitude toward Claude Lanzmann's *Shoah*.

Lanzmann had spent 12 years locating survivors, perpetrators, eyewitnesses, and scholars for his nine-and-a-half-hour film, released in 1985. Critics have called it "a sheer masterpiece" and a "monument against forgetting." *Shoah* was immediately proclaimed a cinematic milestone, and it is widely regarded as the seminal film on the subject of the Holocaust. It is impossible to undermine Lanzmann's achievements in this film, which introduced an entirely new cinematic language and heralded the turn to survivor videos. *Shoah* sought to probe the limits of Holocaust representation and paved the way for new understandings of the mass murder conducted in Nazi-occupied Europe. With its huge and immediate cultural, historical, and aesthetic impact, *Shoah* became almost totally immune to any kind of cultural criticism.

This was true of the academic world as well, which was almost unanimous in its praise. One of the few exceptions was Dominick LaCapra's critical argumentation (which the editors of this book rightly mention in their introduction): "There is in Lanzmann a fascination with the victim and almost the desire to identify with the experience of the victim because Lanzmann himself was not a victim of the Shoah yet somehow feels that he should have been a victim [...] On one level, this is very moving, but it can also lead to a very intrusive kind of questioning in the actual encounter with the victim. It may even lead to an identification with the aggressor."[2] LaCapra was one of the first scholars who posed a radical question with regard to Lanzmann's masterpiece, echoing the famous Nietzschean sentence: "Whoever fights monsters should see to it that in the process he does not become a monster." Another rare critical judgment was voiced by Lanzmann's generational colleague Marcel Ophüls, director of *The Sorrow and the Pity* (1969), the renowned documentary about Vichy France's collaboration with the Nazis: "[Lanzmann] puts himself in the role of judge and jury. That's his own privilege. . . . He's an ideologue, I concentrate on the revelation of the character."[3] Ophüls' comment should be taken seriously since it corresponds not only to *Shoah* itself but also to Lanzmann's famous cinematic trilogy in which *Shoah* plays the second part (the first and the third parts are *Pourquoi Israël* [1973] and *Tsahal* [1994], respectively); all three films echo, implicitly and explicitly, the official Zionist discourse.

The Construction of Testimony: Claude Lanzmann's Shoah *and Its Outtakes* should be understood as a continuation of these attempts to re-view *Shoah* and, in so doing, to deconstruct its mythological aura. Each of the contributors to the anthology suggests a specific critical approach toward Lanzmann's film and its outtakes.[4] Debarati Sanyal and Markus Zisselsberger elaborate an important issue concerning the conspicuous absence of women's voices in *Shoah*, while Erin McGlothlin highlights the way in which Lanzmann uses the technique of montage in the famous interview with former SS guard Franz Suchomel; in the film, he comes across as a one-dimensional perpetrator whereas the outtakes reveal a more complex personality. Another illuminating analysis belongs to Brad Prager, which brings us back to Abraham Bomba, the Jewish barber in Treblinka: Prager reveals that this famous scene—in which Bomba breaks down while cutting someone's hair in a barbershop—was actually a recreation of an earlier interview that took place prior to that scene. Prager's observation can illuminate not only this famous scene, but also Khleifi and Sivan's provocative allusion from 2004: "Can testimony be both an authentic eruption of incontrovertible truth and a dissimulating theatrical performance?"

In another fascinating contribution to this anthology, Tobias Ebbrecht-Hartmann examines *The Last of the Unjust*, a film made by Lanzmann in 2013. Coining the term "temporality of delay," Ebbrecht-Hartman argues that *The Last of the Unjust* is in fact a "delayed" film that brings to life a delayed interview of Benjamin Murmelstein, the infamous *Ältester* (council elder) of the Judenrat in the Theresienstadt concentration camp. Lanzmann shot the interview with Murmelstein in Rome in 1975 for *Shoah*, but didn't include it in the final cut. Ebbrecht-Hartmann argues that, by this delayed act of return to the archive, Lanzmann "revisits his own filmmaking past." It seems as if Lanzmann, then 87 years old, was engaging in self-reflection, looking back on his own film oeuvre in a rather critical manner (mainly in regard to his old attitude toward the use of archival footage). Thus, he depicts the character of Murmelstein as himself going through a (similar and yet different) process of self-reflection.

The term "temporality of delay" captures some of the essence of this fascinating anthology. Both words—"temporality" and "delay"—are surpassingly relevant in analyzing any kind of cinema that deals with historical events, and especially traumatic events. The main question that should be asked has to do with morality: what are the moral routes that bring us back to the past event in light of the present? Time is obviously changing our moral perspectives, hence the act of "delaying" should be regarded as moral in nature. In other words, what cannot be said "morally," at a certain moment and a certain time, should be delayed until the right moment eventually comes. As William Faulkner once said, "The past is never dead. It's not even past."

Were we to further develop Ebbrecht-Hartmann's term, we might arrive at a number of other very interesting questions, such as: is it possible that Lanzmann delayed work on *The Last of the Unjust* until after the death of his old friend and mentor who became known as one of the major critics of the Jewish councils, Raul Hilberg (who died in 2007)? Similarly, is it possible that publication of *The Construction of Testimony* was delayed until after Lanzmann's death in 2018? And last but not least, might it be the case that Khleifi and Sivan were not the first ones to "steal" the image of the barber from the history of cinema—that it was Lanzmann himself who preceded them by "stealing" it from Charlie Chaplin's 1940 masterpiece, *The Great Dictator*? In terms of "temporality of delay," it seems to me that, instead of being fashionably late, as is the filmmaker's habit, Chaplin was embarrassingly early.

EREZ PERY
Sapir College

Notes

1. "Route 181" refers not to an actual road, but rather to UN General Assembly Resolution #181—the November 1947 partition plan.
2. Dominick LaCapra, *Writing History, Writing Trauma* (Baltimore: 2001), 146.
3. Marcel Ophüls, quoted in André Pierre Colombat, *The Holocaust in French Film* (Metuchen: 1993), 307.
4. The United States Holocaust Memorial Museum purchased the *Shoah* outtakes from Claude Lanzmann on October 11, 1996; the footage contains 185 hours of interview outtakes and 35 hours of location filming.

Thomas Pegelow Kaplan and Wolf Gruner (eds.), *Resisting Persecution: Jews and Their Petitions during the Holocaust*. New York: Berghahn, 2020. 251 pp.

Petitioning by Jews to authorities during the Holocaust was a widespread phenomenon that, up to now, has been little researched by scholars. *Resisting Persecution* opens the discussion and highlights the fact that Jews employed varied responses to the measures taken against them and that these reflect Jewish agency and often defiance.

Jews petitioned various authorities throughout the Holocaust, beginning with calls for respecting rights early in the Nazi regime through entreaties during the war, and this form of behavior carried on in demands for better treatment in postwar Germany. The sheer volume of petitions in itself supports the importance of researching this material. Who wrote petitions? Under what circumstances? To whom were they addressed? What were the petitioners' goals? What light can these petitions shed on Jews' responses to the Holocaust? How did the various authorities involved respond? Such questions and more are addressed in this volume.

The book is composed of eight chapters on specific places, sandwiched between an introduction and a conclusion by editors Thomas Pegelow Kaplan and Wolf Gruner, who also each wrote a chapter. The places addressed in the essays include the Greater Third Reich (Gruner); France (Stacy Renee Veeder); the Nazi Protectorate of Bohemia and Moravia (Benjamin Frommer); Romanian and Jewish community leader Wilhelm Filderman (Ştefan Cristian Ionescu); the Łódź ghetto (Svenja Bethke); Budapest (Tim Cole); the Philippines (Kaplan); and postwar Germany (Maximilian Strnad). The articles are interesting and informative and merit closer attention than it is possible to provide in this brief review.

At first glance, the book might seem uneven geographically. For example, three essays address Germany and the "Protectorate," but only one deals with Poland. France is the sole representative of Western Europe, and no region east of Poland is mentioned. This said, there is only so much that can be accomplished in one small volume on such a huge subject. Within these limitations, the book succeeds in being informative and provocative.

Both the introduction and Wolf Gruner's opening chapter on petitions as protest in the Greater German Reich argue that filing petitions and entreaties was part of the larger picture of *'amidah*, active unarmed resistance by individuals or groups. Citing

Yehuda Bauer's analysis of *'amidah*, which includes such acts as smuggling food into ghettos and clandestine education, Gruner argues for petitions as another form of unarmed resistance, since they involved initiative and risks. Yet one might also claim that these courageous acts of Jewish agency were within the norms permitted by the Nazi regime and were therefore not acts of resistance. Are agency and resistance the same in the Holocaust? Most of the chapters in the book address agency more than resistance, though the question of agency versus resistance is not the central issue.

Gruner's fine chapter covers a large geographic and temporal space—the Greater Third Reich and most of the Nazi period. Petitions to local, regional, and federal officials were made mostly by men until November 1938, reflecting the traditional societal structure in Germany. However, after 30,000 Jewish men were arrested in the Kristallnacht pogrom, many more petitions and protests came from women. In this role reversal in Jewish families, analyzed in the past by Marion Kaplan, women continued to petition after the men were released, a fact that is reflected in other chapters as well. For instance, Stacy Renee Veeder's well-constructed chapter on France during the war highlights Jews' efforts to free arrested men from detention camps such as Drancy. Women wrote many of these petitions to French officials, often emphasizing the French acculturation or assimilation of the interned Jewish man and his service in the First World War (if relevant). Acculturation, love for country, and military service were also highlighted in many of the petitions in Germany and in other countries discussed in this book.

Benjamin Frommer looks at a group of some 1,000 Czech citizens who requested recognition as "honorary Aryans" or "Aryans" because they were Christians, albeit considered Jewish by race. Their petitions were sent to the puppet Czech government, which recommended approving only 41 of the applications; *Reichsprotektor* Konstantin von Neurath rejected all of them. Here, too, the applicants highlighted their assimilation into the "Aryan" environment. However, since they did not regard themselves as Jewish and sought removal from that status, the question arises whether their petitions fit within the book's general framework.

The essays of Ştefan Cristian Ionescu (on Romanian Jewish leader Wilhelm Filderman) and Svenja Bethke (petitions to the Judenrat in the Łódź ghetto) differ from the others; Ionescu highlights one Jewish leader, and Bethke focuses on petitions to a Jewish authority rather than German or other non-Jewish authorities. Whereas few of the petitions discussed in other chapters succeeded, Ionescu's piece analyzes several of Filderman's successes with Romanian dictator Ion Antonescu and other Romanian leaders. Alongside personal—though not particularly friendly—connections with these people, Filderman had a sense of how to frame an appeal in order to achieve his goals. His major success was the suspension of the planned deportation of the Jews of the Banat to Transnistria and Poland in the fall of 1942, which he accomplished despite Antonescu's and other Romanian officials' strong dislike for him and his efforts. These officials feared the repercussions of doing this internationally well-connected leader too much harm. According to Ionescu, Filderman "contributed decisively to the survival of many Romanian Jews" (p. 108).

Svenja Bethke aptly suggests using the term "community of coercion," rather than Jewish community, as a more accurate reflection of their coerced conditions. She discusses numerous petitions to Mordechai Chaim Rumkowski that are found in the

Łódź State Archive and remarks on various noteworthy points, such as the large proportion of women among the petitioners. However, the article does not utilize Hebrew sources (save one citation of a letter), the most important of which is Michal Unger's comprehensive book on the Łódź ghetto. Bethke also does not cite Josef Zelkowicz's reportage from Łódź, parts of which are relevant, nor has she consulted the large volume of documentation on Łódź in Israeli archives, which includes numerous first-person accounts. Moreover, "the overly dichotomous categories of resistance and complicity that still prevail in Holocaust research" (p. 117) overstates the case. This dichotomy has not been prominent in Israeli scholarship, or scholarship in general, for many years. Nor did the reevaluation of Judenräte and Jewish responses begin in the late 1970s and 1980s, as Bethke claims. Indeed, the books that she cites marking this change, Isaiah Trunk's *Judenrat* and Jacob Robinson's *And the Crooked Shall be Made Straight*, were published in 1972 and 1965, respectively.

Tim Cole's examination of more than 600 petitions makes for a very interesting analysis of petitions by Jews and non-Jews in Budapest regarding the planned, dispersed ghetto in 1944. Jewish and non-Jewish neighbors often had opposing interests. Jews would petition to have their buildings marked with a yellow star, whereas their non-Jewish neighbors would request the opposite (in each case, the goal was not to be forced to move). Cole also notes additional factors that influenced petitioners' requests, such as the relative desirability of a neighborhood: in some cases, the chance of finding a better location was a factor in seeking to move as opposed to staying in place. There were also collective petitions on the part of residents in a given building who asked that their dwelling be regarded as a "mixed house," a status that would allow them all to stay in place. Some of these petitions were approved, and many were taken seriously by the authorities—a worthy point for future comparative research.

Thomas Pegelow Kaplan's essay deals with the book's most unusual subject: petitions relating to the 1,300 refugees who reached the Philippines in 1938–1941. Kaplan received access to the as yet little explored archive of Manuel Quezon, the president of the Philippines during that time. In presenting this "history of constant forced border crossings," and the petitions by and on behalf of Jewish refugees, Kaplan engages in a global and interactive analysis that goes beyond specific nation-states. Quezon and the local Jewish Refugee Committee were very selective regarding whom they agreed to admit to the country—mostly young people with specific professions and trades, aided by the Joint Distribution Committee (JDC). Ironically, the roles between local Jews and refugees were reversed after the Japanese military government arrested 250 Jews (among them, the rabbi and the cantor) who held U.S. passports. A refugee rabbi, Josef Schwarz, was able to step in to run the synagogue, and to organize aid and write petitions on behalf of the interned Jews, because the Japanese initially viewed the refugees as friendly Germans.

Maximilian Strnad examines intermarried German Jews in the immediate postwar years who fell between the cracks for aid. They survived because they were married to "Aryans"; some had converted to Christianity. The American occupying forces viewed them as Germans who did not merit assistance, while former German political prisoners believed they had not suffered sufficiently to receive aid. The re-emerging Jewish communities regarded them as people who had left the community and should not share in its meager resources, a perspective shared by the JDC. Finally, Christian aid organizations were reluctant to aid people of Jewish background. Notwithstanding, many of them petitioned for aid, arguing that they, too, had suffered. Most of these petitions were unsuccessful. In contrast to the Nazi period, when it was the non-Jewish spouse who petitioned on behalf of the Jewish spouse, thus emphasizing detachment from Jews, in the postwar years the Jewish spouse would petition Jewish organizations and UNRRA on behalf of the non-Jewish spouse, thereby emphasizing Jewish connection and suffering. Still, we might wonder if this topic, worthy as it is, fits in the rubric of "resisting persecution."

Taken together, these essays highlight a generally neglected subject that clearly merits more scholarly attention. Despite the few caveats noted above, *Resisting Persecution* makes a worthy contribution to scholarship and is well worth the read.

DAVID SILBERKLANG
Yad Vashem

Cultural Studies, Literature, and Religion

Steven E. Aschheim, *Fragile Spaces: Forays into Jewish Memory, European History, and Complex Identities*. Berlin: Walter de Gruyter, 2018. 279 pp.

Reviewing a collection of 20 essays is challenging, especially when they are as engaging and wide-ranging as those in this volume. Given that all but four were published previously, one may wonder: How compelling is the case for this collection? Steven Aschheim anticipates the question, suggesting that the essays share "a certain unity of thematic concerns," revolving around "the consequences of political, cultural, and personal ruptures" in various contexts and the ensuing, "sometimes tortured," responses, which introduced often new, "sometimes profound, sometimes fantastical options" (p. 1). Divided into four parts—"History, Memory and Genocide," "Culture and Complex Identities," "Politics," and "Scholarly Dilemmas and Personal Confrontations"—the book's most rewarding essays address issues of politics, philosophy, Holocaust memory, and the history of German-speaking Jewish intellectuals in relation to European culture and modernity. Aschheim views rupture as "a constitutive ingredient of modernity," leading, unsurprisingly, to a "sense of contingency" and, far more suggestively, to a new "awareness of the fragility of things" (ibid.). That sense of *fragility* runs through the pages of this volume, permeating many of Aschheim's inquiries into the past and present.

Fragile Spaces is bookended by an exploration of Theodor Adorno and Max Horkheimer's renowned study, *The Dialectic of Enlightenment*, and an essay on various European-born actors in the Middle East around the time of the First World War, some of whom stretch credulity. It tells, for instance, of Max von Oppenheim, a Jewish-born convert and, in the Nazi period, an "honorary Aryan," who tried to incite anti-British jihad in the Middle East during the First World War and anti-British, anti-Jewish jihad two decades later, during the Second World War. Several essays deal with Gershom Scholem and Hannah Arendt, whose *Correspondence* (*Der Briefwechsel*, 2010) reveals that Arendt, not Scholem, as usually believed, severed their contact. A playful, yet extensively researched "unwritten letter" to Arendt and Scholem by Victor Klemperer, the posthumously famous diarist of day-to-day survival in Nazi Germany (thanks to his marriage to a non-Jew), provocatively adopts the perspective of this assimilationist who chose, postwar, to remain in the German Democratic Republic. The last part of the book contains illuminating reviews of books authored by Yosef Hayim Yerushalmi, Saul Friedländer, Moshe Idel, Pierre Birnbaum, Hans Jonas, and Anthony David's biography of Salman Schocken. There, Aschheim questions certain

Book Reviews In: *Becoming Post-Communist.* Edited by: Eli Lederhendler, Oxford University Press. © Oxford University Press 2023. DOI: 10.1093/oso/9780197687215.003.0014

sweeping judgments about German (and other Western) Jews who were not "sufficiently" Jewish.

Aschheim revisits material here he has dealt with previously, but in provocative new ways. The following focuses on the essays I find most rewarding, from which I quote liberally.

In Chapter 1, Aschheim analyzes Adorno and Horkheimer's *Dialectic of Enlightenment* on both a theoretical and historical level. Its well-known thesis: Enlightenment reason begins as a liberatory force, but eventually undermines itself, turning into oppressive "instrumental reason" in service of "totalitarian" domination in liberal democratic no less than fascist societies. Aschheim finds this too vague, general, and ultimately, undialectical. Acknowledging Enlightenment influences on fascism (modern sciences, for instance, enabled notions of racial purity, degeneration, eugenics, and "bio-politics"), he argues that a "proper historical dialectic" would also account for the " 'irrationalist' impulses" neglected by the authors: "extreme nationalism, vitalism, the cult of force and sacrifice, overt mythology" (p. 22). These re-directed the rational sciences into fascism, Nazism, aggression, violence, and "mechanisms of superiority and exclusion" (ibid.). Adorno and Horkheimer's chapter "Elements of anti-Semitism" provides an "a-historical shopping cart" of possible " 'origins,' 'elements,' concepts and contemporary events" melded together. Aschheim's withering critique:

"The principled difficulty with this kind of philosophical *Kulturkritik* consists of its generality, its insistence upon the (entirely speculative) notion of a repressed phenomenological condition at the heart of an undifferentiated West" (p. 30).

Notwithstanding, in Chapter 6, "The Weimar Kaleidoscope—And, Incidentally, Frankfurt's Not Minor Place in It," Aschheim acknowledges the importance of Adorno, Horkheimer, and other Frankfurt School associates (among them, Walter Benjamin, Ernst Bloch, Leo Löwenthal, and Sigfried Kracauer). In this, the strongest of three essays on Jews in 20th-century Central European culture, Aschheim stresses the "co-constitutive" role these intellectuals played in Weimar Germany (a thesis dating to a 1998 article), which he describes as "a virtual kaleidoscope of multiple shifting patterns, a fascinating panoply of dynamic cultural and intellectual currents and diverse political tendencies, ranging from the *völkisch* and conservative through liberal to radical, revolutionary, and existential impulses" (p. 83). Jews from both the Right (such as Ernst Kantorowiz and Leo Strauss) and Left (apart from Western Marxists, there were also "critically concerned liberals" such as Ernst Cassirer, Erwin Panofsky, and Aby Warburg) contributed to Weimar's twofold image, "half of danger and warning" (politically, socially, etc.), half a "daring experimental spirit, the critical, dissenting radicalized temperament," bursting with creativity, responding to postwar trauma, rupture, and a "[f]ragility" seemingly "built not only into the social fabric but the psyche itself" (pp. 85, 90). Still others sought specifically to revitalize Jewish life—among them Martin Buber, Gershom Scholem, and other cultural Zionists, and Franz Rosenzweig and associates of his *Jüdisches Lehrhaus*. Most of these intellectuals were progressive or close to progressive circles.

Aschheim's discussion of the Brit Shalom Zionist movement in his excellent essay "Zionism and Europe" is highly relevant here. Noting that its predominantly Central European adherents "were most acutely sensitive to the moral problem of Zionism in relationship to the Arab inhabitants of Palestine," Aschheim finds it especially remarkable that they somehow combined an organic, *völkisch* vision with a "peculiar appropriation of the German[-Jewish] tradition of Bildung." This "humanizing" legacy, in turn, informed their ideas of a Jewish essence and ethics, inspiring them to focus on moral-spiritual and cultural matters and to "shear [. . .] their *völkisch* ideology of its hierarchical and political dimensions" (p. 171)—which also explains their advocacy of a bi-national solution to the Arab–Jewish conflict.

All this supports in its own way the "co-constitutive" thesis, though questions do arise. Take the case, discussed in a chapter on Vienna, of Ludwig Wittgenstein, whose three Jewish grandparents *all converted* at an early age (one was raised Catholic) and actively dissociated from the Jewish world. In 1931, Wittgenstein voiced a worry, in racially antisemitic terms, that his Jewish heritage hindered his creativity (p. 133), only to thoroughly abandon this concern thereafter.[1] In what sense is his "Jewish" connection truly relevant?

These essays often touch on questions of the particular and the universal in Jewish history. Chapter 9, "Between the Universal and the Particular: Rescuing the Particular from the Particularists and the Universal from the Universalists," tackles the subject head on, outlining "radical assaults" on "more normatively conceived notions of the particular and the universal and their complex relationship" (p. 141) before coming to their defense. In radically redefining the Universal, French Marxist philosopher Alain Badiou "surprisingly" resurrects the ostensibly long-abandoned "Jewish question." His re-definition displays an "inherited distaste for Jewish separateness," also found in some texts by Slavoj Žižek and Giorgio Agamben, and re-introduces a "supersessionist impulse in a secular key" (p. 146). Badiou attacks a "victim ideology" held by Jews who seek exceptional status and exhibit particularity "summed up crudely . . . as SIT – the Shoah, the State of Israel and the Talmudic Tradition." These hinder the advent of "any genuine universalist and egalitarian mode of being" (pp. 147–148). Yet Badiou's universalism posits "a highly elitist, bi-polar view of 'Man,' as either a pitiful, contemptible victim or—at the other extreme—as inhabiting a kind of ecstatic Nietzschean state of transcendence," excluding any view of "quotidian reality." In response, Aschheim notes the impossibility of "a universal form of life." Complex, dependent on multiple sources, irreducible to a single essence, "cultures and identities" nonetheless arise from "a cluster of particular experiential materials[:] language, tradition, family, friends, religion, nation, profession, norms, customs, and so on" (p. 152).

After tackling Badiou, Aschheim addresses equally problematic definitions of the "particular," since one needs no less to "rescue a defensible particularism from some of its present Israeli protagonists and their exclusive religious and nationalist postures" (p. 155). He cites former Minister of Justice, Ayelet Shaked, who in 2017 admonished the Israeli Supreme Court: " 'Zionism should not continue, . . . and it will not continue to bow down to the system of individual rights interpreted in a universal way' " (ibid.). Noting Shaked's disregard for Israel's "declared goal and responsibility for non-discrimination of all its citizens" (alas, never fully adhered to), Aschheim describes such assaults as "tribal particularism run amok," magnified "by a continuing occupation, the de-legitimization of critics of that policy, and an accompanying non-recognition, at times demonizing, of the Palestinians" (ibid.). Such assaults, he believes, lend some truth to Badiou's claims about "a privileging victim ideology" and the role of the Shoah today, an ideology that "too often serves to muffle or even prevent recognition of Palestinian suffering" (ibid.). Seeking to salvage a valid particularism, Aschheim enlists various intellectuals who, like Leszek Kolakowski, acknowledge the complex, inescapable interplay of the particular and the universal. Those seeking ultimate theoretical resolution here will be disappointed: "No simple answers exist" (p. 161). Instead, Aschheim enters a plea for a "modest but hopeful ameliorative liberalism . . . for both greater empathy *and* discerning judgment . . . for 'moral imagination,'" while suggesting what "any particularism or universalism worthy of emulation" would do—recognize "the dignity [of] . . . all human beings," further human creativity and happiness, and express the "shame that we should feel when these are both individually and collectively abused" (p. 162).

The word "shame" is not used lightly here. In an essay on "Lessons of the Holocaust," Aschheim argues that people of various political persuasions, whether Jewish or non-Jewish, tend to invoke such lessons in problematic ways that lack "concrete historical underpinnings" (p. 60). Here again he brings the discussion back to Israel, forcefully reiterating his point on particularism. In Israel, he finds Holocaust commemoration to be so "suffuse[d]" with "the lesson of endemic anti-Semitism and peculiar Jewish victimization . . . that it threatens to overwhelm the culture and channels virtually all its empathic energies," threatening as well to "muffle" or prevent "the far more difficult task of present political empathy and even act as a justification for ongoing domination of the Palestinians" (pp. 59–60).

Aschheim re-introduces shame when clarifying his own "personal [lesson]" regarding "all acts of indecent atrocity." Quoting Primo Levi, he speaks of "carry[ing] . . . 'the shame that the Germans never knew, the shame which the just man experiences when confronted by a crime committed by another, and he feels remorse because of its existence, because of its having been irrevocably introduced into the world of existing things, and because his will has proven non-existent or feeble and was incapable of putting up a good defense'" (p. 66).

Even more revealing is the essay that follows, "Empathy, Autobiography, and the Tasks and Tensions of the Historian," which begins by reflecting both on the responsibilities of the historian and on tensions in Weber's "Science as a Vocation" between "passionate devotion" and "value neutrality," before venturing into autobiography. Growing up in apartheid South Africa, the child of German Jewish émigrés, Aschheim (as well as many of his acquaintances) turned to Zionism as a form of anti-bourgeois rebellion that fulfilled what were perceived as "very authentic needs," providing a means to psychologically detach from the loathed apartheid system (p. 73). Against this background, Aschheim explores his decision to become a historian and the role of empathy it involves, as historical understanding requires empathy with the "(usually subjugated) Other" and, hence, the capacity to "interrogate one's own narrative, the immense normative power of one's own common-sense 'plausibility structure'" (p. 72). It means accounting for one's own inevitable sympathies or biases, and also being able to empathize on some level with perpetrators. Yet "empathy" has further complexities, which, if not balanced with other considerations, such as justice and the search for truth, limit its value. One can empathize with one's enemies, but still go to battle, vanquish, and oppress them. Conversely, the fact of being a victim does not in itself make one's own account correct or oneself "morally flawless" (pp. 76–77). Such reflections, addressing challenges faced in all historical writing, together with the essay's glimpse into Aschheim as a person and historian, make it one of the most worthwhile in the volume.

Overall, the essays of *Fragile Spaces* make for a compelling volume, precisely because of the way Aschheim draws upon an extensive cast of characters in a highly charged historical drama or, rather, several dramas, whom he explores and confronts amidst the aforementioned—often urgent—responses they offered to rupture and fragility in society, politics, and culture, Jewish and otherwise. Various personages, ideas, events, and concerns reappear in various essays, continually re-arranged to form a new and dynamic pattern ("kaleidoscopically"), so that the essays become mutually illuminating, while reflecting Aschheim's own urgent concerns with the task of the historian, the value and limits of empathy, historical understanding, critical analysis, and the social and political conditions of recent years, especially the "Israel-Palestinian imbroglio," but much else as well. His concerns and approach to these issues show him to be a true heir to the German Jewish intellectual legacy he so often explores.

JEFFREY A. GROSSMAN
University of Virginia

Note

1. See also Ray Monk, *Wittgenstein: The Duty of Genius* (New York: 1990), 316–317.

Manuela Consonni and Vivian Liska (eds.), *Sartre, Jews, and the Other: Rethinking Antisemitism, Race, and Gender.* Berlin: Walter de Gruyter, 2020. xii + 292 pp.

Scholars have long recognized the centrality of Jean-Paul Sartre's *Réflexions sur la question juive* (1946). Sartre in this work applies the existentialist ideas of his *L'Être et le néant* (1943), characterizing the antisemite and the Jew as bound by their relationship with one another. Anxious concerning his place in a changing material world, the antisemite explained his mediocrity through passionate yet irrational "bad faith" arguments about the Jew as the Manichean "other," exploitative and foreign. Claiming the purest of motives, the antisemite thus "made" the Jew, for within this Hegelian/Marxist dialectic, Sartre defined the Jew as a product of his oppressors' gaze. Whatever distinct historical consciousness the Jew had, Sartre argued, had faded long ago; antisemitism now formed his identity. Thus the Jew's "authenticity" for Sartre depended on the degree to which he rejected the contempt imposed from without. For despite the restoration of republicanism in France, democracy there was a poor protector against antisemitism; its unwavering republican universalism in Sartre's view "saves the [Jew] as a man and annihilates him as a Jew."

Réflexions was daring for its time. Sartre aimed to lay bare the antisemitism that led to the deportation and murder of more than 70,000 Jews from France. But understanding antisemitism as a system of thought was also critical in forging human solidarity, as the fate of the Jews could ultimately be the fate of all. In this broader sense, *Réflexions* anticipated postmodern notions of how binary thinking constructed the "other." It thus remains a lodestone in the study not only of antisemitism but also of racism, sexism, and how the victims of these systems navigate oppression. Yet how are we to weigh *Réflexions* after decades of scholarship on everything from Holocaust memory to postcolonial readings of the West to postmodern gender scholarship? And where should we look for intersections between the Holocaust and other forms of oppression in our own fraught age? The volume under review comprises 18 papers presented at the Vidal Sassoon International Center for the Study of Antisemitism on the 70th anniversary of *Réflexions* in 2016. Their interdisciplinary nature—philosophical, historical, psychological, literary—reflects the subject's depth. While the papers do not always speak to one another, some do so while attempting to navigate the major problems at hand.

As Renée Poznanski argues in her essay, Sartre broke the imposed republican silence concerning the wartime fate of France's Jews, a phenomenon rooted in the reluctance to endanger a republican anti-Vichy consensus. Sartre was right about democratic universalism. Still, several of the volume's other authors discuss his superficial understanding of the Jews themselves. By viewing them as an abstract community based on outside perceptions, Sartre, whatever the nobility of his motives (and not everyone saw them as entirely noble), ignored the depth of Jewish culture, replacing it with a trope—what Sarah Hammerschlag has called the "figural Jew." As Bruno Chaouat points out in his essay, which analyzes older critiques of Sartre from André Neher and Emmanuel Levinas, the "anthropological reality [of the Jews] cannot be reduced to ... the imaginary projection of the antisemite" (p. 91). Sartre's existential reading of the Jew, Chaouat argues further, could not yield even "a genuine encounter with Levinas," who understood that Jewishness meant being "riveted and bound to past generations" (p. 101).

Still, as Ethan Katz and Jonathan Judaken argue in their essays, it was Sartre's figural Jew that created the linkages to the anti-colonial struggle, so much so that Michael Rothberg's 2009 notion of "multidirectional memory," the means by which major anticolonialist writers mobilized the memory of the Holocaust by rhetorically connecting Nazi and colonial oppression, must be broadened. Yes, Frantz Fanon's *Black Skin White Masks* (1952) and Albert Memmi's *The Colonizer and the Colonized* (1957) were heavily influenced by Sartre's notion of the objectifying gaze by which the oppressor defines and transforms the oppressed to the point of neuroses, but linkages to the Holocaust spanned to Gillo Pontecorvo's film *The Battle of Algiers* (1966). Sartre's own anticolonialism and antiracism permeated his postwar writing and his journal, *Les Temps Modernes*; the Jewish question was ultimately a question of humanity. But unlike more doctrinaire anticolonialists, Sartre supported Israel, viewing Zionism as an anticolonial liberation movement in its own right and hoping for an equitable settlement between Israel and the Arabs. It never added up for Israel's enemies, Edward Said in particular, but as Judaken points out, Sartre's existentialist, multidirectional antiracism "remains a model for confronting the global racisms of the present" (p. 129).

Other authors in the volume, in particular Vinzia Fiorino and Yael S. Feldman, argue for the effect of Sartre's *Réflexions* on postwar feminism; it must be read, they say, not only in conjunction with Fanon, but also with Simone de Beauvoir's *The Second Sex* (1949). For Fiorino, there is an indirect genealogy from Sartre to Fanon to Italian feminist Carla Lonzi, who sought Sartre's "authenticity" by challenging the "male gaze that ... colonized the female being," all the while recognizing Fanon's belief in the "metaphysical anguish" (p. 196) caused by the dialectical relationship's erosion of the self. For Feldman, the fact that *The Second Sex* was not translated into Hebrew until 2001 matters less than the fact that de Beauvoir's thought was internalized by feminist writers such as Amalia Kahana-Carmon, a major Hebrew writer who challenged categories of gender and racial difference even in those signifiers in the Hebrew Bible.

As political scientist Itamar Ben-Ami has pointed out, the new 2020 Hebrew translation of *Réflexions* affirms its timelessness but also its challenges; in a new afterward, Yehuda Meltzer warns of the xenophobia among the grandchildren of victims of antisemitism toward, among others, Israeli Arabs. The broad analysis of Sartre's consideration of antisemitism, as reflected in the essays in this fine volume, is similarly timely.

NORMAN J.W. GODA
University of Florida

Dina Danon, *The Jews of Ottoman Izmir: A Modern History*. Stanford: Stanford University Press, 2020. 241 pp.
Malte Fuhrmann, *Port Cities of the Eastern Mediterranean: Urban Culture in the Late Ottoman Empire*. Cambridge: Cambridge University Press, 2020. 404 pp.

Traces of a remarkable Jewish past are still to be found in a number of Eastern Mediterranean port cities of the former Ottoman empire. Two recent books on the region, Malte Fuhrmann's *Port Cities of the Eastern Mediterranean*, a sweeping panorama of the region, and Dina Danon's *The Jews of Ottoman Izmir*, a microhistory of Izmir, reveal the broad spectrum of this history and hint at its continuing appeal.

Fuhrmann's ambitious undertaking looks at modern Ottoman culture in relation to "the West" in Salonica, Smyrna, and Constantinople. An unusual array of archival material, supplemented by the author's vast knowledge of literature, is called upon to depict the urban space as a site of ambivalence and as a stage for the multitude of identities intimately intertwined with the European landscape. Fuhrmann's focus is on the lower classes, the European poor—and, in particular, women whose lives crossed cultural and physical borders in search of work and security. A captivating wealth of details about such matters as brothels and beerhouses, opera and the *corso* (promenade) illustrates the urban cultures of the port cities. The conceptualization of the

Eastern Mediterranean as "seascape," a geographical entity shaped by human agency, reinforces Fuhrmann's argument about the fluidity of borders and identities.

One of the book's noteworthy sections is that dealing with the perceived "civilizing" role of opera. In late Ottoman culture, opera reflected both the cosmopolitanism of the empire and its international appeal. Foreign visitors who attended performances in Izmir and wrote about them with admiration included Hans Christian Andersen, Gerard de Nerval, and Gustave Flaubert. The celebrated Naum Theatre in Istanbul, led by a Maronite dynasty, was supported by the Porte and had a semi-imperial status, reflecting the ethnic mosaic of the country. As with opera, architectural modernization was a pursuit shared by the Ottomans and the great powers that built their missions, both political and cultural, in Ottoman cities. Modern buildings, many of which are visible to this day, mark the old and new city centers.

Fuhrmann details the poetics and practicalities of modern travel in the port cities, making use of travelers' accounts to provide insights into the impact of one form of modern travel—the steamship—that became a medium of public transport between the center and the suburbs. Interestingly, in Istanbul, the *vapur*, as it was called, was partly sponsored by the wealthy Jewish Camondo family, though Fuhrmann does not discuss this specific contribution by Jews to the city's network of modern public transportation. Rather, his focus is on Ashkenazi immigrants from Lithuania (in particular) through the prism of the grand-scale poverty in Central Europe in the first half of the 19th century, which propelled them to seek jobs in the Ottoman empire. There are gems of description of the Jewish poor in Istanbul, as when Fuhrmann writes of the "ragged Jewish scavengers from Galata in search of clothes" (p. 92). Perhaps the most fascinating discussion concerns the Ashkenazi prostitutes and the controversial synagogue allotted to them. This synagogue is still standing, albeit in ruins, in the red-light district of Istanbul. The prevalence of Jewish prostitution is further highlighted via a quote from a diary entry of 1911 made by David Ben-Gurion: on a visit to Salonika, he writes, he was hesitant to reveal his Ashkenazi origin, lest he be mistaken for a pimp (p. 385). The U.S. ambassador to Turkey, Henry Morgenthau—himself an Ashkenazi Jew—was the one who took steps to end prostitution.

Port Cities of the Eastern Mediterranean is a non-nostalgic ode to a bygone past, to its lack of single authority, interpretations of modernity, and to the spirit of the Eastern Mediterranean. It highlights a culture in flux, full of contrasts, crises, paupers, and imperialists. Replete with colorful descriptions and analysis, including numerous references to European, American, and Ottoman literary works, it persuasively shows how Eastern Mediterranean port cities form part of the European cultural space, albeit with a twist. As a 19th-century traveler remarks: "What one finds at Smyrna is all the appeal of the Orient and the comfort of Europe, the varying spectacle of Muslim populations and the salons of Paris" (p. 107). Through examples and extensive analysis, Fuhrmann's study attempts to achieve what great art does (to paraphrase Orhan Pamuk)—to change the landscape of our minds.

In *The Jews of Ottoman Izmir*, Dina Danon provides a unique panorama of single port city via the perspective of a Jewish community on the cusp of modernity. Within the heterogenous social fabric of the Ottoman empire, Jews did not particularly stand out. They were one of the smaller groups—it was the Armenian, Greek, and Levantine communities that dominated the city—and their economic and social situation was precarious. Danon's study, drawing upon the booming Ladino press and on the archives of the Jewish charitable (*sedaka*) societies, reintroduces the city's Jews into the discussions of the modern city and to modernizing efforts in the Ottoman empire, from the Tanzimat modernizing reforms beginning in 1839 until the series of wars extending from the Balkans to Trablus (Tripoli), and ultimately, the First World War that brought an end to the empire.

An examination of everyday encounters between rich and poor provides unusual angles of approach to the workings of the community, reinforcing Danon's central argument that the salient characteristics of Izmir's Jews in the modern era, and by extension, modernity, are best revealed through "the mundane, the routine and the ordinary" (p. 27). The city's multiethnic mercantile elite also receives attention, as do modern neighborhoods such as Kordon (with its exclusive clubs and hotels) and the newly established Karataş. One of the landmarks in Karataş was the Asansör building built by the philanthropist Nissim Levi in 1907, a symbol of Jewish imprint on the city to this day. The short-lived Rothschild hospital, the Alliance school and the Grand Synagogue, also in the Karataş neighborhood, are all monumental markers of the modern community. Despite Western influence, the Jewish *dolce vita* had an Ottoman inflection, as shown, for instance, in an ad featuring the Cafe l'Abri that speaks of fresh fish, cold raki, daily live music and nightly sea swimming, except on Shabbat (p. 95).

Danon's work is noteworthy for its intimate and detailed study of the *djuderia* in the 19th century, a period in which the once vibrant Sephardi settlement had fallen into destitution, with a third of its community living off charity. The penury of the Jewish community is given sight and sound, ranging from descriptions of the Russian refugees who put a further strain on charitable resources (displaying behavior that was at odds with community norms and becoming a nuisance to the community) to the carnivalesque Purim festivities stretching over a number of days—a delight for Izmir's non-Jewish residents, but less so for the Jews, as they featured beggars parading throughout the *djuderia*, exposing its poverty. Danon also introduces readers to the remarkable humor and Ottoman-inflected Ladino of Izmir's Jews via a description of a rewriting of the Haggadah in the 1909 Passover issue of the satirical *El Soytari* (The Clown), which, among other things, poked fun at the communal meat tax (*gabela*) benefiting the kosher butchers ("siervos fuimos al kasap en Izmir"—we were slaves to the butcher).

The Jews of Ottoman Izmir expands previous studies on the topic, notably Daniel Goffmann's *Izmir and the Levantine World, 1550-1650* (1990), which focuses on the mercantile classes in the early modern period, and Maureen Jackson's article on the musical cultures of 19th-century Izmir (through a Jewish lens), as part of historiography from the ground up.[1] Danon's work also extends the discussion of Jewish philanthropy in the Ottoman empire beyond the Camondo family and their international connections, which was explored in detail by Nora Şeni in *Les Camondo, ou, L'eclipse d'un fortune* (1997). Thematically organized chapters provide kaleidoscopic views of the vulnerability of Izmir's Jews and how acts of charity were reconfigured by newly formed public associations, notably the *sedaka* organizations and vocational schools, to befit the modernizing efforts of the empire. A recurring theme is the *gabela* meat tax; another is the continual negotiating with regard to leadership and organization of the *kehillah*, notably after the passing of R. Haim Palacci in 1868 and his son

Abraham Palacci in 1898. Despite their lack of conclusiveness, debates on leadership and communal rules between the more traditional members of the community and those who were more progressive promoted modernization. The community itself was to undergo profound changes as the Ottoman empire came to an end. Danon's narrative, as noted, essentially concludes with the First World War, and thus invites further research about the decades that followed.

A remarkable achievement of this study is to turn the panorama of Izmir into an analytical tool on Jews and modernity. The view from Izmir, a recurrent phrase in the study, including beggars, rabbis, and their collaboration toward progress, modifies our understanding of the Jewish world in the Ottoman empire. Equally important, the city serves as a vantage point to contest conceptions of modernity, particularly through the role of class and periphery. The study has a personal dimension as well. Danon credits her grandmother with introducing her to Ottoman Izmir. Her book proves that she has inherited her grandmother's storytelling skills to evoke the city.

Featuring extensive analysis and critical insights, *The Jews of Ottoman Izmir* and *Port Cities of the Eastern Mediterranean* are significant contributions to the literature on modern Izmir and the Eastern Mediterranean, each of them making use of multiple contexts to explore the ways in which one port city—and an entire region—came to face the modern era. Both books are highly recommended to those specializing in this region and, more generally, to scholars dealing with contesting conceptions of modernity.

Esra Almas
Bilkent University (Ankara)

Note

1. Maureen Jackson, "'Cosmopolitan' Smyrna: Illuminating or Obscuring Cultural Histories?" *Geographic Review* 102, no. 3 (2012), 337–349.

Daniela Flesler and Adrián Pérez Melgosa, *The Memory Work of Jewish Spain.* Bloomington: Indiana University Press, 2020. 373 pp.

This book is a combination of rigorous scholarship and artistic sensibility, applied to an in-depth, multifaceted study of "Spain's current efforts to reclaim the memory of Sepharad through the analysis of a comprehensive range of cultural practices, political initiatives, and institutions" (p. 5). It is an extremely rich volume relating with wit and depth to the most up-to-date research, with insights and contributions nurtured by in-situ observations and encounters with some of the protagonists of the complex and elusive stories that fill out its pages.

The book consists of an introduction, six chapters, and a short conclusion. The opening chapter, titled "The Long Journey of Sephardi Myths," is a genealogy of the different myths underlying Spanish initiatives of rapprochement toward Jews and its own Jewish past. With a timeline stretching from the end of the 18th century to the years following the Second World War, the authors show that both the recent initiatives attempting at "bringing back the Jews" and the rhetoric underlying these efforts "obey a powerful cyclical pattern with a long history of evolving iterations" (p. 36). Interestingly, the latter part of this chapter shows how the Jewish construction of Sephardi Jews as a talented and powerful community and as a positive model of Jewish emancipation "would shift in Spain to Spanish nationalistic appropriation" (p. 76).

The next chapter, "Tourism and the Embracing of Spain's Jewish Legacy," focuses on tourism as a key sector of the Spanish economy, which also plays an important role in the construction of local, regional, and national identities. At the core of this chapter is an analysis of the creation in 1995 of a national tourist route, "Paths of Sepharad: Network of Jewish Quarters of Spain," and its further developments. In different case studies, the contradictions generated by the marketing of an idealized medieval *convivencia* between Christians, Muslims, and Jews in loci that are also marked by violence, persecution, and absence are shown to be fundamental in nature: "Although nothing could be further from the celebratory intentions of these cities' officials, these Jewish Quarters without Jews can be visited as places of mourning . . . " (p. 120). Furthermore, the simultaneous presence of different mnemonic signifiers bearing dissimilar interpretations of the past can sometimes be striking. In Segovia, for example, attempts at making visible the traces of a Jewish past coexist with the city's reactivation of an "antisemitic legend [. . .] as a foundational moment of its history and identity" (p. 131).

Chapter 3 centers on the Sephardi Museum of Toledo, established in 1964 and situated inside the Synagogue of the Transit. The authors analyze the many transformations experienced by the synagogue since its construction in the second half of the 14th century, as well as the different narratives articulated around it in its most recent role as Spain's national Jewish museum. Here the authors demonstrate the deep interconnection between the fate of the synagogue and that of the *conversos*, a fact often ignored in the design of the museum's exhibitions. This denial is highly significant: "The underplaying of the converso memory of the building that houses the Sephardi museum amounts to a resistance to research into the very origins of the modern relationship of Spain and Jewishness" (p. 189). In contrast to this resistance, "the space of the museum continues to be haunted by the memory of the conversos" (p. 189).

The following chapter, "Exhibiting Jewish Heritage at the Local and Regional Levels," analyzes the proliferation of exhibitions on the Jewish legacy at the regional and local levels as particular ways of embracing a Sephardi past. As these exhibits reinforce different identity narratives, "[m]edieval Jews become once again instrumentalized as witnesses" of the "essentially righteous character of each town's present society" (p. 197).

The fifth chapter focuses on the annual "Los Conversos" festival celebrated in the city of Hervás since 1997. In this popular festival, "town residents stage a play about the local Jewish past, re-create a medieval 'Jewish market,' and dress up 'as Jews'" (p. 247). The authors convincingly argue that this festival illustrates how the memories of Jewish Spain, the Holocaust, the Spanish Civil War, and the oppressive regime of Francisco Franco function as a tangled complex. The book analyzes four different plays that were staged between the years 1997–2015 to trace the evolution of the festival vis-à-vis Spain's engagement with its Jewish past. This thorough exploration leads to the understanding that "the plays are also doing more than 'performing' the town's distant past. In them, past and present enter into a dance of memory in which each period becomes both shown and concealed, its conflicts mobilized and contained once again" (p. 284).

The last chapter, "Returns to Sepharad," looks at how different people in Spain address two basic questions: "What does it mean to return to Sepharad in contemporary Spain? What are the means of return for different groups in Spain today?" (p. 287). The analysis here is focused on the works of Esther Bendahan, a Spanish writer of Sephardi-Moroccan descent; Wolf Vostell, a German-born artist who lived intermittently in Spain for several decades; and Daniel Quintero, a prominent Spanish painter who converted to Judaism. All of their works are haunted "by a set of historical paradoxes" (p. 328), and in all of them, the traces of a Jewish past are appropriated and interpreted in multiple ways, following different political, religious, and personal sensibilities.

In the closing pages of the book, its authors acknowledge that, from their point of view, it is not the Sephardi Museum of Toledo but the nearby Synagogue of Santa María la Blanca, an empty building belonging to the Archdiocese of Toledo, that better encapsulates the "paradoxes of the splendor, destruction, and fragmentary survival of Jewish Spain" (p. 336). As they sensitively show throughout their book, this Jewish past "has always been ripe for resonances with other histories of destruction and loss" (p. 337). This is precisely one of the main contributions of this book for anyone interested in memory works in general and in the Spanish case in particular: its ability to effectively address not only the visible traces and narratives of a Jewish past, but also the more subtle meanings conveyed by silence, emptiness, and liminality.

Martina L. Weisz
The Hebrew University

Eran Kaplan, *Projecting the Nation: History and Ideology on the Israeli Screen.* New Brunswick: Rutgers University Press, 2020. 203 pp.

Projecting the Nation, a new addition to the bookshelf about Israeli cinema, presents the thematic and chronological developments in Israeli fiction films "over the past eight decades or so" (p. 8). Eran Kaplan defines Israeli cinema as a "national industry: the state and various other public institutions support filmmakers as part of the state's overall investment in the arts" (p. 2). In his view, in order to convince such institutions of the viability of their projects, Israeli filmmakers seek to tackle "big issues" that offer a cinematic treatment of the very nature of the Israeli experience. *Projecting the Nation* explores "how movies have operated within the broader historical and ideological frameworks in Israel—as works of art that were chosen (funded) to engage those questions" (p. 4). Kaplan refers briefly to films that do not deal with "big" top-ics. The vast majority of his book is devoted to the depiction of key features of Israeli identity in realistic films, those which "tend to focus on the social and political reality around them" (p. 4).

The first five chapters of *Projecting the Nation* are both thematic and chronolog-ical, covering a period that ranges from the 1930s to the 2000s. Each chapter analyzes several key films that, in Kaplan's opinion, encapsulate a specific topic.

The first chapter, "Pioneers, Fighters, and Immigrants," deals with Zionist prop-aganda films from the 1930s to the 1950s that focus on Hebrew labor and the trans-formation of the "diasporic Jew" to the "New Jew"; in addition, it examines the emergence of "Bourekas" comedies, which highlighted ethnic conflicts, in the 1960s. The second chapter, "Looking Inward," explores the "new sensitivity" films of the 1960s and 1970s: intimate art house films, or "art for the sake of art," as Kaplan terms them (p. 36). In the following chapter, "Present Absentees," Kaplan turns to repre-sentation of the Israeli–Arab conflict and of "the other," especially in films produced from the 1980s to the 2000s. Chapter 4, "The Post-Zionist Condition," examines the 1990s postmodern turn in Israeli cinema, which, in Kaplan's opinion, was manifested both in the depiction of gratuitous violence that does not seem to support any political or social cause, and in films that represent identity politics in Israeli society. In the fol-lowing chapter, "The Lebanon Trilogy and the Postpolitical Turn in Israeli Cinema," Kaplan introduces three movies from the first decade of the 21st century that depict the first Lebanon war (1982) as well other films from the 2000s that tackle the Israeli–Palestinian conflict.

The last two chapters are thematic: "Eros on the Israeli Screen" deals with the rep-resentation of sex, romance, and relationships, while "In the Image of the Divine" examines religion in the 2000s. In his epilogue, Kaplan turns to the development of the Israeli commercial television industry since the 1990s, global trends, and streaming devices and their influence on contemporary and future Israeli film industry.

Projecting the Nation gives the English reader access to the main subjects and films in the history of Israeli cinema. The historical, socio-cultural background Kaplan pro-vides for each of these periods, and his discussion of changes in government invest-ment in the film industry over the years, are all useful for non-Israeli readers seeking to understand these films in a broader context. In a global era of multimarket chan-nels and streaming services, Israeli films are increasingly accessible to non-Israeli audiences. In this regard, it is unfortunate that Kaplan's analysis in the two thematic chapters does not extend back to 1948: the chapter on Eros starts with films produced in the 1970s, and the chapter on religion deals solely with films produced in the 2000s. Thus, these chapters do not enable readers to comprehend developments over the decades in the representation of these two specific realms.

English-speaking readers would have benefited even more had the book dealt in more depth with previous research pertaining to Israeli cinema. *Projecting the Nation* is not the first book in English on this topic. Kaplan mentions two books in the text proper and many more in the endnotes. In the endnotes he also mentions other works on Israeli cinema in Hebrew—though not, surprisingly, Nurith Gertz's seminal book of 1993, *Sipur mehaseratim* (Motion Fiction: Israeli Fiction in Film), which has in-spired many film researchers.

In his introduction, Kaplan points to the "need for a wider perspective on Israeli cinema and its relationship to major developments in the nation's history" (p. 8). And yet, whereas all the films analyzed in the book have been discussed in previous research, Kaplan mainly uses them as references rather than engaging in comparison and contrast. This approach makes it difficult to understand where he stands in relation to previous research. Does he agree with former analyses? Does he dispute them? Is he suggesting a new perspective? Answers to these questions could have offered the reader an opportunity to examine the current research in a wider cinematic context.

LIAT STEIR-LIVNY
Sapir Academic College
Open University of Israel

Louis Kaplan, *At Wit's End: The Deadly Discourse on the Jewish Joke*. New York: Fordham University Press, 2020. 312 pp.

The title of Louis Kaplan's fascinating and challenging book sets the tone for his argument. He examines "discourses" about Jewish *Witz*—meaning both "wit" and "joking"—in German-speaking Central Europe during the first half of the 20th century. He does not focus on jokes themselves (though some are discussed), but rather the disputes surrounding them in an age of mounting antisemitism. His sources are cultural observers and critics; indeed, only one—the cabaret impresario Kurt Robitschek—was a practitioner of *Witz*. One theme that Kaplan highlights is the debate about the difference between (and relative merits of) Jewish *Witz* and German *Humor*. Gentile Germans coded the latter as positive and affirmative (with overtones of benevolence and *Gemütlichkeit*) in contrast to Jewish *Witz*, which was perceived as destructive, biting, sarcastic, malicious, and cynical. By contrast, Jews and philosemites considered *Witz* to be either a weapon of the weak against a hostile environment or a testament of strength, signaling a self-confidence that could engender and sustain a high degree of self-irony. According to Kaplan, this variegated landscape of competing discourses was a product of the slippery nature of jokes themselves. Indeed, his major assertion is that the polysemy, ambivalence, and ambiguity of jokes made them impossible to control. Hence the same jokes could readily change hands between Jews practicing self-irony and antisemites casting aspersions.

Kaplan has assembled a mixed crew of Jews and Gentiles, philo- and antisemites to make his points. He begins with Arthur Trebitsch, born into a wealthy Viennese Jewish family, who not only denied his Jewishness but turned virulently against his tribe: he was an early political and financial supporter of Hitler, whom the future Führer treated with respect. In a chapter of *Geist und Judentum* (1919), Trebitsch considered the jokes told by Jews to be prime expressions of the unstable and mobile "Semitic" character (as opposed to "Aryan" solidity). Here Kaplan begins a mode of argument that characterizes his book, inasmuch as he highlights the ways in which attempts to analyze something as shifty as jokes can easily backfire: in this case, they boomeranged against Trebitsch qua "self-hating" Jew. Kaplan next turns to Eduard Fuchs, a Marxist Gentile who paradoxically made a fortune by producing a series of best-selling volumes of *Sittengeschichte* (history of mores), whose profuse illustrations bordered on soft-core pornography. Fuchs also published a volume on *Juden in der Karikatur* (1921); the book surveys Gentile caricatures of Jews, though its very last chapter—and a very short one, too, with less than five pages of text—deals with "Jewish self-irony." It relates only two jokes, and Kaplan considers significant the fact that both refer to wealthy Jews—in line with Fuchs' belief that modern antisemitism targeted "the Jew as capitalist." By accepting the antisemitic trope that Rothschild was the symbol of money dominating the world (the subject of one of the jokes, as well as of many caricatures by Gentiles reproduced in his book), Fuchs undermined his self-perceived philosemitism.

The dangers of Jews joking about themselves—the fact that their witticisms could, and were, used by antisemites as "proof" of bad Jewish character and behavior—becomes explicit in the next chapter. Kaplan recounts the attacks of Alfred Wiener, a leading member of the Centralverein deutscher Staatsbürger jüdischen Glaubens (the major German Jewish anti-defamation league), against cabaret artists in Berlin in 1926, among them, Kurt Robitschek. Wiener, writes Kaplan, was a "watchman," an arbiter of Jewish taste and opinion at a time of burgeoning antisemitism; in response, Robitschek appealed for freedom of expression, seeing unconstrained joking as a sign of liberation in the new democracy. But part of the problem—though Kaplan does not underscore it—was the fact that Wiener, like so many leaders of Germany's assimilated Jewish community, was a *Bildungsbürger*. With all due respect to the educated German bourgeoisie, whether Jewish or Gentile, it must be said that *Bildung* relates to Jewish *Witz* in the same way that the Moderna vaccine relates to COVID-19: the former suppresses the latter with 94.1 percent effectiveness.

This becomes clear in the ensuing chapter, which concerns Erich Kahler, a Germanophone Jew from Prague. His book *Israel unter den Völkern* (1933) infuriated the Nazis, inasmuch as he asserted that educated Jews would be the ones to rescue German culture: *Judentum* would save *Deutschtum* by defeating barbaric *Germanentum*. Kahler's faith in *Bildung* inflected his short section on Jewish wit, which he considered valid only when it had overtones of sorrow and seriousness: indeed, he contended that Jews' "dialectics and witticism" originated from their dialogues with God. Like Wiener, Kahler despised frivolous and self-contemptuous Jewish jokes, regarding these as playing into the hands of antisemites. Kaplan's next chapter, dealing with Siegfried Kadner's Nazi-era *Rasse und Humor* (1936), demonstrates that this could be the case: Kadner's book included a section on Jewish "cynicism" in which he argued that Jewish jokes revealed the "true" nature of the Jewish character.

With such a history, it was obvious that, in the aftermath of the Holocaust, the discussion of Jewish jokes would continue to be fraught. Kaplan concludes with an examination of the heated discussion of *Der jüdische Witz: Soziologie und Sammlung* (1960; many later expanded editions), an anthology and analysis of Jewish jokes by the Swiss Jewish Salcia Landmann. It was a best-seller in the Federal Republic of Germany, though it provoked consternation among Jewish critics. Incredibly, Landmann claimed she was performing a "requiem" for the Jewish joke, which she asserted had died in the Holocaust. To be sure, there was Israel—but since she considered jokes a weapon of the weak, she blithely stated that Israel had no need of jokes because it had military weapons. Kaplan coins the terms "joke mourning" and "joke reparations" to characterize Landmann's work as part of the larger project of helping Gentile Germans come to terms with the immensity of the Holocaust. But the older issues were revived as well, as Jewish critics wondered whether postwar Germans who consumed the volume were laughing with, or laughing at, Jews. Moreover, they expressed consternation with regard to Landmann's claim that Jewish *Witz* was dead: Isaac Bashevis Singer dryly responded that it was still "very much alive" in New York, Tel Aviv, Buenos Aires, and Moscow. Indeed, as Friedrich Torberg vehemently asserted, if anyone had killed the Jewish joke, it was Landmann herself: she invariably chose the flattest versions of well-known quips, or penned even worse ones herself. Landmann was bad, if not for the Jews, then definitely for the Jewish joke.

Torberg documented Landmann's "punchline-massacre" (*Pointenmassaker*) by comparing her versions of jokes with successful (and more authentic) ones. Throughout his book, Kaplan, too, deftly compares variants of jokes, though with a different goal in mind: to show how subtle inflections and word choices can swing them between self-irony and hostile aspersion. One of his greatest achievements is his discovery of new domains amid the field of discourses. To be sure, he integrates into his investigation the classic analyses of Jewish jokes, such as those of Sigmund Freud; but he primarily addresses lesser-known texts, those that complicate and deepen our appreciation of the issues. He thereby substantiates his thesis that Jewish jokes, and the disputes surrounding them, were a barometer of Jewish–Gentile relations and attitudes in Central Europe in the first decades of the past century.

Kaplan underscores the continued relevance of some of those issues in his epilogue, titled "The Jewish Joke in Trump's America." But the contexts and the discourses have changed significantly, and in retrospect, we realize that many of the earlier debates were forced and contrived, a product of the ideologies of the day. To ascertain what is Jewish *Witz* and German *Humor*, today's readers can safely revert to the old rule of thumb: If you laugh at a joke, it's Jewish *Witz*—if you don't . . .

PETER JELAVICH
Johns Hopkins University

James McAuley, *The House of Fragile Things: Jewish Art Collectors and the Fall of France.* New Haven: Yale University Press, 2021. xii + 301 pp. +18 plates + 47 illustrations.

Edmund de Waal, *Letters to Camondo.* London: Chatto & Windus, 2021. 182 pp. + 32 illustrations.

As these lines are being composed in October 2021, a heated controversy is brewing in Switzerland over the collection of Impressionist and post-Impressionist art (works by Degas, Monet, Cézanne, van Gogh, Modigliani, Picasso, Gauguin, and many others) being shown in the recently (and vastly) expanded Zurich Kunsthaus.[1] Emil Georg Bürhle had created this collection during the 1940s and early 1950s, and his foundation has now loaned more than 170 paintings to the museum. At the time of his death in 1956, Bürhle was most often described as one of the wealthiest individuals in Switzerland, but now it is his past that hovers—negatively—over his collection. Having sold arms to the Nazis, and having bought and sold art that was looted by them, he has been the target of numerous accusations of unsavory behavior over the last decades. Given the current-day concern of scholars and museums to uncover the fate of stolen art, it is not incidental that Bürhle's past has galvanized an extensive out-pouring of opinion and recrimination. In the past year alone, several books have been published (two will be reviewed here) that treat aspects of the involvement of Jews as dealers and collectors of art, and their dispossession by the Nazis; in addition, at the time of writing, a major exhibition on display at the Jewish Museum in New York traces the spoliation and the restitution of works of art and books.[2]

Pierre-Auguste Renoir's painting *Mlle Irène Cahen d'Anvers* (1880), which is currently a part of the Bürhle collection, provides an intriguing connection to the "afterlife" of a stolen work of art. The story of this painting appears at the conclusion of the two very different volumes under review. James McAuley's *The House of Fragile Things* is an academic study of wealthy French Jewish families that engaged in art collecting during the 19th and 20th centuries until their dispossession by the Nazis and/or Vichy. In contrast, *Letters to Camondo*, written by a descendant of the wealthy Ephrussi family whose home was nearby that of Moïse de Camondo (and whose previous book, *The Hare with Amber Eyes: A Hidden Inheritance* [2010], recounts the life of the Ephrussi family from Odessa and how their priceless collection of Japanese netsuke was successfully hidden from the Nazis), is a collection of fictional letters written to the man once married to the subject of Renoir's portrait. The provenance of the painting, its theft by the Nazis, and its eventual legal acquisition by Bührle in 1949 is described in both studies, but it is in McAuley's elaborate and thorough narrative that we perceive the full extent of the drama associated with the painting's many changing of hands.

As McAuley explains, Renoir was commissioned by Louis Cahen d'Anvers, whose family figures prominently in his book, to paint a portrait of his young daughter, Irene, who later married (and subsequently divorced) Moïse de Camondo. The portrait was eventually passed on to Irene and Moïse's daughter, Béatrice, who proudly owned it for many years. She herself married (and later divorced) Léon Reinach, the son of another wealthy and distinguished Jewish family. The interrelationship of these three families (Cahen d'Anvers, Camondo, and Reinach) engages McAuley's attention beyond the specific story of Irene's portrait. In addition, his wonderful study details the doings of yet another compelling French Jewish family, the Rothschilds. The cosmopolitan worlds of these upper-class French Jewish families, their dwindling Jewishness via conversions and intermarriages alongside their art collecting, are at the heart of his attempt to understand "one of the central and unresolved dilemmas in modern French history: the place of minority communities in a society of 'universal' citizens (at least in theory) that emerged from the French Revolution" (p. 6).

McAuley is concerned with the public persona of elite Jewish families who lived in close proximity, the nature of their collections, what they built and what they donated to France out of love for their country—and how their edifice "turned out to be a house of fragile things" (p. 8). He details their rise to fame and success, and the portraits they commissioned of family members, but is deeply troubled by the opposition and anti-semitism these families constantly encountered. Renoir, for instance, who benefited greatly from their commissions, felt no love for his Jewish clients and often gave voice to his antisemitic feelings. Such feelings were echoed even more vociferously by the Goncourt brothers, Edmond and Jules, who jointly attributed falseness to the Jewish sense of aesthetics, and by the infamous Édouard Drumont, the author of *La France juive* (1886). McAuley insightfully depicts the latter as having formulated a "material antisemitism" that stressed Jewish penetration into the French cultural patrimony, its foreign nature, and its design to dominate France culturally, politically, and finan-cially. Drumont's attacks on the "foreign" style of the Rothschilds' estate, and on the Reinachs' unwitting involvement in helping the Louvre acquire a fake tiara for an enormous sum, were complemented by those of the Goncourt brothers regarding Edmond de Rothschild's lack of taste in collecting art ("these people can only con-quer the beautiful things of industrial art") (quoted in McAuley, p. 73). In contrast is de Waal's nostalgic depiction written more than a century later: "The Jewish fam-ilies who move to this district come from elsewhere. This place offers a chance to bring your family to secular, republican, tolerant, civilized Paris and build something with self-confidence, something with appropriate scale, something public" (de Waal, p. 25).

The Dreyfus Affair did not minimize the attachment that Jews in France felt to their country, and thus, with the outbreak of the First World War, it was only natural that members of these four families joined the war effort in one way or another. Two were killed in action: Nissim de Camondo, the son of Moïse; and Adolphe, the son of Joseph Reinach, who had written extensively on the Affair, publicly supporting Dreyfus. Nissim, shown in both these books in a variety of photographs—as a young-ster, and in his military uniform with family members—is now memorialized by the family mansion (Musée Nissim de Camondo) that his father bequeathed to France. Describing the impact of Nissim's death on both his father and his sister, Béatrice, McAuley quotes in full the moving letter of sympathy addressed to Moïse by Marcel Proust (de Waal does the same, albeit more briefly and in slightly distorted fashion; from the text he presents, it appears as though Nissim is missing in action rather than dead). For the father, Nissim's death was a "catastrophe" that caused him to turn in-ward, resulting in his transforming the family mansion into a private kingdom and Nissim's room into a "shrine," as noted by de Waal.

Moïse Camondo's origins are thoroughly sketched by McAuley, as are the repeated antisemitic jabs thrown at him and his family, enabling the reader to realize how he made every effort to distance himself from his Constantinople background and to shape his mansion, his art collection, and his personality into that of a French aris-tocrat of Jewish origins. He divested himself of Judaica objects in his possession, as his sense of belonging was to the *ancien régime*, in the style and art of the late 18th century, and he worked closely with his architect and with art dealers to fashion the family house in that spirit. McAuley shows how all the objects Moïse pursued, chose, and purchased reflected his own personal taste; he had no desire to offer objects to be shown elsewhere. This personal quality emerges as well from de Waal's letters as he roams through the Musée Nissim de Camondo in the present time—as his book is essentially a series of reflections relating to his own life ("I thought that I'd left all this flâneuring around Paris forever . . . but here I am again in your street, this hill of families, writing to you, talking to the dead, archiving" [p. 36]).

In willing the mansion to the French state to be conserved as a whole, perpetuating his father (also named Nissim) and his son, Camondo stated explicitly that it be named after his son, who was meant to inherit both the house and its collection. McAuley links the name of the museum and its entire holdings to Moïse's desire to categorically counter antisemitic claims: "Jews . . . could indeed know and curate a true, authentic beauty" (p. 195) Or, as de Waal puts it: "You want to make a perfect stage set for conversation, enlightenment, for that moment when French culture was at its most refined, most searching" (p. 111).

Béatrice, who married Léon Reinach in 1919, was overlooked by her father, possibly because of his desire to link Nissim's fate to France, and possibly because she entered a most wealthy family on her own; de Waal remarks that Léon "is absurdly rich, even by Camondo standards" (p. 86). McAuley devotes a remarkable and beautifully composed chapter to the Reinachs, focused in particular on Leon's father, Théodore, and on the Greek-style Villa Kérylos in Beaulieu-sur-Mer that he had built, with utmost elaboration and care, in the post-Dreyfus years. A distinguished scholar of Greek culture, Théodore also wrote a book on Jewish history that emphasized how the Jewish spirit merged with that of the French in its *"mission civilisatrice* that had emanated from the ruins of the Second Temple throughout the foreign lands of the Diaspora, carrying with it the precepts and the promise of spiritual and intellectual liberation" (p. 145). Although Théodore, like his brothers, was maligned by Drumont and others, he was elected to the Institut de France and recognized by his peers for his remarkable erudition, and he also helped found the Liberal synagogue in Paris in 1907. Years later, both his prized home in Kérylos (which he had bequeathed to the Institut) and the archive within it were severely ravaged by the Nazis. One of his sons, who was in the house at the time, was captured and sent to Drancy.

Any book about Jewish elite families in France during this period cannot avoid the Rothschilds. McAuley details the life of one of the lesser-known members of the family, Béatrice Éphrussi de Rothschild, who was married (and later divorced from) Maurice Éphrussi, focusing on her pet project, Villa Île de France. A year before her death in 1934, Béatrice bequeathed the mansion (characterized by de Waal as "an absurd pink palace," p. 126), together with her paintings and decorative objects and a sum of money to turn it into a museum—to be named in memory of her Rothschild parents. McAuley argues persuasively that this act indicated her "desire to challenge, even subtly, the strain of French antisemitism that insisted that Jews could never know true beauty" (p. 211).

De Waal and McAuley turn at the end of their books to the tragic fate of Béatrice de Camondo Reinach, the daughter of Irene, the young girl painted by Renoir. Although Béatrice, a passionate horseback rider, had converted to Catholicism in 1942 (the year of her divorce), she, Léon and their children all perished during the Vichy years. Léon had tried to recover the Renoir painting that was seized by the Nazis; both authors comment on the letter he sent to a Vichy official in August 1941. McAuley provides a detailed description of its content, which elaborates on the many gifts the Camondo and Reinach families had given to France and how they "have considerably enriched the artistic legacy of their adopted country" (p. 222), while stressing the family's unique attachment to the Renoir. The painting was by then in the hands of Hermann Göring. Irène Cahen d'Anvers survived the war hiding in Paris. She was able to retrieve the painting in 1946, but she had become by then so distant from the world in which it was created that, alas, she sold it three year later via an agent to Bührle.

Anyone who visits the Château de Champs-sur-Marne, outside of Paris, bequeathed to France in 1935 by the son of Louis Cahen d'Anvers, or the Camondo mansion, or the Villa Île de France, or the Villa Kérylos, or who sees the Renoir painting after having read these two books, will be engaged by their beauty, and also haunted by their provenance and their evocation of the drama of Jewish acculturation in modern times. Clearly, both McAuley and de Waal have been entranced and disturbed, albeit from very different perspectives. The result is two additional works of art, one a masterpiece of scholarship and the other an imaginative reconstruction of family memories.

RICHARD I. COHEN
The Hebrew University

Notes

1. See, for instance, Catherine Hickley, "An Arms Dealer Casts a Shadow over Kunsthaus Zurich," *The Art Newspaper* (27 Jan. 2021); idem, "A Nazi Legacy Haunts a Museum's New Galleries," *The New York Times* (11 Oct. 2021); Sarah Hugounenq, "Confused Story of a Collector," *La Gazette Drouot* (20 April 2019); Thomas Buomberger and Guido Magnaguagno, *Schwarzbuch Bührle: Raubkunst für das Kunsthaus Zürich?* (Zurich: 2016).

2. Charles Dellheim, *Belonging and Betrayal: How Jews Made the Art World Modern* (Waltham: 2021); *Afterlives: Recovering the Lost Stories of Looted Art* opened in August 2021. See also Darsie Alexander and Sam Sackeroff, *Afterlives: Recovering the Lost Stories of Looted Art* (New Haven: 2021).

Mirjam Rajner, *Fragile Images: Jews and Art in Yugoslavia, 1918-1945*. Leiden: Brill, 2019. xxvi + 446 pp.

Fragile Images is first and foremost a labor of love. Reading this book, one is amazed at the sheer amount of effort that has gone into recovering as much of the legacy of the visual artists treated here as is conceivably possible, despite all the destruction wrought by the Holocaust and by the subsequent cultural policies of Communist-era Yugoslavia. Mirjam Rajner has scoured private collections and obscure museums, has interviewed relatives and acquaintances, and has pored over letters and diaries to reconstruct the tragic lives and fraught visual legacy of artists that even the most well-read specialist in South Slavic culture is unlikely ever to have come across.

The artists discussed in the book were born between 1890 and 1912 in various territories belonging to the Austro-Hungarian empire as well as in independent Serbia.

All came of age in the interwar period, and almost all perished during the Shoah. As Rajner shows, however, these basic biographical similarities hide a wealth of differences related to background (Sephardic vs. Ashkenazic), class (rich, poor, or in the middle), attitudes vis-à-vis Jewish identity (assimilationist, Zionist, internationalist), and artistic approach. Rajner carefully delves into the life and work of each of her "heroes," showing both their attitude toward their Jewish identity and their artistic development (as well as the interrelationship between the two), and how these developed during their short careers.

Informative as it is, however, there are some major issues regarding the book's implied reader, the interpretations provided, and its ultimate purpose. Let us start with the first. The artists discussed are, to put it mildly, obscure, and the analysis of their work is dense. As a result, it is unlikely that a casual reader is going to pick up this book. Nevertheless, Rajner spends many pages explaining in detail the political and social background of interwar and wartime Yugoslavia, information that the book's likely audience (namely, specialists on the former Yugoslavia) simply do not need. This is especially true in Part 3, which is devoted to the wartime years. As there is heartbreakingly little art that survived from this period, Rajner is reduced to exceptionally long and often tedious descriptions of concentration camp life of a type that is already (unfortunately) depressingly familiar.

In her interpretations of the artists' work, Rajner is frequently hamstrung by the fact that much of it did not survive. As a result, she is often reduced to analyzing tantalizing clues and hints, which do not yield the kind of information she would like to provide. Thus, for example, in explaining a change in the approach of the artist Daniel Kabiljo, Rajner conjectures: "Now thirty, he *may have felt more acutely* the need to prove to his father that he could support himself as an artist. As a Jew, he began to feel a need to preserve his roots . . . As a former recipient of La Benevolencia's scholarship, *he may also have been obliged to do so*. Moreover, the rising conflict in Sarajevo's Jewish community *may also have influenced* Kabiljo's change of direction" (p. 69, emphasis mine). Of course, in the absence of sources one must do what one can, but here and in many other places there are too many "may also haves" to sustain a convincing argument.

In the end, though, the biggest problem with this book is its inability to repay the investment one must make to read it. There is nothing wrong with having a scholarly obsession, but if you want readers to wade through 400 + pages, they need to know why. This is particularly true if you are obsessed with the art and lives of obscure Yugoslav painters. To my mind, there could be two potentially convincing reasons: either you want to argue that the artwork itself is of a level of quality that requires it to be appreciated qua art; or you could show the reader that the work (and perhaps lives) illuminate something about the period that cannot be discovered otherwise. Regarding the first possible point, it is difficult to make the case that any of these artists was a figure whose creative legacy must be reckoned with. If we compare them, for example, to such Yugoslav Jewish writers as Isaak Samokovlija, Danilo Kiš, Filip David, or David Albahari, all of whom produced work that anyone with an interest in European 20th-century literature should reckon with, I am afraid that we find nothing comparable in the visual material reproduced here. And if we ask whether the lives of these artists, tragic as they mostly were, tell us something that we don't already know about the

Jewish experience in Eastern Europe or even in Yugoslavia, I am afraid that again the answer is no.

In the end, if you are curious about the visual work produced by Yugoslav Jewish artists, you will find much to admire in this meticulously researched and well-written study. But I fear that you will not leave it convinced that the life and works of such artists as Moše Pijade (an extremely interesting figure, to be sure), Daniel Kabiljo, Adolf Weiller, Bora Baruh, Ivan Rein, and Daniel Ozmo provide you with a new perspective on Yugoslav Jewish identity, the Shoah, or introduce you to unknown masterpieces you will hold in your mind's eye forever.

ANDREW WACHTEL
Compass College (Bishkek, Kyrgyzstan)

Diego Rotman, *The Yiddish Stage as a Temporary Home: Dzigan and Shumacher's Satirical Theater (1927-1980),* trans. Rebecca Wolpe. Oldenbourg: Walter de Gruyter, 2021. 321 pp.

The legendary Solomon Mikhoels, the brightest star of the Soviet Yiddish theater, used to say, "When an actor engages and controls the audience, he feels like he is a leader. And what does it mean to be a leader? It means to be in charge, to lead. And it is precisely this, that the actor seeks to accomplish."[1] Mikhoels proved his thesis throughout his life and career on the stage. It was he—not his contemporaries, the Soviet Yiddish writers, poets, artists, nor the Jewish Communists and activists—who represented the new Jewish life under Communism. Ordinary Soviet Jews considered Mikhoels an unofficial leader and defined their Jewishness through him.

Diego Rotman's book on the lives and theatrical careers of Shimon Dzigan and Israel Shumacher, the famous Yiddish theatrical duo, takes Mikhoels's thesis to a new level by carefully and masterfully analyzing the development and impact of the duo's satirical theater. Starting out in the elite avant-garde Yiddish theater of Lodz in the 1920s, Dzigan and Shumacher became "emissaries of Yiddish culture" in the 1950s–1960s and were also, paradoxically, representatives of the state of Israel, where Yiddish was considered a vestige of the exile. For critics and public alike, Dzigan and Shumacher were social therapists, political commentators and critics, and a bridge connecting the Yiddish-speaking Jewish communities scattered around the globe. In a word, they were their leaders.

Rotman's book is the first comprehensive study to examine the art of Dzigan and Shumacher as a cultural, political, and social phenomenon in historical and artistic context, from Jewish humor and parody to modernist non-Jewish theatrical trends such as *kleinkunst* (miniature) theater and cabaret, to satirical and Yiddish theater in Israel. Context is also crucial to Rotman's approach to his sources, which include rare audio and video recordings of the duo's performances, contemporary critical reviews and popular responses, and memoirs and autobiographical accounts, such as Dzigan's *Der koyekh fun yidishn humor* (The Power of Jewish Humor, 1974). In this approach, the artistic endeavor, the public performance, and the personal story are all interwoven, thus allowing for analysis rather than mere reconstruction of the actual performances.

The book's first chapter discusses the origins of 20th-century avant-garde Yiddish theatre and, in particular, the development of the Lodz Acting Studio, founded in 1922 by Moshe Broderzon, which eventually become the Ararat Theater. These two entities shaped Dzigan and Shumacher as actors and future cultural producers. From very early on in their careers, they learned the politics of acting and acting as politics. In contrast to the popular Yiddish theater known as *shund* (low-brow, or "trash"), which flourished in Eastern Europe and North America in the 1890s–1920s, modernist Yiddish art theater had neither foundations nor tradition, nor any established system to support its development. Amid the political and social upheavals in the years following the First World War, Broderzon imagined a new theater as a portable Jewish polity that would provide some measure of stability, collective identity, and direction. Rotman argues that the name Ararat—both a Yiddish acronym for Artistisher revolutsyonerer teater (Revolutionary Artistic Theater) or, according to others, the Artistisher revyu-teater (Artistic Revue Theater) and the name of the biblical mountain—was symbolic in many respects: "The name transformed the theater at once into a real and mythological place. Broderzon, akin to Noah in the Bible, chose to realize a similar yet unique vision: to establish in Poland a Jewish revolutionary artistic autonomy that was itself a wandering territory" (pp. 25–26).

The Ararat revolutionized both Yiddish theater and Jewish life in Poland. The repertoire for the most part did not include Yiddish classics, "really boycotting Yiddish literature" as one critic put it. Instead, there were works by contemporary authors, mainly Broderzon himself. As for the audience, Rotman maintained that the Ararat was an "arena for encounter between opposing and even ambiguous perspectives" where "the spectators . . . were highly active," playing a "role in creating the meaning of a performance" (p. 36). The Ararat troupe was a collective of equals working for minimum wage, thus maintaining a subversive attitude toward mainstream Yiddish theater and embodying the spirit of political and cultural opposition. Even the language—the Lodz Yiddish deliberately used on stage—"undermined the reigning convention that Yiddish theater required a uniform language" (p. 42). Rotman compellingly argues that both the cultural awareness of the Ararat and its spirit of opposition molded the political and aesthetic approaches of Dzigan and Shumacher.

Chapter 2 traces the post-Ararat career of Dzigan and Shumacher in 1930s Poland. Rotman shows how in these years the duo developed their own voice and honed their unique style of stage dialogue, which "built on oppositions and reflected the traditional Jewish discourse . . . making their joint skits extremely powerful" (pp. 50–51). In the hostile political, social, and economic environment of pre-Second World War Poland, Dzigan and Shumacher "contributed to creating a discourse of opposition in the face of the oppressive reality" (p. 79). In the theater, their audiences were able to find a home, albeit a temporary one, "in which change was possible on stage or in the audience's imagination" (p. 66). It was "a place of catharsis for the soul" (p. 81).

In Chapter 3, Rotman analyzes the duo's tribulations during times of homelessness in wartime Soviet Union from 1940 and in postwar Poland up until 1949. After fleeing the advancing German army and settling in the USSR, Dzigan and Shumacher became the leading actors of the state-sponsored Byalistoker melukhisher yidisher minyatur-teater (Białystok National Jewish Miniature Theater). However, after the German invasion of the Soviet Union, the two men, along with many other "bourgeois" Polish nationals labeled as "potentially disloyal" to the Soviet Union, were imprisoned. They spent six years, from 1941–1947, as inmates of a labor camp in Aktiubinsk (Kazakhstan). Compared with hostile prewar Poland, the "welcoming" Soviet Union was even less of a home for the duo, effectively neutralizing their satire through heavy ideological censorship. According to Rotman, Dzigan and Shumacher "needed to divest themselves of the external signs of Polish Jewry, the substance of the bourgeois identity, merging with the Soviet model and refraining from critical expressions" (p. 93). When they were released from the camp and allowed to return to Poland, they found the remnants of the Polish Jewish community "almost literally, homeless" (p. 109). The duo helped to reconstruct the world around them, reclaiming "the central and classic element of the theater—the actor," as reflected in their film "Unzere kinder" (1948), a pioneering artistic representation of the Holocaust (p. 107).

Paradoxically, as Chapter 4 shows, after they first came to Israel in the 1950s and eventually settled there in the 1960s, Dzigan and Shumacher did not find an actual home in the Jewish homeland. Israel's cultural politics viewed "diasporic" manifestations of Jewish culture as corrupt and doomed to extinction. From 1949–1950, Israeli actors (as opposed to guest artists from abroad) were not allowed to perform in Yiddish, so the duo postponed their official immigration to Israel until the 1960s. As was the case in Poland before and after the war, Dzigan and Shumacher had to create a new theater as a home for themselves and their audiences. Once again, Rotman argues, their Yiddish performance was "an act of defiance, a cultural protest against the official policy" (p. 147). In addition to providing Yiddish-speaking immigrants with a home at their theater, Dzigan and Shumacher offered sharp critiques of the new Jewish state. In his meticulous analysis of "Der nayer dibek" (The New Dybbuk), the duo's famous Israeli skit, Rotman claims that they themselves personified a kind of dybbuk, as they demanded "the voice that was denied to them and those they represented in Israel . . . " (p. 242). In short, Dzigan and Shumacher were "a metonymy of a refugee in a decimated world"; they "did not belong to any specific place and at the same time created an alternative space in which they and their audience felt at home" (pp. 258–259).

Dzigan and Shumacher's performances offered an intangible alternative to the regnant cultural and linguistic order—ultimately becoming a lasting framework for at least one form of collective Jewish identity in the modern age. With his thorough discussion of the wider context of the duo's history and art, Rotman makes a major contribution to the historiography of Yiddish theater. *The Yiddish Stage as a Temporary Home* is likely to become an indispensable resource for academics working in the larger fields of cultural, theater, and Jewish studies.

VASSILI SCHEDRIN
Queen's University (Kingston)

Note

1. Quoted in Konstantin Rudnitskii (ed.), *Mikhoels: Stat'i, besedy, rechi* (Moscow: 1981), 68.

Lynne M. Swarts, *Gender, Orientalism and the Jewish Nation: Women in the Work of Ephraim Moses Lilien at the German Fin de Siècle*. New York: Bloomsbury Publishing Inc., 2020. 328 pp.

Scholars and others familiar with the early Zionist movement have long recognized the work, and often the name, of its leading artist, Ephraim Moses Lilien. Some of Lilien's images are justifiably termed iconic. One, a soft-focus photograph of Theodor Herzl leaning over his Basel hotel balcony in 1901 at the Fifth World Zionist Congress, became the definitive image of the visionary leader. Another Lilien creation, a "Congress card" commissioned by the Zionist Organization the same year as Herzl's photo, translated the movement's ideology into a dramatic vignette: a winged angel emblazoned with a Star of David rests one white hand on the shoulder of a stooped, weary old man, ensnared in the thorns of the Jewish exile. With the other hand, the angel points meaningfully toward the old man's hale and hearty "twin," who is pushing a plow with erect back against an image of the sun rising (presumably) over the Land of Israel. Despite the Zionist movement's secular bent, a Hebrew phrase from traditional Jewish liturgy scrolls across the bottom of the image: "May our eyes witness Your return to Zion in mercy."

In *Gender, Orientalism and the Jewish Nation*, Lynne M. Swarts contends that Lilien "single handedly fashioned a modern and Jewish artistic style" (p. 41) by combining contemporary, representational styles such as Jugendstil (the German version of the French Art Nouveau) with classic Jewish symbols such as the Magen David and the menorah. At first, her writing evokes well-traversed narratives focusing on Lilien's most famous works—the aforementioned "From Ghetto to Zion" tableau and the Herzl portrait, as well as Lilien's illustrations for Börries von Münchhausen's poetry collection *Juda* and Morris Rosenfeld's *Lieder des Ghetto*. Like other scholars, Swarts argues that Lilien's early work is the visual incarnation of Max Nordau's *Muskeljuden*, with his "strong, heroic, muscular Jewish male bodies. . . as if made to order" for Nordau's "aesthetics of the ideal body" (p. 55).

Fortunately, however, the similarities between Swarts' scholarship and prior studies of the Zionist movement's favorite artist are of a limited nature. Following an enlightening discussion about the place of art in Jewish culture and a brief biography of Lilien, Swarts trains her lens on a pair of underappreciated yet profoundly significant themes in his work. She offers a detailed exploration of Lilien's female images in all their sensuality and physicality, charting a steady development from his earlier, sexualized, biblical-era temptresses to more mature, realistic women who exercise agency in their romantic relations and elsewhere. Second, she considers fine art seriously, on its own terms—not as window dressing or as a mere reflection of historical trends, but as a driving force shaping political and social realities. In doing so, she elevates fine art as an element of general historical inquiry, rather than relegating it solely to art history.

The book discusses gender as its own subject and also in conversation with the concept of Orientalism—the calculated use or distortion of "Eastern" figures by people from the West—in early Zionism and the art of the period. Swarts interrogates the relationship between types of portrayals of women in art and their relative powerlessness in society, and the ubiquity of misogynist views in fin-de-siècle Europe. She reveals some shockingly misogynist tropes in late Imperial Germany, which incorporated a range of wildly divergent attitudes about the proper place and capabilities of women. Perhaps unsurprisingly, some of the most strident voices critiquing women (especially women who advocated female suffrage and women in the workforce) would later embrace Fascist ideas, advancing antisemitic visions of effeminate male Jews as a corollary to the unnatural, dominating Jewess. In a provocative twist, Swarts posits that shapers of Zionist art and culture such as Martin Buber, Boris Schatz, and Max Nordau had internalized many of these antisemitic critiques in their analysis of the "weak diaspora Jew." Lilien's evolution beyond these stock images, in the author's view, not only shifts the focus to strong women but actually provides an alternative view of the "new Jew."

Readers are introduced to a cast of characters whose varying interests and perspectives widen the book's purview beyond the expected early Zionist founders or turn-of-the-century fine artists. Poet Else Lasker-Schüler, for instance, is well-known in literary contexts. But here, she is the subject of an entire chapter that compares her aesthetics, her Zionist convictions, and her progressive views on gender—which often made use of transgendered imagery—to those of Lilien. Lasker-Schüler challenged boundaries on an intensely personal plane, even creating an alter ego named "Prince Jussuf." She often dressed in Arab male garb for photos and signed letters with her alternate moniker, blurring the lines between male and female, Arab and Jew, Orient and Occident. In comparing the two artists, Swarts contends that Lilien is as daring as Lasker-Schüler in his images of Jewish femmes fatales, maintaining that this resembles Lasker-Schüler's "vision of a transgendered Orient" (p. 126). Placing the two artists in the same space is not wishful thinking on Swarts' part. Lilien and Lasker-Schüler inhabited the same circles and both published in the seminal journal *Ost und West* in 1901, so it is both appropriate and eye-opening to evaluate them in relation to each other. The result broadens the scope of what can be considered "early Zionist art" far beyond many other scholarly discussions of the subject.

Swarts' contentions are supported by ample references to aesthetics, political and social theory, European and Zionist history, and shifting views of Orientalism as either a tool of cultural imperialism or as a refreshingly "authentic" link to the Land of Israel. It was this latter aspect that Martin Buber and Boris Schatz emphasized in fashioning a unique "Zionist art." Some of Swarts' discussions range too far afield and occasionally become weighed down with the plethora of names, scholarly works, and theoretical frameworks that she incorporates. Essentially, the book is less a cohesive work than a series of thoroughly researched scholarly articles centered around the overall themes of Lilien, Orientalism, and gender representation in art. The volume's physical form treats art as seriously as its author does: abundant black and white illustrations are augmented by a selection of gorgeously reproduced color plates that not only reveal Lilien's work at its most vivid but also give a sense of his artistic milieu, including examples from the work of Gustav Klimt, Oscar Kokoschka, and Max Liebermann, among others.

Reading Swarts' book requires an investment of time, an appreciation of theory, and a willingness to expand the dramatis personae of important early Zionist cultural figures. The volume also offers an important critique of fin-de-siècle European art movements, not only in the realm of aesthetics, but in the degree to which they reflected contemporary ideas about gender and stereotypical representations of Jews. Swarts convincingly argues that these movements — with E. M. Lilien as one of their most important practitioners—played a vital role in creating a visual image of Jews in the eyes of other Europeans. Even more crucially, they helped to advance the self-reflective vision of modern Jews, Zionists and others, as they crafted a new identity at the start of what would ultimately be their most consequential century.

LAUREN B. STRAUSS
American University, Washington, D.C.

History, Biography, Social
and Gender Studies

Barry R. Chiswick, *Jews at Work: Their Economic Progress in the American Labor Market*. Cham: Springer, 2020. xiv + 353 pp.

Jews have done remarkably well economically in the United States: compared with other ethnic and religious groups, their occupational status is higher; they earn more; and they are wealthier. Why? There have been three favored possible explanations: Perhaps Jews do well for the same reasons as non-Jews—by getting more education and working long hours, for example. Perhaps there's something special about Jewish life—the proverbial Jewish focus on education may provide Jews with problem-solving skills uniquely helpful in the modern economy. Or perhaps it's Jewish marginality—Jews' status as never-quite-insiders may make them unusually observant and creative, able to see opportunities that others miss.

What's the answer? We have had little idea, for at least three reasons. Social scientists analyzing economic outcomes focus on groups that do badly, especially racial minorities and women. It's very difficult to find quantitative data on Jews—they are a very small fraction of the U.S. population, so most data sets include too few Jews to study. And Jews may avoid studying Jews, out of fear that their work will be seen as parochial and that highlighting Jewish success may provoke a backlash.

That's why we owe a great deal to Barry Chiswick, an economist currently at George Washington University. Decades ago he decided to apply the theoretical and methodological tools used to study other minorities to the study of Jews; he devoted a tremendous amount of effort to finding Jews in large data sets in which they were not explicitly identified; and he thought that the value of the knowledge gained by analyzing Jewish economic success would far outweigh the consequences of any possible backlash. The result was a series of articles published in a wide variety of journals in economics, religion, and Jewish studies, edited and brought together with new material, in *Jews at Work: Their Economic Progress in the American Labor Market* (co-authors of the original articles included Michael Wenz, Eliezer B. Ayal, Stella Koutroumanes Hofrenning, Carmel U. Chiswick, and Jidong Huang).

Chiswick's work is broad in scope. He studies Jews' labor market outcomes, mostly for men (for reasons he explains), from 1860 almost up to the present day. He considers both earnings and occupational attainment; the experiences of Soviet Jewish immigrants in the late 20th century; the rise and fall of the Jewish Ph.D.; the efforts Jewish couples make to help their children do well; how Jewish women compare with

Book Reviews In: *Becoming Post-Communist*. Edited by: Eli Lederhendler, Oxford University Press. © Oxford University Press 2023. DOI: 10.1093/oso/9780197687215.003.0023

non-Jewish women; how Jews compare with a number of racial and ethnic groups; and, going well beyond the work of most other economists, the relationship between labor market outcomes and involvement in Jewish life.

What does he find? Some of his conclusions will not surprise anyone; others run contrary to the predictions of economic theory or commonsense understandings of Jewish life; and a great many are interesting because they arise from ideas widely shared among economists but surprising to many of the rest of us.

Findings that are unsurprising can be important nevertheless, when they are backed up by much more data than were available previously. Among such findings: male Jewish immigrants started out economically behind native-born whites and immigrants from Northern and Western Europe, but caught up quickly and soon surpassed them, during both the mass migration around the beginning of the 20th century and the Soviet Jewish migration toward the end. Young Jews were getting more education than others by the second decade of the 20th century. And over the course of a generation, Jews moved very rapidly from sales, clerical, and production work to managerial and professional occupations, far surpassing other groups.

An important finding running contrary to conventional beliefs: It is often said that Jews in Europe got so much education partly because it was a kind of insurance; if they were forced to move, they could bring knowledge with them, in contrast to factory equipment or land, which they would have to leave behind. If that were true, economic theory tells us, then Jews should have lower rates of return to education than other groups; they "purchased" more education than needed on a day to day basis, but the extra education pays off only if they have to move. Instead, Jews get a higher rate of return to education than do other groups.

Some possibly surprising findings: Jewish parents—mothers, really—make decisions about labor market participation seemingly intended, at least in part, to enhance their children's labor market outcomes; when children are little and need a lot of quality time with their parents, Jewish mothers, more than others, tend to reduce their labor force participation to spend more time at home; when children are older and need financial support (especially for college tuition), their mothers increase their labor force participation. Jewish men who identify as Conservative earn substantially more than those who identify as Orthodox or secular. Those who attend Jewish day schools at least part of the time during grades 8–12 earn substantially more than those who get no Jewish education.

Overall, Jewish men (and perhaps women) do better than others for obvious reasons—getting more education, for example. But there seems to be something special about Jews as well; they get better returns to education than others do, and half the difference in economic outcomes between them and others cannot be explained in conventional ways (in terms of differences in education, experience, and the like). What's going on? Perhaps, according to Chiswick, Jews are better at what economists call "allocative efficiency"—because of traditional Jewish training in analyzing texts, they may be especially good at analytical reasoning and the kind of decision-making that enables them to spot economic opportunities and take advantage of them. According to Chiswick, skills and values that enable Jews to do well economically can be passed on from generation to generation even when relatively few Jews study texts in traditional ways: the skills and values are simply built into the culture of co-herent Jewish communities.

Chiswick raises questions about whether Jewish success can be sustained. Judaism is a time-intensive religion, and it is often difficult to convince Jews that devoting so much time to Jewish education and practice is worthwhile; as Jews assimilate, the community becomes less cohesive and skills needed for allocative efficiency are less likely to be passed on; and, except for the Orthodox, Jews are reproducing at well below the replacement level. At this point, Chiswick goes well beyond the boundaries of standard economic analysis to draw on his knowledge of Jewish life, providing an especially broad picture of connections between Jewish economic performance and Jewish community and culture.

Barry Chiswick is a winner of the Marshall Sklare award, given by the Association for the Social Scientific Study of Jewry to recognize social scientists whose careers have added greatly to our understanding of Jewish life. It is easy to see why he won the award.

PAUL BURSTEIN
University of Washington, Seattle

Zev Eleff, *Authentically Orthodox: A Tradition-bound Faith in American Life*. Detroit: Wayne State University Press, 2020. xiii + 311 pp.

The cover teaser to this book claims that it "challenges the current historical paradigm in the study of Orthodox Judaism" in the United States, and in his introduction, Zev Eleff asserts that his approach departs from examining what "is fashionably known as the 'slide to the right' of American Orthodox Judaism" (p. 19). Such a view, he argues, provides a "narrow view of history [that] seems too simple"—although, to be sure, he also claims, a few lines down on the same page (p. 23) that an "aggressive Orthodox right" has emerged of late. Leaving aside the seeming contradiction of these two argu-ments, I must admit in all fairness that I am the one whose book *Sliding to the Right: The Contest for the Future of American Orthodox Judaism* (2006) promoted, if not coined, the thesis that Eleff seeks to discredit. This, of course, puts an extra burden on the author, to persuade me of his alternative explanation—and on my book, to stand up under his explicit critique.

Eleff is not the first to challenge my argument regarding the passage of American Orthodox Jewry toward more aggressive cultural conflict with modernity, increasing political and ritual conservatism, and a kind of active fundamentalist either/or posi-tion that argues that one either adheres to such views or one is not truly Orthodox. Some have suggested that the more liberal Modern American Orthodoxy that I pos-ited as having lost its once-dominant voice and veered to the Right was actually a transitional and anomalous phenomenon characteristic only of the period between the two world wars. According to that view, the postwar influx of Orthodox survivor-refugees who finally came to the America they had once shunned as a *trefe medina*, an unkosher country, pulled American Jewish Orthodoxy back to its more normative, conservative stringency. Others have argued that my view of Orthodoxy is too New York-centric, and that elsewhere in the country, where far fewer Orthodox Jews live, a more liberal and "modern" Orthodoxy still persists. Still others point to a countertrend in American Orthodoxy, represented by phenomena such as the Chovevei Torah rabbinical seminary, Yeshivat Maharat, women's *batei midrash*, and partnership *minyanim*, as signals that the slide to the Right was neither the whole nor the inevitable story. I shall not revisit my responses to these interesting and fruitful theses; indeed, I am gratified that my book and thesis are still being debated 15 years after its publication.

I now turn to Eleff's argument, which he begins by asserting that American Orthodoxy has always sought to describe itself as "authentic Judaism," implying that Judaism in any other form was inauthentic. To illustrate the point, he cites words written by an obscure Orthodox rabbi from Delaware, published in 1961. Of course, 1961 is about the time that post-Holocaust Orthodox refugees in America were beginning to experience the first presentiments of what I have called Orthodox triumphalism: a feeling that they could succeed, where earlier American Orthodox Jews did not, in keeping their young people from abandoning Orthodoxy in favor of Conservative or Reform Judaism, the dominant movements. Eleff observes that the rabbi rested his claim to Orthodox authenticity on the worshippers' " 'soul-stirring cry of repentance' " on Yom Kippur (p. 3). I am not sure what kind of evidence this is. It echoes the oft-cited passage in Haym Soloveitchik's article "Rupture and Reconstruction" in which he described Yom Kippur at the American Orthodox synagogue he attended as a boy. Soloveitchik's impression, as he put it, was of a "courtroom" display of contrition, where

> at the closing service of Yom Kippur, the *Ne'ilah,* the synagogue filled and a hush set in upon the crowd. The tension was palpable and tears were shed. What had been instilled in these people in their earliest childhood, and which they never quite shook off, was that every person was judged on Yom Kippur, and, as the sun was setting, the final decision was being rendered (in the words of the famous prayer) "who for life, who for death, / who for tranquility, who for unrest." These people did not cry from religiosity but from self-interest, from an instinctive fear for their lives. Their tears were courtroom tears, with whatever degree of sincerity such tears have.[1]

Soloveitchik further opined that it was actually those Jews who came rarely to the synagogue, whose observance "had been washed away," who cried the most, adding that during "the subsequent thirty-five years . . . attending services in *haredi* and non-*haredi* communities alike," he had not encountered that degree of soul-stirring fear. And they were anything but "authentic" Orthodox Jews. To this testimony, I would add that I have witnessed such tears in congregations not at all affiliated with Orthodoxy, and that, in Orthodox synagogues I attended over the years, I too have noticed that the ones who cried most were the worshippers I only saw once or twice a year. At the same time, as my book *Synagogue Life* (1976) documents, Orthodox services are often places where gossip, joking, and conversations about the latest news find their ways into the prayers and often dominate over genuine worship. It remains unclear, therefore, what "soul-stirring cries of repentance" indicate about what is authentically Orthodox and how any of this might serve to bolster Eleff's thesis.

Eleff then connects American Orthodoxy with developments in early 19th-century America—before the influx of German Jewry, East European Jewry, and, of course, post-Holocaust Jews. Leaving aside the question of whether those earlier developments bear any real significance for the analysis of later phenomena, his picture of that tiny minority sometimes seems off-key. Early American Orthodox Jews were "summoned," as Eleff states, "to partake in specific rituals, like the palm and citron on Sukkot" (p. 5). In fact, these ritual objects were very hard to find in America, especially in the early 19th century. Even when I was a boy in an Orthodox synagogue in the 1950s and 1960s, few congregants had these, even though "summoned" by Jewish law. Only in the next decade, as the demands of Orthodoxy increasingly became answered, did these begin to be ubiquitous, a sign of the growing ritual punctiliousness of an increasingly haredi American Orthodoxy.

Eleff also cites the writings of Jacob Mordecai, who in 1826 made the claim that "his authentic Judaism fit well in American environs" (p. 6). This is a puzzling idea, for if so, why was it that, more than anywhere else, Conservative and Reform Judaism flourished in the United States for more than 150 years afterwards, while Orthodoxy steadily declined in its numbers? Only in the last decades has Orthodoxy rebounded, although the number of American Orthodox is less than that of American Jews who intermarry or who claim that they do not identify as Jews by religion, as the latest Pew Research Center survey and others have shown.

Another puzzling contention made by Eleff is that the basic approach of early American Orthodoxy that "helped decide what was religiously authentic or not" was to "shut the Talmud and open the Bible." He continues that, "most often Orthodox leaders in the United States did not quote verses from the Talmud or the teachings of Maimonides to oppose Reform rivals and quell the concerns of their adherents." Instead, they appealed to the Bible because, as Isaac Leeser, a 19th-century Orthodox leader in Philadelphia put it, the "*true orthodox...*thinks with the Bible. . . ." (pp. 10–11). I would suggest that, if Eleff concurs that this narrow view is "authentic" Orthodoxy, this is an Orthodoxy at odds with that of a majority of Orthodox Jews for whom the Bible has in practice always been secondary to the Talmud and to Maimonides, whose determination of what the Torah demands defines Orthodoxy in America today.

Eleff writes that authentic American Orthodoxy "abided by a strong sense of pluralism" (p. 14). Maybe so. I recall a time when there were institutions such as the Va'ad Harabonim in Boston, a kosher supervision service that included rabbis from a variety of denominations including Orthodoxy; or the Synagogue Council of America, which had representatives from Orthodox institutions among its members along with those from non-Orthodox ones. But if that was "authentic Orthodoxy," today's norm must be *inauthentic* Orthodoxy, as pluralism is practiced less and less, abhorred by the rightward-tilting Jews who have embraced the fundamentalist, intolerant model of "you're either with us or against us." Pluralism in Orthodoxy today is not the default position. And whereas Eleff contends that the "sliding to the right" thesis is "shortsighted" or "unsubstantiated," many of the case studies he presents depict struggles between groups pulling Orthodoxy toward a more punctilious and restrictive direction against those trying to go the other way. Eleff is correct that the terms of the battle often concern what is truly "authentically" Orthodox. Yet in most cases, it is the progressives and modernists who lose the battle to what Eleff calls the "Europeanized view."

Indeed, Orthodoxy in America today—during what is arguably its most influential period—is being shaped by its most politically and religiously right-wing elements, who regard European Jewish behaviors (mythologized with a kind of sacred nostalgia in this post-Holocaust era) as authentic and true. Moreover, American Orthodoxy seems increasingly to reflect the influence of powerful conservative and extremist right-wing forces in both America and Israel, never more than during the Trump and Netanyahu years, but continuing into the present time. To his credit, Eleff admits near the end of his book that "authenticity remains elusive" (p. 206). The rightward trend, however, is always visible.

Eleff sometimes seems to finesse evidence of a relentless rightward movement by using terms such as "the Hungarian inclination toward stringency," in explaining, for instance, the halakhic ruling that peanut oil—once acceptable on Passover—is now prohibited (a similar logic has led some Orthodox groups to exclude quinoa, which was not known in rabbinic times, from the list of permissible Passover products). In my view, this is simply more evidence of the slide to the Right. Moreover, Eleff's claims for a countertrend strike me as unconvincing. He argues, for example, that despite a backlash against the acceptability of bat mitzvah as truly Orthodox, "by the 1980s it became increasingly clear that bat mitzvah did not present a challenge to the spirit of Orthodox Judaism" (p. 59). That would be a surprise to many of those belonging to synagogues that eschew the "Modern Orthodox" label (these comprise the majority of Orthodox synagogues today), where bat mitzvah is regarded as status of religious responsibility—as it always was—but certainly not a chance for a young woman to read the Torah in public or "conduct services," which is still seen as a "deviation of the congregation from orthodoxy" (p. 61).

Space does not permit me to discuss the many interesting chapters in this book that deal with case studies on Jewish law and change, on Orthodox children's culture and education, and on Orthodox reactions to feminism and women's engagement with Judaism and ritual in new ways. Eleff raises important questions in these chapters, though I fail to see what his conceptual emphasis on the matter of "authenticity" (which he calls "a moving target") adds to our understanding.

What *Authentically Orthodox* actually shows is how American Orthodoxy has made itself comfortable in America even as it has become more religiously punctilious, inward-looking, and politically oriented toward the Right. As such, it tests the tolerance of the American "melting pot." Perhaps Orthodox Jews are what Michael Novak once referred to as "the rise of the unmeltable ethnics" at home in a multi-cultural and diverse America.[2] Or, maybe they are simply more at home in a conservative and right-wing America that embraces religious fundamentalism. Eleff concludes by saying that this "tension with the cultural forces that surround it . . . is the stuff of religious authenticity" (p. 209). I say it is more evidence of Orthodoxy's slide to the Right, albeit at a time when America too has been pulled by similar trends. Let the debate continue.

SAMUEL HEILMAN
Queens College, CUNY
The Graduate Center, CUNY

Notes

1. Haym Soloveitchik, "Rupture and Reconstruction: The Transformation of Contemporary Orthodoxy," Tradition 28, no. 4 (Summer 1994), 64–130.
2. Michael Novak, *Unmeltable Ethnics: Politics and Culture in American Life* (New York: 1996).

Elisabeth Gallas, *A Mortuary of Books: The Rescue of Jewish Culture after the Holocaust,* trans. Alex Skinner. New York: New York University Press, 2019. x + 285 pp.

This thorough and thoughtful study deals with the efforts of Jewish intellectuals and scholars to recover the millions of Jewish books, periodicals, archives, documents, and items of Jewish ritual art looted by the Germans during the course of the Second World War. Most of these cultural treasures were discovered by U.S. military forces in 1945 in Frankfurt and in the nearby town of Hungen, where they had been stored by the Nazi-sponsored Institute for the Investigation of the Jewish Question. The Americans transferred them and other looted books discovered in the American zone of occupied Germany to a "central collection point" in Offenbach, a suburb of Frankfurt, which became known as the Offenbach Archival Depot (OAD). The depot aspired, in the words of its administration, to be "the antithesis of the plundering Nazi Einsatzstab Reichsleiter Rosenberg [. . . .] the biggest book restitution operation in library history" (p. 19).

The first part of Gallas' book is a history of the OAD, an institution directed by officers affiliated with the U.S. military's Monuments, Fine Arts and Archives Unit, but staffed almost entirely by German librarians and workers. The OAD's restitution of non-Jewish books, stolen mainly from national libraries and state archives, was straightforward: these were returned to the governments of their countries of origin. Certain Jewish collections from Western Europe were treated similarly. Thus, the archive of the Alliance israélite universelle and the library of the Parisian École rabbinique were restituted to France, whose government returned them to the institutions that owned them. An exception regarding the "return to the country of origin" principle was made for the library and archive of the Yiddish Scientific Institute (YIVO), whose headquarters had moved from Vilna to New York in 1940; after recognizing the New York YIVO as the direct continuation of the Vilna YIVO, the OAD eventually restituted the collection to New York.

But the vast majority of Jewish books and cultural treasures were either of unknown origin (without ex libris) or were "heirless." They belonged to communities and organizations that were now defunct, or to individuals who had been murdered along with all their heirs.

Enter Jewish Cultural Reconstruction (from 1944, the Commission of European Jewish Cultural Reconstruction, and from 1947, Jewish Cultural Reconstruction Inc.), the main focus of Gallas' book. The organization was the brainchild of the historian Salo W. Baron, with the active participation of other academics (notably, City College philosopher Morris Raphael Cohen, and Columbia law professor Jerome Michael). JCR was the arm of organized American Jewry and later of world Jewry concerned with the retrieval of Jewish books and cultural property. It argued successfully before the American authorities that, in the Jewish case, blanket restitution of cultural property to the government of its country of origin would only compound the original crime. It would transfer ownership of Jewish treasures from prewar German Jewish and Austrian Jewish institutions to the former perpetrators, the emerging German and Austrian states. And the massive shipment of Jewish books back to Poland—a country whose remnant of surviving Jews was leaving in droves—would cut the treasures off from the Jewish people. As a JCR memo argued: "Europe is no longer [. . .] a center of Jewish spiritual and cultural activity. The great centers of such activity are now, and will continue to be, Palestine and the United States" (p. 105).

JCR set forth a legal and moral argument that these cultural treasures were the property of the Jewish people, and that JCR should be recognized as the books' trustee on behalf of the Jewish people, to assume ownership and redistribute them. The U.S. government accepted this principle in November 1947, and transferred the heirless Jewish items to JCR's ownership in 1949, shortly before the end of the U.S. military government regime and the establishment of the Federal Republic of Germany. During the course of the next few years, according to Baron's estimate, the organization redistributed 500,000 books, 1,200 Torah scrolls, and 700 artistic and ceremonial objects (p. 216). It was guided by an allocation formula of 40 percent to the United States, 40 percent to the newly established state of Israel, and 20 percent to the rest of the world (with special attention to Great Britain).

The book's final chapter deals with the role played by four scholars and intellectuals who were central to this entire endeavor: Salo W. Baron and Gershom Scholem (both of whom were already established Jewish scholars, and who represented the interests of American Jewry and the Yishuv within JCR), and Lucy Dawidowicz, and Hannah Arendt (at the time, staff members who worked for months on the ground in Germany, either at OAD or on behalf of JCR, and whose subsequent careers were transformed by that experience).

This history has been known in its broad strokes, and Gallas builds upon a large, diverse body of literature, including recent work by Dan Diner, David Engel, Anna Holzer-Kawalko, Dov Schidorsky, Nancy Sinkoff, and Noam Zadoff, among others. A Mortuary of Books adds layers of detail, nuance, and sophistication in its mining of vast archival sources, most notably the Salo W. Baron Papers, records of the Hebrew University's Committee to Rescue Diaspora Treasures (Otzarot hagolah), the Office of the U.S. Military Government for Germany, and Hannah Arendt's articles and correspondence.

Gallas brings into strong relief the full and multifaceted significance of this chapter in postwar Jewish history: Jewish scholars and intellectuals devoted themselves tirelessly to salvaging Jewish books because they considered books to be the core repository of Jewish culture and heritage, and because these specific books were "sites of memory" for the destroyed Jewish communities of Europe. (As Gallas notes in passing, JCR never considered selling some of its duplicate books to provide material relief to Holocaust survivors and displaced persons—a policy pursued by the Jewish Restitution Successor Organization when it obtained title to other types of heirless Jewish property during those years.) JCR's leaders were able to form a strong international coalition of organizations that shared their commitments. While there were disagreements and occasional tensions between the organization's American and Israeli wings, the two collaborated constructively. The organization's crowning political achievement was the recognition by the U.S. government of the Jewish people—a non-territorial, non-governmental, entity—as the legal heir to Jewish cultural property in Europe. The restitution agreement between the United States and JCR laid the conceptual and political groundwork for the subsequent reparations agreement between the Federal Republic of Germany, Israel, and the World Jewish Congress in 1952, to which diaspora Jewry was a party. In Gallas' words, JCR's work to retrieve Jewish books looted by the Nazis "brought to the fore crucial aspects of postwar Jewish existence; here rupture and loss became just as visible as the dedicated efforts to ensure continuity and survival" (p. 253).

DAVID E. FISHMAN
Jewish Theological Seminary of America

Dvora Hacohen, *To Repair a Broken World: The Life of Henrietta Szold*. Cambridge, Mass.: Harvard University Press, 2021. 388 pp.

To Repair a Broken World is a fascinating, wide-ranging biography of Henrietta Szold (1860-1945), one of the most prominent figures in both the American Jewish community and the Yishuv. Few individuals, if any, made their mark so significantly on these two communities. Dvora Hacohen offers a survey of Szold's long life against the background of the multitude of events in the history of American Jewry, American Zionism, and mainly the Yishuv (the pre-state Jewish community in Palestine), from the beginning of the 20th century until Szold's death shortly before the end of the Second World War. The book also illuminates various aspects of Szold's personal and inner life.

The first eight chapters (about a third of the book) examine Szold's life in the United States, over the first five decades of her life. Hacohen details Szold's parents' home and her upbringing in Baltimore, both of which deeply shaped her personality and worldview. Szold's periods of work with immigrants, her intellectual activity among the American Jewish intellectual elite at the Jewish Publication Society (JPS) and the *American Jewish Year Book*, as well as in the Federation of American Zionists, are all covered. The second part of Szold's adulthood, which, according to Hacohen, began with her founding of Hadassah, the Women's Zionist Organization of America in 1912, is explored in the second (and longer) section of the book. Szold's numerous roles in the Yishuv, including her serving as head of the educational and health and the social departments of the Vaad Leumi (national council) and leading Youth Aliyah, are examined against the backdrop of the political and social situation of the Yishuv, waves of immigration to Palestine, and developments within the Zionist movement.

An important novelty of the book is its suggested gendered interpretation of Szold's life. Hacohen depicts Szold's adulthood before becoming a major Zionist leader as frustrated and unhappy, mostly as the consequence of her being an extraordinary woman ahead of her time. She experienced long periods of loneliness and was frustrated both by her lack of opportunity to acquire higher education and her inability to find a suitable marriage partner. Over a period extending nearly two decades, she worked within exclusively male milieus, alongside American Jewish intellectuals and the American Zionist leadership. Although her extraordinary intellectual and organizational abilities were thoroughly acknowledged, Szold was nonetheless greatly deprived in terms of status and financial recompense. Working as what would nowadays be described as chief editor at the Jewish Publication Society while at the same time managing the publication, editing, and handling the technical aspects of publication, Szold held the official title of "secretary" and was paid accordingly. No better was the situation at the *American Jewish Year Book*. She was never named as author or translator for the many articles she produced; although she co-edited the annual with Cyrus Adler, his was the only name that appeared in print, leaving her important writing and editing unacknowledged. Similar deprivation occurred within the American Zionist Federation she was invited to rehabilitate. Most traumatic was her relationship with Louis (Levi) Ginzberg, the prominent scholar of the Jewish Theological Seminary and an influential figure in the Conservative movement. Hacohen describes how Ginzberg allowed Szold to work her fingers to the bone without pay on his renowned *Legends of the Jews*. In the end, he totally rejected her love by marrying another, younger, woman.

Hacohen further shows how, as a result of this relationship and of her understanding that she would never marry, Szold underwent a period of deep depression, from which she rose as a women's and Zionist leader: confident, determined, and an exemplary figure. In contrast to the previous periods of her adulthood, Szold's life as a Zionist leader was full of substantial activities on a national scale. Furthermore, it was "filled with admiration and acclaim" (p. 326) both in the Yishuv and in the United States. Her importance and scope of activities, and the respect felt for her in Palestine, are reflected in Hacohen's account of Szold's funeral, "one of the biggest Jerusalem had ever seen" (p. 320). Thousands of people from all walks of life attended: heads of the Yishuv and members of the Zionist executive, Hebrew University professors, mayors, nurses and social workers, Youth Aliyah workers, high-ranking British officials (including the high commissioner), and Jewish, Christian, and Muslim religious leaders. In the United States, too, Szold's passing was marked by numerous tributes.

Notwithstanding, Hacohen's assessment is that Szold was not happy in this thriving part of her life, either. She had a personal sense of missed opportunity and even described her own life on her deathbed as rich but not happy. Another important insight presented by Hacohen is that Szold was doubly deprived of a sense of home, never marrying or having children, and never feeling quite at home either in the United States or in Palestine.

Hacohen's biography is based on archival materials from three countries, personal letters, diaries, and an array of scholarly studies largely dealing with the history of the Yishuv. Additional citations would enable the reader to better trace the sources on which Hacohen bases her descriptions and arguments; more discussion of Szold's Zionist and gender views would also be welcome, along with further analysis of Szold's American values and beliefs, all of which deeply affected her public activity and the many organizations and institutions she was involved with.

The author deserves much praise for undertaking the task of solving the hard riddle of such an accomplished, diverse, and complex figure during so long and significant a period of Jewish history. In addition, Hacohen's fascinating narrative style makes this a book of interest not only for historians but for much larger audiences as well.

MIRA KATZBURG-YUNGMAN
The Open University of Israel

Rachel Manekin, *The Rebellion of the Daughters: Jewish Women Runaways in Habsburg Galicia*. Princeton: Princeton University Press, 2020. 304 pp.

> *Farewell, and if my fortune be not crossed,*
> *I have a father, you a daughter, lost*
> — Jessica, *The Merchant of Venice*, Act 2, Scene 5

Shylock's daughter Jessica is probably the most famous runaway Jewish daughter in world literature. In Shakespeare's *The Merchant of Venice*, she elopes with Lorenzo, steals her father's fortune, and—adding insult to injury—converts to Christianity. Jessica was obviously on the mind of Felix Salten, the Austrian writer (and creator of *Bambi*), when he penned the screenplay for *Der Shylock von Krakau* (The Shylock of Kraków), a 1913 silent film about the daughter of a Galician Jewish moneylender who runs away to Berlin with her Polish lover. But she was surely not the only runaway daughter on Salten's mind. Indeed, when he wrote the screenplay on the eve of the Great War, sensational (and sensationalist) tales of Jewish women runaways filled the pages of newspapers across the Habsburg monarchy, thanks to a series of court trials that brought the phenomenon of runaway Jewish daughters to the attention of the wider public. These women are the subject of Rachel Manekin's riveting and painstakingly researched book, *The Rebellion of the Daughters: Jewish Women Runaways in Habsburg Galicia.*

Manekin identifies "the rebellion of the daughters" as a widespread phenomenon in late imperial Galicia, one that was intimately linked to the so-called Daughters' Question. The Daughters' Question does not feature among the Big Questions of the 19th century (for instance, the Jewish, Polish, Woman, Eastern, and Macedonian Questions), but this Jewish corollary to the Woman Question was the subject of vigorous debate and hand-wringing in late Habsburg Galicia. As Manekin explains, the

Daughters' Question was about how to offer young Jewish women a modern education without weakening their Jewish observance or attenuating their ties to the Jewish community. Jewish women runaways, who tended to be "highly educated but Jewishly ignorant," served as a glaring reminder that a certain "equilibrium" had been "knocked off kilter" (p. 130).

In Chapter 1, Manekin traces the origins of the Daughters' Question in Galicia, setting the stage for her discussion in Chapters 2–4 of three women runaways from Kraków and its environs. In Galicia, Orthodox Jewish parents tried to "protect" their sons from state-mandated secular education, but when it came to their daughters, they saw no need to worry, at least not until the early 20th century. In fact, the most prominent hasidic leaders sent their daughters to non-Jewish schools—even convent schools!—where they learned secular subjects and foreign languages. These young Jewish women studied and socialized with their Polish Catholic peers, and they found themselves straddling two worlds (and two cultures) that often clashed or conflicted with one another. Some of these women managed to reconcile the two worlds, but others experienced a sense of "dissonance," "bifurcation," or "alienation"—to use some of the terms Manekin employs to describe the psychological toll taken by a divided life. For the would-be runaways, the breaking point was often a looming arranged marriage, one that threatened to trap them in the traditional Jewish world, foreclosing any possibility of pursuing romantic love or higher education.

Running away often meant conversion, and the Felician Sisters' Convent in Kraków plays an outsize role in Manekin's narrative. Known colloquially in Yiddish as a *shmad fabrik* ("apostasy factory"), the convent was a way station for three of the book's protagonists who found temporary refuge with the Felician Sisters (two of them converted to Catholicism). Between 1873 and 1914, 340 people converted at the convent, of whom 324 were Jewish women, most between the ages of 14 and 20. Their individual stories are impossible to retrieve, which is why the three court trials between 1900 and 1910—and their sizable paper trails—are a remarkable find. They enable Manekin to reconstruct, in vivid detail, the personal sagas and inner lives of three Jewish runaways: 15-year-old Michalina Araten, 18-year-old Debora Lewkowicz, and 19-year-old Anna Kluger.

Manekin devotes a chapter to each of these women, creating a kind of typology of runaway Jewish women: Michalina was driven by "religious ardor," Debora by "romantic love," and Anna by "intellectual passion." None of these women, however, was a typical runaway, with the possible exception of Debora, the daughter of tavern-keepers in a small village outside of Kraków. Michalina and Anna, by contrast, were daughters of wealthy and prominent hasidic families, which is one reason why their cases became *causes célèbres*. Michalina's father, a Ger hasid, made every possible effort to bring his daughter home; he turned to the police, the courts, the Austrian parliament, and he even had a much-publicized audience with Emperor Franz Joseph I. Anna's mother was the great-granddaughter of Hayim Halberstam, founder of the hasidic Sanz dynasty, making Anna's rebellion all the more scandalous.

All three cases unfolded on the backdrop of the Daughters' Question, in part, because the Jewish press often blamed higher education for leading the young women astray. Michalina was "stuffed" with foreign subjects and languages, claimed an article in the Orthodox press, and thereby inclined to "follow strangers" and their "immoral views" (p. 59). Debora wrote love letters in Polish, a language she acquired at the public school for girls. In the case of Anna, the Daughters' Question was front and center, because she (and her sister Leonore) ran away from home after falling in love, not with Jesus or a Catholic Pole, but with the prospect of a higher education. The Kluger case is remarkable because the sisters not only ran away, but also sued their parents to allow them to live outside of their parental home and to attend university. And they won. In 1910, the case reached the Viennese Supreme Court, which not only upheld Anna and Leonore's request, but also obliged the father to support the sisters financially, citing an Austrian law that obligated fathers to provide a decent livelihood for their children. In 1914, Anna received her doctoral degree at the University of Vienna, with a dissertation on Giuseppe Mazzini; she went on to marry a Jewish Social Democratic politician and to become a gymnasium teacher in Kraków.

These causes célèbres, especially the Kluger case, were a turning point in the Daughters' Question, because they catapulted the issue of higher education for women into the non-Jewish public sphere. It was after the Kluger case, in particular, Manekin argues, that "gymnasium and university education for women became a red flag for the Orthodox leadership" (p. 164). While Zionists hoped to solve the Daughters' Question by establishing Jewish schools that offered a strong Jewish national curriculum, the Orthodox press increasingly advocated limits on the instruction of secular subjects and foreign languages (as well as the increased supervision of the schoolgirls in order to prevent them from socializing with non-Jewish men). Manekin sees this as the beginning of a "counter-revolution" in women's education, culminating in the establishment of the Beit Yaakov (Bais Yaakov) schools, which emphasized Jewish observance and enthusiasm, while aiming to "extinguish the desire for a higher education" among Jewish women.

If Michalina Araten, Debora Lewkowicz, and Anna Kluger were the rebels, then Sarah Schenirer, founder of the Beit Yaakov schools, was the counter-revolutionary. Manekin devotes an entire chapter to Schenirer, whose first school, founded in Kraków in 1917, serves as the model for ultra-Orthodox girls' schools to this day. The curriculum included Jewish and secular subjects, but, as Manekin points out, it offered no option for a matriculation exam, thereby blocking the path to gymnasium, university, or other institutions of higher learning. It was meant to inculcate an enthusiasm for Judaism, not a thirst for knowledge. It was a solution, in Manekin's view, to the Daughters' Question.

Manekin's monograph is an exemplary work of social and cultural history, drawing on an impressive range of court files, legal documents, halakhic literature, memoirs, and novels—along with the contemporary Polish-, German-, Hebrew-, and Yiddish-language press—to identify and investigate a deep crisis in Galician Jewish family life at the beginning of the 20th century. Manekin has discovered intimate, heart-wrenching letters and testimonies that reveal the inner lives and inner torments of young Jewish women, whose life stories would have otherwise been inaccessible and inaudible. So much of the recent scholarship on Galician Jewry focuses on Jewish politics or anti-Jewish violence, and Manekin's focus on education and daily lives is a refreshing change. Nevertheless, I would have wanted her to provide more of the broader social and political context, such as the impact of the 1898 anti-Jewish riots in Galicia, which is the subject of recent books by Daniel Unowsky and Tim Buchen.

Did this wave of violence affect choices made by young Jewish women? Did it make running away more or less likely?

Manekin gives us a remarkable window into the lives of the three runaways, mostly focusing on the court battles and their immediate aftermaths. I wish we knew more about Debora, whose trail seems to run dry after she returned to Judaism. Anna taught history and geography at a coeducational Hebrew gymnasium in Kraków, and published prolifically, but her remarkable life was cut short when she and her husband were murdered by the Germans at Kremenets (Krzemeniec) in 1942. Michalina's subsequent life is the most fascinating, and was even the subject of a novel, *Michalina: Daughter of Israel*, published in 1986. Written by Michalina's sister-in-law, Rachel Sarna Araten, the novel asserts that Michalina was kidnapped by the family's Catholic maid and forcibly converted to Catholicism, and thus attempts to silence the runaway narrative that Manekin so meticulously details. In the novel, as in real life, Michalina marries, moves to Belgium, survives the war, immigrates to Israel (in 1960), and returns to Judaism. This redemptive ending eluded Shakespeare's Jessica, and it also eluded most of the runaway Jewish women in Galicia who opted for conversion over "dissonance," "bifurcation," and "alienation."

MICHAEL L. MILLER
Central European University

Rafael Medoff, *The Jews Should Keep Quiet: Franklin D. Roosevelt, Rabbi Stephen S. Wise, and the Holocaust*. Lincoln: University of Nebraska Press, 2019. xvi + 387 pp.

Arthur Morse's *While Six Million Died* (1967) inaugurated the project of historical revisionism that undermined the exalted reputation of America's 32nd president, Franklin Delano Roosevelt, among its Jewry. Until that point, American Jews, in the words of a Republican judge, Jonah Goldstein, had believed in three *veltn*, or worlds: this world (*di velt*), the world to come (*yene velt*), and Roosevelt. Morse, a television journalist, was followed by academicians, among them Saul S. Friedman, Henry L. Feingold, David S. Wyman, and Monte Noam Penkower, all of whom highlighted the limitations of the official U.S. response to the refugee crisis of the 1930s and to the Final Solution in the 1940s. In so doing, they peeled away the halo of humanitarianism that Roosevelt earned during the Great Depression. At the same time, there are other historians— Richard Breitman, Allan Lichtman, Robert Rosen, and William D. Rubinstein —who have mounted defenses of FDR's record. How much, these writers have asked, could *any* administration have done for beleaguered European Jewry, given the nativism, the isolationism, and the antisemitism of the 1930s? To what extent would military and diplomatic measures on the Jews' behalf have been effective against the Axis powers? Such questions haunt the contrast between the Nazi dedication to extermination and the belated, paltry reaction of the United States. American officialdom explained that only a speedy military victory could save Europe's Jews.

By V-E Day, however, only a remnant had survived— so few that historians were bound to consider alternative policies, in the course of which they smashed a presidential pedestal. Revisionists have also inflicted collateral damage upon the memory of Stephen S. Wise (1874–1949), the eminent Zionist and leader of Reform Judaism who was the most prominent tribune of American Jewry during that era. *The Jews Should Keep Quiet* is the first book to entwine FDR and Wise as it examines the singular challenge that the Third Reich posed to victims and bystanders alike.

No historian has detached himself more fully from the appeal that Roosevelt and his rabbinical friend once exerted than Rafael Medoff, although his own interpretation of their relationship does not break sharply from that offered in the first scholarly biography of Wise, Melvin I. Urofsky's *A Voice That Spoke for Justice* (1982). Urofsky presented a sympathetic account of a liberal activist who had warned— early and eloquently—of the international danger of Nazism. Wise had cherished (while also exaggerating) his access to Roosevelt, the Democratic savior of millions of impoverished citizens during the crisis of American capitalism. As was the case for the approximately 80–90 percent of Jewish voters whom Roosevelt consistently galvanized, Wise was so grateful for the domestic programs of the New Deal that a public break with FDR over foreign policy was unimaginable. The rabbi "believed the president's political and social agenda was best for society, and therefore Jews needed to support him when they cast their ballots," Medoff writes (p. 242). Wise was therefore ill-equipped to demand anything of "the Chief," even in private, at a time when Nazi Germany engaged in the systematic destruction of Jewish life in Europe. Moreover, in serving as a pivotal figure in too many causes, Wise was exhausted and increasingly beset by medical problems. Corroborating Urofsky's portrayal, Medoff makes it evident that more vigorous leadership, independent of slavish loyalty to the Democratic Party, would have better served the Jewish community. The emergence of Rabbi Abba Hillel Silver (1893–1963), an advocate for swinging Jewish support to the Republicans and Wise's main rival to American Jewish leadership, suggested that such a transfer of authority was happening anyway.

The Jews Should Keep Quiet is punctuated with its author's polemical gifts, as Medoff skewers the excuses for inaction and political paralysis that the Roosevelt administration offered. The Johnson–Reed Immigration Act of 1924 had installed barriers to Jews seeking entry into the United States. Yet from 1933 until Pearl Harbor, the German and Austrian quotas for admission were unfulfilled every single year (except for 1938–1939). Medoff remarks that nearly 200,000 Jews might have found refuge without changing the quota law inherited from the Republican Party. Why were so many Jews barred? Two successive assistant secretaries of state, as well as many of the consuls who served under them, deliberately kept Jews out, and Roosevelt was frequently briefed on this policy of denying them visas. The Department of State thus validated the adage of the modus operandi of administration: "personnel *is* policy." Its rationale in this instance was that too many refugees might deprive Americans of jobs. But children posed no threat to anyone's employment; and after Kristallnacht, the Wagner–Rogers bill was intended to admit 20,000 Jewish children outside the quota. The president refused to support the bill, and it died. During the Battle of Britain, the executive and legislative branches agreed to the rescue of thousands of English children. No extra credit for guessing their religion. But when it came to Jews fleeing the

Nazis, the question was posed: how could refugees be transported during wartime to the Western Hemisphere? Medoff points out that the Liberty Ships that transported U.S. materiel to Britain returned empty, even though insufficient ballast entailed the risk of capsizing. Those ships might have been filled with Jewish refugees, always assuming that they could reach England. Is it fair to ask a democratic politician to get ahead of public opinion? Medoff cites a Gallup poll taken in the spring of 1944, when seven in ten Americans came around to supporting the idea of emergency shelters for Jewish refugees. That prospect of receptivity came tragically late, however; most of the Jews murdered in the Holocaust had already been killed in 1942.

Perhaps the most novel feature of *The Jews Should Keep Quiet* is its attempt to tie statecraft to prejudicial remarks that Roosevelt made about Jews. The snobbery that he harbored toward lesser "races," the lame jokes with which he regaled associates (plus even Stalin and Ibn Saud) revealed a mindset that, according to Medoff, made it difficult for FDR to appreciate the horrific plight of Jews. Here the author's case is too one-sided to be convincing. The president was willing to risk the onus of a "Jew Deal" by making prominent appointments of Jews to his cabinet and to the Supreme Court. That even Roosevelt was infected with a mild dose of antisemitism hints at how pervasive such bigotry was. Its ubiquity helps explain the timidity of Stephen S. Wise, as well as the official refusal to name European Jews as the prime targets of paranoiac frenzy—lest Nazi propagandists continue to blame the most helpless victims for causing the war. Nearly half a century would be needed before AIDS activists came up with the resonant slogan that "silence = death."

STEPHEN J. WHITFIELD
Brandeis University

Michael A. Meyer, *Rabbi Leo Baeck: Living a Religious Imperative in Troubled Times*. Philadelphia: University of Pennsylvania Press, 2021. xi + 262 pp.

Book reviewers seldom acknowledge the predispositions that color their attitudes to the work under their consideration. In the case of Michael A. Meyer's sympathetic biography of Rabbi Leo Baeck, it is necessary to render these explicit. Intellectual historians—I include myself among them—have devoted a great deal of attention to 20th-century German Jewish intellectuals such as Gershom Scholem, Franz Rosenzweig, Martin Buber, Theodor Adorno, Hannah Arendt, Walter Benjamin, and Leo Strauss, to mention only the most prominent few. These figures have all achieved widespread posthumous fame in both Jewish and more general matters. By and large, Leo Baeck (1873–1956) has been conspicuously absent from this pantheon, despite the fact that, as Meyer ably demonstrates, this liberal rabbi is regarded as the most courageous and dignified persona of 20th-century German Jewry, especially in its most tragic times. Why then this intellectual neglect? To be sure, Baeck has by no means been forgotten—in his name there are schools in Haifa and Toronto, a Liberal rabbinical seminary in London, a street in the Zehlendorf section of Berlin, a temple in Los Angeles and, most familiarly, the international Leo Baeck Institute, whose goal is the preservation and critical study of the legacy of German Jewry. Yet his oeuvre is seldom, if at all, discussed. Perhaps this has to do with Baeck's essentially "establishment" role and leadership responsibilities. There was little in him of the challenging restless radicalism, the subversive impulse characteristic of these other "free-floating" intellectuals. Acceptable to virtually all sectors of German Jewry— scholar and thinker though he may have been—it was not in his thought but in his integrity and temperate leadership, his indispensable role in a plethora of organizational, communal, and rabbinical affairs, that he really made his mark.

Indeed, though Meyer analyzes in respectful detail Baeck's works of scholarship and his liberal religious worldview, the point of the biography is not, I believe, a plea for his inclusion in the above-named pantheon. Even though he concludes the book by noting that Baeck's "assertion of the powerful connection between a God dwelling in mystery but known to Jews and others through the imperative to act justly and strive toward a messianic horizon seems more relevant than ever in our own time" (p. 215), he is aware of Baeck's limited posthumous intellectual influence, that most of his works go unread and that he established no school of thought. The real aim and gist of the biography must therefore be sought elsewhere. For Meyer—a veteran scholar of the German Jewish religious experience especially qualified to render the life and thought in measured and judicious manner—Baeck's special quality consisted precisely of a remarkable integral combination: a personal philosophy that went organically hand in hand with both public and private action. For this liberal (and universalist) Jew, faith in God implied a consistent moral obligation in all areas of life, and a messianic emphasis on future justice. The book diligently documents the ways in which this unity manifested itself throughout Baeck's life and actions.

Given this special quality, the genre of biography demands an investigation into the formation and nature of Baeck's personality. While correctly shunning all reductive psychologizing, Meyer defines the task of the volume as that of integrating the contradictory elements of Baeck's psychological make-up (despite the moral unity of his actions): a gentleness and kindness that could co-exist with combativeness; courage and selflessness that contrasted with a "streak of puritanism and an outsize veneration for martyrdom" (p. x); an inevitably dignified, if not stolid, stance occasionally punctured by humor (surprisingly, his first article was published in the popular satirical weekly *Simplicissimus*). He was, incidentally, a typical bourgeois *yekke*— before being ordered to Theresienstadt, he insisted upon paying his electricity and gas bills!—yet also a fervent admirer of the nobility. I am not certain that his biographer has entirely succeeded in this self-imposed task of penetrating Baeck's psyche. Meyer himself emphasizes the exceedingly private nature of this public personality, his immense distaste for self-revelation, his dogged refusal to confide matters of a private and intimate nature (his marriage to his wife, Nina Hamburger, was a deeply comforting aspect of that area of his life), and his almost instinctive posture of dignified distance. As his younger rabbinical colleague, Joachim Prinz, put it: Baeck was "a leader of the people without being of the people." Meyer brings this graphically home, reporting that, upon his visit to the United States, when American photographers told him to smile, Baeck objected that this turned people into caricatures. The numerous pictures of Baeck that grace this volume almost always reveal a serious countenance.

Indeed, the cover of the book, a 1931 colored portrait of Baeck painted by his friend, Ludwig Meidner, conveys a kind of sad, almost tragic countenance—even prior to the Nazi assumption of power.

Given this personal inscrutability, Meyer correctly concentrates on Baeck's more accessible public career, not only as Germany's leading Liberal rabbi but also—by dint of his measured "above party" posture—his unique acceptability to all sectors of German Jewry, heading in either titular or active form virtually all its communal and representative organizations. His statesmanlike stature was such that it was he who was chosen to give Walther Rathenau's funeral address. His tolerance toward all branches of identified Jewish life included the Zionist option. Although initially he regarded its nationalism as a narrowing of the universal role that Judaism as a world religion was destined to play, over the years his attitude became less ambivalent, affirming the necessity for Jews to find a secure place (while also concerned with improving Jewish–Arab relations and seeking to alleviate the suffering of post-1948 Palestinian refugees).

Meyer also analyzes Baeck's lifelong scholarly endeavors. These include his polemical writings in which he contrasted "Classical Judaism" and its monotheistic valorization of a single humanity and social justice with what he dubbed "Romantic Christianity" and its putatively uncritical relationship to, and dependence upon, power and the state. In this contrapuntal narrative, Jews were rendered as inherently a people of nonconformists. Baeck also entered into heated contemporary Weimarian debates regarding morality and relativism. There he neatly inverted the conventional secular order of things. Historicism, he declared, made revelation a predicate of history, whereas in fact history becomes a predicate of revelation. Meyer does not mention this, but Baeck, rather surprisingly, even invoked Martin Heidegger in his defense of Judaism: "The philosopher Heidegger has—intentionally or unintentionally— expressed a biblical thought by saying . . . : 'Dasein, that is not a being present-at hand (*Vorhandsein*), but a being ready-to-hand (*Zuhandsein*), something that is laid down before the human, something he forms, makes, shapes.' This is Jewish thinking."[1] In all of Baeck's writings, his overarching conception of Jewish existence, *Heilsgeschichte*, as Meyer sums it up, consisted of a partnership between God and humanity aimed at justice and a kind of messianic collective salvation. At least in terms of his religious vision, this temperamentally conservative and distant man was actually a dissenter, a social democrat, a critic of the *Machtstaat*.

For all his deep respect for his subject, Meyer does not neglect to discuss the rabbi's detractors and underminers and, most importantly, some of his later life-and-death decisions under Nazi rule that remain controversial to this day. Indeed, apart from specialists in the field and the research institution that carries his name, Baeck has frequently been associated with Hannah Arendt's notorious depiction of him as the Jewish "Führer" under the Nazis (a deeply unfair description that she later regretted) and the fact that, as their spiritual leader, he refrained from divulging information he had obtained regarding their horrible future fate in the East. This was an unbearably painful dilemma. There were those who argued that making public the murders in the East could have saved lives by enabling the possibility of escape or resistance (even if it would have cost Baeck's own life). And yet, Meyer argues, such a revelation could have had the "negative effect of multiplying suicides and would be a denial of the possibility that some, despite all odds, might nonetheless survive in Germany or in Poland, or even that the Nazi regime might come to an end before a particular individual was put to death" (p. 141). Moreover, who could be capable of reminding people daily that they were destined to death? To this day there is no clear-cut resolution to this tragic dilemma.

Whatever else may be said, Meyer makes Baeck's courage and integrity under Nazi rule very clear. Despite numerous offers and opportunities to leave Germany he refused to so, regarding his leadership responsibilities as paramount. At first, he was actively involved in the urgent task of forging Jewish unity. In September 1933, it was clear that he was the only figure who could fill the role of president of the newly formed Reichsvertretung der deutschen Juden (National Representation of German Jews, mandated by the regime). In this representative role he engaged in helping Jews to emigrate and, when that became impossible, worked to uphold morale, reinforce pride in an often attenuated Judaism, and alleviate suffering. Upon being dispatched to Theresienstadt (where he was *not* the official so-called "Jewish elder"—that post was held by Paul Eppstein, a man not much admired by Baeck), he continued to play the same pastoral role (officiating, among other things, at the funeral of Theodor Herzl's daughter). Throughout, the dignity of the man—if not all his decisions—remained exemplary. Arrested five times, he remained unbowed, even gaining the grudging respect of the authorities. Allegedly, after a surprise encounter with Eichmann in Theresienstadt in April 1945, the Nazi arrogantly blocked the door: "Baeck simply put his hand on Eichmann's arm just below the shoulder, lightly pushed him aside, and passed through the doorway. As he walked down the street, Baeck could feel the astonished glance following his departing steps" (p. 162).

For all that, Baeck temperamentally suppressed any emphasis on evil; during the Weimar years, he avoided references to the obviously growing antisemitism. Even after the Holocaust, he tended to turn away from such discussions. In its earliest stages—like many others—he was reluctant to recognize the depth of National Socialist depravity. Indeed, he affirmed the need for Germany's renewal and initially "harbored the illusion that what had happened was not a reversal but only an unfortunate but manageable change of regime" (p. 85). As late as 1937, he argued that 80 percent of the German people were opposed to persecution of the Jews but were simply afraid to express their opinion. In the immediate postwar period, this perception was to change dramatically. "The history of German Jewry is decisively at an end," he declared. "The clock cannot be turned back. . . . Too much stands between the German Jews and the Germany of the period 1933–45—so much murder, theft, and plunder, so much blood and tears, so many tears. That cannot be erased. . . The nurturing layer of soil is no longer there" (p. 169). To be sure, he later adopted a more reconciliatory attitude to Germany and the possibility of renewing some Jewish life there.

Michael Meyer's biography of Baeck is clearly a labor of love. This is not to say it is hagiographical in nature. Where criticism is needed, he voices it, and he does not romanticize his subject. Yet his admiration clearly shines through. Ultimately he views Baeck as the "incarnation of all that was admirable in German Jewry and in Liberal Judaism" (p. 209). Baeck may not belong to the intellectual giants of the German

Jewish experience, but Meyer has definitively succeeded in demonstrating his indispensable representative role in its creative, compelling, and ultimately tragic history.

STEVEN E. ASCHHEIM
The Hebrew University

Note

1. Quoted in Daniel M. Herskowitz, *Heidegger and His Jewish Reception* (Cambridge: 2021), 93.

Sharon Pardo and Hila Zahavi (eds.), *The Jewish Contribution to European Integration*. Lanham: Lexington Books, 2020. 196 pp.

In situating the notion of *The Jewish Contribution to European Integration* in scholarly discourse, this volume, edited by Sharon Pardo and Hila Zahavi, makes its mark. It comprises (more or less) verbatim presentations from workshops held in Jerusalem and Beersheva from 2013 to 2015, hosted by the Israeli Office of the Konrad-Adenauer Stiftung and the Simone Veil Research Centre for Contemporary European Studies of Ben-Gurion University of the Negev. Pardo and Zahavi, however, had the bad luck of compiling their work around the time of Brexit and the Trump election, which upended many previous assumptions about international relations and diplomacy surrounding Jews, Europe, and Israel.

In some respects, the central weakness of this volume mimics its post-1945, European subject. It has a bureaucratic, box-ticking feel, and it focuses more on structures and operations than on people and events. To the extent that the book does reflect on "unsung heroes"—Walther Rathenau, Fritz Bauer, and Simone Veil—none of these are approached by appropriate scholars, and their treatment reveals a lack of familiarity with the relevant historiography.

It is also telling that the chapter the editors regard as an outlier is by far the most outstanding of the volume: Diana Pinto's "The Jewish World's Ambiguous Attitude toward European Integration." Pinto is distinctive among the contributors for tracing the genealogy of the visceral anti-European-ness of the neocons as (supposedly) pro-Israel advocacy, and the way in which hostility to Europe was raised to fever pitch under Benjamin Netanyahu, which negated any possibility of an ongoing "Jewish contribution to European integration." By aligning himself so vociferously with Vladimir Putin and Donald Trump, both the Israeli prime minister (who was Trumpian in advance of Trump), along with those Jews who insist that Jewishness is compatible only with a right-wing incarnation of greater Israel, style themselves as foes of European integration. Not surprisingly, they are ill-disposed to George Soros' efforts to promote open societies. Indeed, in September 2017, acting as a mouthpiece for his father, Yair Netanyahu demeaned Soros through grotesque antisemitic stereotypes, which have continued in other tweets and speeches (by Yair and other Bibi allies) since then.

The potential value of this book is also constrained by a narrowness of vision. Jews, including Israeli Jews, have contributed to European integration in such areas as sports and entertainment—but this point is entirely overlooked. As it happens, Israeli athletes in Europe, few in number as they are, are not regarded as being out of the ordinary. In addition, Israel not only is included, but has also been a four-time winner in the wacky but weighty Eurovision song contest. This has been part of a pronounced cultural affinity between Israel and Europe, and especially the gay subcultures of each. Certainly Israel and Eurovision, from Ofra Haza to Dana International to Neta Barzilai, deserves a chapter. In addition to pop music, the extent to which translated Hebrew literature has become part of the European intellectual landscape is certainly noteworthy.[1]

Another dimension of European integration that receives strangely subdued treatment is Judaism's relationship to the major Christian denominations. The editors have underestimated the individual and institutional efforts underlying the transformation of (most of) Europe's churches into anti-antisemitic bulwarks. On the one hand, progressive varieties of Judaism have often been slighted by the European states as compared with Orthodoxy, Habad, and other "traditional" alternatives—such as in Hungary, in giving Habad control over military chaplaincy. But on the other hand, British Jewish rabbis such as (the late) Albert Friedlander, Julia Neuberger, and Jonathan Wittenberg have been tireless in their attempts to engender a liberal Europe through contact with, and fertilization of, the more open-minded varieties of European Judaism.

One of the reasons why something akin to the Holocaust is hard to imagine in post-Second World War Central Europe is because the churches, along with political parties, have been weaned from antisemitism with the deliberate assistance of local and European-wide Jews. Gerhard Riegner and the World Jewish Congress have been critical in this regard.[2] Along with Judaism in itself, the academic study of Judaism and Jewish studies, broadly conceived, should be considered as an important factor in making Jewry a rightful part of the European mosaic. In this realm, it would have been intriguing to refer to scholars such as Gershom Scholem, Theodor Adorno, John Klier, Ulrich Beck, Barbara Kirshenblatt-Gimlet, Antony Polonsky, Vivian Liska, Dan Diner, Marc Gelber, Susannah Heschel, Michael Brenner, Aron Rodrigue, Esther Benbassa, Liliane Weissberg, Sander Gilman, George Mosse, Jonathan Webber, and Matti Bunzl, who have enabled Jewish history and literature to materialize in the emerging whole cloth of European academe. The omission of Bunzl is especially troubling because he has produced seminal articles about the changing self-perceptions of Jews in Austria and elsewhere as Europeans.[3]

Sharon Pardo and Hila Zahavi earnestly dedicate their book to "Lars Hänsel and Michael Mertes, the past directors of the Konrad-Adenauer Stiftung Israeli Office. It is the work and the writings of these two staunch Europeanists, as well as their commitment to the idea of Europe, for which we express our admiration," and which inspired this volume. Incorporating the efforts of Hänsel and Mertes, and their circle, would have made this a better book. The editors might also have expended more energy in exploring those who have sought to undermine the vision that was so dear to them and to their predecessors. Much work remains in order to develop a historically driven, comprehensive, nuanced, and perhaps more somber reflection on the Jewish contribution to the European integration process.

MICHAEL BERKOWITZ
University College London

Notes

1. See Derek Penslar, "Hebrew Fiction and the World Market," posted on June 14, 2015, at derekpenslar.com/2015/06/14/hebrew-fiction-and-the-world-market/ (accessed 10 January 2021).
2. Gerhard M. Riegner, *Never Despair: Sixty Years in the Service of the Jewish People and the Cause of Human Rights*, trans. William Sayers (Chicago: 2006).
3. See Matti Bunzl, "Austrian Zionism and the Jews of the New Europe," *Jewish Social Studies* 9, no. 2 (Winter 2003), 154–173.

Joel Perlmann, *America Classifies the Immigrants: From Ellis Island to the 2020 Census*. Cambridge, Mass.: Harvard University Press, 2018. viii + 451 pp.

America Classifies the Immigrants: From Ellis Island to the 2020 Census, by historian Joel Perlmann, is a well-written, compelling analysis of how the U.S. statistical system grappled with the increasing heterogeneity of the origins of immigrants and their U.S.-born descendants from the turn of the 20th century to the present. It is a story that tells us as much (or more) about America—including its political decisions, the federal bureaucracy, attitudes toward race, and the social sciences over this period—as it does about the immigrants themselves. How people were classified depended less on how they thought of themselves than on how the political system and social sciences regarded them.

The book consists of four parts. It begins with the "List of Races and Peoples" (starting in 1898) and its implementation by the immigration authorities; the U.S. Immigration Commission Reports (1911), commonly referred to as the Dillingham Commission; and the U.S. decennial censuses. The list differentiated not only what we would today consider racial categories, but also among the myriad European ethnic groups, with special interest in the increasing numbers from Southern and Eastern Europe starting in the 1880s. Classification of immigrants was a nature versus nurture issue: would the adjustment in the United States of these new immigrants be determined by their origins (biology) or would they adjust (and if so, how quickly) to the American norms? Classification based on country of origin would not be sufficient, given the heterogeneity of peoples (language, culture, religion, etc.) within the pre-First World War European empires.

Part 2 focuses on "institutionalizing race distinction" in immigration law, especially with regard to the country of origin quotas established in the National Origins Acts of

1921 and 1924, which remained largely in effect until the immigration reforms instituted in 1965. Based on eugenics and race theory popular in the 1920s, the objective was to use country of origins as a proxy for European "races" to restrict the entry of South and East European immigrants in particular.

Part 3 focuses on the evolution of the concept of "race" into that of "ethnicity" during the 1920s through the early 1960s, emphasizing the evolution and assimilation to the American scene among the immigrants and their descendants. The concept of ethnicity led to concerns about the persistence of identifiable ethnic groups ("ethnic survival"), as distinct from an assimilation approach where ethnic differences among immigrants and their descendants would diminish across generations due to assimilation and intermarriage, although the rate of erosion would differ across groups.

Part 4 focuses on the implications of two major, interrelated developments in the 1960s, the civil rights movement and the 1965 immigration reform, which opened the United States to immigrants from Asia and, to a lesser extent, other Third World countries. This new consciousness of race and ethnicity, and the increased heterogeneity of the origins of the U.S. population, compelled new modes of classification. So, too, the greater incidence and recognition of intermarriage across racial and ethnic groups resulted in a rethinking of what had been considered conventional single race/ ethnic categories. Both the civil rights movement and the increased immigration from Latin America led to the establishment of the Hispanic ethnicity category, comprising immigrants and their descendants from the quite heterogeneous Spanish-speaking countries of Latin America.

America Classifies the Immigrants may be of particular interest to the readers of *Studies in Contemporary Jewry* since it highlights various attempts to identify Jews in the immigration and census data. The length of the entries on Jews and Jewish organizations in the book's index is larger than for any other demographic group. Debates relating to the Jews revolved around the question of whether they should be considered a "race" (in the late 19th century and early 20th century use of the term), a nationality, a "people," an ethnic group, or merely a religious group. Nor was there consensus among Jews or Jewish organizations as to how the community preferred to be defined. Indeed, in the late 19th and early 20th centuries, for various reasons, the German Jewish (religiously Reform) elite opposed any mechanism for identifying, directly or indirectly, Jews in immigration or other government data. Judaism, they argued, was merely a religion. In contrast, both the Yiddish-speaking, more Orthodox, and more recently arrived East European Jews and the secular Zionists advocated for the separate identification of Jews. They insisted that Judaism was more than just a religion—Polish Jews, for instance, were different from Polish Catholics.

The result was attempts to identify Jews without the government asking what might be a constitutionally prohibited question on religion. The immigrant authority "List of Races and Peoples" included Hebrew as one category, as did the surveys and reports conducted by the Dillingham Immigration Commission. When the "mother tongue" question was added to the decennial census in 1910, Yiddish was among the languages coded.

Perlmann's analysis does not include a discussion of an earlier (1890) attempt to learn about the adjustment in the United States of a relatively new immigrant group that started arriving in larger numbers in the 1880s—Jews. This was an Office of the Census report titled "Vital Statistics of the Jews in the United States, commonly referred to as the Billings Report, after the statistician who directed the project.[1] The Billings Report indicates that the purpose of surveying 10,000 Jewish households was to learn the characteristics and adjustment of this new immigrant group, which they knew would not be separately identified in the upcoming 1890 census. The respondents were identified as Jews by rabbis and presidents of Jewish congregations.

America Classifies the Immigrants is much more than the tale of how people were identified. It is a sophisticated, yet non-technical, study of the debates over immigration policy over the last 120 years. It is well written; a good read. It presents the overarching issues together with much fascinating detail. It can be read as a complete book or by sub-period for those with more specialized interests. Moreover, it is of considerable value to both the immigration/demographic specialist and the interested lay reader.

BARRY R. CHISWICK
George Washington University

Note

1. See John S. Billings, *Vital Statistics of the Jews in the United States* (Washington, D.C.: 1890). See also Barry R. Chiswick, "The Billings Report and the Occupational Attainment of American Jewry, 1890," *Shofar: An Interdisciplinary Journal of Jewish Studies* 19, no. 2 (Winter 2001), 53–75, reprinted as ch. 3 in idem (ed.), *Jews at Work: Their Economic Progress in the American Labor Market* (Cham: 2020), 33–50.

Anne C. Schenderlein, *Germany on Their Minds: German Jewish Refugees in the United States and Their Relationships with Germany, 1938–1988*. New York: Berghahn, 2020. 245 pp.

Following the rise of National Socialism, the annexation of Austria and Czechoslovakia, and the outbreak of the Second World War, some 90,000 Jewish refugees from the Third Reich entered the United States in the 1930s and early 1940s. Anne Schenderlein's informative *Germany on Their Minds* sheds light on a major subgroup of these refugees, namely, those who held German citizenship before 1933, and who, as she convincingly shows, continued to maintain convoluted relationships with "the old homeland." Referring to five decades of German Jewish life in America, from the late 1930s to the late 1980s, Schenderlein explores the refugees' reflections on Germany and its place in their self-perceptions as Americans and as Jews. The book makes use of a remarkable variety of sources, from the writings and speeches of intellectuals, rabbis, and community leaders, to retrospective interviews with "ordinary" immigrants. It cleverly highlights the roles played by local organizations in facilitating and directing the refugees' discussions about their relationships with

Germany and America. In underscoring the distinctive experiences of refugees of different generations and in different locations—particularly, in Los Angeles as opposed to New York—Schenderlein's study offers a nuanced and, at times, revealing account of the refugees' "Americanization."

Germany on Their Minds argues that the refugees' lasting attachment to Germany went beyond nostalgic longing for the lost home. The first five chapters, covering roughly one decade, from the late 1930s to the late 1940s, show how the various perceptions of such "attachment" shaped the refugees' position in America and as "Americans." For the refugees who arrived from the Third Reich in the 1930s, Americanization, both in terms of acculturation and of naturalization, was a "practical necessity" (p. 27). While Americanization did not require the refugees to conceal or renounce their German background, they often understated it in order to ease their integration into American society. The main publications of the refugee community—the *Aufbau* in New York and the *Neue Welt* in Los Angeles—recommended playing down the German (and Jewish) background of the newcomers in order to link "their story to that of many others who have found haven in the United States" (p. 26). During the war, some German Jewish soldiers in the U.S. armed forces went so far as to "Americanize" their names so they would not be recognized as Germans. Yet, despite the urgent necessity to "Americanize," some German Jewish organizations continued to emphasize the connection of the refugees to German culture, language, and even nationality. The refugees' "clubs" maintained cultural events in German (this was presented as an act of defiance against Nazism); some referred to the German language as an anti-Nazi bridge between Jewish and non-Jewish German immigrants in America; and, in the face of American antisemitism, some organizations sought to help the refugees by presenting them as "Germans."

Throughout the 1930s, and particularly after September 1939, German Jewish organizations and their publications closely monitored the atrocities of the Nazi regime in Germany and in German-occupied territories. The outbreak of war in Europe expedited Jewish acculturation in the United States as the refugees struggled both to demonstrate loyalty to the new homeland and to criticize the seeming American reluctance to intervene. Yet articles and letters published in the New York-based magazine *Aufbau* testify that even the successfully Americanized refugees often suffered depression and anxiety as Nazi Germany strengthened its position in Europe. When the United States entered the war, many refugees once again highlighted their background as both German and Jewish. On the one hand, they hoped to utilize their knowledge as Germans to help American wartime intelligence; on the other hand, they accentuated their situation as victims of the Nazi regime to affirm their loyalty to the United States. These efforts proved fruitful by 1943, as many German Jewish refugees were recruited to the Office of Strategic Services (OSS) and to other military intelligence units.

On the home front, refugee organizations initiated donations of money and maps to support the war effort. Before 1943, however, the war seemed to undermine the Americanization endeavor. When the war began, most refugees were still in the process of naturalization and, as non-citizens with German background, were classified as "enemy aliens" and subject to distrust and restrictions. Schenderlein here makes a noteworthy point: whereas scholars of German Jews in America normally refer to this classification as a negligible nuisance without any substantial implications, they most frequently have been looking at the refugees who resided in New York. However, a closer look at the second-largest German Jewish community in America— that of Los Angeles—offers a different picture. The city's proximity to military bases and muni- tions factories, together with the presence of a large Japanese population in southern California, brought military authorities in the region to dictate curfew and other restric- tions on "enemy aliens." Schenderlein notes the ironic fact that, when the Los Angeles Jewish Community organized an anti-Nazi mass meeting in August 1942, German Jewish refugees could not participate because it took place after the 8 p.m. curfew.

While the classification as "enemy aliens" frustrated refugees' endeavor to be- long in America—"I wasn't German anymore, I wasn't American either," one ref- ugee reminisced (p. 69)—the post-1942 developments both accelerated the refugees' Americanization and led to a thorough revision of their relationships with Germany. The German Jewish soldiers who fought the Wehrmacht had already received their American citizenship. Many of them relished the reversal of power embedded in their encounters with Germans soldiers, prisoners of war, and defeated civilians. Nevertheless—and not surprisingly—in interviews conducted a few decades after the fact, they emphasized their determination to act in a humane fashion. Encountering the actual Germany of 1945—rather than the place their parents remembered from the 1930s—the soldiers' German and Jewish background was once again brought to the fore. As "Germans," they could interrogate suspected adherents of Nazism and also aid in the establishment of the occupation authorities' bureaucratic structure. As Jews, they maintained a critical position vis-à-vis the local population's reluctance to assume responsibility for the atrocities of Nazism. Many reflected on the future of Germany in their letters home. Most of them, however, were dismissed from the occupation government because they were perceived as "insufficiently impartial and objective" (p. 102).

The last two chapters of the book consider the refugees' relationships with Germany in the aftermath of the war. In the 1950s and 1960s, German Jewish mag- azines and organizations in the United States engaged in heated debate about the future of Germany and the place of refugees in it. While the refugees debated their new relationships with the "old homeland," Konrad Adenauer, the chancellor of West Germany (1949–1963), sought their help in legitimizing the American alliance with the Federal Republic of Germany. West German diplomats in the United States fol- lowed the German Jewish publications closely (Schenderlein notes that the German Jews they observed matched these diplomats' vision of the "new" German citizen better than the more nationalist, non-Jewish Germans in America). While the Jewish refugees, especially on the East Coast, were skeptical of these efforts, they continued to monitor German politics and were sensitive to the differences between individual politicians and parties. Beyond the East Coast elite, however, many more refugees now interacted with West German authorities in the course of applying for repara- tions, and this led them, despite the bureaucratic hurdles they encountered, to develop a more nuanced understanding of Germany.

The final chapter in the book offers an intriguing analysis of the most ambitious attempt to bolster the relationships between German Jewish refugees and West

Germany, namely, the municipal visitor program, which started as local initiatives in the 1960s. Schenderlein indicates that the programs took place only after German Jewish refugees had started to visit Germany privately. Now retired, the older generation of refugees had the time and the means to travel to Germany. The "normalization" of West Germany as reflected in German Jewish publications—which occasionally reported on tourist attractions without any references to the Nazi past—also contributed to the willingness to visit. Rather than being a watershed development in the history of German Jewish refugees, the popular municipal visitor program belongs to an ongoing, complex process of "normalization."

Germany on Their Minds is a thorough survey of the different approaches to Germany held by German Jewish refugees in America from the New Deal to the end of the Cold War. The book nevertheless opens with a few misleading statements. Schenderlein argues that her study examines "the lives of . . . ordinary people who have mostly been neglected by scholars" (p. 2). This statement is not accurate: first, "ordinary" German Jewish immigrants have been the subject of several studies;[1] second, many of the book's sources quote prominent intellectuals, artists, and activists (for instance, Leopold Jesner, Manfred George, and Max Nussbaum) rather than "ordinary" refugees. In addition, Schenderlein states that "[a]t the center of this book is the refugee community in Los Angeles" (p. 5). To be sure, many of her insights concerning the Los Angeles community are intriguing, yet many of the sources she quotes—and, subsequently, the experiences and views she discusses—are from East Coast publications. Despite and arguably because of the book's diversion from its initial statements, the outcome is a rich, multilayered account that includes a variety of perspectives, experiences, and reactions to Germany by a diverse community of refugees.

OFER ASHKENAZI
The Hebrew University

Note

1. See, for instance, Sibylle Quack (ed.), *Between Sorrow and Strength: Women Refugees of the Nazi Period* (Cambridge: 2002); Lori Gemeiner Bihler, *Cities of Refuge: German Jews in London and New York, 1935-1945* (New York: 2018); Rhonda F. Levine, *Class, Networks, and Identity: Replanting Jewish Lives from Nazi Germany to Rural New York* (Lanham: 2001).

Harvey Schwartz (ed.), *The Jewish Thought and Psychoanalysis Lectures*. Bicester: Phoenix Publishing House, 2020. 156 pp.

A book consisting of a lecture series often serves as a kind of tombstone for a past event, a respectable but pallid rendition of what had once been a vivid exchange between speaker and audience. This, however, is not the case with the volume under review. I read it with pleasure (except for one chapter) and felt engaged in a spirited and instructive exchange. Several factors contribute to the book's successful presentation of what transpired in the lecture series held in Philadelphia beginning in 2013. Chief among them are the introductions to each of the chapters and to the volume as a whole by Harvey Schwartz, the initiator and host of the series. These introductions skillfully combine personal experience and anecdotes with psychoanalytic illustrations that are both surprising and learned. They serve as appetizers for the material to come, which is typically scholarly and profound. They do not "introduce," anticipate, or provide the gist of the next topic; rather, each is a variation on the theme—the relationship between Jewish thought and psychoanalysis—that is about to be played.

Exploring the links between Jewish thought and psychoanalysis is a bold undertaking. Notably, it is not the relationship between *Jews* and psychoanalysis (though this is touched upon), nor between *Judaism* and psychoanalysis, which would have gone in very different trajectories. Rather, the leitmotiv of the volume is *Jewish thought*. As both Jewish thought and psychoanalysis are multilayered and inexhaustible, one must be selective and confine one's focus to aspects of both. The attractiveness of the book is enhanced by the way this has been navigated: each chapter takes up a facet of the diamond, with its author displaying a certainty that comes from knowledge and expertise.

Psychoanalysis and its relationship and relatedness to Jews and Jewish thought is dealt with by Harvey Schwartz in his general introduction. Although this connection is informally and historically undeniable, he notes, the topic itself has largely been avoided. The specter of being identified as a "Jewish science" hovered over Freud and instructed his socio-political moves (as, for instance, his anointment of Carl Jung as his would-be successor), and yet Nazi persecution and the attempt to obliterate Freud's teaching by fire only strengthened this linkage. Reflecting on how this theme reaches into the present, it may be noted that the reluctance to note openly the fact that so many psychoanalysts are Jewish may be a current politically correct attempt to avoid antisemitism, but it cannot change reality. This lecture series and publication are therefore an act of courage that puts these links out in the open and asks readers to consider them, albeit, as said, within the limited scope of specific issues.

The brief scope of this review does not allow for in-depth appraisal of each chapter, and I will thus confine myself to cursory comments and a few highlights, leaving the richness of the various presentations to be discovered by the curious reader.

Eli Zaretsky's study of *Moses and Monotheism* is nothing less than a tour de force, which can certainly also be said about this late masterpiece of Freud. Zaretsky's analysis of the place and meaning of *Geistigkeit*—an essentially untranslatable term involving both intellectuality and spirituality, which plays such an important role in Freud's analysis—is a key to unraveling the mystery of the place of Jewish thought both in the world of ideas and in actuality. Connected to the emergence and centrality of paternity, *Geistigkeit*, in Freud's conception, replaced the maternal goddesses' order. The paternal monotheistic order ushered in a profound change in civilization, in which Jews are a centerpiece, both hated and admired and usually persecuted.

Psychoanalysis is the later manifestation of this *Geistigkeit*, inheriting much of the ambivalence directed at it.

Steven Frosh explores the place of forgiveness in Judaism and psychoanalysis. His "clinical" example comes from an International Psychoanalytical Association (IPA) congress in 2007, which marked a return to Berlin. A Large Group event in the congress suffered serious administrative setbacks, which, he argues, represented the unconscious ambivalence of the planners and organizers about being in Berlin. Frosh sees psychoanalysis as a critical discipline that "raises a lens to individuals and to society that challenges them to think honestly." The difficulties enacted around the Large Group event suggest that "there remains something lacking in the psychoanalytic heritage, which is a genuine coming-to-terms with the Jewish part of that heritage." Frosh goes on to compare the kabbalistic notion of *tikun* with Melanie Klein's idea of reparation: *tikun* necessitates the repair of the shattered vessels that contained the light of creation, which can be seen as an antecedent to forgiveness.

Sander Gilman's essay on "Freud, the Jewish Body and Hysteria" is highly instructive, combining historical research with psychoanalytic discoveries in a way that sheds new light on both. Freud's assertion that hysteria was not exclusively a feminine affliction, thus challenging the prevailing notion that it was caused by the displaced uterus, played out against the backdrop of prevalent medical assumptions about Jewish males—namely, that they were characterized by bodily weakness and nervous, hysterical behavior. Gilman shows the links between this "scientific" discourse and later Nazi propaganda. In this wider historical perspective, he argues, Freud's discovery of the unconscious roots of hysteria foreshadowed the struggle against the future denigration of the Jews and set the stage for both the Holocaust and the relationship between trauma and hysteria.

Marsha Aileen Hewitt's chapter left me with unresolved questions. It builds a continuum from unconscious communication to telepathy to religious experience, and from there to what I consider the mystical strand within psychoanalysis. A brief review cannot develop the argument and do justice to the thesis, so I will mention only this: in a volume that deals with and searches for connections, both overt and hidden, between psychoanalysis and Jewish thought, this chapter is the least concerned with what may be regarded as Jewish thought. In fact, it seems somewhat Christian in its otherworldly preoccupation. The existence of states of merger and union is explainable psychoanalytically without resorting to the notion of a mystical union with the Absolute (*unio mystica*). As she herself notes, the fact that Freud referred to the "mysterious unconscious" in no way was intended to imply that it is mystical.

The last two chapters are by Israeli authors. Eran Rolnik deals with the intricate relationship between an ineffable "Jewish essence," Zionism, Freud's Jewishness, and current political developments in Israel. This relationship undergoes an involutional course, beginning as a love affair between Zionism and early psychoanalysis and declining into the present dilemmas of working psychoanalytically under conditions of dominating and ruling over conquered territories. Freud's ambivalence toward Zionism and Jewish settlement in Palestine is prophetic in the face of subsequent developments: "Palestine" he wrote, "has never produced anything but religious sacred frenzies."[1]

The final chapter is a dialogue between Ruth Calderon and Harvey Schwartz that revolves around a talmudic discussion concerning whether it is permissible to "marry" a woman for a one-night stand. This discussion is especially timely and pertinent, as it links with current issues regarding the exploitation of women by authority figures and idealized male personas. The dialogue between the two protagonists—one, a female talmudic scholar, the other a clinically practicing psychoanalyst—is fascinating. This final discussion also serves to complete the circle of looking at the ways in which Jewish thought and psychoanalysis have influenced and fertilized one another, and how some aspects of this union are viewed through the lens of current social issues.

SHMUEL ERLICH
The Hebrew University

Note

1. Letter from Sigmund Freud to Arnold Zweig, quoted in Eran Rolnik, *Freud in Zion: Psychoanalysis and the Making of Modern Jewish Identity* (London: 2012), 66.

Augusto Segre, *Stories of Jewish Life: Casale Monferrato–Rome–Jerusalem, 1876-1985*, trans. Steve Siporin. Detroit: Wayne State University Press, 2020. 252 pp.

Augusto Segre's *Stories of Jewish Life* is a remarkable autobiographical collection of brief family and personal stories of interest to historians, literature scholars, and the general public. Glimpses of life and tragi-comic figures from the small ghetto of Casale Monferrato—where Segre's father was the community rabbi—are followed by his experiences of Fascism, the Second World War, and the national Jewish Italian organizations where he worked until the late 1970s, when he immigrated to Israel. Episodes and figures from the book give the reader an insight into the challenges and inner dilemmas of generations, allowing for an original understanding of the multiple aspects and voices of Italian Jewry in tensions between integration, acculturation, and assimilation; patriotism and Zionism; and secularism and religious orthodoxy. These challenges of modernity, both positive and negative, go beyond the small world of the Casale ghetto and speak to more universal themes of Jewish modernity.

Segre was a well-known 20th-century educator, journalist, writer, and rabbi who held important institutional roles in the postwar Italian Jewish community. However, in contrast to his earlier memoir,[1] his career and formal education do not appear in this second autobiographical work. Written in the third person, the book starts forty years before Segre's birth, recounting oral stories of his family and community, populated by figures whose voices do not usually appear in history books: as in a theater piece, we meet *minianistim* (people who were paid to pray), recipients of charity, marginalized intellectuals, non-Jewish peasants whose loyalty and help saved Segre and his family during the war, and droll bureaucrats in Israeli offices. These figures appear in what Segre himself defines as a "midrash," as it "frequently offers authentic interpretations but above all because it knows how to find the direct and immediate path to the heart and can be understood by everyone, without distinction" (p. 227). This call for authenticity is one of the strengths of the stories he tells.

Segre's religious upbringing frames his nostalgic description of the lost world of the ghetto, as well as his harsh stand against assimilation and the anti-Zionist narrative of community leaders and the Jewish press. This focus on observant Jewish Italian culture is another strength of the book and a welcome rarity within the literary production of Italian Jewry, although Segre's linear association of liberals as mere assimilationists has been challenged by historiographical works on Jewish liberalism and secularism.[2] Segre's book is also a significant contribution to the growing number of Jewish Italian autobiographies of intellectuals—both male and female—that reveal the remarkable variety of 20th-century Italian Jewry, most of which are still available only in Italian.

The book is preceded by an interesting introduction by the translator, Steve Siporin, who has done a great job in his literary translation as well as in rendering nuances of the Piedmontese dialect. As noted, it is likely to find an appreciative audience among students and scholars interested in Jewish and Italian history and literature, as well as the wider public. I would recommend it as a whole or in its individual chapters as part of syllabi in modern Jewish European and Italian history.

LUISA LEVI D'ANCONA MODENA
European Forum at the Hebrew University

Notes

1. Augusto Segre, *Memories of Jewish Life: Casale Monferrato–Rome–Jerusalem, 1918–1960*, trans. Steve Siporin (Lincoln: 2008).

2. See, for instance, Abigail Green and Simon Levis Sullam (eds.), *Jews, Liberalism, Antisemitism: A Global History* (London: 2020); Ari Joskowicz and Ethan B. Katz (eds.), *Secularism in Question: Jews and Judaism in Modern Times* (Philadelphia: 2015).

Nancy Sinkoff, *From Left to Right: Lucy S. Dawidowicz, the New York Intellectuals and the Politics of Jewish History*. Detroit: Wayne State University Press, 2020. xix + 518 pp.

In Nancy Sinkoff's masterful biography of Lucy Schildkret Dawidowicz, we encounter a scholar and public intellectual who strode purposefully within 20th-century Jewish communal life and thought. Sinkoff takes us along on these journeys through a lively narrative that explores and celebrates the vitality of the last century's Yiddish intelligentsia both in Poland and later in the United States. She also comprehensively shows how her protagonist's visions influenced renowned American Jewish men and women of letters to reconsider their ancestral ties. Most critically, she demonstrates how Dawidowicz's work on the history of the Holocaust caused these thinkers, as well as readers of all backgrounds, to rethink the origins of the European destruction during the Second World War.

With Sinkoff as our guide, we learn of the young Schildkret's commitment to Yiddish culture, a devotion that was "so very different from that of many other East European Jewish immigrant children" (p. 24). The author takes us into the world of Yiddish schools, camps, and youth organizations in interwar New York, where Schildkret was initially inculcated with a love for her East European heritage. We get to travel with Schildkret to Vilna where, in 1939, the aspiring modern Yiddishist scholar met up with some of the greatest minds of prewar Poland who headed the Yiddish Scientific Institute known as YIVO. Although Max Weinreich was her most important mentor in Vilna, the thought and writings of historian Simon Dubnov had the most enduring influence upon her work; the latter deepened her commitment, through the critical study of their past, to the continuity of Jews' lives and identity wherever they resided. Blessed with an American passport, Schildkret got out of Eastern Europe just before the Nazi invasion that led to the murder of so many of the YIVO luminaries, including Dubnov, who perished in the Riga ghetto. Back on the friendly soil of the United States, she was on the scene after the war as the YIVO reconstituted itself in New York. There, at YIVO, she benefited from associations with survivor scholars, especially Weinreich.

The chapters focusing on Dawidowicz (she took her husband's surname when they were wed in 1947) and her teachers explain the deep origins of the sensibilities that informed her subsequent life experiences as a public intellectual and scholar of the Holocaust. As the book's title and subtitle suggest, she became part of a group of thinkers known as the "New York Intellectuals." From the moment these provocative thinkers appeared in the 1930s, they debated the future of the world in universalistic terms. Though all of them were born Jewish, and some had some facility with Jewish languages and culture, they evinced a studied alienation from any connection to a positive ancestral identity. Later on in their careers, as they moved "Left to Right" in their intellectual orientations and adopted entirely new visions of society, they still maintained a wide distance from questions of Jewish survival. Dawidowicz was the outspoken, unrepentant outlier within and apart from the group, determined as she was to project Judaism's particularism.

Indeed, due to her influence, Dawidowicz's colleagues began to seek "a balance between their commitments to universalist and particularistic values" (p. 190). This personal and scholarly agenda was manifest not only to the New York intellectuals who granted her a seat at their "table," but also to a wide reading audience, beginning with the publication of *The Golden Tradition,* a work that became a classic. Published in 1967, this volume of primary sources drawn from a wide trove of East European Jewish cultural contributions "cast Dawidowicz as the 'authentic' historical voice of murdered European Jewry and a sought after lecturer in both academic and public venues" (p. 153).

With the publication in 1975 of her magnum opus, *The War against the Jews,* Dawidowicz gave full voice to her being more than a "representative" of Polish Jewry—to use Sinkoff's term. In the role of "defender" of her doomed brethren, she argued the particularity of the Holocaust against those who depicted the destruction in universal terms. She also emphasized, through extensive documentation, how Jews "responded as best they were able to the virulent antisemitism that aimed at their complete extermination" (p. 173). Dawidowicz significantly became one of the first to promote an "intentionalist" understanding of the Final Solution. Other historians (the "functionalists") argued that the Holocaust was an evolving process that had much to do with competing voices within the Reich as the regime engaged in its titanic battle with the Soviet Union. For Dawidowicz, however, a direct line could be drawn from the antisemitism in Hitler's *Mein Kampf* to the death camps of Poland; there was no "twisted road to Auschwitz." Dawidowicz had much less to say about a third dynamic of the European Jewish destruction: the passivity of the world in standing by while six million were murdered. Only five years after *The War against the Jews* appeared did she criticize the U.S. government's failure to take action at the time of the war.

With Sinkoff providing the very useful historiographical contexts, we are given a front row seat as Dawidowicz engages in vital intellectual combat with Raul Hilberg, Hannah Arendt, and others who had written about the universality of Nazi atrocities, the banality of those within the Reich who perpetrated the Holocaust, and the fatalistic reaction on the part of Jews to what was happening to them. In making her points, Dawidowicz would always emphasize that her opponents erred in relying on non-Jewish sources. She, for her part, invoked the wealth of Jewish sources to which her training gave access.

In her tireless, unstinting battle against the "functionalists," Dawidowicz "played a central role in the creation of Holocaust consciousness." Such advocacy constituted a fitting reconnection to the exposition of the vibrancy of Polish Jewish life—one that was "initiated by Dubnov and fostered by the community of scholars associated with the YIVO" (p. 168). All told, Sinkoff's work constitutes a major contribution to 20th-century Jewish intellectual history both of the lamented East European community and of the provocative thinkers who have interpreted life in the United States.

JEFFREY S. GUROCK
Yeshiva University

Stephen J. Whitfield, *Learning on the Left: Political Profiles of Brandeis University*. Waltham: Brandeis University Press, 2020. 581 pp.

Stephen Whitfield has spent a lifetime, first as a graduate student and then, for more than forty years, as a professor of American studies, at Brandeis University. He unquestionably writes this book as the consummate "insider" whose familiarity has been honed by five decades spent on the campus. At the same time, his knowledge and understanding of American history, literature, politics, philosophy, and culture—as a lifetime of scholarly output attests—is plainly vast. Whitfield is the ideal person to write this book.

In this learned and engaging volume, Whitfield combines encyclopedic erudition, keen analytical skills, and clarity of prose to present a dynamic and crucial history of the contributions to American politics made by persons affiliated with Brandeis since the founding of the university in 1948. As chronicled by Whitfield, the sheer volume and importance of the political thinkers and figures associated with Brandeis is nothing less than astonishing. Indeed, this book is more than a history of one university and its outsized influence on politics and political theory in America. *Learning on the Left* is an indispensable political history of the Left and other sectors of American politics—in thought and in deeds—over the past 75 years.

At a moment when moderate-liberal and progressive wings of the Democratic Party in the United States are vying with one another for political dominance, Whitfield's portraits of the Brandeis faculty and alumni are particularly instructive. His work illustrates the multivocality of the Left and demonstrates that the disagreements that have divided the more moderate from the more progressive elements of the Left have been present for decades. *Learning on the Left* traces and illustrates the directions and evolution of these elements over time.

Whitfield opens his book by pointing out that Brandeis was created in a crucible of post-Second World War liberal optimism. America, it was believed, was capable of creating a true meritocracy in which persons would be judged as individuals and where atavistic barriers of racial discrimination and economic injustice would increasingly be removed. Moreover, by the time Brandeis opened in 1948, the prevalent social and cultural antisemitism of pre-1940s America was beginning to lessen, and elite institutions of American higher education were beginning to open themselves up to Jews. It is against this background that Whitfield details the events that fortuitously led Brandeis to select Abram Leon Sachar as its founding president. It was his leadership and foresight that transformed Brandeis almost immediately, and seemingly against all odds, into a virtually unprecedented success story in the history of American higher education. Sachar advocated a liberal ethos that espoused *Emet* (truth) as the highest value of the university and allowed for an unbridled commitment to the virtues of tolerance, openness, and intellectual exploration even during the repressive atmosphere of the time, as evidenced in the activity of the House Un-American Activities Committee (HUAC) and Senator Joseph McCarthy.

It was upon this foundation of classical liberalism that Brandeis was constructed, and this groundwork quickly led the university to a premiere position in the world of political thought and action—most often liberal in nature, but occasionally conservative and at times even extremist. Brandeis students, graduates, and faculty were center-Left or progressive Democrats, Communists or Weathermen. At least one, Aafia Siddiqui, was a jihadist fanatic. Many were champions of civil rights for women and racial minorities; not a few raised their voices in opposition to governmental torture at Guantanamo or in defense of constitutional rights for all Americans, writing their views in periodicals as varied as *Dissent*, *The New Republic*, and *The National Review*. Whitfield discusses and illuminates them all.

Indeed, a veritable "Who's Who" of American political thought and deed has been associated with Brandeis. The names are too many to list. However, just consider that Whitfield provides portraits of persons on all sides of the political spectrum— C. Wright Mills, Phillip Rieff, Frank Manuel, Felix Browder, Ray Ginger, Eleanor

Roosevelt, Walter Laqueur, Abbie Hoffman, Irving Howe, Herbert Marcuse, Phillip Rahv, Evelyn Fox Keller, Stephen Solarz, Pauli Murray, Angela Davis, Anita Hill, Max Lerner, Lawrence Fuchs, Michael Walzer, Michael Sandel, Susan Miller Orkin, Naomi Jaffe, Katherine Power, Susan Saxe, Michael Ratner, John Roche, Marty Peretz, and Sidney Blumenthal, among many others in this book.

In discussing each of these figures, Whitfield displays an absolute genius in summarizing clearly and correctly the often complex political and social thought of each of these persons in terms that are accessible to specialist and non-specialist alike. As I read his work, I was reminded of the late Harvard anthropologist Stephen Jay Gould, who, in works such as *The Mismeasure of Man*, displayed the rare ability to explain dense scientific theory in straightforward language. Whitfield, like Gould, offers clear summaries, in this case, of the political thoughts and deeds of each person and their critics, whom he presents by successfully contextualizing each actor and thinker within the broader framework of their decade. Finally, Whitfield, again like Gould, is a riveting raconteur who employs countless anecdotes to entertain the reader and capture the spirit and background of a particular moment or person in Brandeis history. For example, I loved learning that the chauffeur for the Marcuse family in Berlin was later the driver for Goebbels after the Marcuse family was forced by the Nazis to leave the German capital, and that the interview of Irving Howe for a position in the English department began awkwardly—until the interview moved on into Yiddish! However, my favorite anecdote involved Abbie Hoffman, whose "favorite piece of hate mail," Whitfield reports, stated: "Dear Abbie—Wait till Jesus gets his hands on you—you little bastard—Anonymous." These stories and his crisp explications of actions and theories capture the humanity as well as the intellectual vitality and effervescence of the Waltham campus.

In *Learning on the Left*, Whitfield points to a Brandeis that was designed to create a society that would be tolerant and diverse, respectful of individuals and free speech, allowing for the protection of their rights and the flourishing of their talents. Its ethos embodied a liberal optimism about the world, the American nation, and human potential. However, Whitfield also confronts the fact that these liberal dreams failed to materialize as anticipated. African-Americans, other persons of color, and women simply did not succeed quite as well as had been hoped. Indeed, Whitfield describes in significant detail the confrontations and conflicts that arose on the Brandeis campus in the early 1970s between Sachar's administration and many members of the faculty who championed a liberal ethos that assigned priority to the individual, along with African-American students who issued numerous demands for minority empowerment. His candid account shows how the liberalism of Sachar and others did not anticipate the failure of minorities to realize equality of results once the barriers of discrimination were legally lifted.

Whitfield indicates that, in our day, forces on the Left are increasingly mobilized on behalf of restorative justice aimed at eliminating "privilege." The ethos of liberal individualism, it seems, is slowly but inexorably being discarded by the Left, with preference now being granted to distributive policies that achieve racial justice and gender equity for less fortunate groups in American society. Whitfield seems wistful about elements of these directions as he recounts these contemporary trends. However, his analysis of this trajectory in liberal-progressive circles over the last decades allows

Learning on the Left to be much more than a narrative about Brandeis alone. Rather, this excellent volume reaches far beyond Waltham, providing genuine insight into the overarching political trajectory of the United States during our day.

DAVID ELLENSON
Hebrew Union College–Jerusalem Institute of Religion
Brandeis University

Steven J. Zipperstein, *Pogrom: Kishinev and the Tilt of History*. New York: Liveright Publishing Corporation, 2018. xx + 261 pp.

In this volume, Steven J. Zipperstein explores one of the most notorious episodes in the long history of anti-Jewish violence, one that was perceived as a turning point in Jewish and East European history right from the moment news regarding the violence in Kishinev was disseminated across the world. In the weeks and months that followed the pogrom of April 1903, a swell of urgent letters and petitions from Jewish individuals and communities were dispatched to local police and officials in the Polish lands, expressing fear, if not panic, about the possibility of similar occurrences in towns and cities hundreds of kilometers away from Bessarabia. These letters were written in an entirely different tone than those of previous years. From the time of the wave of pogroms in the Russian empire in the 1880s, Jewish communities had understood that there was always going to be the possibility of a "riot." But Kishinev was a massacre, immediately understood as a fundamental shift in the broader framework of Jewish–non-Jewish relations.[1]

This is why the pogrom has been well covered in scholarship, most notably by Edward H. Judge in his 1992 monograph about the Kishinev pogrom. Zipperstein frequently cites this pioneering study and does not challenge its core findings. In summarizing the factors contributing to the pogrom, Judge pointed, first and foremost, to pervasive prejudice and hostility toward Jews. Second, there was the specific social dynamic in Kishinev, whose very rapid demographic development left little time for Moldavians, Russians, and Jews to encounter and come to know each other. Judge also emphasized the antisemitic incitement by Pavel Krushevan, editor of the local daily, the infamous *Bessarabets*; in addition, as if anticipating the growing attention of later theoreticians of interethnic violence, he noted the significance of chronology in the violent pogrom dynamic as it played out on Easter Sunday and the following day.[2] Another important source that, somewhat surprisingly, goes unmentioned by Zipperstein is the volume published in 2000 by the Institute for Interethnic Studies at the Moldovian Academy of Sciences—more than 500 pages of mostly Russian-language documents of very varied provenance, including reports by local administrators as well as central authorities, broadsheets inciting to anti-Jewish violence, petitions and letters of the local Jewish community, and interventions by political parties in Russian and abroad, including a pamphlet by the Bund.[3]

The obvious question arises as to whether the awful events in Kishinev deserved a new account, and whether Zipperstein's volume provides relevant new insights. For this reviewer, the answer is in the affirmative. *Pogrom* offers new and relevant source material; contributes significantly to a better understanding of the social and political context; and explains why the pogrom proved to be a pivotal moment in the broader framework of Jewish history in Russia and abroad, leading to ever more brutal and lethal instances of anti-Jewish violence. The structure of the volume is clear and helpful, opening with a reflection on the way that Kishinev informed what Jews think about when they hear or say "pogrom." Zipperstein argues that the word evokes serious references to a difficult past, but functions as well as a literary topos, or to illustrate a sarcastic take on everyday challenges. The next chapter takes the reader quite literally on a walk through the present-day Kishinev, now known as Chişinău. The author brings the place to life, showing, with the aid of maps and historical and contemporary photographs, that Kishinev/ Chişinău is a real place where real people lived—and where one day at the beginning of the 20th century, a real mob killed more than four dozen Jews in horrific ways, raping women, randomly destroying Jewish homes and shops, robbing and pillaging.

In the third chapter, Zipperstein details the cruelty of the perpetrators, the randomness of their attacks, the active participation of adolescents and even children, and the horrific dimension of sexual violence, in itself a departure from the violent events leading to the coining of the term "pogrom" in the late 19th century.[4] Included in this chapter is a necessary discussion of the alleged dispatch sent by Minister of the Interior Vyacheslav von Plehve to local government officials, instructing them not to intervene; publication of this document, which scholars today believe to be a forgery, was particularly damaging to tsarist Russia's international reputation. A lesser-known story features Georgi Pronin, both a local businessman of dubious reputation and Krushevan's partner in the anti-Jewish incitement. Zipperstein portrays Pronin as a crucially important networker in fomenting antisemitic hatred. In documenting this man's claim to bourgeois prominence—among the most striking pieces of evidence is a photograph showing Pronin's impressive villa—Zipperstein helps us to understand better those whom Paul Brass has so convincingly described as "pogrom specialists" who "institutionalised riot systems."[5] A more detailed examination of this topic might have further illuminated the "tilt of history" that Zipperstein encapsulates, on the one hand, in the disillusionment of Jews in Russia and abroad with the tsarist regime, and, on the other, in the transition from widespread but self-limiting interethnic violence to extreme lethal force culminating in mass killings.[6] For this reviewer, Pronin's villa seems a fitting, counterintuitive illustration of this specific tilt.

In the following chapter, Zipperstein contrasts the two most important chroniclers of the events, Michael Davitt and Hayim Nahman Bialik. It takes a seasoned author such as Zipperstein to build the *vitae parallelae* of these two authors—the former, a journalist with the ambition to inform as broadly and precisely as possible, while also respecting the dignity of those who had suffered horrific and dehumanizing violence; the latter a highly gifted emerging poet and author who would make the shamefulness of unheroic survival his central theme in "In the City of Slaughter." Bialik's poem is magisterially presented and analyzed, with Zipperstein showing its lasting impact on Hebrew (and more specifically, Israeli and Zionist) culture.

Pavel Krushevan is the subject of the book's penultimate chapter. Integrating the most relevant recent and exhaustive scholarship regarding the infamous *Protocols of Zion*, Zipperstein further corroborates the argument that Krushevan, who published the antisemitic screed in his other newspaper, the St. Petersburg weekly *Znamia*, was also one of its co-authors. Zipperstein quotes the recently discovered diary of the young Krushevan, which among other things reveals the presence of Jews in his immediate family context, including the marriage of his widowed father with a Jewish woman. Perhaps more so than in other European regions, deep-seated resentment and hatred toward Jews could go hand-in-hand with social proximity to Jews. The final chapter of *Pogrom* introduces another fascinating perspective in its account of how events at Kishinev were perceived among liberal Jewish and non-Jewish Americans, leading them to a growing awareness that anti-African American violence, vigilantism, and lynchings were not only comparable to anti-Jewish violence, but substantially identical. Zipperstein here presents the insights of William Walling and Anna Strunsky, experts on contemporary Russia and vehement critics of tsarist authoritarianism, who became co-founders of the National Association for the Advancement of Colored People (NAACP).

In summary, the author offers a rich array of hitherto unused materials that he analyzes with precision and passion, exploring a seemingly familiar place where Jewish and non-Jewish European history indeed entered a new, darker period.

FRANÇOIS GUESNET
University College London

Notes

1. Werner Bergmann explicitly excludes the pogrom of Kishinev from his investigation of anti-Jewish violence in 19th century Europe because of the new quality of interethnic violence; see *Tumulte-Excesse-Pogrome. Kollektive Gewalt gegen Juden in Europa, 1789-1900* (Göttingen: 2020), 16.

2. Edward Judge, *Easter in Kishinev: Anatomy of a Pogrom* (New York: 1992).

3. Yakov Mikhailovich Kopanskii et al. (eds.), *Kishinevskii pogrom 1903 goda: Sbornik dokumentov i materialov* (Chișinău: 2000).

4. On this, see John D. Klier, *Russians, Jews and the Pogroms of 1881–1882* (Cambridge: 2010), 46–47, 236–237. Cf. Steven Zipperstein's contribution to *Pogroms: A Documentary History*, ed. Eugene M. Avrutin and Elissa Bemporad (New York: 2021), ch. 3.

5. Paul Brass, "Introduction: Discourses of Ethnicity, Communalism, and Violence," in *Riots and Pogroms*, ed. Paul Brass (London: 1996), 1–55.

6. For two fine studies on interethnic violence, see Darius Staliunas, *Enemies for a Day: Antisemitism and Anti-Jewish Violence in Lithuania under the Tsars* (Budapest: 2015); Tim Buchen, *Antisemitism in Galicia: Agitation, Politics, and Violence against Jews in the Late Habsburg Monarchy* (New York: 2020 [German edition, Berlin: 2012)].

Zionism, Israel, and the Middle East

Yonatan Mendel, *Safah miḥutz limkomah: orientalizm, modi'in veha'aravit beyis-rael* (Language out of Place: Orientalism, Intelligence and Arabic in Israel). Tel Aviv: The Van Leer Institute and Hakibbutz Hameuchad, 2020. 282 pp.

Yuval Evri, *Hashivah leAndalus: maḥlokot 'al tarbut vezehut yehudit-sefaradit bein 'araviyut le'ivriyut* (The Return to Al-Andalus: Disputes over Sephardic Culture and Identity between Arabic and Hebrew). Jerusalem: Magnes Press, 2020. 357 pp.

Is Israel a Middle Eastern state? Geographically it is located in the region but culturally it is not, argues Yonatan Mendel. Very few Israeli Jews, including the second and third generations of immigrants from Arab countries, speak, read, or write in Arabic. Under the British Mandate and in Israeli Basic Law up until July 2018, both Hebrew and Arabic enjoyed the status of official languages. However, in 2018, the Knesset enacted a new Basic Law that downgraded Arabic to having a "special status," with Hebrew remaining the sole official state language. This well-written book, a revised edition of the author's volume in English,[1] deals with the history and politics of Arabic studies in Jewish Israeli mainstream schools. Ultraorthodox schools do not teach Arabic, and in most national-religious schools it is either not taught or else is offered as an elective subject. Both systems are therefore not included in Mendel's discussion.

As Mendel shows, methods introduced by Hebrew University professors back in the 1920s and 1930s continue to shape the teaching of Arabic in Israeli schools and universities. Almost all of these professors had been trained in the Oriental studies departments of German universities, where the emphasis was exclusively on the phil-ological, grammatical, and syntactical analysis of texts. Colloquial language, with its many regional and status dialects, was considered too "popular" (that is, non-scholastic) to be included in the faculties of liberal arts.

Whereas other scholars have focused on the study of Arabic in Israeli universities,[2] Mendel is mostly interested in high school education. Based in the main on archival documents from the mid-1930s up to the mid-1980s, his book is organized chrono-logically. The first chapter deals with the pre-statehood period, the second from 1948 to the Six-Day War of 1967, and the third on the combined impact of the Six-Day War and the Yom Kippur War of 1973. Chapter 4 centers on the decade from 1976–1986. From there, Mendel moves to a discussion of two prestigious informal educa-tional institutions aimed at promoting peaceful coexistence between Jews and Arabs in Israel, Giv'at Havivah and Ulpan Akiva. The last chapter, based on interviews and newspaper articles, deals with Arabic teaching in the 21st century.

Book Reviews In: *Becoming Post-Communist.* Edited by: Eli Lederhendler, Oxford University Press. © Oxford University Press 2023. DOI: 10.1093/oso/9780197687215.003.0037

Up to 1948, Palestinian Jews spoke Arabic in their everyday life encounters with their neighbors' hegemonic culture. Two developments dramatically changed this situation. The first was the philological methods of teaching Arabic that took hold in Jewish educational institutions; the second was the Zionist/Israeli–Arab conflict. Both led to what Mendel defines as the "Latinization" of Arabic; that is, relating to Arabic as a textual language that students translate.

Mendel exposes and critiques the symbiotic relationship between Arabic studies and the security establishment. The opportunity for future service in military intelligence is a prime factor motivating young Israelis to study Arabic, and the Ministry of Education and school principals willingly accept army funds covering not only the cost of Arabic classes but also extracurricular activities. At the ministerial level, military intelligence officers take part in planning how to increase the number of Jewish high school students learning Arabic. In consequence, the intelligence corps of the Israeli army has a major role in determining how Arabic is taught; this, according to Mendel, contributes to the militarization of Israeli society in general and high school students' education in particular. For the vast majority of Israeli Jews, the army–school symbiosis is natural and necessary, considering Israel's conflict with most of its neighboring countries. The boundaries between civilian and military spheres are thin and easily crossed.

In the pre-statehood era, as noted, the situation was different. With Arabs constituting a majority of the population, Arabic was the lingua franca, according to Mendel. It was spoken as well by urban Ashkenazic Jews, with no particular security importance. But as the conflict between Zionism and the Palestinian national movement (already manifest in the 1936–1939 Arab Revolt) escalated from 1945 onward, Arabic became the "language of the enemy." It was increasingly taught in order to spy, control, and occupy rather than as an expression of communication, an aspect of a rich culture, and as a potentially integrative tool. Ashkenazic Jews who were leaders of both the Zionist movement and the state of Israel adopted an Orientalist view on Arab language and culture that distanced the young state from encounters with Arab native culture, art, and intellectual life. In addition, whereas the younger members of the first generation of Jewish immigrants from Arab countries preserved their original language and culture and thus could serve in Israeli intelligence units, the second and third generations acceded to hegemonic social pressure, abandoning their Arab cultural origins in order to integrate into the Hebrew national culture. Growing intelligence needs after 1967 and 1973 wars were what led the army to collaborate with the Ministry of Education to establish a multi-layered network to expand the study of Arabic.

The education system–intelligence network largely excludes Israeli Arabs, who are perceived as a security risk. According to Mendel, only a marginal number of Israeli Palestinians teach Arabic in Jewish schools, and they are not allowed to accompany their students to meetings with army officers on issues pertaining to their Arabic education, or to participate in joint social gatherings. What this means is that the vast majority of teachers do not speak Arabic at home, nor do they regularly consume Arab culture and media or write in Arabic. Consequently, a new type of Arabic has developed: "Israeli Arabic," as Mendel calls it, which stands as a barrier between Jews and Arabs. If Mendel had instead used the term "Israeli-Jewish Arabic" he would have been more accurate and in line with his own argument on behalf of Jewish–Arab integration and mutual respect.

There are a few other problems in the book. Though Mendel's writing is fluent and his book is well-documented, he frequently hammers at his main argument. He over-emphasizes his thesis to the extent that readers are apt to conclude that he is mainly interested in campaigning against dominant Israeli educational institutions and their methods of teaching Arabic. He argues, for instance, that both Giv'at Havivah and Ulpan Akiva collaborated with the army intelligence corps in a manner similar to that of the Ministry of Education. However, he does not provide data on the extent of such collaboration in each of these institutions' activity. Moreover, Mendel himself notes that, in 2001, UNESCO awarded Giv'at Havivah its Peace Education Prize; several years earlier, in 1992 and 1993, a group of EU members of parliament and U.S. Congressional representatives, respectively, nominated the founder of Ulpan Akiva for the Nobel Peace Prize (pp. 201–201). Mendel does not speculate as to their motives for doing so, or whether they had any knowledge concerning alleged collaboration.

Finally, the book is somewhat short on nuance. It fails to take account of certain possibilities—for instance, that some of those who serve in army intelligence and then go on to study Arabic in a university program might come to respect the richness of Arab culture or learn colloquial Arabic, or that certain texts can serve to build bridges between people rather than hierarchically dividing between "us" and "them."

Whereas Mendel deals with teaching Arabic and social history, Evri is interested in Arabic as identity expression and intellectual history. Based on several of Evri's articles published in English, *Hashivah leAndalus* covers a time frame extending from the end of the 19th century to the 1930s as it probes several case studies pertaining to Sephardic enlightenment and Sephardic identity in the context of the Ottoman and British empires.[3] Evri takes the 21st-century new historians to a different direction, demonstrating that Jewish enlightenment was not limited to Western Europe, and that its Sephardic wing had reached different conclusions regarding native Palestinian Jews and Arabs than those adopted by the Ashkenazic-European Zionist modernization project.[4] As opposed to the colonial–Orientalist approach of European Zionists that perceived Palestine's inhabitants as passive and conservative, he argues, members of the Sephardic enlightenment felt a kinship with the Arab renaissance (*al-Nahdah*) and raised their voices in favor of their approach to Jewish–Arab medieval collaboration in West European learning centers such as Madrid, Frankfurt, and Heidelberg. In contrast to the current scholarly consensus, Evri convincingly argues that Sephardic intellectuals were agents, not mere victims, of Western colonialism. This said, his definition of "Sephardic" is fluid and less convincing. He writes that it is a "mobile category" with "multi-representations" (p. 6), and his discourse moves freely from "Sephardic" as the identity of a European geographical unit to Jewish–Spanish medieval culture, to an Israeli identity based on Oriental origins, and to the category of "Arab-Jews." Is this "mobile category" a unique Sephardic phenomenon or it is applicable as well to Ashkenazic Jews? Aren't all identities multi-representational? The author does not relate to this matter.

Following an introductory first chapter, Chapters 2 and 3 deal with the late Ottoman period and Chapter 4 with the early British Mandate. The second chapter—twice as long as any of the others—focuses on two individuals, Shaul Abdallah Yosef

(1849–1906), an autodidact merchant from Baghdad who settled in Southeast Asia, and Dr. Avraham Shalom Yehuda (1877–1951). Both of them fundamentally disagreed with Ashkenazic Jewish scholars who, regarding themselves as cultural heirs to the Sephardim of the Golden Age, analyzed Hebrew Andalusian poetry and literature according to Western Orientalist philological methods. Yosef and Yehuda each argued that the Golden Age of Hebrew Sephardic heritage should be seen in the context of the medieval Arab culture to which Jews of the region belonged, and about which German and Russian scholars were ignorant. The latter contended that Jewish cultural creativity was frozen in the period between medieval Andalusia and the 18th-century Enlightenment. According to Yosef and Yehuda, there was no break in Sephardic integration in Arab, or the dominant Muslim, culture.

The Sephardic intellectuals favored Jewish renaissance through integration in the Orient. They heavily criticized the Zionist policy of isolation from, and superiority over, native Palestinians. This was an intra-Jewish multidimensional conflict revolving around status, waged between Ashkenazic newcomers and Sephardic natives—but entailing, as well, a conflict over Palestinian Hebrew identity and its orientation toward its environment, in which an integrative stream that saw Arabs as potential partners squared off against a separatist, pro-Western approach that viewed Arabs as bitter enemies. The Sephardic approach failed, Evri argues, mainly because of the Ottoman defeat in the First World War. The Sephardim in Palestine, who had once enjoyed an official status as the representative Jewish community (vis-à-vis the Ottoman authorities), lost ground to the majority Ashkenazic communities in Palestine and, more crucially, to the Zionist leadership abroad that tied itself to Britain. Notwithstanding, Sephardic intellectuals opted to remain loyal Zionists rather than cooperating with Palestinian Arab partners against the separatist Zionist approach. They translated (from Arabic) and published about five hundred critical newspaper articles warning that Zionist methods would lead to negative consequences, which were ignored by the Zionist leadership. Frustrated, they accepted the role that the more recently arrived Zionist leaders allocated to them: namely, mediating between the new elite and Arab natives as propagandists and intelligence agents. Had Sephardic leaders accepted the Palestinian Arab leaders' offer to cooperate (p. 207–208) the two peoples' history might have been less bloody.

Evri's analysis is innovative but also repetitive, and he fails to integrate previous scholarly studies into his text, as opposed to citing them in footnotes. He also ignores the fact that many Zionist settlers spoke Arabic even if they did not read or write it, and they also imitated popular Bedouin and *falah* (rural) customs, though not those of the urban elite (*efendiyah*), the national movement's powerbase. In other words, as was the case with other settler-colonial societies, the dichotomy was less sharp than Evri's Sephardic primary sources describe.

Finally, according to Evri, the logic of partitioning Palestine between Jews and Arabs guided British policy from the establishment of the Mandate in 1922. In fact, the League of Nations Mandate states that Great Britain is responsible "to put into effect" the Balfour Declaration on establishing a national home for the Jewish people in Palestine—that is, a single state. Only the 1936 Arab revolt brought the Peel commission of 1937 to suggest the partition plan that the British cabinet endorsed. In the late Ottoman period, Evri concludes, people had mixed, if not competing, identities made up of Ottomanism, Arabism, religion, and local patriotism. However, following Sephardic primary sources and new historical studies, Evri rightly gives primacy to local patriotism, frequently referring to Palestinian Jews as "sons of the land" (*benei haaretz*).

Hashivah leAndalus is relevant to current-day Israel. Evri shows that the conflict between Mizrahi and Ashkenazic Jews that continues to divide Israeli society did not start in the 1950s with the hegemonic Ashkenazic establishment's discrimination against, and marginalization of, immigrants from Middle East countries. Decades before, in the early 20th century, the Ashkenazic elite already perceived Sephardim as a problem. In the eyes of the elite, the Sephardim would have to change; they were obliged to integrate into the dominant culture that the Ashkenazic newcomers created in order to be considered true sabras.

MENACHEM KLEIN
Bar-Ilan University

Notes

1. Yonatan Mendel, *The Creation of Israeli Arabic: Political and Security Considerations in the Making of Arabic Language Studies in Israel* (London: 2014).

2. Menahem Milson, "Reshit limudei ha'aravit vehaislam bauniversitah ha'ivrit," in *Toledot hauniversitah ha'ivrit birushalayim: shorashim vehathalot*, ed. Shaul Katz and Michael Heyd (Jerusalem: 1997), 575–588; Amit Levi, "A Man of Contention: Martin Plessner (1900–1973) and His Encounters with the Orient," *Naharaim* 10, no.1 (2016), 79–100; Eyal Clyne, *Orentalism, Zionism and Academic Practice: Middle East and Islam Studies in Israeli Universities* (London: 2019); Gil Eyal, *The Disenchantment of the Orient: Expertise in Arab Affairs and the Israeli State* (Stanford: 2006).

3. Yuval Evri, "Return to al-Andalus beyond German-Jewish Orientalism: Abraham Shalom Yehuda's Critique of Modern Jewish Discourse," in *Modern Jewish Scholarship on Islam in Context: Rationality, European Borders, and the Search for Belonging*, ed. Ottfried Fraisse (Berlin: 2018), 339–354; idem, *Translating the Arab-Jewish Tradition: From al-Andalus to Palestine / Land of Israel* (Berlin: 2016); idem and Almog Behar, "Between East and West: Controversies over the Modernization of the Hebrew Culture in the Works of Abdallah Yosef and Ariel Bension," *Journal of Modern Jewish Studies* 16, no. 2 (2017), 295–311.

4. Menachem Klein, "The 21st Century New Critical Historians," *Israel Studies Review* 32, no. 2 (Autumn 2017), 146–163.

Tal Elmaliach, *Hakibbutz Ha'artzi, Mapam, and the Demise of the Israeli Labor Movement*, trans. Haim Watzman. Syracuse: Syracuse University Press, 2020. 299 pp.

Tal Elmaliach's *Hakibbutz Ha'artzi, Mapam, and the Demise of the Israeli Labor* deals with the roots of the collapse of the Israeli Labor movement in a defined period—from 1956 to 1977. The first of two significant events taking place in 1956 was the "secret speech" of Soviet leader Nikita Khrushchev to a closed session of the 20th Congress of the Communist Party of the Soviet Union, in which he denounced acts of terror carried out by the Stalinist regime. The speech, which very soon was leaked to the West, led to a split in the Israeli Left between those who continued to adhere to a radical Moscow-oriented party line and those who hewed to a Western-style democratic socialism. The second event was the Sinai War, in which Israel collaborated with Britain and France, the main imperialist European powers at the time—an act regarded by many in the socialist Zionist Left as a betrayal of its principles. Two decades later, Israel underwent a political upheaval in the 1977 Knesset elections, when the right-wing Likud Party headed by Menachem Begin took power. As Elmaliach explains, this event marked the end of 44 years of Labor dominance, which he dates back to the Mapai (Labor) victory in the elections to the pre-state 18th Zionist Congress of 1933.

Elmaliach's goal is to show the dynamic of the Labor movement's collapse via the internal history of Mapam (United Workers Party), a left-Zionist party, and its affiliated kibbutz movement, Hakibbutz Haartzi. Established in 1927, Hakibbutz Haartzi comprised 60 kibbutzim in 1955, with a total population of 25,000 members. One of three large kibbutz movements, it was the flagbearer of Mapam's pioneering ethos. Its mother party, Mapam, had been established in January 1948, following the union of two socialist Zionist parties, Hashomer and Ahdut Ha'avodah. In 1949, after elections to the First Knesset, Mapam became the second-largest party (following Mapai). However, it was not part of the ruling coalition. During the 1950s, Mapam underwent a grave crisis known as the "Mordechai Oren affair." Oren, a member of Kibbutz Mizra and a senior activist in Mapam, was arrested in Prague as a "Zionist spy." He was imprisoned following a show trial and spent four and a half years in prison. Upon his release and return to Israel, Oren wrote a book that laid bare the dark side of the Communist "world of tomorrow." These revelations further deepened the Israeli Left's disenchantment with the Communist bloc.

In the elections to the Sixth Knesset in November 1965, Mapam's power declined from nine Knesset representatives to eight. The Sixth Knesset included a new party known as Gahal, formed by a merger of two parties, the right-wing Herut and the centrist Liberal Party. According to Elmaliach, "Gahal actually received more votes in some places than labor-movement parties" (p. 123). Such was the case, for example, in Ashdod, a development town where the majority of residents were of Oriental (Mizrahi) origin. In Elmaliach's view, the Sixth Knesset election results were the first indicator of the labor movement's impending decline. Following the elections, Mapam joined the coalition headed by Mapai leader Levi Eshkol, with two of its representatives becoming ministers.

In January 1968, three parties on the Left—Mapai, Ahdut Ha'avodah and Rafi (Israeli Workers List)—merged to form Ha'avodah (the Labor Party), which, with 59 representatives, became the largest party in the Knesset. One year later, fearing further erosion of its electoral power, and possibly even its disappearance from the Israeli political map, Mapam joined the party, now renamed Hama'arakh (the Alignment). Yet Mapam's position within the governing party was problematic, since its moderate, dovish political stance found no favor with Golda Meir, a political hawk who became prime minister in March 1969 following Eshkol's death. The situation became even more complicated in the wake of elections to the Seventh Knesset in November 1969. Once again, Meir formed a coalition government—but this time it was a "unity government" that included Gahal as well as Mapam, with the right-wing party having more power and influence than Mapai's ostensible "sister party." Mapam's weakness was clearly shown in its reluctant support of free-market policies that ran counter to its socialist ideology, "in contrast with the 'partnership while in conflict' stance Mapam had taken during its previous stint in government" (p. 158). A further blow to the labor movement as a whole took place with the establishment of the Gush Emunim (Bloc of the Faithful), the national-religious movement in 1974. Gush Emunim's goal, the creation of a string of Jewish settlements in the heart of the West Bank, made use of the historic symbolism of the settlement ethos of the Labor Zionist kibbutz movement, thus discrediting some of the erstwhile prestige of Hakibbutz Haartzi.

And finally: "On Election Day, May 17, 1977, the labor movement's worst fears were realized. . . . Twenty years earlier, the stage for the upheaval had been set. Now it played out" (p. 221).

The process of the decline of the labor movement is a decisive phase in Israel's history. Elmaliach succeeds in analyzing the process via an examination of Mapam, which stood at the very heart of the movement. His book is an important contribution to the research pertaining to Israeli society and the Israeli political world.

YECHIAM WEITZ
University of Haifa

Sharon Geva, *Haishah mah omeret? Nashim beyisrael bishnot hamedinah harishonot* (Women in the State of Israel: The Early Years). Jerusalem: Magnes Press, 2020. 293 pp.

Written from the perspective of a contemporary feminist, Sharon Geva's engaging book offers a critical review of women's status and rights in Israel of the 1950s, through the lens of women's magazines and newspaper columns. Geva provides ample empirical proof for the justified criticism voiced by Israeli feminists as early as the 1970s—namely, women's equality in Israel was nothing but a myth. Geva's book covers significant topics pertaining to gender inequality and women's everyday lives. She validates previous studies, and therefore this book is not a revisionist history.

Geva dedicates the first chapter to women as citizens, describing Israel's few female Knesset members and their parliamentary work as well as that of the single female cabinet member, Golda Meyerson (Meir); local council members (and one mayor); and their female constituencies. Women who were elected to office, argues Geva, were loyal to the national cause more than to the advancement of women's rights and status. Moreover, those who wished to promote women's rights needed to convince their own party members, as they were unable to collaborate with women across party lines.

In the following chapter, Geva examines women's role as mothers, criticizing Israeli women for adhering to the dictate that a woman's main role in life is motherhood. She opens the chapter with the depiction of a small minority of subversive women who supported peace and vehemently condemned any kind of violence, whether that of Palestinian "infiltrators" killing Jewish women and children, or violence on the part of the Israeli Defense Forces (IDF). Most of these women were Communists. In what follows, Geva criticizes the majority of Jewish Israeli mothers for their deep devotion to their nation and for raising their children to become loyal soldiers. The chapter covers additional issues, ranging from the physical conditions in maternity wards (dreadful) to those in schools (poor) to public campaigns aimed at increasing the Jewish birthrate (for Geva, an unfathomable infringement of women's control over their bodies, though most Jewish women of that time did not complain). She also discusses the legal status of abortions (illegal, though the law was not enforced). Geva traces the hierarchy of motherhood constructed by the hegemonic veteran Ashkenazi society in the 1950s. Mizrahi mothers (and fathers, for that matter) were at the bottom of the ladder, considered unfit to fulfill their roles without guidance.

Chapter 3 presents women's role both as housewives and in the labor market. During the early 1950s, most Jewish women felt that a woman's role was to keep house. Only 25 percent of married women held paid jobs, most of them in "feminine" occupations such as nursing or teaching. Men were considered to be the main providers, whereas women's work was perceived merely as a complimentary source of income. Even women who developed a career were expected to take care of household chores, since performing such tasks was felt to detract from a man's masculinity.

Most columnists, Geva finds, guarded the wall separating women from men. "Without a woman there is no home," wrote Sara Tsur in *Laishah* magazine (quoted on p. 187), while a columnist for '*Al hamishmar* warned against the lack of domestic training for girls: "How do girls make their way in the business of keeping a home, when for 12 years, they have been trained for different things entirely?" (p. 199). At times, however, criticism over the lack of equality was voiced: "It would a good thing if a boy learned to lend a helping hand and perform some household chores. He should learn how to sew a button or prepare a light meal by himself. He should not be raised as a parasite . . . " (p. 202). Rachel Galek voiced her grievances more explicitly: "I hate myself for being so compulsive toward myself; for the emotional weakness that stems the rebellious fire burning within me. I hate myself for not having enough courage to allow myself just once to escape the daily cycle" (pp. 224–225). Geva presents these lone voices with much enthusiasm. In her book's conclusion, she argues that Israeli women played the role they were assigned by men, with only a few of them rebelling against the hegemonic patriarchal order.

Geva's book offers a first-of-its-kind feminist history of Israeli women in the 1950s. It has, however, a few weaknesses, the main one being its judgmental tone. Historians, as Marc Bloch argued, should attempt to understand the society they are studying rather than judging it.[1] Blaming women (who are clearly victims of patriarchy) for their own marginalization is akin to blaming the poor for being poor. The role of the historian is to offer cultural, psychological, or economic explanations, not to cast blame. Geva's methodological strategy—relying almost solely on the press for her sources—is also problematic, as it yields a black and white picture. Had she chosen to rely on archival sources, or at least more broadly on previous research, a more nuanced picture would have emerged.[2]

When discussing her methodology, Geva acknowledges the fact that only veteran Ashkenazi women held paid jobs as journalists, and therefore only their point of view was actually heard. We learn much less about immigrants from Muslim countries. The latter are mostly presented in this book as victims of the oppressive and racist Ashkenazi hegemony. Tracing the voices of immigrants from Muslim countries is indeed a difficult task.[3] Yet even when an opportunity presents itself, Geva misses out. While she focuses on the oppressors, she disregards the message conveyed by Mizrahi women. One such striking example is brought in a survey among female veterans in *Haaretz*. Geva writes: "New immigrants saw their military service as a major contribution to their nation and an empowering experience," and adds a quote by a young woman from Morocco: "Moving from a makeshift housing unit [*badon*] to the IDF is like immigrating from a Moroccan village to Tel Aviv" (p. 77). Like most scholars, Geva argues that female soldiers in the 1950s were marginalized in the Israeli army. Notwithstanding, a more complex approach would have been able to accommodate the voices of immigrant women who felt differently, and thus grant them agency. As some scholars have already shown, the myth of gender equality itself enabled some women, Mizrahi included, to improve their status and sense of control over their lives.[4]

ORIT ROZIN
Tel Aviv University

Notes

1. Mark Bloch, *Apologie Pour L'Histoire*; in Hebrew version, *Apologiyah 'al hahistoriyah o miktzo'o shel hahistoriyon*, trans. Zvia Zmiri (Jerusalem: 2002), 156–160.

2. See, for example: Dana Olmert, *Kehomah 'amodnah: imahot lelohimim basifrot ha'ivrit* (Tel Aviv: 2018); Tagrid Kaedan, "Teguvot hatzibur hamuslemi kelapei hahok leshivuy zekhuyot haishah" (master's thesis, The Hebrew University, 2013); Yael Broude-Bahat, Me'oravutam shel irgunei hanashim behakikat hok yahasei mamon bein benei zug bashanim 1948–1973, *Mishpat umimshal* 16 (2013), 27–89.

3. For a discussion of sources and the use of oral history, see, for example, Hila Shalem Baharad, "'Hitukh behom namukh': safah, dat, hinuch veyahasim bein-'adatiyim bemahanot uma'abarot ha'olim" (Ph.D. diss., The Hebrew University, 2019), 47–50; Rachel Sharaby and Na'ama Hadad-Kedem, "Hahalutzot mimoshavei ha'olim: sipuran shel 'olot mizrahiyot bemoshavei perozdor yerushalayim," in *Bein haperati letziburi: nashim bakibutz uvemoshav*, ed. Sylvie Fogiel-Bijaoui and Rachel Sharaby (Jerusalem: 2013), 251–283.

4. See, for example, Inbal-Esther Sicurel, "Temurot behavnayat yahasei migdar: hevrah, dat, va'avodah bekerev nashim bemoshav karai," in ibid., 284–300.

Walter L. Hixson, *Israel's Armor: The Israel Lobby and the First Generation of the Palestine Conflict*. Cambridge: Cambridge University Press, 2019. xi + 313 pp.

Israel's Armor is an extraordinarily strange and problematic book. Its main goal, as its author emphasizes from the first page, is "to analyze the foundations and early history of a critical component of a special relationship: the pro-Israeli lobby," which, he claims, played a "crucial role in mobilizing US support for the Zionist state" (p. 1). From the outset, Walter L. Hixson's distorted view of Jewish history is on display, as he informs us that he does not believe Zionism is a national movement of the Jewish people. He regards Israel as nothing but a "settler state," a "Zionist state," a "colonial project." Zionism, he claims, was the product of Russian pogroms, and Herzl was overly influenced by the Dreyfus affair. Entirely disregarding the heritage of the Jewish people, who since the time of the Bible have considered themselves a nation, he makes no mention of the Lovers of Zion or 19th-century forerunners of the Zionist movement.

Basing his work on "evidence drawn from multiple US archives," Hixson targets the American Israel Public Affairs Committee (AIPAC)—headed during the "first generation of the Palestinian conflict" by Isaiah (Si) Kenen—as the main player in a powerful lobby that "glossed over Israel's aggressiveness in the Palestine conflict while depicting its own advocacy as purely defensive" and which "typically proved effective in achieving its aims" (p. 2). Unaware of the facts, or choosing to ignore them, Hixson excoriates the "Zionist attitude" toward the Palestinians, accusing "Zionist settlers" of treating them as *Untermenschen* (p. 25). He does not appear to know that the Palestinians began to consider themselves a nation only in the 1930s, after giving up the idea of being part of the new Syrian state. He makes basic mistakes in chronology (claiming, for instance, that the Arab states invaded Palestine in January 1948). He also consistently shows his bias, with terms such as "aggressiveness" and "intransigence" applied solely to the "Zionist" side of the conflict. Thus, Hixson's sole reference to Haj Amin al-Husseini, the grand mufti of Jerusalem who was recognized as the leader of the Palestinian national movement, characterizes him as a "spiritual leader" (p. 23), ignoring al-Husseini's cordial meeting with Adolf Hitler in November 1941.[1] Similarly, Hixson neglects to note Egyptian president Gamal Abdel Nasser's repeated threats to annihilate Israel during the 1950s and 1960s at such public forums as the Cairo summit of January 1964 (at which Nasser promised the "final liquidation" of Israel) and the Alexandria summit in September 1964.

Hixson, in brief, appears to have conducted his research with a ready-made conclusion firmly in place. While his book purports to examine the "Israel lobby," there is no attempt made to examine the copious documentation found in Israeli cabinet protocols or the correspondence between the Israeli embassy in Washington, D.C. and the Israeli foreign ministry in Jerusalem. To be sure, much of this material is in Hebrew, but the Israel State Archives also contains companion volumes in English to supplement its series of books on the history of Israeli foreign policy. Here, a serious researcher can find ample evidence to counter Hixson's claim that a powerful, U.S.-based lobby worked to undermine U.S. interests in the period between 1948 and the Six-Day War of June 1967. Even Hixson, limiting himself to "multiple US archives," might have discovered just how flimsy America's security commitments to Israel really were. During the Kennedy administration, the concept of "special relationship" was very different from what Israel might have imagined or desired. It did *not* include security guarantees: Kennedy had been advised against this by the officials at the State Department, the Pentagon, and the National Security Council, all of whom argued that granting such guarantees might cause the radical Arab states to side with the Soviet bloc. Contrary to Hixson's claims that AIPAC was successful in its (un-American) mission ("By the time of [John F.] Kennedy's assassination . . . Israel and AIPAC had solidified the now officially proclaimed special relationship" [p. 31]) and that Lyndon B. Johnson, who took office after the assassination, was not merely pro-Israeli, but "a savior presiding over the security of the Jews in their return to the Promised Land" (p. 234). The maximum Israel achieved in terms of U.S. support was the Memorandum of Understanding signed on March 10, 1965. This provided for a very limited special relationship, in which the U.S. government "reaffirmed its concern for the maintenance of Israel's security and . . . renewed its assurances that the United States firmly opposes aggression in the Near East and remains committed to the independence and integrity of Israel."[2]

Two years later, at the peak of the May 1967 crisis. President Johnson was convinced that America should not encourage Israel to initiate a war—and AIPAC, for its part, did not urge U.S. intervention. In the event, apart from surplus Patton tanks supplied indirectly via Germany, the only significant military assistance offered by the United States to Israel at that time was a supply of defensive, surface-to-air Hawk missiles. Had it not been for the French military aircraft it was able to purchase, Israel would not have won the Six-Day War. Johnson sided with Israel only *after* the Six-Day War, and then only because of Cold War considerations—specifically, the massive military and political support granted to the defeated Arabs by the Soviet Union.

Finally, how far AIPAC was from advocating an "undermining" of U.S. policy is apparent in a remark made on July 2, 1962 by Armin Meyer, the American ambassador to Beirut, who was no particular friend of the Jewish state. Writing to McGeorge Bundy (President Kennedy's national security adviser) about ways to counter arguments on behalf of Israel, Meyer made mention of "my old friends Si Kennen [*sic*] of the America-Israel Public Affairs Committee and Label Katz of B'nai B'rith." In Meyer's assessment: "I've always found that when you lay out the facts to such responsible citizens they are ready to stand by their country."[3]

Full of historical errors and omissions and marked by unremitting bias, *Israel's Armor* is not worthy of review—save for the troubling fact that it was published by the prestigious Cambridge University Press.

JOSEPH HELLER
The Hebrew University

Notes

1. In contrast, Hixson takes the trouble to mention Avraham Stern's tragic attempt to make an alliance with Hitler (p. 25), even though Stern headed a group numbering fewer than 100 people. See Joseph Heller, *The Stern Gang: Politics, Ideology and Terror* (London: 1995).
2. Full text in *Foreign Relations of the United States, 1964–1968,* vol. 18, *Arab-Israeli Dispute 1964–1967,* ed. Harriet Dashiell (Washington, D.C.: 2000), 398–399.
3. Quoted in Warren Bass, *Support Any Friend: Kennedy's Middle East and the Making of the U.S.–Israel Alliance* (Oxford: 2013), 56–57.

Nir Kedar, *Law and Identity in Israel: A Century of Debate*, trans. Haim Watzman. Cambridge: Cambridge University Press, 2019. 236 pp.

What makes "Israeli law" "Israeli"? Is it sufficient that it developed in the setting of legal institutions operating in the state of Israel? Does it become "Israeli" by virtue of legislation of statutes with "Jewish" content, such as the Pig Raising Prohibition Act of 1962, the Passover Act of 1986, or even the Law of Return of 1950? Did the Israeli legal system begin evolving only upon the declaration of the establishment of the state of Israel, or are its roots planted in the early history of Zionism? These questions and others are at the heart of Nir Kedar's book, *Law and Identity in Israel*. In fact, the book's subtitle—*A Century of Debate*—suggests at least a partial answer to these questions, implying not only that Israeli law was not created out of thin air on May 14, 1948, the day the state was established, but that a perusal of its historical roots returns one to the earliest days of Zionism, which saw the first attempts to create a national legal system.

Indeed, already in the book's introduction, Kedar informs the reader: "The story of Israeli law is in fact the story of Zionism itself" (p. 2). The common denominator between the Zionist movement and Israeli law is, in his opinion, the fact that they both "swung between the desire and need to address questions of modern Jewish identity in a profound way and the need to stifle, or at least mute, these very same debates so that they would not become hindrances to the building of the Israeli state and society and thus frustrate the goal of establishing a free Jewish life" (p. 5). Kedar's conclusion is that not only did the institutions of Israeli law—like those of the Zionist movement and the Yishuv—refrain from making decisions about deeply controversial questions of identity and culture in Israeli society, but that they do not even have the tools to debate these questions. Consequently, Kedar considers it inappropriate to resolve such questions in the legal arena. This is not to say that Israeli law is neither national nor Jewish; indeed, the case is quite the opposite. According to Kedar, it is the formation of the legal system in the national state of the Jewish people; in Hebrew; by Israeli citizens; in a cultural environment that suits their needs, interests, and values—this is what distinguishes the system as "Israeli law."

Kedar supports his conclusion with a historical review of the efforts to express the Israeli nature of the Israeli legal system from the beginning of Zionism up until today, whether by infusing the law with Jewish–Hebrew content, or through incorporating cultural and national elements into legislation. The first part of the book (Chapters 1–6) describes the historical efforts to establish a comprehensive national-Jewish-Israeli legal system, which can be divided into three chronological periods: the first of days of the Zionist movement, the first period of the Yishuv, and the first decades of the state. The second part of the book (Chapters 7–8) deals with the return of discourse regarding identity to Israeli law in the 1980s, and how this discourse found expression in the enactment of the Foundations of Law Act of 1980. In this context, Kedar describes the legislature's attempts to base Israeli law on Jewish content and on various sources of Jewish law, and the practical manifestations of the declarative dimension of this Act (or, more correctly, the absence of it) in case law. In the third and final part of the book (Chapters 9–10), Kedar abandons the chronological narrative and examines Zionism's complex relationship with the issue of culture, and the delicate interaction between Israeli law and Jewish heritage. The conclusion of these chapters, and, indeed, of the entire book, is that, notwithstanding the fact that periodic attempts to imbue Israeli law with content based on the principles of Jewish law had mostly failed, ultimately, Israeli law serves as a *lieu de mémoire*, in Pierre Nora's phrase denoting the mapping of collective memory, in this case with regard to Jewish heritage (p. 186). This has been accomplished through the incorporation of symbols, concepts, and norms derived from traditional Jewish sources into Israeli law, as well as by ensuring the independence of the Israeli legal system. In this sense, Israeli law today constitutes "the most important preserve of and monument to Jewish law" (p. 197).

Kedar's wide-ranging and deeply thought-out book makes an important contribution to the understanding of the discourse concerning questions of national culture and identity within the legal sphere, in general, and the place of Jewish nationalism, Jewish law, and Jewish–Israeli culture in the development of Israeli law, in particular. To show that this is an age-old discourse, Kedar masterfully weaves a number of legal events into one historical narrative, demonstrating that they all shared a common goal of bestowing legal validity on the basic values of Jewish heritage, or shaping Israeli law to reflect the principles of Jewish law. But this goal, according to Kedar, was destined to fail. Kedar's coherent, clear, and thought-provoking analysis makes this book a significant milestone in the historical and legal research of the issues discussed.

Nonetheless, some of the book's assumptions may be open to debate. First, the central argument of the book remains on the theoretical-ideological level, and is not sufficiently grounded in primary historical sources. One might expect, for example, that the discussion of the fascinating historical phenomena of the "Hebrew Peace Courts" (Chapter 2) and the "Hebrew Law Society" (Chapter 3) would be based on relevant archival sources. With few exceptions, however, Kedar chose to rely on secondary sources for his analysis. Moreover, his argument that these attempts to revive Jewish law were doomed to failure because the law is not the appropriate arena to discuss questions of identity and culture (p. 38) is not consistent with the conclusions of some historical scholarship indicating that such failure can be attributed to historical circumstances of time and place.[1] A similar criticism can be leveled at the discussion of the legislative process behind the Foundations of Law Act and its implementation by the courts (Chapter 7), for which Kedar relied primarily on existing legal research. This discussion could have been enriched by a more wide-ranging and deeper analysis of case law following the Act, beyond the most familiar and well-known judgments.

Second, the discussion throughout the book refers to "Israeli law" in a broad sense, without separating it into its various branches, whereas it may have been appropriate and enlightening to distinguish the legislature from the judiciary. Kedar does not draw this obvious distinction. For him, "the law," as a singular entity, "is not the appropriate arena for deciding between different takes on identity or views of Jewish culture" (p. 200). While there are those who will agree with this position regarding case law (although even this is certainly debatable), it is more difficult to accept the claim in relation to legislation, as long as it is enacted in accordance with constitutional standards. Moreover, Kedar does not address questions of Jewish and Israeli identity and culture in semi-judicial forums, such as national committees of inquiry, which use legal tools to examine important historical and public events.

And finally, and perhaps most importantly, in the 74 years of its existence, the Knesset has enacted a considerable number of acts that, to one extent or another, anchor cultural symbols and motifs related to the Jewish identity of the country.[2] It is not unusual for discussions of the issues underlying these acts to cross the threshold of Israeli courts. At least in some situations, the discussion has not been limited to "formal" issues such as in the famous cases discussed in the Israeli Supreme Court, for instance, drafting yeshiva students or allowing businesses to be open on Shabbat. In any event, the final enactment of the Basic Law: Israel – The Nation-State of the Jewish People, which coincided (as Kedar recounts) with the completion of the book (pp. 102–101), alongside the recent Supreme Court ruling concerning the law's constitutionality,[3] casts doubt on the strength of Kedar's central claim. The Nation-State Act declares that the land of Israel is the historical homeland of the Jewish people. It also adds and secures symbols and values from Jewish heritage, including the Hebrew language, the return from the diaspora, ties with Jewish people in the diaspora, Jewish settlement, reliance on the Hebrew calendar, the status of Shabbat and Jewish holidays, and more. Even if it is possible, then, to argue about *the propriety* of Jewish and national symbols and fundamental principles being anchored and embedded in statute and case law, there is no doubt that the Nation-State Act represents *the actualization* of this process. Thus, even if we accept that Kedar's claim was correct in the past, it is difficult to dispute that today, with the establishment and stabilization of the Israeli legal system, the time is ripe to reopen the debate on questions of identity and culture and their place in the law.

YEHUDIT DORI DESTON
The Hebrew University

Notes

1. Ronen Shamir, "Lex Moriendi: 'al moto shel mishpat yisreeli," in *Rav-tarbutiyut bimdinah demokratit vihudit: sefer hazikaron leAriel Rosen-Zvi z"l*, ed. Menachem Mautner, Avi Sagi, and Ronen Shamir (Tel Aviv: 1998) 589–632, esp. 589, 593, 628–632. See also Assaf Likhovski, "Mishpat 'ivri veideologiyah tziyonit beeretz-yisrael hamandatorit," in ibid., 633, 639.

2. See, for instance, the State Flag, Symbol and National Anthem Act 1949 (5709); Law of Return 1950 (5710); Hours of Work and Rest Act 1951 (5711); Status of the World Zionist Organization and the Jewish Agency Act 1952 (5713); Holocaust Remembrance – Yad Vashem Act 1953 (5713); Holocaust Remembrance Day Act 1959 (5719); Use of the Hebrew Calendar Act 1998 (5758); Museum of the Jewish People Act 2005 (5766); Independence House Act 2009 (5769); Immigration to Israel [Aliyah] Day Act 2016 (5776), and many more.

3. HCJ 5555/18, *Hason v. The Knesset* (8 July 2021).

Fredrik Meiton, *Electrical Palestine: Capital and Technology from Empire to Nation*. Oakland: University of California Press, 2019. xiv + 305 pp.

This book is one of a long line of studies dealing with the question of Israel/Palestine and the Israeli–Palestinian conflict that view economic, social, or cultural issues as the prime explanation for the deep rift between two rival nationalities. For example, Jacob Norris' *Land of Progress, Palestine in the Age of Colonial Development, 1905–1948* (2013) advances a historical-economic narrative in which competition over natural resources is the prime mover of the conflict, as if economic competition was what stood behind the Arab opposition to the Zionist enterprise. Norris also pursues a classic postcolonial explanation: that empires play a key role in intensifying the conflict by means of their allocation of resources to one side or another, in an effort to strengthen their clout.

In *Electrical Palestine*, Fredrik Meiton analyzes one of the key factors underlying the progress and prosperity of British Mandate Palestine: its electricity grid, which was established formally in 1923 but had been developed gradually over two decades. He aims to convince his readers that this grid is crucial to understanding a long and painful historical process that ended when the Jews established an independent state and the Palestinians lost their opportunity to do the same. Through electrification, the Jewish state had an infrastructure in place several decades before its establishment, and this served as a counterbalance to the huge demographic gap between the Arab majority and the Jewish minority. "The central argument of this book," Meiton writes, "is that the story of Palestine's transformation is largely a story of the precipitous and uneven development of its infrastructures, and that its ethnonational conflict is largely a story of diverging economies coevolving with those technologies" (p. 6). This statement implies that egalitarian economic and technological development—assuming there is such a thing—could have changed the history of this parcel of land. It suggests that the Arabs, both those living in Mandate Palestine and those of neighboring states, might have welcomed Zionist settlement and the Jewish national aspiration for a national home, or at least a bi-national state.

Meiton has done diligent work in researching the 140-year-old historic confrontation over this piece of land by putting it on the tip of the power line. The seven chapters of the book, along with its introduction and conclusion, are based on primary sources that he found in Israeli archives, in the Hebrew, Arabic, and English press, and in previous studies that have dealt with the electrification of Palestine. The first chapter focuses on Pinhas Rutenberg, a Russian-born engineer and revolutionary who was the key figure in the building of the grid. Rutenberg arrived in Palestine in 1919 and became a prominent leader and activist among Zionist circles. It was he who initiated the idea of acquiring concessions on electrical production and power stations, along with constructing an electrical grid under a single authority.[1] In the second chapter, Meiton concentrates on the complex and intricate process by which Rutenberg obtained the concession from the British; in the following chapter, he discusses the "thin circles" (hinting at electrical circuits?) of the debates in England, mainly with regard to granting the concession to "Zionists," thus in effect giving them the keys to the local economy and affording them a significant initial advantage over the Arabs. "Light in Tel-Aviv, darkness in Jaffa" captures the concept that the author uses metaphorically throughout the book: the light of Tel Aviv radiated over the entire Zionist enterprise and gave it a competitive edge; whereas Jaffa (or Nablus), which chose for ideological reasons not to join the grid, were left in the dark. The Arabs' decision arose from an unwillingness to depend on the Zionist movement, but it also corresponded to a conscious choice of technological inferiority, and hence, political weakness, on their part—a choice that would lead to their adversity in later years.

In the fourth chapter, Meiton presents his view of the relationship between the electrification of the land and Zionist supremacy, pointing to the first hydroelectric power station in Naharayim, on the confluence of the Jordan and Yarmouk rivers, as the factor that dictated the image of the land as a Jewish national space and the status of the Arabs as "secondary beneficiaries" of the country's development. The fifth chapter details the economic and industrial boom caused by the establishment of the Palestine Electric Corporation (PEC) and the expansion of its network. At the conclusion of this chapter, Meiton offers an astonishing parallel between the tripling of Jewish population in Palestine between 1931 and 1939 and the doubling in size of the electrical grid and the tenfold increase in electricity consumption during that period (p. 186). He makes no mention of the dramatic political shifts occurring in Europe, nor of the increasingly severe persecution of Central European Jews that caused many of them to flee. Following the lines of his presentation, the Fifth Aliyah can be regarded as nothing more than a consequence of electrification, just as the Arab Revolt of 1936–1939 was the outgrowth of accumulated Arab resentment as a result of their economic inferiority.

The sixth chapter discusses the special case of the building of an electrical power plant in Jerusalem, a private initiative that offered an alternative to Rutenberg's centralized, countrywide system. The Jerusalem Electric Company never managed to meet demands for consumption in the period before 1948 and in the years following the establishment of the state of Israel, the shortfall became worse. The short, seventh chapter (it could have been merged with the conclusion), is mainly a political-historical narrative of the various partition proposals prior to the war of 1948–1949, followed by a summary of events up until the nationalization of the Palestine Electric Corporation in September 1954.

The concluding chapter is instructive. In it, Meiton presents his claim that British policy vis-à-vis Palestine was in complete alignment with the aims of the Zionist movement. That is, European Jews would go to Palestine to serve as an avant-garde for development and progress, and as a "light" to the local Arabs—since the latter were perceived as "natives" who were unable to take steps in the name of their own prosperity. Put more succinctly, the land was backward, and the only way to engender progress was through an Anglo-Zionist alliance. Thus, in Meiton's view, the British "squared the circle" of the Mandate for Palestine with the Balfour Declaration, which had called for a national home for the Jews in Palestine alongside preservation of the rights of the local, non-Jewish population. The electricity grid "produced what it illuminated: a Jewish national space, a frame for Jewish–Arab relations, and a powerful model of economic development. ... The electric supply in Palestine contributed certain necessary conditions for the making of a Jewish state, without which such a state might not have been" (pp. 219–220). In addition, the countrywide electricity grid provides the answer to the question of how the Zionists managed in such a short period of time to gain control of and establish a state in an area with an Arab majority. The book's punch line is without a doubt its last two sentences, which summarize the disaster that befell the Palestinian Arabs because they did not take part in the national network's initiative, did not integrate into it, and opposed it: "From their perspective, centralized large-scale electrification was hardly 'better.' It cost them the land" (p. 223).

Given this conclusion, it is no wonder that two prominent Arab historians, Rashid Khalidi and Marwa Elshakry, praise the book on its back cover, though I doubt whether Derek Penslar, who also expressed his appreciation, truly agrees that it was the power grid that "set the stage" for 1948. In fact, Meiton's (re-)reading of history ignores a number of important matters. He does not investigate why the Arabs did not present a worthy alternative to the economic development of the country put forward by the Zionists. He also fails to prove his basic claim for alleged preferences of Jewish economic initiatives over Arab proposals: was there, in fact, any Arab entrepreneur who proposed an infrastructure projects that was rejected by the British authorities? Further, Meiton does not compare the situation in Mandate Palestine to that of other Arab territories such as Syria and Lebanon, in which concessions were allocated almost totally to European entrepreneurs, and where Zionism had no role to play. Finally, he does not consider the fact that the British were given a mandate to develop the country, and they sought to do so in a way that would not place the cost of development on the shoulders of British taxpayers. They thus adopted the Zionist economic initiatives; their preference did not necessarily stem from any particular sympathy for the Jewish cause.

Other studies on the Palestine Electric Corporation and its establishment can be found in the literature. For instance, Ronen Shamir's work of 2013, *Current Flow: The Electrification of Palestine*, contains a number of insights that are similar to those presented by Meiton. According to Shamir, the separation between Jewish and Arab localities can be explained—to some extent—by the Rutenberg power plant, but he does not regard the grid as the primary factor in the non-establishment of a Palestinian state. Another relevant work is Eli Shaltiel's comprehensive biography of Pinhas Rutenberg, which appeared (in Hebrew) in 1990. Most of the material found in Meiton's book has long been known to scholars and readers in the field. Although the author claims to differentiate himself by the fact that he, unlike his predecessors, researched material written in Arabic, an in-depth look at his sources shows that, with the exception of the Nablus Municipality archives, most of these sources are newspaper articles discussing the pros and cons of hooking up to the "Zionist" electrical grid.

The most important innovation in this study, therefore, is its attempt to serve as a general model for understanding postcolonial outcomes. Meiton's use of the Palestinian case soon escalates into a classic indictment of imperialism, Zionism, and their nefarious merger in order to explain the inability of the Palestinians to begin to develop the infrastructure for their own nation-state when the UN proposed the Partition Plan. One must be innocent or blind to history to hang the Palestinians' short-sightedness on the electricity grid. The Jewish nation in its Zionist form would have made efforts to establish a national home even in a world of oil lamps. The regional alternative to that of a national network that allegedly gave a tremendous advantage to Jews (or Zionists, as Meiton defines it), stands in ruins in Shuafat, the site of the local, regional, and non-Zionist Jerusalem Electric Company. Its consumers, who never received the amount of electricity they needed, can testify that Rutenberg's idea was professionally correct. Palestinian entrepreneurs or a Palestinian power union that could have competed for the concession that was granted in 1926 were not to be found, and this fact—rather than electricity lines—reflects the depth of the difference between the two rival sides.

YOSSI BEN ARTZI
University of Haifa

Note

1.   See Michael Aran, "Hamasa-umatan lehasagat zikayon leḥevrat haḥashmal," *Cathedra* 26 (December 1982), 133–176.

Rachel Rojanski, *Yiddish in Israel: A History*. Bloomington: Indiana University Press, 2020. 453 pp.

Yiddishists and Hebraists alike tend to assume that Yiddish was suppressed in Israel, even as their ideological assessments of the matter differ greatly. The former see it as another chapter in the longstanding struggle for the Yiddish language, whereas for the latter, it was a fully justified battle for the triumph of Hebrew as the exclusive national language of the Jewish people in Israel. In *Yiddish in Israel*, Rachel Rojanski sets out to revise this conception about the way Yiddish was regarded in Israel and to demonstrate the issue's much greater complexity.

While the vast majority of Zionists supported the idea of Hebrew as their national language, accepting (with different degrees of sadness or satisfaction) the inevitable demise of Yiddish, the preservation of the cultural legacy of the Jewish Exile (*galut*) was a more complicated issue. Some Zionists rejected nearly everything created outside the Jews' ancestral homeland as worthless for the born-again nation, while others, who believed in the value of cultural continuity, worked to preserve and translate into Hebrew the heritage of bygone days. The Holocaust also had a significant impact on attitudes toward the Jewish past, even among the most zealous Exile-rejectionists. The need to commemorate murdered families and home communities, as well as the fact that Yiddish was no longer regarded as a real threat to Hebrew hegemony in Israel, made space for both Yiddish and the Jews of the diaspora in Israeli memory.

In the first chapter of her book, Rojanski discusses the variety of Zionist attitudes toward Yiddish. As she points out, the young Israeli government of that time did not always speak in one voice on the subject. David Ben-Gurion, for instance, was known for his belief in a biblical cultural revival—*mehaTana"kh laPalmaḥ* — that is, moving directly from the Bible to the pre-state Palmach fighting force, skipping over the centuries of exile, as it were. Others, however, such as Ben-Zion Dinur, the minister of education, did not agree, arguing that the diaspora heritage was a necessary component of Israel's identity and should serve as a source of inspiration to the new Israeli culture.

At the heart of *Yiddish in Israel* is Rojanski's examination of whether the state of Israel used coercive measures to suppress the use of Yiddish in public culture, and if so, what was the impact of such measures. Her research thus focuses on evidence to be found among policies, by-laws, and their implementation, rather than in the ideological field as such. In Chapter 2, she concentrates on the Yiddish press in the young state; in the following chapter, she follows the trials and tribulations of several Yiddish theater groups active at that time in Israel. Her findings are that, while hostility to Yiddish definitely existed in some official quarters, it had little (if any) effect on the legal status of the language. To be sure, there were attempts to limit the publication of Yiddish newspapers in the first years of the state, with a general censorship directive inherited from the British Mandate being used to regulate their publication. A similar attempt to limit theater performances in Yiddish was also debated— it, too, drawing its legal basis from British Mandate regulations. But as Rojanski shows, attempts at such legislation failed and the proposed limitations on publishing newspapers and producing shows were soon put aside.

This said, it is important to acknowledge the other side of the issue. Though legal means proved ineffective, the fate of Yiddish in Israel was nonetheless shaped by the power of hegemony and through informal sanctions. Seeking to ensure the triumph of Hebrew, as this was perceived to be crucial in the development of an Israeli identity, both teachers and Hebrew-language public media denigrated Yiddish as ridiculous, outdated, weak, and "ungrammatical." Side by side with the belittling of Yiddish was the effort to assimilate its speakers to the normative use of Hebrew. A case in point is the strategy pursued by the then-dominant Mapai (Labor) Party. In 1949, Mordechai Tsanin founded *Letste nayes*, which, for four decades, was Israel's most influential Yiddish daily. In its first few years the paper was seen as a threat to Mapai's hegemony, but eventually, instead of fighting against *Letste nayes* and other Yiddish newspapers, Mapai chose to dominate the discourse by putting out its own Yiddish-language publications. This move turned out to be effective: Yiddish lost its power as a language of opposition, and thus its potential appeal for certain readers—who, in any event, were in the process of acquiring the new national language. Rojanski reveals in her book that Tsanin actually sold his newspaper to a Mapai-controlled publishing firm in 1960 (though he remained the editor): a deal he was reluctant to discuss until the end of his life. This anecdote seems to tell, in a nutshell, the entire story of Yiddish in Israel.

The story of Yiddish theater in Israel follows along similar lines. Rojanski describes the government's attempts to limit the performance of local actors in Yiddish (only Hebrew was allowed), countered by the Avrom Goldfaden Theater (founded by Nathan Wolfovich), which successfully appealed to the Supreme Court. Still, in later years, the absence of state-sponsored support meant that Yiddish theater had to choose between popular entertainment, which brought in audiences and paid the bills, and artistic theater that might have had no commercial means of support. The result of this predicament was a reaffirmation of the stigma imposed on Yiddish as a popular language supposedly devoid of real cultural value. Informal sanctions again proved more effective than official ones.

In Chapters 4 and 5, Rojanski examines two major projects associated with the Yiddish poet Abraham Sutzkever—the quarterly *Di Goldene Keyt*, the world's leading post-Holocaust Yiddish literary journal, and the establishment of the writers' group known as Yung Yisroel (young Israel). *Di Goldene Keyt* was not only tolerated but was actually founded and supported by the Mapai-dominated General Labor Federation (Histadrut), which aspired not only to organize and represent all the workers in Israel but also to play a role in the creation of Israel's national culture. Rojanski surmises that this sponsorship was undertaken as part of a plan to establish Israel as the world center for Yiddish, thus strengthening the connections with Jewish communities around the world and affirming the centrality of the state. Her discussion is vital in illuminating not only how Yiddish was seen as a resource by highly placed Zionist leaders, but also the unique situation of Yiddish in Israel—where practical necessities, and perhaps a sense of responsibility to the past, justified supporting a high-quality Yiddish periodical at the same time as people in the streets of Tel Aviv were expected to speak only in Hebrew.

Rojanski relates how Sutzkever immigrated from the Soviet Union to Israel believing that he could help reattach the unique and abiding Jewish "soul" ("the Golden Chain" in the journal's title is a literary reference to the unbroken chain of Jewish creativity) to the "body" of the newly established Jewish state. Unlike the re-born spirit of Israeli nationhood as imagined by many Zionists, Sutzkever's vision was embodied in the ideals of modern Yiddish culture. Whether Sutzkever's idea was ever feasible is another issue. What is undeniable is that Sutzkever was not only one of the greatest Yiddish poets of the century, but also an active agent of Yiddish cultural revival after the Holocaust. Rojanski's portrayal of Yiddish activists in Israel, especially Tsanin and Sutzkever, defy the image of passivity and victimhood often attributed to Yiddish and Yiddish-speakers. Despite the marginalization of Yiddish, these individuals' struggle contributed to the shaping of Israeli culture in its early years.

The Yiddish writers of Yung Yisroel, founded in 1951, were also part of this effort, although the group itself disbanded after eight years without managing to create a distinct school of writing. Adopting Zionist rhetoric in their work, the members of Yung Yisroel employed it to offer a Yiddish alternative voice, as Rojanski writes: "For them, redemption from the *galut* was not achieved merely by settling in Israel. The Israeli experience led to the healing of wounded souls, comfort, and closure. The memory of the *galut* was not to be abandoned but reworked and integrated into the present. This was the true redemption" (p. 274). Since Rojanski's study is mainly historical rather than literary, further analysis of the poetry and prose of Yung Yisroel would certainly be welcomed; some research along this line appears in a recent book by Gali Drucker Bar-Am.[1] The same is true with regard to an analysis of Yiddish theater in Israel. Of all the actors mentioned by Rojanski, only the renowned Yiddish comedians Dzigan and Shumacher have so far merited a comprehensive study, authored by Diego Rotman.[2]

In the sixth chapter Rojanski discusses the production of Itsik Manger's Yiddish musical play, *Di megile*, in Jaffa in 1965 and its impressive commercial and artistic success. Her final chapter, essentially a summary, brings the 20th century to a close with an account of later developments of Yiddish culture in Israel. Here, too, there is room for further research that might account for the interest aroused by Yiddish and Yiddish culture in the later decades of the century, possibly along the lines suggested by Jeffrey Shandler and his concept of *post-vernacularity*.[3]

What does the history of Yiddish in Israel teach us? This history, it seems, is less dramatic than what some might have imagined as a crusade by Zionists against anti-Zionists, a cosmic struggle between nationalists and internationalists, or even be-tween hegemonic "perpetrators" and oppressed "victims" in colonial contexts. It was more like a family feud. While it is easy to see how Palestinians, Communists, and some Mizrahi Jews may adopt an unequivocal anti-Zionist stance, it is much harder to define the subtle ways in which Yiddishists took up the cause of Yiddish language and culture in Israel, or the complexity of the alternative they offered to mainstream Zionist ideology in Israel. For what is the place of such an alternative? Can it exist in any form beyond fighting for the mere survival of Yiddish? How should it be seen in the context of economic and political struggles? It seems that a different terminology still needs to be constructed in order to describe the predicaments of Yiddish in the Hebrew state.

YAAD BIRAN
Haifa University
Beth Shalom Aleichem, Tel Aviv

Notes

1. Gali Drucker Bar-Am, *Ani afarekh: yisrael basiporet hayidish hayisreaelit, 1948–1967* (Jerusalem: 2021).
2. Diego Rotman, *The Yiddish Stage as a Temporary Home: Dzigan and Shumacher's Satirical Theater (1927-1980)* (Berlin: 2021).
3. Jeffrey Shandler, *Adventures in Yiddishland: Postvernacular Language and Culture* (Berkeley: 2006).

Marc Volovici, *German as a Jewish Problem: The Language Politics of Jewish Nationalism.* Stanford: Stanford University Press, 2020. 352 pp.

This book is about "the Jewish history of the German language" (p. 3), or more pre-cisely, "the place of German in Jewish nationalism" (p. 12).

As a teaser, Marc Volovici has used a scene from the chronicles of the Israeli Knesset. In March 2008, in the course of a state visit to Israel, German Chancellor Angela Merkel gave a speech in the Knesset in German, at which several Knesset members demonstratively left the chamber. One of the most vociferous among the protesters was right-wing MK Arieh Eldad, who exclaimed: "This was the language in which my grandparents were killed." Former Knesset speaker Avrum Burg retorted: "It is also the language in which Theodor Herzl wrote."

Avrum Burg's father, Volovici reminds us, was the German-born politician Yosef Burg, who opposed boycotting his mother tongue. But Volovici could have named as well Arieh Eldad's father, Israel Eldad—a right-wing ideologist who trans-lated Nietzsche into Hebrew, and yet also taught his son to hate anything German. Moreover, Volovici does not mention a public opinion poll (carried out by the Koebner Center for German History at the Hebrew University) that would have added further weight to his opening. This poll found that approximately 50 percent of Israel's Jews had no objection to Merkel's German-language speech, with an additional 20 percent objecting to German only when used on formal occasions. Only 12 percent of the respondents, most of them Orthodox Jews, supported an all-out boycott against the use of German in Israel. In sum, the use of German in Israel is less of a problem than it used to be. Israeli Jewish attitudes toward Germany appear to have normalized. This is true not only with regard to German industrial products widely sold in Israel, but also to cultural assets connected with the German language. Netflix films in German, for instance, are readily available to Israeli subscribers. In addition, the German language does not seem to disturb the large number of Israeli tourists who travel to Austria, to Switzerland or, for that matter, to the Black Forest region or Berlin.

Volovici's book has much to recommend it. His point of departure is a paradox: German as a language was decisive in Jewish history both in the Middle Ages, when it provided the major basis for the Ashkenazi Jewish lingua franca, Yiddish, and then again in the early modern period—as the language of Jewish religious reform and Haskalah (enlightenment). In other words, German appears to have been historically associated with Jews living in the diaspora and with Jewish assimilation, not with Jewish nationalism or a return to Palestine. The question Volovici sets out to answer is how the German language became relevant to Jewish nationalism. His chronological focus is on the years 1870–1945 (or, more precisely, 1870–1918) with an emphasis on those who *read* rather than spoke German.

The first chapter, "Jews and German since the Enlightenment," serves as an introduction and general background. The next chapter revolves around Leo Pinsker's *Auto-Emancipation* (1882) as the textual link between German and early modern Jewish nationalism. The following chapters are devoted to German's repute as the language of knowledge and its relevance for the rise of Hebraism; the language dispute (*Sprachenstreit*) in the Zionist Yishuv in the years prior to the First World War; Martin Buber's dilemma with regard to his translating the Bible into German (together with Franz Rosenzweig) and his writing in German; and the role of German and Yiddish in the discourse of Jewish nationalists. The last chapter concentrates on "German as a Jewish problem" since the rise of Nazism, and beyond.

According to Volovici, advocates of the Haskalah wanted German to replace Yiddish as the Jewish lingua franca. And indeed, their fight for Jewish emancipation brought about a profound change in the influence of the German language on Jewish life, not only in Germany but in Central and Eastern Europe, in general. Paradoxically, German became a tool of auto-emancipation, that is, something *beyond* emancipation. Thus, the Odessa-based herald of Jewish national awakening, Leo Pinsker, wrote his book in German not only to circumvent the Russian censors but also, and mainly (according to Volovici), because his Jewish nationalism was influenced by German Romanticism, especially that of Herder and Fichte. Nor was the influence of German nationalism confined to Pinsker and other so-called "precursors of Zionism." Rather, it continued to be a feature of Zionist ideology and rhetoric. To cite just one example: in the early 1940s, the text of posters put up by members of the Etzel (Irgun Zvai Leumi) underground movement in Palestine contained both the Hebrew slogan "This is the Only Way!" (*rak kakh*!") and the first stanza of German national poet E.M. Arndt's "Fatherland Song": "God, who created iron, did not want His people to be slaves!"

Another paradox explored by Volovici is that, of all languages, it was German that helped establish Hebrew as the national Jewish language. Once again, German historical experience was a precedent for Jewish nation-building: Volovici brings up Peretz Smolenskin, an opponent of the Haskalah, as an example of a Jewish-nationalist Hebraist for whom Martin Luther's historic embrace of German provided a well-known example of how a language might be turned into an essential tool of nation-building. Within the Zionist movement, German competed both with Yiddish and with Hebrew. Until 1935, the minutes of the Zionist congresses appeared in German (in the Yiddish-inflected *patois* humorously and patronizingly dubbed *Kongressdeutsch*), a measure that was supported even by Orthodox Zionists such as Ezriel Hildesheimer, on the grounds that it would be unseemly to publish such proceedings in "the holy tongue" (*lashon hakodesh*). The competition between German and Hebrew reached its peak on Palestinian soil in the so-called *Sprachenstreit* prior to the First World War. Influential figures, among them Ahad Ha'am and Hayim Nahman Bialik, defended Hebrew monolingualism against the more characteristic Jewish multilingualism for which German was a stand-in (Bialik even referred to German as a form of "historical treason" to the Jewish people, and railed against "Germanising the Hebrew spirit") (pp. 102, 127, 152), while at the same time acknowledging German's importance as a language of knowledge. Ahad Ha'am, for his part, translated Pinsker's *Auto-emancipation* into Hebrew but left the original German title page untouched, as he could not find a proper Hebrew translation for *Selbst-Emanzipation*—thus showing how delicate the "German problem" was for national Jews.

Volovici gives special attention to Buber's role in the debate. He regards the German translation of the Bible done by Buber and Rosenzweig as, on the one hand, an attempt "to come to terms with modern Hebrew" (p. 171) but, on the other hand, as a balancing act between Hebrew and German. The real challenge for many Zionists, as we know, was not the competition between Hebrew and German, but that of distancing themselves from Yiddish. This challenge explains to a great extent the debate about German as a Jewish or national-Jewish language. Inculcated with the legacy of the Haskalah's pejorative attitude toward Yiddish, Zionism was inclined to be positive toward German. No wonder that Ber Borochov, the Russian-born Yiddish linguist and Marxist-Zionist leader, suspected that the spread of the German language in the East was a tool to "Germanize" East European Jews. The author's conclusion: German was in one form or another an influential factor in maintaining the concept of a rift between Western and Eastern Jews, now within the framework of the common national-Jewish movement.

The last chapter revolves around an emotional question: Is it proper for Jews to use the language of Goethe (and Herzl), given that it is also the language associated with Hitler? The popular ban on the use of German in the public sphere in Palestine since 1933, or the Hebrew University's decision, at that time, to suspend teaching German as a foreign language as of 1934, serve as examples of a linguistic "turn" against German that left its imprint on Israeli society until long after the Second World War. At the same time, Volovici's mention of the cancelation of actor Albert Bassermann's visit to Israel in 1950 as an example of this anti-German tendency ignores many examples to the contrary. Another actor, Elisabeth Bergner (who was both Jewish and born in Austria), was cheered by the Israeli audience *because* she used the German language, and Marlene Dietrich, the celebrated German movie star and wartime anti-Nazi cultural icon who visited Israel about a decade after Bergner, encountered similar enthusiasm when she sang "Lili Marleen" in German. During the 1950s, German films produced in Austria (especially the *Sissi* trilogy) enjoyed great popularity, ignoring the fact that many of the actors were old Nazis. Against this background, a scene from Adolf Eichmann's trial, in which the defendant discusses a legal matter with the three judges (all of them born in Germany) in German, appears to be quite natural. German eventually regained its status as a language that Jewish nationalism could at least tolerate.

German as a Jewish Problem is an original, well-researched, and multifaceted work of intellectual Jewish history. A reader might well be surprised by the large number of well-known people whose books, articles, and pamphlets are analyzed by Volovici. To be sure, there are still a number of lacunae—for instance, what was the role of German in Jewish, then Zionist, colloquial discourse? A discussion of relevant writings by S.Y. Agnon, Salman Schocken, Gershom Scholem, Fritz Mordecai Kaufmann, and Sammy Gronemann, among others, might provide further support for Volovici's thesis concerning the paradoxical role of German as an expression, or at least a tool, of Jewish nationalism. And finally, Volovici's brief comment concerning the Zionist fight against the German language as being indirectly aimed at Arabic should definitely be considered more thoroughly.

MOSHE ZIMMERMANN
The Hebrew University